Craig McMurtry
Marc Mercuri
Nigel Watling

C0-ARF-915

Microsoft®
Windows®
Communication
Foundation

Hands-on!

Beta Edition

800 East 96th Street, Indianapolis, Indiana 46240 USA

Microsoft Windows Communication Foundation: Hands-On

Copyright © 2006 by Sams Publishing

International Standard Book Number: 0-672-32877-1

Library of Congress Catalog Card Number: 2006922041

Printed in the United States of America

First Printing: May 2006

09   08   07   06   4   3   2

Trademarks

All terms mentioned in this book that are known to be trademarks or service marks have been appropriately capitalized. Sams Publishing cannot attest to the accuracy of this information. Use of a term in this book should not be regarded as affecting the validity of any trademark or service mark.

Warning and Disclaimer

Every effort has been made to make this book as complete and as accurate as possible, but no warranty or fitness is implied. The information provided is on an "as is" basis. The authors and the publisher shall have neither liability nor responsibility to any person or entity with respect to any loss or damages arising from the information contained in this book.

Bulk Sales

Sams Publishing offers excellent discounts on this book when ordered in quantity for bulk purchases or special sales. For more information, please contact

U.S. Corporate and Government Sales
1-800-382-3419
corpsales@pearsontechgroup.com

For sales outside of the U.S., please contact

International Sales
international@pearsoned.com

Associate Publisher
Greg Wiegand

Acquisitions Editor
Neil Rowe

Development Editor
Mark Renfrow

Managing Editor
Patrick Kanouse

Senior Project Editor
Matthew Purcell

Copy Editor
Cheri Clark

Indexer
Aaron Black
Lisa Stumpf

Proofreader
Tracy Donhardt

Publishing Coordinator
Cindy Teeters

Book Designer
Gary Adair

Page Layout
Nonie Ratcliff

Table of Contents

Foreword

In order to keep in touch with customer concerns early in the product cycle, many Microsoft teams periodically hold Software Design Reviews (SDRs). Very early on, SDRs are about information flowing in to the product team: we invite a dozen industry experts in for a day or two of meetings, ask them for extensive feedback, and fold their thought into the product. As the product firms up, SDRs are about information flowing out to customers: we invite a couple hundred analysts and experts and early adapters to Seattle for a couple days of presentations, hands-on labs, and parties.

The hands-on labs at our last SDR, in March 2005, were created by our developer evangelist, Craig McMurtry, one of the authors of the book whose foreword you are now reading. Now, I've never been to South Africa (where Craig grew up), but after working with his hands-on labs, I feel like I've learned something about the South African educational system. They must give the kids a lot of homework. A lot. An overwhelming lot. Enough to make a child bitter. Extremely bitter. The kind of bitter that waits a lifetime for a chance at revenge. What else could explain a 11-part lab intended to be solved in an hour? What else justifies the haggard souls struggling to finish part 8 of that lab late on the first night of the SDR while the rest of us return to the conference hotel after dinner and frivolity? Why else would Craig rub his hands and chuckle at the sight?

Satisfied with their effect, Craig teamed up with his colleague, Marc Mercuri, who had been innocently working on organizing the SDR and helping drive customer adoption of the technology (albeit in a more kindly fashion). They set to work to evolve the March 2005 SDR labs into the larger set of labs presented at the PDC in September, and then again into the material that makes up the bulk of this book. Marc and Craig spent the holiday season with an additional guest at their dinner table: the manuscript. Now that you'll be able to take the material home and work on it at your own pace, Craig's bitterness becomes your gain. The material he wanted to torture you with in six one-hour timeslots, thanks to their joint effort, becomes a rich, deep introduction to WCF that you can explore at home. Over a period of months. In peace.

Have fun.

Steve Swartz
Microsoft Windows Communication Foundation Architect

We Want to Hear from You!

As the reader of this book, *you* are our most important critic and commentator. We value your opinion and want to know what we're doing right, what we could do better, what areas you'd like to see us publish in, and any other words of wisdom you're willing to pass our way.

As an associate publisher for Sams Publishing, I welcome your comments. You can email or write me directly to let me know what you did or didn't like about this book—as well as what we can do to make our books better.

Please note that I cannot help you with technical problems related to the topic of this book. We do have a User Services group, however, where I will forward specific technical questions related to the book.

When you write, please be sure to include this book's title and author as well as your name, email address, and phone number. I will carefully review your comments and share them with the author and editors who worked on the book.

Email: feedback@samspublishing.com

Mail: Greg Wiegand
            Associate Publisher
            Sams Publishing
            800 East 96th Street
            Indianapolis, IN 46240 USA

Reader Services

Visit our website and register this book at www.samspublishing.com/register for convenient access to any updates, downloads, or errata that might be available for this book.

Introduction

The Windows Communication Foundation, which was code-named *Indigo*, is a technology by which pieces of software can communicate with one another. There are many other such technologies, including COM and DCOM, RMI, MSMQ, and WebSphere MQ. Each of those works well in a particular scenario, not so well in others, and is of no use at all in some cases. The Windows Communication Foundation is meant to work well in any circumstance in which software entities must be made to communicate with one another. In fact, it is meant to always be the very best option: It provides performance that is about as good as, if not better than, any other alternative; it offers at least as many features and probably several more; and it will certainly always be the easiest solution to program.

Concretely, the Windows Communication Foundation consists of several new sets of classes added to the second version, the 2.0 version, of the Microsoft .NET Framework Class Library: principally, the Service Model, the Channel Layer, the XML Formatter, and the Extensible Security Infrastructure. It also adds some facilities for hosting Windows Communication Foundation solutions to Internet Information Services (IIS), the Web server that is built into Windows operating systems.

The Windows Communication Foundation will be released concurrently with the Windows Vista operating system in the second half of 2006, as part of a package called *WinFX*. WinFX includes several other technologies, including the Windows Presentation Foundation, which was code-named *Avalon*, the Windows Workflow Foundation, and InfoCard. Interim releases of WinFX, which are updated every month or two, can be downloaded from the Microsoft Windows Vista Developer center, at http://msdn. microsoft.com/winfx/. Those interim releases are available free, and so too will be the finished version.

One can install the Windows Communication Foundation on any Windows operating system on which the 2.0 version of the .NET Framework is supported. Those include Windows XP Service Pack 2, Windows Server 2003, Windows Server 2003 R2, Windows Vista, and the successor to Windows Server 2003, which is code-named *Windows Longhorn Server*. A very small number of features will be available only on Windows Vista and later operating systems.

Because the Windows Communication Foundation is meant to accommodate any circumstance in which software entities must be made to communicate with one another, it has a considerable number of features. However, the design of the Windows Communication Foundation makes it easy to understand how they all relate to one another. Nonetheless, this book is not intended to serve as an encyclopedic reference to the technology. Instead, it is meant to provide the understanding and knowledge required for most practical applications of the Windows Communication Foundation.

The book is written so as to explain the Windows Communication Foundation while showing how to use it. So, in each chapter, there are the precise steps for building a solution that demonstrates a particular aspect of the technology, along with a thorough explanation of each step. Readers who can program in C#, and who like to learn by doing, will be able to follow the steps. Those who prefer to just read will get a detailed account of the features of the Windows Communication Foundation, and be shown how to use them.

To follow the steps in the chapters, one should have any version of Visual Studio 2005 installed. Free copies are available at http://msdn.microsoft.com/vstudio/express/.

The January Community Technology Preview (CTP) Release of WinFX is also required. The instructions in the chapters assume that all the runtime and developer components of WinFX have been installed. The set of components may vary from one release of WinFX to another. The components of the current pre-release version of WinFX are clearly enumerated on the downloads page that is accessible from http://msdn.microsoft.com/winfx/.

A most important component of WinFX is the pertinent material in the Microsoft Windows Software Development Kit (SDK). By default, the SDK material installs into a folder called Microsoft SDKs\Windows in one's Program Files folder. Somewhere below that folder, one should find an archive called AllSamples.zip. That archive is usually located, by default, in the v1.0\samples subfolder. The archive contains a large number of Windows Communication Foundation samples.

Starting points for the solutions built in each of the chapters are available on this book's companion web page (www.samspublishing.com). Because the first version of the Windows Communication Foundation had yet to be completed at the time of writing, the authors pledge to keep providing updates to the text and the code via one of the author's Web logs at http://blogs.msdn.com/craigmcmurtry/archive/category/11914.aspx.

Many people contributed to this book. Among them are the folks on the Windows Communication Foundation development team, who were not actually aware they were contributing to a book. The reason is that the authors did not know, at the time they were doing the research, that they were, in fact, writing a book. What they produced just happened to be one.

The authors would like to thank Joe Long, Eric Zinda, Angela Mills, Omri Gazitt, Steve Swartz, Steve Millet, Mike Vernal, Doug Purdy, Eugene Osvetsky, Daniel Roth, Ford McKinstry, Craig McLuckie, Alex Weinert, Shy Cohen, Yasser Shohoud, Kenny Wolf, Anand Rajagopalan, Jim Johnson, Andy Milligan, Steve Maine, Ram Pamulapati, Ravi Rao, Andy Harjanto, T. R. Vishwanath, Doug Walter, Martin Gudgin, Giovanni Della-Libera, Kirill Gavrylyuk, Krish Srinivasan, Mark Fussell, Richard Turner, Ami Vora, Ari Bixhorn, Vic Gundotra, Neil Hutson, Steve DiMarco, Gianpaolo Carraro, Steve Woodward, James Conard, Vittorio Bertocci, Blair Shaw, Jeffrey Schlimmer, Matt Tavis, Mauro Ottoviani, John Frederick, Mark Renfrow, Sean Dixon, Matt Purcell, Cheri Clark, Mauricio Ordonez,

Neil Rowe, Donovan Follette, Pat Altimore, Tim Walton, Manu Puri, Ed Pinto, Suwat Chitphakdibodin, Gowind Ramanathan, Ralph Squillace, John Steer, Brad Severtson, Gary Devendorf, and Al Lee. Any mistakes in the pages that follow are not their fault. The authors also owe a great debt of gratitude to their wives, Marta MacNeill, Kathryn Mercuri, and Sylvie Watling.

CHAPTER 1

Prerequisites—Generics and Transactions

In November 2005, Microsoft released version 2.0 of the .NET Framework. WinFX and the Windows Communication Foundation are built on top of that framework and leverage key additions to the functionality version 2.0 provided.

To get the most out of this book, you will need to have an understanding of two features: Generics and System. Transactions. This chapter provides an overview of these features, providing the prerequisite knowledge to complete the exercises in future chapters.

> **NOTE**
>
> For those wanting to go deep in these areas, it is recommended that you visit http://msdn.microsoft.com. There you can find documentation and whitepapers on these subjects.

Generics

When you design classes, you do so without a crystal ball. Classes are designed based on the available knowledge of who the consumers of the class likely could be, and the data types those developers would like to use with your class.

While developing a system, you may have a need to develop a class that stores a number of items of the integer type. To meet the requirement, you write a class named Stack that provides the capability to store and access a series of integers:

```
using System;

public class Stack
{
    int[] items;

    public void Push (int item) {...};
    public int Pop() {...};

}
```

Suppose that at some point in the future, there is a request for this same functionality, only the business case requires the support for the double type. This current class will not support that functionality, and some changes or additions need to be made.

One option would be to make another class, one that provided support for the double type:

```
public class DoubleStack
{
    double[] items;

    public void Push (double item) {...};
    public int Pop() {...};

}
```

But doing that is not ideal. It leaves you with two classes, and the need to create others if requests to support different types arise in the future.

The best case would be to have a single class that was much more flexible. In the .NET 1.x world, if you wanted to provide this flexibility, you did so using the object type:

```
using System;

public class Stack
{
    object[] items;

    public void Push (object item) {...};
    public int Pop() {...};

}
```

This approach provides flexibility, but that flexibility comes at a cost. To pop an item off the stack, you needed to use typecasting, which resulted in a performance penalty:

```
double d = (double)stack.Pop;
```

In addition, that class allowed the capability to write and compile the code that added items of multiple types, not just those of the double type.

Fortunately, with version 2.0 of the .NET Framework, Generics provide us a more palatable solution. So what are Generics? Generics are code templates that allow developers to create type-safe code without referring to specific data types.

The following code shows a new generic, GenericStack<M>. Note that we use a placeholder of M in lieu of a specific type:

```
public class GenericStack<M>
{
    M[] items;

    void Push(M input) { }
    public M Pop() {}
}
```

The following code shows the use of GenericStack<M>. Here, two instances of the class are created, stack1 and stack2. stack1 can contain integers, whereas stack2 can contain doubles. Note that in place of M, the specific type is provided when defining the variables:

```
class TestGenericStack
{

    static void Main()
    {
        // Declare a stack of type int
        GenericStack<int> stack1 = new GenericStack<int>();

        // Declare a list of type double
        GenericStack<double> stack2 = new GenericStack<double>();

    }
}
```

This provides support for us to use the functionality for the types we know we must support today, plus the capability to support types we'll be interested in in the future. If in the future, you create a class named NewClass, you could use that with a Generic with the following code:

```
// Declare a list of the new type
 GenericStack<NewClass> list3 = new GenericStack<NewClass>();
```

In GenericStack<M> class, M is what is called a generic-type parameter. The type specified when instantiating the GenericStack<M> in code is referred to as a type argument. In the code for the TestGenericStack class, int and double, are both examples of type arguments.

In the preceding example, there was only one generic-type parameter, M. This was by choice and not because of a limitation in the .NET Framework. The use of multiple generic-type parameters is valid and supported, as can be seen in this example:

```
class Stock<X, Y>
{
    X identifier;
    Y numberOfShares;

    ...


}
```

Here are two examples of how this could then be used in code. In the first instance, the identifier is an int, and the number of shares a double. In the second case, the identifier is a string, and the number of shares is an int:

```
Stock<int,double> x = new Stock<int,double>();
Stock<string,int> y = new Stock<string,int>();
```

In these examples, we've also used a single letter to represent our generic-type parameter. Again, this is by choice and not by requirement. In the Stock class example, X and Y could have also been IDENTIFIER and NUMBEROFSHARES.

Now that you've learned the basics of generics, you may have a few questions: What if I don't want to allow just any type to be passed in, and want to make sure that only types deriving from a certain interface are used? What if I need to ensure that the type argument provided refers to a type with a public constructor? Can I use generic types in method definitions?

The good news is that the answer to each of those questions is yes.

There will undoubtedly be instances in which you will want to restrict the type arguments that a developer may use with the class. If, in the case of the Stock<X, Y> generic, you wanted to ensure that the type parameter provided for X was derived from IStockIdentifier, you could specify this, as shown here:

```
public class Stock<X, Y> where X:IStockIdentifier
```

Although this example uses a single constraint that X must derive from IStockIdentifier, additional constraints can be specified for X, as well as Y.

In regard to other constraints for X, you may want to ensure that the type provided has a public default constructor. In that way if your class has a variable of type X that creates a new instance of it in code, it will be supported.

By defining the class as

```
public class Stock<X, Y> where X:new()
```

you ensure that you can create a new instance of X within the class:

```
X identifier = new X();
```

As mentioned earlier, you can specify multiple constraints. The following is an example of how to specify that the Stock class is to implement both of the constraints listed previously:

```
public class Stock<X, Y> where X:IStockIdentifier, new()
```

In the GenericStack<M> example, you saw that there were Push and Pop methods:

```
public class GenericStack<M>
{
    M[] items;

    void Push(M input) { }
    public M Pop() {}
}
```

Push and Pop are examples of generic methods. In that code, the generic methods are inside of generic types. It is important to note that they can also be used outside of generic types, as seen here:

```
public class Widget
{
    public void WidgetAction<M>(M m)
    {...}
}
```

> **NOTE**
>
> It should be noted that attempts to cast a type parameter to the type of a specific class will not compile. This is in keeping with the purpose of generics—casting to a specific type of class would imply that the generic-type paremeter is, in fact, not generic. You may cast a type parameter, but only to an interface.

Inheritance is the last area we'll cover on Generics in this chapter. Inheritance is handled in a very straightforward manner—when defining a new class that inherits from a generic, you must specify the type argument(s).

If we were to create a class that inherited from our Stock class, it would resemble the following code:

```
public class Stock<X,Y>
{...}
public class MyStock : Stock<string,int>
{...}
```

System.Transactions

The definition of a transaction is "an action or activity involving two parties or things that reciprocally affect or influence each other." In developing software systems, there is regularly the need to have transactional behavior.

The canonical example for a software transaction is that of transferring funds. In that scenario, you are decrementing money from a savings account and crediting money to a checking account. If an issue were to occur sometime after decrementing the money from your savings account but before adding it to your checking account, you would expect the transaction to roll back. Rolling back the transaction would place the funds back in your savings account.

The topic of transactions and transactional messaging is discussed in Chapter 5, "Reliable Sessions, Transactions, and Queues," but before you go to that chapter, it will be helpful to have an understanding of the added functionality around transactions in version 2.0 of the framework, specifically the functionality exposed via System.Transactions.

This next section begins with an overview of how transactions are managed in the .NET Framework, and then discusses how to implement transactions in code.

Transaction Managers

Version 2.0 of the framework introduced two new transaction managers: the Lightweight Transaction Manager and the OleTx Transaction Manager.

The Lightweight Transaction Manager (LTM) is a two-phase commit coordinator that provides transaction management within a single app domain. It is used for scenarios in which there is only a single durable resource involved, and there is no requirement for the Transaction Manager to log. This offers the capability to incorporate transaction management into an application without Microsoft Distributed Transaction Coordinator (DTC) and the overhead associated with it.

The OleTx Transaction Manager can handle those scenarios not handled by the LTM. The OleTx Transaction Manager is used for transactions that involve more than one durable resource, or span beyond a single app domain.

As a developer, you will not interact with the transaction managers directly, but instead through the objects in the System.Transactions namespace. One of the key benefits of this approach is the capability to support transaction promotion.

By default, every System.Transactions transaction begins utilizing the Lightweight Transaction Manager. If there comes a point in the scope of the transaction where it involves a second durable resource, that is, a second database connection, or crosses the app domain boundary, it is promoted and enlisted in a new OleTx transaction. This lets you, as a developer, focus on writing transactions, and lets the .NET framework use the best manager for a given scenario.

Coding System.Transactions Transactions

To utilize System.Transactions in your solutions, there are two ways to go about the task: by defining them declaratively using attributes or by explicitly defining them in code.

Declarative Coding of Transactions

If you've developed using Enterprise Services in the past, you will already be familiar with adding transactions in a declarative way. Declarative coding for transactions is done by applying attributes.

The following code is an example from an Enterprise Services application. In it you can see that two attributes are assigned, one at the class level and one at the operation level:

```
[Transaction(TransactionOption.Required)]
public class WireTransfer : ServicedComponent
{
    [AutoComplete]
    public double Transfer(int sourceAccountNbr, int targetAccountNbr, double
➡ amount);
    {
        ...
    }
}
```

At the class level, the [Transaction] attribute is applied. This serves as an instruction indicating that calls to any method within the class will occur within a transactional context.

At the operation level, the [AutoComplete] attribute is placed on the Transfer method. This serves as an instruction to automatically commit a transaction if the Transfer method does not end in error.

Explicit Coding of Transactions

System.Transactions also provides the capability to explicitly code transactions. Transactions will occur within a TransactionScope. TransactionScope provides a definition of the boundaries of the transaction, with all the code contained within it becoming part of the transaction:

```
using (TransactionScope scope = new TransactionScope ())
{
    //Code that will be part of the transaction
}
```

In the preceding code, the transaction is assumed complete when the using statement has been completed. To explicitly state that the scope was completed, use the Complete method on the TransactionScope object:

```
using (TransactionScope scope = new TransactionScope ())
{
    //Code that will be part of the transaction
    scope.Complete();
}
```

Transaction scopes can be nested, and when a TransactionScope is defined, there is the capability to specify how this scope will work with any ambient transactions. For example, you may want to utilize an ambient transaction, or you may demand that a new transaction be created for a particular scope of work—regardless of any existing transactions. You may even want to suppress the ambient transaction context for this scope of work.

You can introduce this when defining your scope, by specifying the appropriate value of the TransactionScopeOption enumeration. In the following listing, you can see an example in which there are nested transaction scopes and the innermost scope requires that it be part of a new transaction:

```
using (TransactionScope scope = new TransactionScope
➥ (TransactionScopeOption.Required))
{
    //Code that will be part of the transaction
    using (TransactionScope scope = new TransactionScope
➥ (TransactionScopeOption.RequiresNew))
    {
        //More work that exists inside of a new transaction;
    }

}
```

You can also specify additional options, such as isolation level or timeout, by passing in an instance of the TransactionOptions class to the TransactionScope constructor. This provides the capability to specify values for things such as isolation level and timeout. The next listing shows the setting of the isolation level of the transaction to ReadCommitted:

```
public double Transfer(int sourceAccountNbr, int targetAccountNbr, double
➥ amount)
{
        TransactionOptions options = new TransactionOptions();
        options.IsolationLevel = IsolationLevel.ReadCommitted;
        using (TransactionScope scope = new TransactionScope
        ➥ (TransactionScopeOption.Required, options))
        {
            //Code that will be part of the transaction
        }
}
```

Summary

In this chapter you were introduced to two key pieces of functionality in the second version of the .NET Framework: Generics and System.Transactions.

If you were unfamiliar with Generics before starting the chapter, you should now have an understanding of what they are, why they're important, and how they can be used. Generics are very visible in WCF, and you'll see quite a bit of them in the following chapters.

You should now also have an understanding of System.Transactions in the framework. The Lightweight Transaction Manager and the OleTx Transaction Manager were introduced, as was how to write transactional code. This will be helpful as you navigate through Chapter 5, which covers transactions within the context of WCF.

With these two prerequisite areas behind you, you're now ready to learn the ABC's of the Windows Communication Foundation.

CHAPTER 2

The Fundamentals

Background

Dealing with something as an integrated whole is self-evidently easier than having to understand and manipulate all of it parts. Thus, to make programming easier, it is commonplace to define classes that serve as integrated wholes, keeping their constituents hidden. Doing so is called *encapsulation*, which is characteristic of what is known as *object-oriented programming*.

The C++ programming language provided syntax for encapsulation that proved very popular. In C++, one can write a class like this one:

```
class Stock
{
private:
    char symbol[30];
    int number;
    double price;
    double value;
    void SetTotal()
    {
        this->value = this->number * this->price;
    }
public:
    Stock(void);
    ~Stock(void);
    void Acquire(const char* symbol, int number, double
price);
    void Sell(int number, double price);
};
```

The class hides away its members, symbol, number, price, and value, as well as the method SetTotal(), while exposing the methods Acquire() and Sell() for use.

Some refer to the exposed surface of a class as its *interface*, and to invocations of the methods of a class as *messages*. David A. Taylor does so in his book *Object-Oriented Information Systems: Planning and Integration* (1992, 118).

Using C++ classes to define interfaces and messages has an important shortcoming, however, as Don Box explains in *Essential COM* (1998, 11). There is no standard way for C++ compilers to express the interfaces in binary format. Consequently, sending a message to a class in a dynamic link library (DLL) is not guaranteed to work if the calling code and the intended recipient class were built using different compilers.

That shortcoming is significant, because it restricts the extent to which the class in the DLL can be reused in code written by other programmers. The reuse of code written by one programmer within code written by another is fundamental, not only to programming productivity, but also to software as a commercial enterprise, to being able to sell what a programmer produces.

Two important solutions to the problem were pursued. One was to define interfaces using C++ abstract base classes. An *abstract base class* is a class with pure virtual functions, and, as Box explained, "[t]he runtime implementation of virtual functions in C++ takes the [same] form[...]in virtually all production compilers" (1998, 15). One can write, in C++, the code given in Listing 2.1.

LISTING 2.1   Abstract Base Class

```
//IStock.h
class IStock
{
public:
     virtual void DeleteInstance(void);
     virtual void Acquire(const char* symbol, int number, double price) = 0;
   virtual void Sell(int number, double price) = 0;
};

extern "C"
IStock* CreateStock(void);

//Stock.h
#include "IStock.h"

class Stock: public IStock
{
private:
    char symbol[30];
    int number;
    double price;
    double value;
    void SetTotal()
```

LISTING 2.1   Continued

```
    {
        this->value = this->number * this->price;
    }
public:
    Stock(void);
    ~Stock(void);
    void DeleteInstance(void);
    void Acquire(const char* symbol, int number, double price);
    void Sell(int number, double price);
};
```

In that code, IStock is an interface defined using a C++ abstract virtual class. IStock is an abstract virtual class because it has the pure virtual functions Acquire() and Sell(), their nature as pure virtual functions being denoted by having both the keyword, virtual, and the suffix, = 0, in their declarations. A programmer wanting to use a class with the IStock interface within a DLL can write code that retrieves an instance of such a class from the DLL using the global function CreateStock() and sends messages to that instance. That code will work even if the programmer is using a different compiler than the one used by the programmer of the DLL.

Programming with interfaces defined as C++ abstract virtual classes is the foundation of a Microsoft technology called the *Component Object Model*, or *COM*. More generally, it is the foundation of what became known as *component-oriented programming*.

Another important solution to the problem of there being no standard way for C++ compilers to express the interfaces of classes in binary format is to define a standard for the output of compilers. The Java Virtual Machine Specification defines a standard format for the output of compilers, called the *class file format* (Lindholm and Yellin 1997, 61). Files in that format can be translated into the instructions specific to a particular computer processor by a Java Virtual Machine. One programmer can provide a class in the class file format to another programmer who will be able to instantiate that class and send messages to it using any compiler and Java Virtual Machine compliant with the Java Virtual Machine Specification.

Similarly, the Common Language Infrastructure Specification defines the Common Intermediate Language as a standard format for the output of compilers (ECMA International 2005). Files in that format can be translated into instructions to a particular computer processor by Microsoft's Common Language Runtime, which is the core of Microsoft's .NET technology, as well as by Mono.

Despite these ways of making classes written by one programmer reusable by others, the business of software was still restricted. The use of COM and .NET is widespread, as is the use of Java, and software developed using Java cannot be used together easily with software developed using COM or .NET.

The Web Services Description Language (WSDL) overcomes that restriction by providing a way of defining software interfaces using the Extensible Markup Language (XML), a format that is exceptionally widely adopted, and for which processors are readily available. Writing classes that implement WSDL interfaces is generally referred to as *service-oriented programming*.

Microsoft provided support for service-oriented programming to COM programmers with the Microsoft SOAP Toolkit, and to .NET programmers with the classes in the System. Web.Services namespace of the .NET Framework Class Library. Additions to the latter were provided by the Web Services Enhancements for Microsoft .NET. Java programmers can use Apache Axis for service-oriented programming.

Yet service-oriented programming has been limited by the lack of standard ways of securing message transmissions, handling failures, and coordinating transactions. Standards have now been developed, and the Windows Communication Foundation provides implementations thereof.

So the Windows Communication Foundation delivers a more complete infrastructure for service-oriented programming than was available to .NET software developers. Providing that infrastructure is important, because service-oriented programming transcends limits on the reuse of software between Java programmers and COM and .NET programmers that had been hampering the software business.

However, this way of understanding the Windows Communication Foundation severely underestimates its significance. The Windows Communication Foundation provides something far more useful than service-oriented programming—namely, a software factory template for software communication.

The concept of software factory templates is introduced by Jack Greenfield and Keith Short in their book *Software Factories: Assembling Applications with Patterns, Models, Frameworks, and Tools* (Greenfield and others 2004). It provides a new approach to model-driven software development.

The notion of model-driven software development has been popular for many years. It is the vision of being able to construct a model of a software solution from which the software itself can be generated after the model has been scrutinized to ensure that it covers all the functional and nonfunctional requirements. That vision has been pursued using general-purpose modeling languages, the Unified Modeling Language (UML) in particular.

A serious shortcoming in using general-purpose modeling languages for model-driven software development is that general-purpose modeling languages are inherently imprecise. They cannot represent the fine details of requirements that can be expressed in natural languages like English. They also are not sufficiently precise to cover things such as memory management, thread synchronization, auditing, and exception management. If they were, they would be programming languages, rather than general-purpose modeling languages, yet memory management, thread synchronization, auditing, and exception management are precisely the sorts of things that bedevil programmers.

Greenfield and Short argue that progress in model-driven development depends on eschewing general-purpose modeling languages in favor of *domain-specific languages*, or DSLs. A DSL models the concepts found in a specific domain. DSLs should be used in conjunction with a corresponding class framework, a set of classes specifically designed to cover the same domain. Then, if the DSL is used to model particular ways in which those classes can be used, it should be possible to generate the software described in the model from the class framework (Greenfield and others 2004, 144).

The combination of a DSL and a corresponding class framework constitute the core of a software factory template (Greenfield and others 2004, 173). Software factory templates serve as the software production assets of a software factory from which many varieties of the same software product can be readily fabricated.

A fine example of a software factory template is the Windows Forms Designer in Microsoft Visual Studio .NET and subsequent versions of Microsoft Visual Studio. In that particular case, the Windows Forms Designer is the DSL, the Toolbox and Property Editor being among the terms of the language, and the classes in the `System.Windows.Forms` namespace of the .NET Framework Class Library constitute the class framework. Users of the Windows Forms Designer use it to model software that gets generated from those classes.

Programmers have been using the Windows Forms Designer and tools like it in other integrated development environments for many years to develop software user interfaces. So Greenfield and Short, in introducing the concept of software factory templates, are not proposing a new approach. Rather, they are formalizing one that has already proven to be very successful, and suggesting that it be used to develop other varieties of software besides user interfaces.

The Windows Communication Foundation is a software factory template for software communication. It consists of a DSL, called the *Service Model*, and a class framework, called the *Channel Layer*. The Service Model consists of the classes of the `System.ServiceModel` namespace, and an XML configuration language. The Channel Layer consists of the classes in the `System.ServiceModel.Channel` namespace. Developers model how a piece of software is to communicate using the Service Model, and the communication components they need to have included in their software are generated from the Channel Layer, in accordance with their model. Later, if they need to change or supplement how their software communicates, they make alterations to their model, and the modifications or additions to their software are generated. If they want to model a form of communication that is not already supported by the Channel Layer, they can build or buy a suitable channel to add to the Channel Layer, and proceed to generate their software as usual, just as a user of the Windows Forms Designer can build or buy controls to add to the Windows Forms Designer's Toolbox.

That the Windows Communication Foundation provides a complete infrastructure for service-oriented programming is very nice, because sometimes programmers do need to do that kind of programming, and service-oriented programming will likely remain popular for a while. However, software developers are always trying to get pieces of software to communicate, and they always will need to do that, because software is reused by sending and receiving data, and the business of software depends on software reuse.

So the fact that the Windows Communication Foundation provides a software factory template for generating, modifying, and supplementing software communication facilities from a model is truly significant.

The Service Model

The key terms in the language of the Windows Communication Foundation Service Model correspond closely to the key terms of WSDL. In WSDL a piece of software that can respond to communications over a network is called a *service*. A service is described in an XML document with three primary sections:

- The service section indicates where the service is located.

- The binding section specifies which of various standard communication protocols the service understands.

- The third primary section, the portType section, lists all the operations that the service can perform by defining the messages that it will emit in response to messages it receives.

Thus, the three primary sections of a WSDL document tell one where a service is located, how to communicate with it, and what it will do.

Those three things are exactly what one specifies in building software communication facilities with the Windows Communication Foundation Service Model: where the software is, how to communicate with it, and what it will do. Instead of calling those things *service*, *binding*, and *portType*, as they are called in the WSDL specification, they are named *address*, *binding*, and *contract* in the Windows Communication Foundation Service Model. Consequently, the handy acronym *a*, *b*, c can serve as a reminder of the key terms of the Windows Communication Foundation Service Model and, thereby, as a reminder to the steps to follow in using it to enable a piece of software to communicate.

More precisely, in the Windows Communication Foundation Service Model, a piece of software that responds to communications over a network is a service, a service has one or more endpoints to which communications can be directed, and an endpoint consists of an address, a binding, and a contract. This chapter explains, in detail, how to use the Windows Communication Foundation Service Model to enable a piece of software to communicate. Lest the details that are provided obscure how simple this task is to accomplish, here is an overview of the steps involved.

A programmer begins by defining the contract. That is done by writing an interface in a .NET programming language,

```
public interface IEcho
{
    string Echo(string input);
}
```

and then adding attributes from the Service Model that designate the interface as a Windows Communication Foundation contract, and one or more of its methods as being included in the contract:

```
[ServiceContract]
public interface IEcho
{
    [OperationContract]
    string Echo(string input);
}
```

The next step is to implement the contract, which is done simply by writing a class that implements the interface:

```
public class Service : IEcho
{
    public string Echo(string input)
    {
        return input;
    }
}
```

A class that implements an interface that is designated as a Windows Communication Foundation contract is called a *service type*. How the Windows Communication Foundation conveys data to and from the service type from outside can be controlled by adding behaviors to the service type definition using the ServiceBehavior attribute:

```
[ServiceBehavior(ConcurrencyMode=ConcurrencyMode.Multiple)]
public class Service : IEcho
{
    public string Echo(string input)
    {
        return input;
    }
}
```

For example, the concurrency mode behavior attribute controls whether the Windows Communication Foundation can convey data to the service type on more than one concurrent thread.

The final step for the programmer is to provide for hosting the service within an application domain. IIS can provide an application domain for hosting the service, and so can any .NET application. Hosting the service within an arbitrary .NET application is easily accomplished using the ServiceHost class provided by the Windows Communication Foundation Service Model:

```
string httpBaseAddress = "http://localhost:8000/EchoService/";
string tcpBaseAddress = "net.tcp://localhost:8080/EchoService/";
```

```
Uri[] baseAddresses = new Uri[] {
    new Uri(httpBaseAddress),
    new Uri(tcpBaseAddress) };

using (ServiceHost host = new ServiceHost(typeof(Service), baseAddresses ))
{
    host.Open();

    Console.WriteLine("The service is ready.");
    Console.ReadKey();

    host.Close();
}
```

Next, an administrator specifies an address and a binding for the service. An editing tool, shown in Figure 2.1, is provided for that purpose.

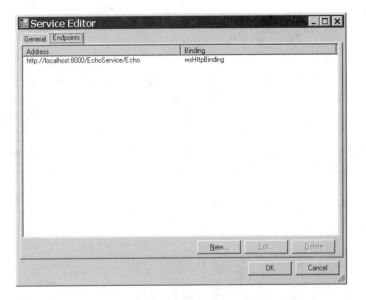

FIGURE 2.1   Defining an address and a binding.

As indicated in Figure 2.2, the administrator can also use the editing tool to add behaviors to control how the Windows Communication Foundation moves data to and from the service.

Now that the address, binding, and contract of an endpoint have been defined, the contract has been implemented, and a host for the service has been provided, the service can be made available for use. The administrator executes the host application. The

Windows Communication Foundation examines the address, binding, and contract of the endpoint that have been specified in the language of the Service Model, and generates the necessary components by which the service can receive and respond to communications from the Channel Layer.

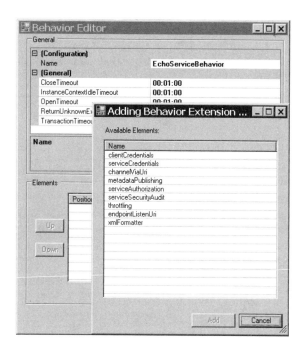

FIGURE 2.2   Adding behaviors to a service.

Among what it generates is WSDL to define the address, bindings, and contracts of the service. A programmer developing an application to communicate with the service can download that WSDL, and generate code for contacting the service, as well as an application configuration file with the address and binding information. That can be done with a single command:

```
svcutil http://localhost:8000/EchService/Echo
```

Then the programmer can use the generated code to communicate with the service:

```
EchoProxy echoProxy = new EchoProxy();
string response = echoProxy.Echo("Hello, World!");
echoProxy.Close();
```

The preceding steps are all that is involved in using the Windows Communication Foundation. The value of using it is in the administrator being able to modify how the service communicates simply by modifying the binding, without the code having to be changed, and by the administrator being able to make the service communicate in an unlimited variety of ways. When the service's host executes again, the Windows Communication Foundation generates the communications infrastructure for the new or modified endpoints. At last, the promise of model-driven development has actually yielded something tangible: a software factory template by which the communications system of an application can be manufactured from a model.

The foregoing provides a brief overview of working with the Windows Communication Foundation Service Model. Read on for a much more detailed, step-by-step examination. That account starts right from the beginning, with building some software with which one might like other software to be able to communicate. To be precise, it starts with developing some software to calculate the value of derivatives.

A Software Resource

A *derivative* is a financial entity whose value is derived from that of another. Here is an example. The value of a single share of Microsoft Corporation stock was $24.41 on October 11, 2005. Given that value, one might offer for sale an option to buy 1,000 of those shares, for $25 each, one month later, on November 11, 2005. Such an option, which is known as a *call*, might be purchased by someone who anticipates that the price of the shares will rise above $25 by November 11, 2005, and sold by someone who anticipates that the price of the shares will drop. The call is a derivative, its value being derived from the value of Microsoft Corporation stock.

Pricing a derivative is a complex task. Indeed, estimating the value of derivatives is perhaps the most high-profile problem in modern microeconomics.

In the foregoing example, clearly the quantity of the stock, and the current and past prices of the Microsoft Corporation stock, are factors to consider, but other factors might be based on analyses of the values of quantities that are thought to affect the prices of the stock, such as the values of various stock market indices, or the interest rate of the U.S. Federal Reserve Bank. In fact, one can say that, in general, the price of a derivative is some function of one or more quantities, one or more market values, and the outcome of one or more quantitative analytical functions.

Although actually writing software to calculate the value of derivatives is beyond the scope of this book, one can pretend to do so by following these steps:

1. Open Microsoft Visual Studio 2005, choose File, New, Project from the menus, and create a new blank solution called DerivativesCalculatorSolution in the folder C:\WCFHandsOn\Fundamentals, as shown in Figure 2.3.

2. Choose File, New, Project again, and add a C# Class Library project called DerivativesCalculator to the solution, as shown in Figure 2.4.

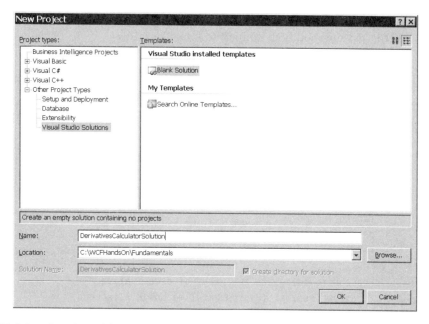

FIGURE 2.3   Creating a blank Visual Studio solution.

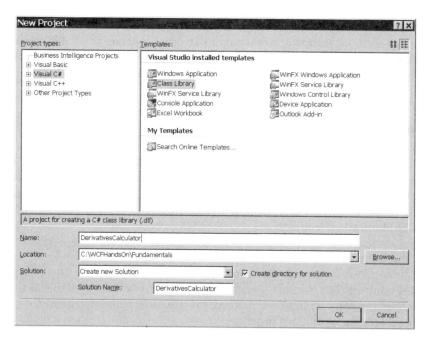

FIGURE 2.4   Adding a Class Library project to the solution.

3. Rename the class file `Class1.cs` in the DerivativesCalculator project to `Calculator.cs`, and modify its content to look like this:

```
using System;
using System.Collections.Generic;
using System.Text;

namespace DerivativesCalculator
{
    public class Calculator
    {
        public decimal CalculateDerivative(
          string[] symbols,
          decimal[] parameters,
          string[] functions)
        {
        //Pretend to calculate the value of a derivative.
            return (decimal)(System.DateTime.Now.Millisecond);
        }
    }
}
```

This simple C# class purports to calculate the value of derivatives, and will serve to represent a piece of software with which one might like other software to be able to communicate. Certainly, if the class really could calculate the value of derivatives, its capabilities would be in extraordinary demand, and one could quickly earn a fortune by charging for access to it.

Building a Service for Accessing the Resource

To allow other software to communicate with the class, one can use the Windows Communication Foundation Service Model to add communication facilities to it. One does so by building a Windows Communication Foundation service with an endpoint for accessing the facilities of the derivatives calculator class. Recall that, in the language of the Windows Communication Foundation Service Model, an endpoint consists of an address, a binding, and a contract.

Defining the Contract

In using the Windows Communication Foundation Service Model, one usually begins by defining the contract. The contract specifies the operations that are available at the endpoint. After the contract has been defined, the next step is to implement the contract, to actually provide the operations it defines.

Defining and implementing Windows Communication Foundation contracts is simple. To define a contract, one merely writes an interface in one's favorite .NET programming language, and adds attributes to it to indicate that the interface is also a Windows

Communication Foundation contract. Then, to implement the contract, one simply programs a class that implements the .NET interface that one has defined:

1. Choose File, New, Project from the Visual Studio 2005 menus again, and add another C# Class Library project to the solution, called DerivativesCalculatorService.

2. Rename the class file `Class1.cs` in the DerivativesCalculatorService project to `IDerivativesCalculator`.

3. Modify the contents of the `IDerivatesCalculator.cs` file to look like so:

```
using System;
using System.Collections.Generic;
using System.Text;

namespace DerivativesCalculatorService
{
    public interface IDerivativesCalculator
    {
        decimal CalculateDerivative(
            string[] symbols,
            decimal[] parameters,
            string[] functions);

        void DoNothing();
    }
}
```

`IDerivativesCalculator` is an ordinary C# interface, with two methods, `CalculateDerivative()` and `DoNothing()`. Now it will be made into a Windows Communication Foundation contract.

4. Choose Project, Add Reference from the Visual Studio 2005 menus; select `System. ServiceModel` from the assemblies listed on the .NET tab of the Add Reference dialog that appears, as shown in Figure 2.5; and click on the OK button. `System. ServiceModel` is the most important of the several new class libraries that the Windows Communication Foundation adds to the .NET Framework Class Library 2.0.

5. Modify the `IDerivativesCalculator` interface in the `IDerivativesCalculator.cs` module to import the classes in the `System.ServiceModel` namespace that is incorporated in the `System.ServiceModel` assembly:

```
using System;
using System.Collections.Generic;
using System.ServiceModel;
using System.Text;

namespace DerivativesCalculatorService
{
```

```
public interface IDerivativesCalculator
{
    decimal CalculateDerivative(
        string[] symbols,
        decimal[] parameters,
        string[] functions);

  void DoNothing();
}
}
```

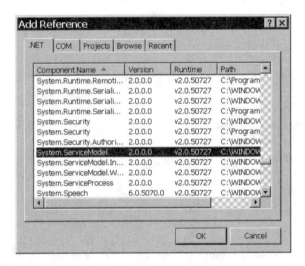

FIGURE 2.5   Adding a reference to the System.ServiceModel assembly.

6. Now designate the IDerivativesCalculator interface as a Windows Communication Foundation contract by adding the ServiceContract attribute that is included in the System.ServiceModel namespace:

```
using System;
using System.Collections.Generic;
using System.ServiceModel;
using System.Text;

namespace DerivativesCalculatorService
{
    [ServiceContract]
    public interface IDerivativesCalculator
    {
```

```
        decimal CalculateDerivative(
            string[] symbols,
            decimal[] parameters,
            string[] functions);

        void DoNothing();
    }
}
```

7. Use the OperationContract attribute to designate the CalculateDerivative()
   method of the IDerivativesCalculator interface as one of the methods of the
   interface that is to be included as an operation in the Windows Communication
   Foundation contract:

```
using System;
using System.Collections.Generic;
using System.ServiceModel;
using System.Text;

namespace DerivativesCalculator
{
    [ServiceContract]
    public interface IDerivativesCalculator
    {
        [OperationContract]
        decimal CalculateDerivative(
            string[] symbols,
            decimal[] parameters,
            string[] functions);

        void DoNothing();
    }
}
```

By default, the namespace and name of a Windows Communication Foundation
contract are the namespace and name of the interface to which the
ServiceContract attribute is added. Also, the name of an operation included in a
Windows Communication Foundation contract is the name of the method to which
the OperationContract attribute is added. One can alter the default name of a
contract using the Namespace and Name parameters of the ServiceContract attribute,
as in

```
[ServiceContract(Namespace="MyNamespace",Name="MyContract")]
public interface IMyInterface
```

One can alter the default name of an operation with the `Name` parameter of the `OperationContract` attribute:

```
[OperationContract(Name="MyOperation")]
string MyMethod();
```

8. Returning to the derivatives calculator solution in Visual Studio 2005, now that a Windows Communication Foundation contract has been defined, the next step is to implement it. In the DerivativesCalculatorService project, choose Project, Add, New Class from the Visual Studio 2005 menus, and add a class called `DerivativesCalculatorServiceType.cs` to the project, as shown in Figure 2.6.

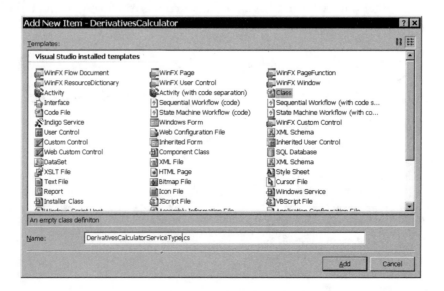

FIGURE 2.6   Adding a class to a project.

9. Modify the contents of the `DerivativesCalculatorServiceType.cs` class file to look like this:

```
using System;
using System.Collections.Generic;
using System.Text;
namespace DerivativesCalculator
{
    public class DerivativesCalculatorServiceType: IDerivativesCalculator
    {
      #region IDerivativesCalculator Members
      decimal IDerivativesCalculator.CalculateDerivative(
```

```
      string[] symbols,
      decimal[] parameters,
      string[] functions)
    {
      throw new Exception(
        "The method or operation is not implemented.");
    }

    void IDerivativesCalculator.DoNothing()
    {
      throw new Exception(
        "The method or operation is not implemented.");
    }
    #endregion
  }
}
```

As mentioned earlier, in the language of the Windows Communication Foundation, the name *service type* is used to refer to any class that implements a service contract. So, in this case, the DerivativesCalculatorServiceType is a service type because it implements the IDerivativesCalculator interface, which has been designated as a Windows Communication Foundation service contract.

A class can be a service type not only by implementing an interface that is a service contract, but also by having the ServiceContract attribute applied directly to the class. However, by applying the ServiceContract attribute to an interface and then implementing the interface with a class, as in the foregoing, one yields a service contract that can be implemented with any number of service types. In particular, one service type that implements the service contract can be discarded in favor of another. If the service contract attribute is instead applied directly to a class, that class and its descendants will be the only service types that can implement that particular service contract, and discarding the class will mean discarding the service contract.

10. At this point, the DerivativesCalculatorServiceType implements the IDerivativesCalculator interface in name only. Its methods do not actually perform the operations described in the service contract. Rectify that now by returning to the DerivativesCalculatorService project in Visual Studio 2005, and choosing Project, Add Reference from the menus. Select the Projects tab, select the entry for the DerivativesCalculator project, shown in Figure 2.7, and click on the OK button.

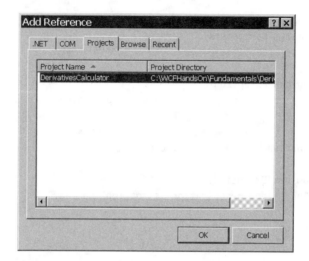

FIGURE 2.7   Adding a reference to the DerivativesCalculator project.

11. Now program the `CalculateDerivative()` method of the
    `DerivativesCalculatorServiceType` to delegate the work of calculating the
    value of a derivative to the `Calculator` class of the DerivativesCalculator project,
    which was the original class with which other pieces of software were to be
    able to communicate. Also modify the `DoNothing()` method of the
    `DerivativesCalculatorServiceType` so that it no longer throws an exception:

```
using System;
using System.Collections.Generic;
using System.Text;

namespace DerivativesCalculator
{
    public class DerivativesCalculatorServiceType: IDerivativesCalculator
    {
        #region IDerivativesCalculator Members
        decimal IDerivativesCalculator.CalculateDerivative(
            string[] symbols,
            decimal[] parameters,
            string[] functions)
        {
            return new Calculator().CalculateDerivative(
                symbols, parameters, functions);
        }

        void IDerivativesCalculator.DoNothing()
```

```
            {
                return;
            }
            #endregion
        }
    }
```

12. Choose Build, Build Solution from the Visual Studio 2005 menu to ensure that there are no programming errors.

Hosting the Service

Recall that the purpose of this exercise has been to use the Windows Communication Foundation to provide a means by which other software can make use of the facilities provided by the derivatives calculator class written at the outset. That requires making a Windows Communication Foundation service by which the capabilities of the derivatives calculator class are made available. Windows Communication Foundation services are collections of endpoints, each endpoint consisting of an address, a binding, and a contract. At this point, the contract portion of an endpoint for accessing the facilities of the derivatives calculator has been completed, the contract having been defined and implemented.

The next step is to provide for hosting the service within an application domain. Application domains are the containers that Microsoft's Common Language Runtime provides for .NET assemblies. So, in order to have an application domain to host a Windows Communication Foundation service, some Windows process will need to initialize the Common Language Runtime on behalf of the service. Any .NET application can be programmed to do that. IIS can also be made to have Windows Communication Foundation services hosted within application domains. To begin with, the derivatives calculator service will be hosted in an application domain within a .NET application, and then, later, within an application domain in IIS:

1. Choose File, New, Project from the Visual Studio 2005 menus, and add a C# console application called Host to the derivatives calculator solution, as shown in Figure 2.8.

2. Select Project, Add Reference from Visual Studio 2005 menus, and, from the .NET tab of the Add Reference dialog, add a reference to the `System.ServiceModel` assembly, as shown earlier in Figure 2.5. Add a reference to the `System.Configuration` assembly in the same way.

3. Choose Project, Add Reference from the Visual Studio 2005 menus, and, from the Projects tab, add a reference to the DerivativesCalculatorService project.

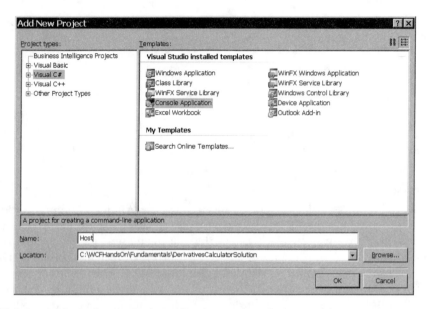

FIGURE 2.8   Adding a host console application to the solution.

4. Modify the contents of the `Program.cs` class module in the Host project to match Listing 2.2.

LISTING 2.2   A Host for a Service

```
using System;
using System.Collections.Generic;
using System.Configuration;
using System.ServiceModel;
using System.Text;

namespace DerivativesCalculator
{
    public class Program
    {
        public static void Main(string[] args)
        {
            Type serviceType = typeof(DerivativesCalculatorServiceType);

            string httpBaseAddress =
                ConfigurationManager.AppSettings["HTTPBaseAddress"];
            string tcpBaseAddress =
                ConfigurationManager.AppSettings["TCPBaseAddress"];
            Uri httpBaseAddressUri = new Uri(httpBaseAddress);
            Uri tcpBaseAddressUri = new Uri(tcpBaseAddress);
```

LISTING 2.2   Continued

```
        Uri[] baseAdresses = new Uri[] {
            httpBaseAddressUri,
            tcpBaseAddressUri};

        using(ServiceHost host = new ServiceHost(
            serviceType,
            baseAdresses))
        {
            host.Open();

            Console.WriteLine(
                "The derivatives calculator service is available."
            );
            Console.ReadKey();

            host.Close();
        }
    }
  }
}
```

The key lines in that code are these:

```
using(ServiceHost host = new ServiceHost(
    serviceType,
    baseAdresses))
{
    host.Open();

    ...
    host.Close();
}
```

ServiceHost is the class provided by the Windows Communication Foundation Service Model for programming .NET applications to host Windows Communication Foundation endpoints within application domains. In Listing 2.2, a constructor of the ServiceHost class is given information to identify the service type of the service to be hosted. The constructor is also given an array of Uniform Resource Identifiers (URIs). Those URIs are Windows Communication Foundation base addresses from which the actual addresses of each hosted Windows Communication Foundation endpoint will be derived. In this particular case, two base addresses are provided, and those base addresses are retrieved from the application's configuration file. Consequently, a configuration file with those base addresses must be created.

5. Use the Project, Add Item menu to add an application configuration file named `app.config` to the DerivativesCalculatorService project, as shown in Figure 2.9.

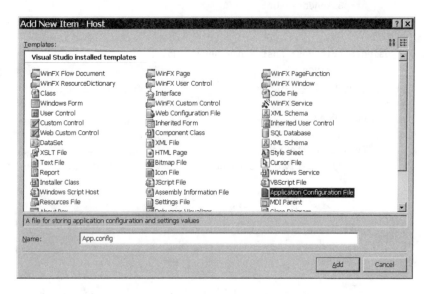

FIGURE 2.9   Adding an application configuration file.

6. Modify the contents of the `app.config` file in this way:

```xml
<?xml version="1.0" encoding="utf-8" ?>
<configuration>
    <appSettings>
        <add key="HTTPBaseAddress"
             value="http://localhost:8000/Derivatives/"/>
        <add key="TCPBaseAddress"
             value="net.tcp://localhost:8010/Derivatives/"/>
    </appSettings>
</configuration>
```

Here, the URIs used as base addresses are http://localhost:8000/Derivatives/ and net.tcp://localhost:8010/Derivatives/. The expression preceding the initial colon of a URI is called the *schema*, so the schemas of these URIs are http and tcp. In providing base addresses to the Windows Communication Foundation ServiceHost, the URI for each base address must have a unique schema.

7. Choose Build, Build Solution from the Visual Studio 2005 menu to ensure that there are no programming errors.

Specifying an Address and a Binding

A Windows Communication Foundation endpoint consists of an address, a binding, and a contract. A contract has been defined and implemented for the endpoint that will be used to provide access to the derivatives calculator class. To complete the endpoint, it is necessary to provide an address and a binding.

Specifying an address and a binding for an endpoint does not require writing any code, and is customarily the work of an administrator rather than a programmer. Providing an address and a binding can be done in code. However, that would require having to modify the code in order to change the address and the binding of the endpoint. A key innovation of the Windows Communication Foundation is to separate how software is programmed from how it communicates, which is what the binding specifies. So, generally, one avoids the option of specifying the addresses and bindings of endpoints in code. The alternative is to specify them in configuring the host.

As indicated previously, an editing tool is provided by which administrators can do the configuration. The use of that tool is covered in detail in Chapter 12, "Manageability." Here, to facilitate a detailed understanding of the configuration language, the configuration will be done by hand:

1. Modify the `app.config` file of the Host project to look as shown in Listing 2.3.

LISTING 2.3   Adding an Address and a Binding

```
<?xml version="1.0" encoding="utf-8" ?>
<configuration>
    <appSettings>
        <add key="HTTPBaseAddress" value="http://localhost:8000/Derivatives/"/>
        <add key="TCPBaseAddress" value="net.tcp://localhost:8010/Derivatives/"/>
    </appSettings>
    <system.serviceModel>
        <services>
            <service type=
"DerivativesCalculator.DerivativesCalculatorServiceType,
            DerivativesCalculatorService">
                <endpoint
                    address="Calculator"
                    binding="basicHttpBinding"
                    contract=
"DerivativesCalculator.IDerivativesCalculator,DerivativesCalculatorService"
                />
            </service>
        </services>
    </system.serviceModel>
</configuration>
```

2. Choose Build, Build Solution from the Visual Studio 2005.

In the XML in Listing 2.3,

```
<service type=
"DerivativesCalculator.DerivativesCalculatorServiceType,
          DerivativesCalculatorService">
```

identifies the configuration of the `DerivativesCalculatorServiceType` hosted by the Host application. The expression

```
"DerivativesCalculator.DerivativesCalculatorServiceType,
          DerivativesCalculatorService"
```

is the name of the `DerivativesCalculatorServiceType` in a standard .NET format, which is called the *assembly-qualified name* format. In the expression, `DerivativesCalculator` is the namespace of the service type, `DerivativesCalculatorServiceType` is the name of the service type itself, and `DerivativesCalculatorService` is the display name of the assembly that contains the service type.

The configuration defines a single endpoint at which the facilities exposed by the service type will be available. The address, the binding, and the contract constituents of the endpoint are all specified.

The contract constituent is identified by giving the assembly-qualified name of the interface that defines the service contract implemented by the service type, `DerivativesCalculatorServiceType`. That interface is `IDerivativesCalculator`, which is in the `DerivativesCalculatorService` assembly:

```
contract=
"DerivativesCalculator.IDerivativesCalculator,DerivativesCalculatorService"
```

The binding constituent of the endpoint is specified in this way:

```
binding="basicHttpBinding"
```

To understand what that signifies, one must understand Windows Communication Foundation bindings.

A Windows Communication Foundation binding is a combination of binding elements. Binding elements are the primary constituents provided by the Windows Communication Foundation's Channel Layer.

One special category of binding element consists of those that implement protocols for transporting messages. One of those is the binding element that implements the Hypertext Transport Protocol (HTTP). Another is the binding element that implements the Transmission Control Protocol (TCP).

Another special category of binding element consists of those that implement protocols for encoding messages. The Windows Communication Foundation provides three such binding elements. One is for encoding SOAP messages as text. Another is for encoding

SOAP messages in a binary format. The third is for encoding SOAP messages in accordance with the SOAP Message Transmission Optimization Mechanism (MTOM), which is suitable for messages that incorporate large quantities of binary data.

Examples of Windows Communication Foundation binding elements that are neither transport protocol binding elements nor message-encoding binding elements are the binding elements that implement the WS-Security protocol and the WS-ReliableMessaging protocol. One of the most important ways in which the capabilities of the Windows Communication Foundation can be extended is with the addition of new binding elements, which may be provided by Microsoft, or its partners, or by any software developer. Later chapters show how to program custom message-encoding binding elements and custom transport protocol binding elements.

Now, a Windows Communication Foundation binding is a collection of binding elements that must include at least one transport protocol binding element, one or more message-encoding protocol binding elements, and zero or more other binding elements. Bindings may be defined by selecting individual binding elements, either in code or in configuration. However, the Windows Communication Foundation provides several classes that represent common selections of binding elements. Those classes may be referred to as the *predefined bindings*.

One of the predefined bindings is the `BasicHttpBinding`. The `BasicHttpBinding` represents the combination of the HTTP transport binding element and the binding element for encoding SOAP messages in text format. The `BasicHttpBinding` class configures those binding elements in accordance with the WS-I Basic Profile Specification 1.1, which is a combination of Web service specifications chosen to promote interoperability among Web services and consumers of Web services on different platforms.

All the current predefined bindings are listed in Table 2.1. They each derive from the class `System.ServiceModel.Binding`.

TABLE 2.1   Windows Communication Foundation Predefined Bindings

Name	Purpose
BasicHttpBinding	Maximum interoperability through conformity to the WS-BasicProfile 1.1
WSHttpBinding	HTTP communication in conformity with WS-* protocols
WSDualHttpBinding	Duplex HTTP communication, by which the receiver of an initial message will not reply directly to the initial sender, but may transmit any number of responses via HTTP in conformity with WS-* protocols.
WSFederationBinding	HTTP communication, in which access to the resources of a service can be controlled based on credentials issued by an explicitly-identified credential provider
NetTcpBinding	Secure, reliable, high-performance communication between Windows Communication Foundation software entities across a network
NetNamedPipeBinding	Secure, reliable, high-performance communication between Windows Communication Foundation software entities on the same machine

TABLE 2.1   Continued

Name	Purpose
NetMsmqBinding	Communication between Windows Communication Foundation software entities via Microsoft Message Queuing (MSMQ)
MsmqIntegrationBinding	Communication between a Windows Communication Foundation software entity and another software entity via MSMQ
NetPeerTcpBinding	Communication between Windows Communication Foundation software entities via Windows Peer-to-Peer Networking

This specification, in the configuration of the endpoint for the DerivativesCalculatorService in Listing 2.3,

```
binding="basicHttpBinding"
```

identifies the BasicHttpBinding as the binding for that endpoint. The lowercase of the initial letter, *b*, is in conformity with a convention of using camel-casing in configuration files.

One can adjust the settings of a predefined binding by adding a binding configuration to the definition of the endpoint like so:

```
<system.serviceModel>
  <services>
    <service type=
"DerivativesCalculator.DerivativesCalculatorServiceType,
          DerivativesCalculatorService">
      <endpoint
        address="Calculator"
        binding="basicHttpBinding"
        bindingConfiguration="bindingSettings"
        contract=
"DerivativesCalculator.IDerivativesCalculator,DerivativesCalculatorService"
     />
    </service>
  </services>
  <bindings>
    <basicHttpBinding>
      <binding name="bindingSettings" messageEncoding="Mtom"/>
    </basicHttpBinding>
  </bindings>
</system.serviceModel>
```

In this case, the settings for the predefined BasicHttpBinding are adjusted so as to use the MTOM message-encoding binding element rather than the default text message-encoding binding element.

The address specified for the endpoint in the configuration of the DerivativesCalculatorService in Listing 2.3 is Calculator. That address for the endpoint is relative to a base address. Which of the base addresses provided to the host of a service is the base address for a given endpoint is determined based on the scheme of the base address, and the transport protocol implemented by the transport binding element of the endpoint, as shown in Table 2.2. The transport protocol implemented by the transport binding element of the endpoint is the HTTP protocol, so, based on the information in Table 2.2, the base address for the endpoint is http://localhost:8000/Derivatives/. Therefore, the absolute address for the endpoint is http://localhost:8000/Derivatives/Calculator.

TABLE 2.2   Mapping of Base Address Schemes to Transport Protocols

Base Address Scheme	Transport Protocol
http	HTTP
net.tcp	TCP
net.pipe	Named Pipes
net.msmq	MSMQ

Anyone who would like to know the complete Windows Communication Foundation configuration language should study the XML Schema file containing the definition of the configuration language. Assuming that the Visual Studio 2005 Extensions for WinFX have been installed, that XML Schema file should be \Program Files\Microsoft Visual Studio 8\Xml\Schemas\DotNetConfig.xsd, on the disc where Visual Studio 2005 is installed. If that file seems to be missing, search for a file with the extension .xsd, containing the expression system.serviceModel.

Deploying the Service

Now an address, a binding, and a contract have been provided for the Windows Communication Foundation endpoint at which the facilities of the derivatives calculator class will be made available. An application domain for hosting the service incorporating that endpoint has also been provided, or, to be more precise, it will be provided as soon as the Host console application is executed:

1. Execute that application now by right-clicking on the Host entry in the Visual Studio 2005 Solution Explorer, and selecting Debug, Start New Instance from the context menu. After a few seconds, the console application window of the host should appear, as in Figure 2.10.

   The Windows Communication Foundation has examined the code in the Host and DerivativesCalculatorService assemblies, as well as the contents of the Host assembly's configuration file. The code and the configuration use the Windows Communication Foundation's Service Model to define a service for accessing the derivatives calculator class. From that code and that configuration, the Windows Communication Foundation generates and configures the service using the programming framework constituted by the classes of the Channel Layer. In particular, it employs the binding element classes used by the `BasicProfileBinding` class that was selected as the binding for the service. Then the Windows Communication Foundation loads the service into the default application domain of the Host console application.

FIGURE 2.10   The Host console application running.

2. Confirm that the Windows Communication Foundation service for accessing the capabilities of the derivatives calculator class is available by directing a browser to the HTTP base address that was provided to the ServiceHost: http://localhost:8000/ Derivatives/. A page like the one shown in Figure 2.11 should be opened in the browser.

   A similar page can be retrieved for any Windows Communications Foundation service with a host that has been provided with a base address with the scheme http. It is not necessary that the service have any endpoints with addresses relative to that base address.

3. Add the query `wsdl` to the URI at which the browser is pointing, by pointing the browser at http://localhost:8000/Derivatives/?wsdl, as in Figure 2.12, and the WSDL for the service should be displayed.

Using the Service

Now a Windows Communication Foundation service is available for accessing the facilities of the derivatives calculator class. The Windows Communication Foundation can be employed to construct a client for the derivatives calculator, a software entity that uses the facilities of the derivatives calculator via the service. Different ways to build the client with the Windows Communication Foundation are shown, as well as ways to build a client in Java for the same Windows Communication Foundation service.

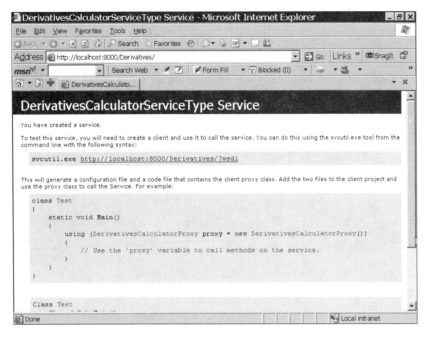

FIGURE 2.11   Help page for a service.

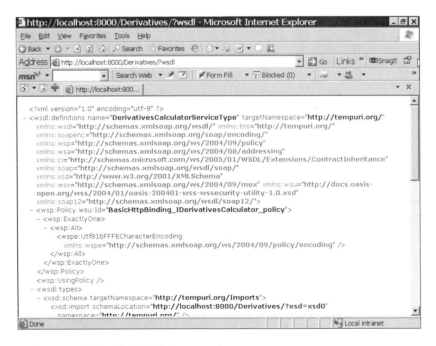

FIGURE 2.12   Examining the WSDL for a service.

Using the Service with a Windows Communication Foundation Client

For the following steps, access to the tools provided with the Windows Communication Foundation from a .NET command prompt will be required. Assuming a complete and normal installation of the Microsoft Windows SDK for the January 2006 WinFX CTP, that access is provided by a command prompt that should be accessible from the Windows Start menu by choosing All Programs, Microsoft Windows SDK, CMD Shell. That command prompt will be referred to as the *Microsoft Windows Vista DEBUG Build Environment prompt*. From that prompt, the Windows Communication Foundation's Service Metadata Tool, SvcUtil.exe, will be used to generate components of the client for the derivatives calculator:

1. If the Host console application had been shut down, start an instance of it, as before.

2. Open the Microsoft Windows Vista DEBUG Build Environment prompt.

3. Enter

   ```
   C:
   ```

   and then

   ```
   cd c:\WCFHandsOn\Fundamentals\DerivativesCalculatorSolution
   ```

   at that prompt to make to the derivatives calculator solution folder the current directory.

4. Next, enter

   ```
   svcutil http://localhost:8000/Derivatives//out:Client.cs /config:app.config
   ```

   The output should be as shown in Figure 2.13.

FIGURE 2.13 Using the Service Metadata Tool.

The command executes the Windows Communication Foundation's Service Metadata Tool, passing it a base address of a service that has the scheme http. In this case, it is passed the base address of the derivatives calculator service constructed by the earlier steps in this chapter. Given a base address of a Windows Communication

Foundation service, provided it is an address with scheme http, the Service Metadata Tool can retrieve the WSDL for the service and other associated metadata and, by default, generate the C# code for a class that can serve as a proxy for communicating with the service. It also generates, by default, a .NET application-specific configuration file containing the definition of the service's endpoints. The switches `/out:Client.cs` and `/config:app.config` used in the foregoing command specify the names to be used for the file containing the C# code and for the configuration file. In the next few steps, the output from the Service Metadata Tool will be used to complete the client for the derivatives calculator.

5. Choose Debug, Stop Debugging from the Visual Studio 2005 menus to terminate the instance of the Host console application so that the solution can be modified.

6. Select File, New, Project from Visual Studio 2005 menus to add a C# Console Application project called Client to the DerivativesCalculator solution.

7. Choose Project, Add Reference from the Visual Studio 2005 menus, and add a reference to the Windows Communication Foundation's `System.ServiceModel` .NET assembly to the client project.

8. Select Project, Add Existing Item from the Visual Studio 2005 menus, and add the files `Client.cs` and `app.config`, in the folder `C:\WCFHandsOn\Fundamentals\DerivativesCalculatorSolution`, to the Client project, as shown in Figure 2.14. Those are the files that should have been emitted by the Service Metadata Tool.

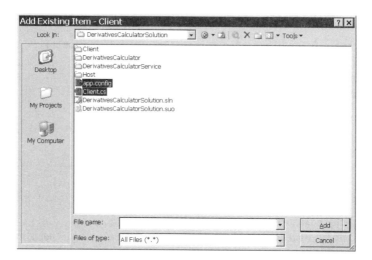

FIGURE 2.14   Adding output from the Service Metadata Tool to a project.

9. Alter the code in the `Program.cs` file of the Client project of the derivatives calculator solution to use the class generated by the Service Metadata Tool as a proxy for communicating with the derivatives calculator service. The code in the `Program.cs` file should be the code in Listing 2.4.

LISTING 2.4   Using the Generated Client Class

```
using System;
using System.Collections.Generic;
using System.Text;

namespace Client
{
    public class Program
    {
        public static void Main(string[] args)
        {
            Console.WriteLine("Press any key when the service is ready.");
            Console.ReadKey();

            decimal result = 0;
            using (DerivativesCalculatorProxy proxy =
                new DerivativesCalculatorProxy("CalculatorEndpoint"))
            {
                result = proxy.CalculateDerivative(
                    new string[] { "MSFT" },
                    new decimal[] { 3 },
                    new string[] { });
                proxy.Close();
            }
            Console.WriteLine(string.Format("Result: {0}", result));

            Console.WriteLine("Press any key to exit.");
            Console.ReadKey();

        }
    }
}
```

In Listing 2.4, the statement

```
DerivativesCalculatorProxy proxy =
                new DerivativesCalculatorProxy("CalculatorEndpoint")
```

creates an instance of the class generated by the Service Metadata Tool to serve as a proxy for the derivatives calculator service. The string parameter passed to the constructor of the class, CalculatorEndpoint, identifies which definition of an endpoint in the application's configuration file is the definition of the endpoint with which this instance of the class is to communicate. Therefore, one must identify an endpoint definition in the configuration file accordingly.

The `app.config` file added to the Client project in step 8 should contain this definition of an endpoint, with a specification of an address, a binding, and a contract:

```
<client>
            <endpoint address="http://localhost:8000/Derivatives/Calculator"
                bindingConfiguration="BasicHttpBinding_IDerivativesCalculator"
                binding="customBinding" contract="IDerivativesCalculator" />
</client>
```

Why does the binding look different here than it does in the configuration file for the service? The Service Metadata Tool does not know about the predefined bindings, which the Windows Communication Foundation provides as a convenience for humans. The Service Metadata Tool examines the metadata for the service and configures a custom binding to match the substance of the binding described in the metadata.

10. Modify the endpoint definition so that it has the name of the endpoint definition passed to the constructor of the proxy class in the foregoing C# code, the name `CalculatorEndpoint`:

```
<client>
            <endpoint name="CalculatorEndpoint"
                address="http://localhost:8000/Derivatives/Calculator"
                bindingConfiguration="BasicHttpBinding_IDerivativesCalculator"
                binding="customBinding" contract="IDerivativesCalculator" />
</client>
```

11. Prepare to have the client use the derivatives calculator by modifying the startup project properties of the derivatives calculator solution as shown in Figure 2.15.

12. Choose Debug, Start Debugging from the Visual Studio 2005 menus.

13. When there is activity in the console for the Host application, enter a keystroke into the console for the Client application. The client should obtain an estimate of the value of a derivative from the derivatives calculator service, as shown in Figure 2.16. Note that the value shown in the Client application console may vary from the value shown in Figure 2.16, due to variations in prevailing market conditions over time.

14. In Visual Studio 2005, choose Debug, Stop Debugging from the menus.

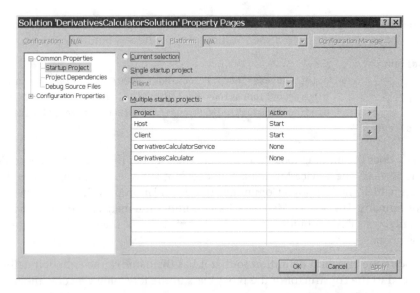

FIGURE 2.15 Startup project properties of the derivatives calculator solution.

FIGURE 2.16 Using the derivatives calculator via a service.

Different Ways of Coding Windows Communication Clients

In the preceding steps for building a client for the derivatives calculator service, the code for the client was generated using the Windows Communication Foundation's Service Metadata Tool. The generated code consists of a version of the IDerivativesProxy interface, and the code of a proxy class for communicating with the derivatives calculator service. The latter code is in Listing 2.5.

LISTING 2.5   Generated Proxy Class

```
public partial class DerivativesCalculatorProxy :
    System.ServiceModel.ClientBase<IDerivativesCalculator>,
    IDerivativesCalculator
{

    public DerivativesCalculatorProxy()
    {
    }

    public DerivativesCalculatorProxy(string endpointConfigurationName) :
            base(endpointConfigurationName)
    {
    }

    public DerivativesCalculatorProxy(string endpointConfigurationName,
        string remoteAddress) :
            base(endpointConfigurationName, remoteAddress)
    {
    }

    public DerivativesCalculatorProxy(string endpointConfigurationName,
        System.ServiceModel.EndpointAddress remoteAddress) :
            base(endpointConfigurationName, remoteAddress)
    {
    }

    public DerivativesCalculatorProxy(System.ServiceModel.Binding binding,
        System.ServiceModel.EndpointAddress remoteAddress) :
            base(binding, remoteAddress)
    {
    }

    public decimal CalculateDerivative(string[] symbols,
        decimal[] parameters,
        string[] functions)
    {
        return base.InnerProxy.CalculateDerivative(symbols,
            parameters,
            functions);
    }
}
```

Naturally, one can write such a class instead of generating it with the Service Metadata
Tool. To do so, one simply defines a class that inherits from the Windows

Communication Foundation's ClientBase<T> generic, and that implements the contract for the service:

```
[ServiceContract]
public interface IDerivativesCalculator
{
    [OperationContract]
    decimal CalculateDerivative(
            string[] symbols,
            decimal[] parameters,
            string[] functions);
    ...
}


public partial class DerivativesCalculatorProxy :
    ClientBase<IDerivativesCalculator>,
    IDerivativesCalculator
{
  ...
}
```

Then, in the class's implementations of the contract, one simply delegates to the methods of the InnerProxy property of ClientBase<T>:

```
public partial class DerivativesCalculatorProxy :
    ClientBase<IDerivativesCalculator>,
    IDerivativesCalculator
{
    public decimal CalculateDerivative(string[] symbols,
        decimal[] parameters,
        string[] functions)
    {
        return base.InnerProxy.CalculateDerivative(symbols,
            parameters,
            functions);
    }
}
```

This way of writing a Windows Communication Foundation client for the derivatives calculator service is one of at least three ways of doing so. The other way of writing a client for the service, given a definition of the IDerivativesCalculator contract, would simply be to write

```
IDerivativesCalculator proxy =
  new ChannelFactory<IDerivativesCalculator>("CalculatorEndpoint").
  CreateChannel();
proxy.CalculateDerivative(... );
((IChannel)proxy).Close();
```

Whereas the first method for writing clients yields a reusable proxy class, this second method merely yields a proxy variable.

A third option for writing the client would be to program it in such a way that it downloads the metadata for the service and configures a proxy in accordance with that metadata while executing. Listing 2.6 shows how to do that using the Windows Communication Foundation's `MetadataResolver` class. A `MetadataResolver` instance is provided with a location for the metadata for the derivatives calculator service, the same metadata shown earlier in Figure 2.12. Then the `RetrieveEndpointsUsingHttpGet()` method of the `MetadataResolver` instance is used to download that metadata and generate a collection of `ServiceEndpoint` objects that describe the service endpoints defined in the metadata. Each `ServiceEndpoint` object is used to configure a proxy variable that is then able to be used for communicating with the service.

LISTING 2.6   Retrieving Metadata Dynamically

```
using System;
using System.Collections.Generic;
using System.ServiceModel;
using System.ServiceModel.Design;
using System.Text;

namespace Client
{
    class Program
    {
        static void Main(string[] args)
        {
            Console.WriteLine("Press any key when the service is ready.");
            Console.ReadKey();

            MetadataResolver metadataResolver = new MetadataResolver(
                new EndpointAddress(
                @"http://localhost/Metadata/DerivativesCalculatorService.wsdl"));
            ServiceEndpointCollection endpoints =
                metadataResolver.RetrieveEndpointsUsingHttpGet();
            IDerivativesCalculator proxy = null;
            foreach (ServiceEndpoint endpoint in endpoints)
            {
                proxy = new ChannelFactory<IDerivativesCalculator>(
                    endpoint.Binding, endpoint.Address).CreateChannel();
                proxy.CalculateDerivative(
                    3,
                    new string[] { "MSFT" },
                    new string[] { });
                ((IChannel)proxy).Close();
```

LISTING 2.6   Continued

```
            }

            Console.WriteLine("Press any key to exit.");
            Console.ReadKey();
        }
    }
}
```

Using the Service with a Java Client

The service by which the facilities of the derivatives calculator class are made available for use by other software entities is configured to use the Windows Communication Foundation's standard BasicProfileBinding. That binding conforms to the WS-I Basic Profile Specification 1.1. Therefore, the service can be used not only by clients built using the Windows Communication Foundation, but by any clients that can consume services that comply with that specification.

The Apache Foundation provides a Web services development toolkit for Java programmers called *Axis*. Axis incorporates a tool called *WSDL2Java*, which, like the Windows Communication Foundation's Service Metadata Tool, will download the WSDL for a service and generate the code of a class that can be used as a proxy for the service. Whereas the Windows Communication Foundation's Service Metadata Tool can generate code in the C#, Visual Basic.NET, VBScript, JScript, JavaScript, Visual J#, and C++ programming languages, the WSDL2Java tool generates code only in the Java programming language.

One can download Axis from http://ws.apache.org/axis/. After it has been installed correctly, and the Host console application of the derivatives calculator solution is running, one can issue this command from a command prompt:

```
java org.apache.axis.wsdl.WSDL2Java http://localhost/Derivatives/?wsdl
```

That command should cause WSDL2Java to download the WSDL for the Windows Communication Foundation derivatives calculator service and generate Java code for accessing the service.

The quantity of that code will be much larger than the quantity of code emitted by the Windows Communication Foundation's Service Metadata Tool. The code for a proxy class for the derivatives calculator service generated by the WSDL2Java tool is 18KB in size, whereas the code for a proxy class for the same service emitted by the Windows Communication Foundation's tool is about 3KB in size.

Given the code emitted by the WSDL2Java tool, one can write a Java application to use the derivatives calculator service. The code for such an application is in Listing 2.7. Figure 2.17 shows the application executing within the Eclipse 3.1 development environment, which is available from http://eclipse.org/downloads/.

LISTING 2.7   WSDL2Java Proxy

```java
import org.tempuri.*;
import java.math.*;

public class Client
{
    public static void main(String[] arguments)
    {
        try
        {
            String[] symbols = new String[1];
            symbols[0] = "MSFT";

            BigDecimal[] parameters = new BigDecimal[1];
            parameters[0] = new BigDecimal(3);

            String[] functions = new String[1];
            functions[0] = "TechStockProjections";

            DerivativesCalculatorServiceTypeLocator locator =
                new DerivativesCalculatorServiceTypeLocator();
            IDerivativesCalculator stub =
                locator.getBasicHttpBinding_IDerivativesCalculator_port();
            BigDecimal[] values = new BigDecimal[1];
            values[0] = stub.calculateDerivative(symbols,parameters,functions);


            System.out.println(String.format("Result: %f", values));
        }
        catch(Exception e)
        {
            System.out.println("Error: " + e.getMessage());
        }

        try
        {
            System.in.read();
        }
        catch(Exception e)
        {
        }
    }
}
```

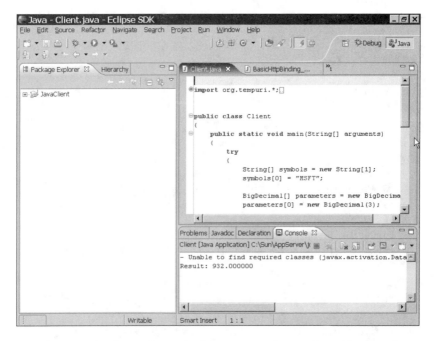

FIGURE 2.17   Using the derivatives calculator service using a Java Client.

Hosting the Service in IIS

Recall that IIS can be made to provide application domains for hosting Windows Communication Foundation services. Having IIS provide hosts for Windows Communication Foundation services is beneficial for several reasons:

- IIS is a scalable host. Its scalability features include central processing unit (CPU) affinity and web gardening.

- IIS is a reliable host. Its reliability features include health management, process isolation, and application domain isolation.

- IIS is a fault-tolerant host. If an unhandled exception occurs in a service, IIS automatically restarts it.

- The security of IIS has been arduously tested, found wanting, and reinforced. Although IIS is notorious for having been the victim of a number of successful attacks in the past, it now incorporates lessons learned from that experience, making it far more trustworthy than untried alternatives.

Only services of which all the endpoints have bindings for communicating using HTTP can be hosted within IIS 5.1 and IIS 6, those being the versions of IIS provided for Windows XP and Windows Server 2003. IIS 7 incorporates a new facility called the Windows Activation Service for routing messages received using any transport protocol to hosted .NET assemblies. Thus, Windows Communication Foundation services can be hosted within IIS 7 regardless of their transport protocols. Even custom transport protocols added to the Windows Communication Foundation's Channel Layer can be supported in IIS 7 through customizations to the Windows Activation Service.

To have IIS host a Windows Communication Foundation service, one must simply identify the service type of the service to IIS. That is done in a file with content very similar to the contents of the `.asmx` file that one would use in creating an ASP.NET Web service. For example, to have the derivatives calculator service hosted within IIS, one would use a file containing these directives:

```
<%@Service Class="DerivativesCalculator.DerivativesCalculatorServiceType" %>
<%@Assembly Name="DerivativesCalculatorService" %>
```

The `Service` directive identifies the service type of the service that IIS is to host, and the `Assembly` directive indicates which assembly contains that service type.

Now, by default, a file with these directives, telling IIS to host a Windows Communication Foundation service, must have the extension `.svc`. In the February CTP and earlier releases of WinFX, that default cannot be modified, but it will be possible to modify it in subsequent releases. Specifically, one will be able to specify any number of extensions by adding the appropriate entries to the system's `web.config` file, which should be in the `CONFIG` subdirectory of the .NET Framework installation folder. For example, entries like these would specify that not only the `.svc` extension, but also the `.asmx` extension should be treated as containing directives for the hosting of Windows Communication Foundation services:

```
<system.web>
  ...
  <compilation>
    ...
    <buildProviders>
      ...
      <add
        extension=".asmx"
        type="System.ServiceModel.ServiceBuildProvider,
              System.ServiceModel, ... " />
      <add
        extension=".svc"
        type="System.ServiceModel.ServiceBuildProvider,
              System.ServiceModel, ..." />
    </buildProviders>
    ...
  </compilation>
  ...
</system.web>
```

Having files with the .asmx extension treated as files with directives for hosting Windows Communication Foundation services would be useful in rewriting ASP.NET Web services as Windows Communication Foundation services. One could rewrite the ASP.NET services as Windows Communication Foundation services and have clients of the original services still be able to refer to those services using URI with a path containing an .asmx extension.

Up to this point, the Windows Communication Foundation service for accessing the facilities of the derivatives calculator class has been hosted within a console application. The steps for hosting the service within IIS begin with these steps for creating an IIS virtual directory by which IIS will map a URI to the location of the derivatives calculator service:

1. Choose Administrative Tools, Internet Information Services (IIS) Manager from the Windows Start menu.

2. Expand the nodes of the tree control in the left pane until the node named Default Web Site becomes visible.

3. Right-click on that node, and choose New, Virtual Directory from the context menu that appears.

4. In the Virtual Directory Creation Wizard, enter DerivativesCalculator in the Virtual Directory alias screen.

5. Enter

   ```
   c:\WCFHandsOn\Fundamentals\DerivativesCalculatorSolution\
   ➡DerivativesCalculatorService
   ```

   as the path on the Web Site Content Directory screen of the wizard.

6. Select the Read, Run Scripts, and Execute permissions on the wizard's Virtual Directory Access Permissions screen; then click Next and follow the instructions to exit the wizard.

The creation of the IIS virtual directory is complete. Here are the remaining steps for having IIS host the derivatives calculator service:

1. Add a text file named Service.svc to the DerivativesCalculatorService project.

2. Add content to that file so that it looks like this:

   ```
   <%@Service Class="DerivativesCalculator.DerivativesCalculatorServiceType" %>
   <%@Assembly Name="DerivativesCalculatorService" %>
   ```

   Those directives tell IIS to host the Windows Communication Foundation service type DerivativesCalculator.DerivativesCalculatorServiceType that is in the assembly DerivativesCalculatorService. IIS will be looking for that assembly in the bin subdirectory of the folder in which the file referring to the assembly is located. Therefore, it is necessary to ensure that the asssembly is located there. The next two steps will accomplish that task.

3. Select the DerivativesCalculatorService project of DerivativesCalculatorSolution in the Visual Studio 2005 Solution Explorer. Choose Project, DerivativesCalculatorService Properties from the Visual Studio menus. Select the Build tab, and set the value of the Output path property to refer to the bin subdirectory of the project directory, as shown in Figure 2.18.

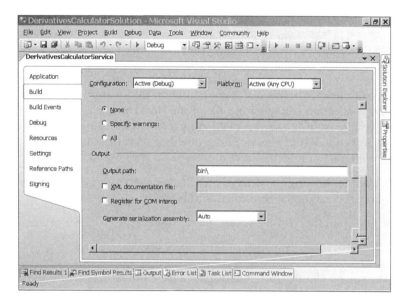

FIGURE 2.18   Altering the build properties of the DerivativesCalculatorService project.

4. Select Build, Build Solution from the Visual Studio 2005 menus.

   The remaining two steps are for configuring the service. In hosting the service within the Host console application, the configuration for the service was incorporated into the configuration file for that application. Now that the service is to be hosted within IIS, the configuration information must be a configuration file named Web.config in the same directory as the file with the directives telling IIS to host the service.

5. Add an application configuration file named Web.config to the DerivativesCalculatorService project in the derivatives calculator solution.

6. Modify the contents of that file in this way, before saving the file:

```xml
<?xml version="1.0" encoding="utf-8" ?>
<configuration>
    <system.serviceModel>
        <services>
            <service type=
"DerivativesCalculator.DerivativesCalculatorServiceType,
    DerivativesCalculatorService">
```

```
        <endpoint
            address=""
            binding="basicHttpBinding"
            contract=
"DerivativesCalculator.IDerivativesCalculator,DerivativesCalculatorService"
            />
        </service>
      </services>
    </system.serviceModel>
</configuration>
```

There is just one difference between this configuration information and the information that was in the application configuration file of the Host console application: The value provided for the address of the service's endpoint is an empty string. The reason is that the address of any endpoint of a service hosted within IIS is the URI of the file containing the directives telling IIS to host the service.

The work required for hosting the derivatives calculator service in IIS is complete. The availability of the service can be confirmed in this way:

1. Choose Run from the Windows Start menu, and enter

   ```
   http://localhost/DerivativesCalculator/Service.svc
   ```

   Internet Explorer should open and display a page similar to the one shown earlier in Figure 2.11. Now that the service is available, the client can be modified to use the derivatives calculator service hosted within IIS.

2. Modify the app.config file in the Client project of the derivatives calculator solution to refer to the address of the endpoint hosted within IIS by changing this entry in the file,

   address="http://localhost:8000/Derivatives/Calculator"

   to this:

   address="http://localhost/DerivativesCalculatorService/Service.svc"

3. Choose Build, Build Solution from the Visual Studio 2005 menus.

4. Right-click on the Client entry in the Visual Studio 2005 Solution Explorer, and select, Debug, Start New Instance from the context menu.

5. When the console application window of the host appears, enter a keystroke into the console. The client obtains an estimate of the value of a derivative from the derivatives calculator service hosted in IIS, with output like that shown earlier in Figure 2.16. Note, again, that the value shown in the Client application console may vary from the value shown in Figure 2.16, due to variations in prevailing market conditions over time.

6. Close the Client executable.

Securing the Service

The only provision that the WS-I Basic Profile 1.1 makes for securing communications is the use of HTTPS. Because that protocol was never applied to the derivatives calculator service, one should not expect that transmissions to and from the service are being kept confidential at this point.

The following steps will prove that the transmissions are not being kept confidential. They will also demonstrate just one of the Windows Communications Foundation's many features for administering services, its facility for logging messages:

1. Provide an empty folder to which the Windows Communication Foundation can log messages. In the following steps, that folder will be assumed to be `c:\logs`.

2. Modify the `Web.config` file of the DerivativesCalculatorService project to look as shown in Listing 2.8, which configures a standard .NET diagnostics trace listener to listen for trace information emanating from the Windows Communication Foundation's message logging facility, `System.ServiceModel.MessageLogging`. The configuration also turns that logging facility on with the diagnostics element within the `System.ServiceModel` element.

LISTING 2.8   Message Logging Configuration

```xml
<?xml version="1.0" encoding="utf-8" ?>
<configuration>
    <system.diagnostics>
        <sources>
            <source
                name="System.ServiceModel.MessageLogging"
                switchValue="Verbose">
                <listeners>
                    <add
                        name="xml"
                        type="System.Diagnostics.XmlWriterTraceListener"
                        initializeData="c:\logs\message.log" />
                </listeners>
            </source>
        </sources>
        <trace autoflush="true" />
    </system.diagnostics>
    <system.serviceModel>
        <diagnostics>
            <messageLogging logEntireMessage="true"
                            maxMessagesToLog="300"
                            logMessagesAtServiceLevel="false"
                            logMalformedMessages="true"
                            logMessagesAtTransportLevel="true" />
        </diagnostics>
```

LISTING 2.8   Continued

```
        <services>
            <service type=
"DerivativesCalculator.DerivativesCalculatorServiceType,
   DerivativesCalculatorService">
                <endpoint
                    address=""
                    binding="basicHttpBinding"
                    contract=
"DerivativesCalculator.IDerivativesCalculator,DerivativesCalculatorService"
                    />
            </service>
        </services>
    </system.serviceModel>
</configuration>
```

3. Build the solution.

4. Start an instance of the Client executable, and enter a keystroke into the console for the Client application. The client should obtain an estimate of the value of a derivative from the derivatives calculator service hosted in IIS, as shown earlier in Figure 2.16.

5. Close the Client executable.

6. Open the file c:\logs\Message.log in Notepad. Search for the string MSFT, which, as should be apparent from Listing 2.4, is a stock symbol that the client transmits to the server in its request to calculate the value of a derivative. That string will be found in the file, because communications with the derivatives calculator service are not being kept confidential.

The Windows Communication Foundation provides at least two principal ways of remedying that problem. One is to secure the transmissions by using a secure transport protocol, substituting HTTPS for HTTP, for example. The other is to encrypt the messages before transporting them, as provided for by the WS-Security protocol, for example.

Securing the Service with a Secure Transport Protocol

The HTTPS protocol uses the Secure Socket Layer/Transport Layer Security (SSL/TLS) protocol. Instructions for configuring the SSL/TLS protocol on IIS are available at http://www.microsoft.com/smallbusiness/support/articles/sec_IIS_6_0.mspx#EDAA.

Assuming that the SSL/TLS protocol has been configured on the IIS hosting the derivatives calculator service, secure transmissions between the client and the service via the HTTPS protocol can be accomplished simply by replacing the contents of the Web.config file in the DerivativesCalculatorService project of the derivatives calculator solution with the configuration in Listing 2.9, and by replacing the contents of the app.config file the Client project with the configuration in Listing 2.10.

LISTING 2.9   Secure Service Configuration

```xml
<?xml version="1.0" encoding="utf-8" ?>
<configuration>
    <system.serviceModel>
        <services>
            <service type=
"DerivativesCalculator.DerivativesCalculatorServiceType,
  DerivativesCalculatorService">
                <endpoint
                    address=""
                    binding="basicHttpBinding"
                    bindingConfiguration="SecureBasicHttpBinding"
                    contract=
"DerivativesCalculator.IDerivativesCalculator,DerivativesCalculatorService"
                />
            </service>
        </services>
        <bindings>
            <basicHttpBinding>
                <binding name="SecureBasicHttpBinding">
                    <security mode="Transport">
                        <transport clientCredentialType="None"/>
                    </security>
                </binding>
            </basicHttpBinding>
        </bindings>
    </system.serviceModel>
</configuration>
```

LISTING 2.10   Secure Client Configuration

```xml
<?xml version="1.0" encoding="utf-8"?>
<configuration>
    <system.serviceModel>
        <client>
            <endpoint
            name="CalculatorEndpoint"
            address="https://localhost/DerivativesCalculatorService/Service.svc"
            bindingConfiguration="SecureBasicHttpBinding"
            binding="basicHttpBinding" contract="IDerivativesCalculator" />
        </client>
        <bindings>
        <basicHttpBinding>
            <binding name="SecureBasicHttpBinding">
                <security mode="Transport">
```

LISTING 2.10   Continued

```
                <transport clientCredentialType="None"/>
            </security>
        </binding>
    </basicHttpBinding>
    </bindings>
    </system.serviceModel>
</configuration>
```

Both configurations incorporate these two lines:

```
binding="basicHttpBinding"
bindingConfiguration="SecureBasicHttpBinding"
```

The first line should be familiar from the foregoing: It simply says that the standard Windows Communication Foundation BasicHttpBinding is the binding for the derivatives calculator endpoint. The second line is new. It says that the properties of the standard BasicHttpBinding are to be modified somewhat from their default values, and that the set of modifications are labeled SecureBasicHttpBinding. Elsewhere within the System.ServiceModel element of the configuration, there is this sub-element:

```
<bindings>
    <basicHttpBinding>
        <binding name="SecureBasicHttpBinding">
            <security mode="Transport">
                <transport clientCredentialType="None"/>
            </security>
        </binding>
    </basicHttpBinding>
</bindings>
```

That sub-element could contain any number of different sets of modifications to the default settings of any number of different standard bindings. In this case, it contains just one set of modifications, which is the set with the label SecureBasicHttpBinding, the set to which the line

```
bindingConfiguration="SecureBasicHttpBinding"
```

referred. The modifications to the default settings specify that transmissions are to be secured by the transport protocol. Note that the only modifications that the Windows Communication provides for the standard BasicHttpBinding are modifications that are permitted by the WS-I Basic Profile 1.1 specification.

The only other important change in the configurations is this alteration, in Listing 2.10, to the client configuration:

```
address="https://localhost/DerivativesCalculatorService/Service.svc"
```

2

It uses the scheme https in the URI for the service, thereby directing the request via IIS's SSL/TLS socket.

Encrypting Messages Before Transporting Them

WS-Security is a standard protocol for ensuring the confidentiality of communications through the encryption of messages. Although the WS-Security protocol is widely accepted and despite there being several implementations, it is, nonetheless, not included in the WS-I Basic Profile Specification 1.1, which was meant to ensure interoperability by incorporating only the most fundamental protocols. Yet although the use of a transport security protocol like HTTPS to ensure confidentiality tends to provide better performance, the use of a protocol like WS-Security that works by encrypting the messages before transporting them offers more flexibility. For example, whereas the use of HTTPS presupposes having a Web server like IIS that supports HTTPS, the Windows Communication makes it very simple to apply the WS-Security protocol in scenarios with or without IIS. Follow these steps to see how it is done:

1. Modify the app.config file of the Host project in the derivatives calculator solution to look like the configuration in Listing 2.11.

LISTING 2.11   Configuring for Message Security

```
<?xml version="1.0" encoding="utf-8" ?>
<configuration>
    <appSettings>
        <add key="HTTPBaseAddress" value="http://localhost:8000/Derivatives/"/>
        <add key="TCPBaseAddress" value="net.tcp://localhost:8010/Derivatives/"/>
    </appSettings>
    <system.diagnostics>
        <sources>
            <source
                name="System.ServiceModel.MessageLogging"
                switchValue="Verbose">
                <listeners>
                    <add
                        name="xml"
                        type="System.Diagnostics.XmlWriterTraceListener"
                        initializeData="c:\logs\message.log" />
                </listeners>
            </source>
        </sources>
        <trace autoflush="true" />
    </system.diagnostics>
    <system.serviceModel>
        <services>
<diagnostics>
            <messageLogging logEntireMessage="true"
                            maxMessagesToLog="300"
```

LISTING 2.11   Continued

```
                                logMessagesAtServiceLevel="false"
                                logMalformedMessages="true"
                                logMessagesAtTransportLevel="true" />
            </diagnostics>
                <service type=
"DerivativesCalculator.DerivativesCalculatorServiceType,
  DerivativesCalculatorService">
                    <endpoint
                        address="Calculator"
                        binding="wsHttpBinding"
                        contract=
"DerivativesCalculator.IDerivativesCalculator,DerivativesCalculatorService"
                    />
                </service>
            </services>
        </system.serviceModel>
</configuration>
```

This change to the configuration file of the .NET application for hosting the deriva-tives calculator service substitutes the standard binding WSHttpBinding for the stan-dard binding BasicHttpBinding that had been used before. WSHttpBinding is a standard binding that, by default, uses the WS-Security protocol.

The new configuration also has the service log the messages it receives. Specifically, the service is to log the messages to the file message.log in the folder c:\logs. Change that setting to point to a different file and folder if necessary.

2. Ensure that whatever file is referred to in the configuration for logging the messages does not exist, or has been deleted. Having a fresh log will serve to highlight the effects of the new configuration clearly.

3. Change the app.config file in the Client project to look like this, with a description of the derivatives calculator endpoint matching the description in the server's configuration:

```
<?xml version="1.0" encoding="utf-8"?>
<configuration>
    <system.serviceModel>
        <client>
            <endpoint
            name="SelfHostedEndpoint"
            address="http://localhost:8000/Derivatives/Calculator"
    binding="wsHttpBinding" contract="IDerivativesCalculator" />
        </client>
    </system.serviceModel>
</configuration>
```

4. Choose Debug, Start Debugging from the Visual Studio 2005 menus.

5. When there is activity in the console for the Host application, enter a keystroke into the console for the Client application. The client should again obtain an estimate of the value of a derivative from the derivatives calculator service, as shown earlier in Figure 2.16.

6. Stop debugging.

7. Open the file c:\logs\Message.log in Notepad. Search for the string MSFT, which, as mentioned before, is a stock symbol that the client transmits to the server in its request to calculate the value of a derivative. That string will not be found in the file, because now the messages exchanged with the derivatives calculator service are being kept confidential through encryption.

8. Modify the CalculateDerivative() method of the DerivativesCalculatorServiceType in the DerivativesCalculatorService project to look like this:

```
decimal IDerivativesCalculator.CalculateDerivative(
            string[] symbols,
            decimal[] parameters,
            string[] functions)
{
Console.WriteLine(
            "Message received from {0}.",
            System.ServiceModel.
            OperationContext.
            Current.ServiceSecurityContext.
            WindowsIdentity.Name.ToString());
            return new Calculator().CalculateDerivative(
                symbols, parameters, functions);
}
```

9. Reexecute steps 4, 5, and 6. This time, the console application window of the Host application should show the identity of the user of the client application. That is possible because, by default, the WSHttpBinding uses the Windows identity of the user of the client application to authenticate a client to a service. The Windows Communication Foundation Service Model's OperationContext class provides static properties for retrieving information about the context in which a method of a service is being invoked, and, in the new code for the CalculateDerivative() method, it is the information about the identity of the client that is retrieved and displayed.

The Windows Communication Foundation's OperationContext class may seem familiar to programmers used to Microsoft Transaction Server, COM+, and Enterprise Services programming. The OperationContext class is similar to the ContextUtil class of those earlier programming interfaces.

Debugging

The Windows Communication Foundation's facility for logging messages has already been demonstrated earlier in this chapter. That is a powerful tool for diagnosing problems with services in production, and it should be welcomed by anyone who has attempted the challenging task of logging messages to or from ASP.NET Web Services. Other potent instruments for administering Windows Communication Foundation solutions in production are covered in Chapter 12.

To diagnose problems with Windows Communication Foundation solutions in development, the most important tool is the Visual Studio 2005 debugger. Generally, one can simply set breakpoints in the code for a client or service, and start debugging one's code.

In the case of a service, what happens when one starts debugging it within Visual Studio 2005 is that Visual Studio automatically attaches its debugger to the host process. When the service is being hosted within IIS, one must attach the Visual Studio 2005 debugger to the host process manually. Doing so requires two steps.

The first step is to cause IIS to actually have the service loaded into an application domain. That can be done either by having a client invoke the service, or by browsing to the location of the service's .svc file to view the service's help page.

The remaining step is to actually attach the Visual Studio debugger to the host process. One begins doing that by choosing Debug, Attach to Process from the Visual Studio menus. Then, on Windows Server 2003 one selects w3wp.exe from the list in the Attach to Process dialog, and on Windows XP one selects aspnet_wp.exe, those being the processes in which IIS hosts Windows Communication Foundation services. Finally, one clicks on the Attach button. Then, any breakpoint set in the code for the service can provide a starting point for stepping through it.

Evidently, although it is not especially difficult to debug services hosted in IIS, it is a little more challenging. Therefore, it is recommended to follow the approach shown in this chapter of first hosting the service within one's own .NET application, and thoroughly debugging it within that process, before proceeding to host the service within IIS.

Summary

The Windows Communication Foundation provides a software factory template for software communication, consisting of a modeling language called the Service Model, and a programming framework called the Channel Layer. The Service Model incorporates a class library and a configuration language by which services are described, simply as collections of endpoints defined by an address, a binding, and a contract. Descriptions of software communication solutions expressed in the language of the Service Model are used as input for generating the components of the solution from the lower-level class library that is the Channel Layer. Using the software factory template for software communications that the Windows Communication Foundation provides, one can quickly adapt code to new scenarios. For instance, as demonstrated in the foregoing, one can host the same service within a .NET console application or within IIS without modifying the code for the service at all. One can also easily change how a client and a service communicate, making the communication between them confidential, for example. Being able to adapt software to diverse scenarios with little effort has always been the promise of model-driven development. With the Windows Communication Foundation, that promise is realized for software communications.

References

Box, Don. 1998. *Essential COM*. Reading, MA: Addison-Wesley.

Greenfield, Jack, Keith Short, Steve Cook and Stuart Kent. 2004. *Software Factories: Assembling Applications with Patterns, Models, Frameworks, and Tools*. Indianapolis, IN: Wiley.

Taylor, David A. 1992. *Object-Oriented Information Systems: Planning and Implementation*. New York, NY: Wiley.

Data Representation

Background

The Windows Communication Foundation provides a language, called the *Service Model*, for modeling software communications. Software executables can be generated from models expressed in that language using the classes of a lower-level programming framework called the *Channel Layer*.

In the language of the Service Model, a piece of software that responds to communications over a network is a *service*. A service has one or more endpoints to which communications can be directed. An endpoint consists of an *address*, a *binding*, and a *contract*.

The role of the address component is simple. It specifies a unique location for the service on a network in the form of a uniform resource locator.

The binding specifies the protocols for communication between the client and the server. Minimally, the binding must specify a protocol for encoding messages and a protocol for transporting them.

A contract specifies the operations that are available at an endpoint. To define a contract, one merely writes an interface in one's preferred .NET programming language, and adds attributes to it to indicate that the interface is also a Windows Communication Foundation contract. Then, to implement the contract, one simply writes a class that implements the .NET interface that one has defined.

This contract was used to define the operations of a derivatives calculator service in Chapter 2, "The Fundamentals."

```
using System;
using System.Collections.Generic;
```

```
using System.ServiceModel;
using System.Text;

namespace DerivativesCalculator
{
    [ServiceContract]
    public interface IDerivativesCalculator
    {
        [OperationContract]
        decimal CalculateDerivative(
            string[] symbols,
            decimal[] parameters,
            string[] functions);

        void DoNothing();
    }
}
```

One way of writing code for a client of that service that is to use the CalculateDerivative() operation would be to write this:

```
string[] symbols = new string[]{"MSFT"};
decimal[] parameters = new decimal[]{3};
string[] functions = new string[]{"TechStockProjections"};

IDerivativesCalculator proxy =
  new ChannelFactory<IDerivativesCalculator>("CalculatorEndpoint").
  CreateChannel();
proxy.CalculateDerivative(symbols, parameters, functions);
((IChannel)proxy).Close();
```

When the statement

```
proxy.CalculateDerivative(symbols, parameters, functions);
```

is executed, the data being provided by the client as input to the operation is added to an instance of the Message class of the Windows Communication Foundation's Channel Layer. Within the Message class, the data is represented in the form of an XML Information Set (InfoSet). When the data is ready to be transported from the client to the service, the message-encoding protocol specified in the binding will determine the form in which the Message object containing the data provided by the client will be represented to the service. The message-encoding protocol could conceivably translate the message into a string of comma-separated values, or into any format whatsoever. However, all the standard bindings specify encoding protocols by which the Message object will continue to be represented as an XML InfoSet. Depending on the encoding protocol of the binding, that XML InfoSet may be encoded either using one of the standard XML text encodings, or the standard MTOM protocol, or using a binary format proprietary to the Windows Communication Foundation.

When a transmission is received by a Windows Communication Foundation service, it is reassembled as a Message object by a message-encoding binding element, with the data sent by the client being expressed within the Message object as an XML InfoSet, regardless of the format in which it was encoded by the client. The Message object will be passed to a component of the Windows Communication Foundation called the *dispatcher*. The dispatcher extracts the client's data items from the XML InfoSet. It invokes the method of the service that implements the operation being used by the client, passing the client's data items to the method as parameters.

XmlSerializer **and** XmlFormatter

From the foregoing, it should be apparent that data being sent from the client to the service is serialized to XML within the client, and deserialized from XML within the service. There are two XML serializers that the Windows Communication Foundation can use to accomplish that task.

One of those is a new XML serializer provided with the Windows Communication Foundation. It is the XmlFormatter class in the System.Runtime.Serialization namespace within the System.Runtime.Serialization assembly. That assembly is one of the constituent assemblies of the Windows Communication Foundation. The XmlFormatter class is the XML serializer that the Windows Communication Foundation uses by default.

Given a class like the one in Listing 3.1, one could make the class serializable by the XmlFormatter by adding DataContract and DataMember attributes as shown in Listing 3.2. The representation of instances of a class in XML that is implied by the addition of the DataContract attribute to the class, and the DataMember attributes to its members, is commonly referred to as a *data contract* in the argot of the Windows Communication Foundation.

LISTING 3.1   DerivativesCalculation Class

```
public class DerivativesCalculation
{
        private string[] symbols;
        private decimal[] parameters;
        private string[] functions;

        public string[] Symbols
        {
            get
            {
                return this.symbols;
            }
        }
```

LISTING 3.1   Continued

```
            set
            {
                this.symbols = value;
            }
        }

        public decimal[] Parameters
        {
            get
            {
                return this.parameters;
            }

            set
            {
                this.parameters = value;
            }
        }

        public string[] Functions
        {
            get
            {
                return this.functions;
            }

            set
            {
                this.functions = value;
            }


        }
}
```

LISTING 3.2   DerivativesCalculation Data Contract

```
[DataContract]
public class DerivativesCalculation
{
        [DataMember]
        private string[] symbols;
        [DataMember]
        private decimal[] parameters;
```

LISTING 3.2 Continued

```
    [DataMember]
    private string[] functions;

    public string[] Symbols
    {
        get
        {
            return this.symbols;
        }

        set
        {
            this.symbols = value;
        }
    }

    public decimal[] Parameters
    {
        get
        {
            return this.parameters;
        }

        set
        {
            this.parameters = value;
        }
    }

    public string[] Functions
    {
        get
        {
            return this.functions;
        }

        set
        {
            this.functions = value;
        }

    }
}
```

Although the XmlFormatter is the default XML serializer of the Windows Communication Foundation, the Windows Communication Foundation can also be configured to do XML serialization using the System.Xml.Serialization.XmlSerializer class that has always been included in the System.Xml assembly of the .NET Framework Class Library. To exercise that option, add the XmlSerializerFormat attribute to the definition of a Windows Communication Foundation contract, like so:

```
namespace DerivativesCalculator
{
    [ServiceContract]
    [XmlSerializerFormat]
    public interface IDerivativesCalculator
    {
        [OperationContract]
        decimal CalculateDerivative(
            string[] symbols,
            decimal[] parameters,
            string[] functions);

        void DoNothing();
    }
}
```

The option of using the XmlSerializer class for XML serialization can also be selected just for individual operations:

```
namespace DerivativesCalculator
{
    [ServiceContract]
    public interface IDerivativesCalculator
    {
        [OperationContract]
        [XmlSerializerFormat]
        decimal CalculateDerivative(
            string[] symbols,
            decimal[] parameters,
            string[] functions);

        void DoNothing();
    }
}
```

The XmlSerializer provides very precise control over how data is to be represented in XML. Its facilities are well documented in the book *.NET Web Services: Architecture and Implementation*, by Keith Ballinger (2003).

The XmlFormatter, on the other hand, provides very little control over how data is to be represented in XML. It only allows one to specify the namespaces and names used to refer to data items in the XML, and the order in which the data items are to appear in the XML, as in this case:

```
[DataContract(Namespace="Derivatives",Name="Calculation")]
public class DerivativesCalculation
{
        [DataMember(Namespace="Derivatives",Name="Symbols",Order=0)]
        private string[] symbols;
        [DataMember(Namespace="Derivatives",Name="Parameters",Order=1)]
        private decimal[] parameters;}
        [...]
}
```

By not permitting any control over how data is to be represented in XML, the serialization process becomes highly predictable for the XmlFormatter and, thereby, more amenable to optimization. So a practical benefit of the XmlFormatter's design is better performance, approximately 10% better performance.

The XML Fetish

One might wonder whether the gain in performance is worth the loss of control over how data is represented in XML. That is most certainly the case, and understanding why serves to highlight the brilliance of the design of the Windows Communication Foundation.

A practice that is most characteristic of service-oriented programming is commonly referred to as *contract-first development*. Contract-first development is to begin the construction of software by specifying platform-independent representations for the data structures to be exchanged across the external interfaces, and platform-independent protocols for those exchanges.

Contract-first development is a sound practice. It helps one to avoid such unfortunate mistakes as building software that is meant to be interoperable across platforms, but that emits data in formats for which there are only representations on a particular platform, such as the .NET DataSet format.

However, the sound practice of contract-first development has become confused with one particular way of doing contract-first development, by virtue of which people become excessively concerned with XML formats. That one particular way of doing contract-first development is to use an XML editor to compose specifications of data formats in the XML Schema language, taking care to ensure that all complex data types are ultimately defined in terms of XML Schema Datatypes. Now, as a software developer, one's sole interest in contract-first development should be in defining the inputs and outputs of one's software, and in ensuring that, if necessary, those inputs and outputs can be represented in a platform-independent format. Yet practitioners of contract-first development, working in the XML Schema language in an XML editor, tend to become distracted from those core concerns and start to worry about exactly how the data is to be represented in XML. Consequently, they begin to debate, among other things, the virtues of various ways of encoding XML, and become highly suspicious of anything that might inhibit them from seeing and fiddling with XML. The XML becomes a fetish, falsely imbued with the true virtues of contract-first development, and, as Sigmund Freud wrote, "[s]uch substitutes are with some justice likened to the fetishes in which savages believe that their gods are embodied" (1977, 66).

With the XmlFormatter, the Windows Communication Foundation not only restores the focus of software developers to what should be important to them, namely, the specification of inputs and outputs, but also relocates control over the representation of data to where it properly belongs, which is outside of the code, at the system administrator's disposal. Specifically, given the class

```
public class DerivativesCalculation
{
     public string[] Symbols;
     public decimal[] Parameters;
     public string[] Functions;
     public DataTime Date
}
```

all one should care about as a software developer is to be able to say that the class is a data structure that may be an input or an output, and that particular constituents of that structure may be included when it is input or output. The DataContract and DataMember attributes provided for using the XmlFormatter to serialize data allow one to do just that, as in the following:

```
[DataContract]
public class DerivativesCalculation
{
     [DataMember]
     public string[] Symbols;
     [DataMember]
     public decimal[] Parameters;
     [DataMember]
     public string[] Functions;
     public DataTime Date
}
```

It is by configuring the encoding protocol in the binding of an endpoint that one can control exactly how data structures are represented in transmissions.

Now there are two scenarios to consider. In the first scenario, the organization that has adopted the Windows Communication Foundation is building a service. In the other scenario, the organization that has adopted the Windows Communication Foundation is building a client.

In the first of these scenarios, the Windows Communication Foundation developers define the data structures to be exchanged with their services using the DataContract and DataMember attributes. Then they generate representations of those structures in the XML Schema language using the Service Metadata Tool, introduced in the preceding chapter. They provide those XML Schema language representations to developers wanting to use their services. The designers of the Windows Communication Foundation have expended considerable effort to ensure that the structure of the XML into which the XmlFormatter serializes data should be readily consumable by the tools various vendors provide to assist in deserializing data that is in XML. Thus, anyone wanting to use the services provided by the Windows Communication Foundation developers in this scenario should be able to do so, despite the Windows Communication Foundation developers never having necessarily looked at, or manipulated, any XML in the process of providing the services.

In the second scenario, the Windows Communication Foundation developers use the Service Metadata Tool to generate code for using a software service that may or may not have been developed using the Windows Communication Foundation. If the XML representations of the inputs and outputs of that service deviate from the way in which the XmlFormatter represents data in XML, then the code generated by the Service Metadata Tool will include the switch for using the XmlSerializer instead of the XmlFormatter for serializing data to XML. That code should allow the Windows Communication Foundation developers to use the service, and, once again, they will not have had to look at or manipulate any XML in order to do so.

Should the fetish for XML prove too overwhelming, and one is compelled to look at the XML Schema language that defines how a class will be represented within XML, the Windows Communication Foundation does make provision for that. Executing the Service Metadata Tool in this way,

```
svcutil /datacontractonly SomeAssembly.dll
```

where SomeAssembly.dll is the name of some assembly in which a data contract is defined for a class, will yield the XML Schema language specifying the format of the XML into which instances of the class will be serialized.

The question being considered is whether the gain in performance yielded by the XmlFormatter is adequate compensation for its providing so little control over how data is represented in XML. The answer that should be apparent from the foregoing is that control over how data is represented in XML is generally of no use to software developers, so, yes, any gain in performance in exchange for that control is certainly welcome.

Using the XmlFormatter

To become familiar with the XmlFormatter, open the Visual Studio solution associated with this chapter that you downloaded from www.samspublishing.com. The solution contains a single project, called *Serialization*, for building a console application. All the code is in a single module, Program.cs, the content of which is shown in Listing 3.3. Note that there is a using statement for the System.Runtime.Serialization namespace, and also that the project references the System.Runtime.Serialization assembly.

LISTING 3.3   Program.cs

```csharp
using System;
using System.Collections.Generic;
using System.Data;
using System.Runtime.Serialization;
using System.ServiceModel;
using System.Text;

namespace Serialization
{
    [DataContract(Name="Calculation")]
    public class ServiceViewOfData: IUnknownSerializationData
    {
        [DataMember(Name = "Symbols")]
        private string[] symbols;
        [DataMember(Name = "Parameters")]
        private decimal[] parameters;
        [DataMember(Name = "Functions")]
        private string[] functions;
        [DataMember(Name="Value")]
        private decimal value;

        private UnknownSerializationData unknownData;

        public string[] Symbols
        {
            get
            {
                return this.symbols;
            }

            set
            {
                this.symbols = value;
            }
        }

        public decimal[] Parameters
        {
            get
            {
                return this.parameters;
            }
```

LISTING 3.3   Continued

```csharp
        set
        {
            this.parameters = value;
        }
    }

    public string[] Functions
    {
        get
        {
            return this.functions;
        }

        set
        {
            this.functions = value;
        }

    }

    public decimal Value
    {
        get
        {
            return this.value;
        }

        set
        {
            this.value = value;
        }
    }

    #region IUnknownSerializationData Members

    public UnknownSerializationData UnknownData
    {
        get
        {
            return this.unknownData;
        }
```

LISTING 3.3   Continued

```
            set
            {
                this.unknownData = value;
            }
        }

    #endregion
}

[DataContract]
public class Data
{
    [DataMember]
    public string Value;
}

[DataContract]
public class DerivedData : Data
{
}

[DataContract(Name = "Calculation")]
public class ClientViewOfData : IUnknownSerializationData
{
    [DataMember(Name = "Symbols")]
    public string[] Symbols;
    [DataMember(Name = "Parameters")]
    public decimal[] Parameters;
    [DataMember(Name="Functions")]
    public string[] Functions;
    [DataMember(Name="Value")]
    public decimal Value;
    [DataMember(Name = "Reference")]
    public Guid Reference;

    private UnknownSerializationData unknownData;


    public UnknownSerializationData UnknownData
    {
        get
        {
            return this.unknownData;
        }
```

LISTING 3.3 Continued

```csharp
            set
            {
                this.unknownData = value;
            }
        }


    }


    [ServiceContract(Name = "DerivativesCalculator")]
    [KnownType(typeof(DerivedData))]
    public interface IServiceViewOfService
    {
        [OperationContract(Name="FromXSDTypes")]
        decimal CalculateDerivative(
            string[] symbols,
            decimal[] parameters,
            string[] functions);

        [OperationContract(Name="FromDataSet")]
        DataSet CalculateDerivative(DataSet input);

        [OperationContract(Name = "FromDataContract")]
        ServiceViewOfData CalculateDerivative(ServiceViewOfData input);

        [OperationContract(Name = "AlsoFromDataContract")]
        Data DoSomething(Data input);

    }

    [ServiceContract(Name="DerivativesCalculator")]
    [KnownType(typeof(DerivedData))]
    public interface IClientViewOfService
    {
        [OperationContract(Name = "FromXSDTypes")]
        decimal CalculateDerivative(
            string[] symbols,
            decimal[] parameters,
            string[] functions);

        [OperationContract(Name = "FromDataSet")]
        DataSet CalculateDerivative(DataSet input);
```

LISTING 3.3   Continued

```
    [OperationContract(Name = "FromDataContract")]
    ClientViewOfData CalculateDerivative(ClientViewOfData input);

    [OperationContract(Name = "AlsoFromDataContract")]
    Data DoSomething(Data input);
}

public class DerivativesCalculator : IServiceViewOfService
{
    #region IDerivativesCalculator Members

    public decimal CalculateDerivative(
        string[] symbols,
        decimal[] parameters,
        string[] functions)
    {
        return (decimal)(System.DateTime.Now.Millisecond);
    }


    public DataSet CalculateDerivative(DataSet input)
    {
        if (input.Tables.Count > 0)
        {
            if (input.Tables[0].Rows.Count > 0)
            {
                input.Tables[0].Rows[0]["Value"] =
                    (decimal)(System.DateTime.Now.Millisecond);
            }
        }
        return input;
    }

    public ServiceViewOfData CalculateDerivative(ServiceViewOfData input)
    {
        input.Value = this.CalculateDerivative(
            input.Symbols,
            input.Parameters,
            input.Functions);
        return input;
    }

    public Data DoSomething(Data input)
    {
```

LISTING 3.3   Continued

```
        return input;
    }


    #endregion
}


public class Program
{
    public static void Main(string[] args)
    {
        using (ServiceHost host = new ServiceHost(
            typeof(DerivativesCalculator),
            new Uri[] {
                new Uri("http://localhost:8000/Derivatives") }))
        {
            host.AddServiceEndpoint(
                typeof(IServiceViewOfService),
                new BasicHttpBinding(),
                "Calculator");
            host.Open();

            Console.WriteLine("The service is available.");

            string address =
                "http://localhost:8000/Derivatives/Calculator";

            ChannelFactory<IClientViewOfService> factory =
                new ChannelFactory<IClientViewOfService>(
                    new BasicHttpBinding(),
                    new EndpointAddress(
                        new Uri(address)));
            IClientViewOfService proxy =
                factory.CreateChannel();

            decimal result = proxy.CalculateDerivative(
                new string[] { "MSFT" },
                new decimal[] { 3 },
                new string[] { "TechStockProjection" });
            Console.WriteLine(
              "Value using XSD types is {0}.",
              result);

            DataTable table = new DataTable("InputTable");
            table.Columns.Add("Symbol", typeof(string));
```

LISTING 3.3   Continued

```csharp
table.Columns.Add("Parameter", typeof(decimal));
table.Columns.Add("Function", typeof(string));
table.Columns.Add("Value", typeof(decimal));

table.Rows.Add("MSFT", 3, "TechStockProjection",0.00);

DataSet input = new DataSet("Input");
input.Tables.Add(table);

DataSet output = proxy.CalculateDerivative(input);
if (output != null)
{
    if (output.Tables.Count > 0)
    {
        if (output.Tables[0].Rows.Count > 0)
        {
            Console.WriteLine(
                "Value using a DataSet is {0}.",
                output.Tables[0].Rows[0]["Value"]);
        }
    }
}

ClientViewOfData calculation =
    new ClientViewOfData();
calculation.Symbols =
    new string[] { "MSFT" };
calculation.Parameters =
    new decimal[] { 3 };
calculation.Functions =
    new string[] { "TechStockProjection" };
calculation.Reference =
    Guid.NewGuid();

Console.WriteLine(
    "Reference is {0}.", calculation.Reference);

ClientViewOfData calculationResult =
    proxy.CalculateDerivative(calculation);
Console.WriteLine(
  "Value using a Data Contract is {0}.",
  calculationResult.Value);
```

LISTING 3.3   Continued

```
            Console.WriteLine(
                "Reference is {0}.", calculationResult.Reference);

            DerivedData derivedData = new DerivedData();
            Data outputData = proxy.DoSomething(derivedData);

            MemoryStream stream = new MemoryStream();
            XmlFormatter formatter = new XmlFormatter();
            formatter.Serialize(stream, calculation);
            Console.WriteLine(
              UnicodeEncoding.UTF8.GetChars(stream.GetBuffer()));

            Console.WriteLine("Done.");

            ((IChannel)proxy).Close();

            host.Close();

            Console.ReadKey();

        }
      }
    }
}
```

In Listing 3.3, the static Main() method of the class called Program both provides a host for a Windows Communication Foundation service and uses that service as a client. The hosting of the service is accomplished with this code:

```
using (ServiceHost host = new ServiceHost(
  typeof(DerivativesCalculator),
  new Uri[] {
    new Uri("http://localhost:8000/Derivatives") }))
{
    host.AddServiceEndpoint(
      typeof(IServiceViewOfService),
      new BasicHttpBinding(),
      "Calculator");
    host.Open();
    [...]
    host.Close();
    [...]
}
```

In this code, an endpoint, with its address, binding, and contract, is added to the service programmatically, rather than through the host application's configuration, as was done in the preceding chapter. Similarly, the client code directly incorporates information about the service's endpoint, rather than referring to endpoint information in the application's configuration:

```
string address =
  "http://localhost:8000/Derivatives/Calculator";
ChannelFactory<IClientViewOfService> factory =
  new ChannelFactory<IClientViewOfService>(
    new BasicHttpBinding(),
    new EndpointAddress(
    new Uri(address)));
IClientViewOfService proxy =
  factory.CreateChannel();
```

This imperative style of programming with the Windows Communication Foundation is used here for two reasons. The first is simply to show that this style is an option. The second, and more important, reason is to make the code that is discussed here complete in itself, with no reference to outside elements such as configuration files.

The contract of the service is defined in this way:

```
[ServiceContract(Name = "DerivativesCalculator")]
[...]
public interface IServiceViewOfService
{
  [...]
}
```

The client has a separate definition of the contract of the service, but the definition used by the client and the definition used by the service are semantically identical:

```
[ServiceContract(Name="DerivativesCalculator")]
[...]
public interface IClientViewOfService
{
  [...]
}
```

In both the client's version of the contract and the service's version, there is this definition of an operation:

```
[OperationContract(Name="FromXSDTypes")]
decimal CalculateDerivative(
  string[] symbols,
  decimal[] parameters,
  string[] functions);
```

When the client uses that operation, like this,

```
decimal result = proxy.CalculateDerivative(
  new string[] { "MSFT" },
  new decimal[] { 3 },
  new string[] { "TechStockProjection" });
Console.WriteLine(
  "Value using XSD types is {0}.",
  result);
```

its attempt to do so works, which can be verified by running the application built from the solution. In this case, the inputs and outputs of the operation are .NET types that correspond quite obviously to XML Schema Datatypes. The XmlFormatter automatically serializes the inputs and outputs into XML.

The next operation defined in both the client's version of the contract and the service's version is this one:

```
[OperationContract(Name = "FromDataSet")]
DataSet CalculateDerivative(DataSet input);
```

The client uses that operation with this code:

```
DataTable table = new DataTable("InputTable");
table.Columns.Add("Symbol", typeof(string));
table.Columns.Add("Parameter", typeof(decimal));
table.Columns.Add("Function", typeof(string));
table.Columns.Add("Value", typeof(decimal));

table.Rows.Add("MSFT", 3, "TechStockProjection",0.00);

DataSet input = new DataSet("Input");
input.Tables.Add(table);

DataSet output = proxy.CalculateDerivative(input);
[...]
Console.WriteLine(
  "Value using a DataSet is {0}.",
 output.Tables[0].Rows[0]["Value"]);
```

In this case, the input and output of the operation are both .NET DataSet objects, and the .NET DataSet type does not obviously correspond to any XML Schema Datatype. Nevertheless, the XmlFormatter automatically serializes the input and output to XML, as it will for any .NET type that implements ISerializable. Of course, passing .NET DataSets around is a very bad idea if one can anticipate a non-.NET client needing to participate, and it is never wise to rule that out as a possibility.

In the service's version of the contract, this operation is included:

```
[OperationContract(Name = "FromDataContract")]
ServiceViewOfData CalculateDerivative(ServiceViewOfData input);
```

The input and output of this operation is an instance of the `ServiceViewOfData` class, which is defined like so:

```
 [DataContract(Name="Calculation")]
public class ServiceViewOfData: IUnknownSerializationData
{
  [DataMember(Name = "Symbols")]
  private string[] symbols;
  [DataMember(Name = "Parameters")]
  private decimal[] parameters;
  [DataMember(Name = "Functions")]
  private string[] functions;
  [DataMember(Name="Value")]
  private decimal value;
  [...]
}
```

The client's version of the contract defines the corresponding operation in this way:

```
[OperationContract(Name = "FromDataContract")]
ClientViewOfData CalculateDerivative(ClientViewOfData input);
```

Here, the input and output are of the `ClientViewOfData` type, which is defined in this way:

```
[DataContract(Name = "Calculation")]
public class ClientViewOfData : IUnknownSerializationData
{
  [DataMember(Name = "Symbols")]
  public string[] Symbols;
  [DataMember(Name = "Parameters")]
  public decimal[] Parameters;
  [DataMember(Name="Functions")]
  public string[] Functions;
  [DataMember(Name="Value")]
  public decimal Value;
  [DataMember(Name = "Reference")]
  public Guid Reference;
}
```

The service's `ServiceViewOfData` class and the client's `ClientViewOfData` class are used to define data contracts that are compatible with one another. The data contracts are compatible because they have the same namespace and name, and because the members that have the same names in each version of the contract also have the same types. Because of the compatibility of the data contracts used in the client's version of the operation and the service's version, those operations that the client and the service define in different ways are also compatible with one another.

The client's version of the data contract includes a member that the service's version of the data contract omits: the member named Reference. However, the service's version implements the Windows Communication Foundation's IUnknownSerializationData interface, thus:

```
[DataContract(Name="Calculation")]
public class ServiceViewOfData: IUnknownSerializationData
{
  [...]
  private UnknownSerializationData unknownData;
  [...]
  public UnknownSerializationData UnknownData
  {
    get
    {
      return this.unknownData;
    }

    set
    {
      this.unknownData = value;
    }
  }
}
```

By implementing the IUnknownSerializationData interface, it sets aside some memory that the XmlFormatter can use for storing and retrieving the values of members that other versions of the same contract might include. In this case, that memory is named by the variable called unknownData. Thus, when a more advanced version of the same data contract is passed to service, with members that the service's version of the data contract does not include, the XmlFormatter is able to pass the values of those members through the service. In particular, when the client calls the service using this code,

```
ClientViewOfData calculation =
  new ClientViewOfData();
calculation.Symbols =
  new string[] { "MSFT" };
calculation.Parameters =
  new decimal[] { 3 };
calculation.Functions =
  new string[] { "TechStockProjection" };
```

```
calculation.Reference =
  Guid.NewGuid();

Console.WriteLine(
  "Reference is {0}.", calculation.Reference);

ClientViewOfData calculationResult =
  proxy.CalculateDerivative(calculation);
Console.WriteLine(
  "Value using a Data Contract is {0}.",
  calculationResult.Value);

Console.WriteLine(
  "Reference is {0}.", calculationResult.Reference);
```

not only is the XmlFormatter able to serialize the custom type, ClientViewOfData, to XML for transmission to the service, but the member called Reference that is in the client's version of the data contract, but not in the service's version, passes through the service without being lost.

Two things should be evident from this case. First, the DataContract and DataMember attributes make it very easy to provide for the serialization of one's custom data types by the Windows Communication Foundation's XmlFormatter. Second, implementing the Windows Communication Foundation's IUnknownSerializationData interface is always a good idea, because it allows different versions of the same data contract to evolve independently of one another, yet still be usable together.

The last operation defined for the service is this one, which is defined in the same way both in the code used by the service and in the code used by the client:

```
[OperationContract(Name = "AlsoFromDataContract")]
Data DoSomething(Data input);
```

The input and output of the operation are of the custom Data type, which is made serializable by the XmlFormatter through the use of the DataContract and DataMember attributes, thus:

```
[DataContract]
public class Data
{
  [DataMember]
  public string Value;
}
```

The client uses that operation with this code:

```
DerivedData derivedData = new DerivedData();
Data outputData = proxy.DoSomething(derivedData);
```

That code passes an instance of the DerivedData type to the service, a type which is derived from the Data class, in this way:

```
[DataContract]
public class DerivedData : Data
{
}
```

What will happen in this case is that the XmlFormatter, in deserializing the data received from the client on behalf of the service, will encounter the XML into which an instance of the DerivedData class had been serialized, when it will be expecting the XML into which an instance of the Data class has been serialized. That will cause the XmlFormatter to throw an exception. However, both the service's version of the endpoint's contract and the client's version have a KnownType attribute that refers to the DerivedData class:

```
[ServiceContract(Name = "DerivativesCalculator")]
[KnownType(typeof(DerivedData))]
public interface IServiceViewOfService
{
  [...]
}
[...]
[ServiceContract(Name="DerivativesCalculator")]
[KnownType(typeof(DerivedData))]
public interface IClientViewOfService
{
  [...]
}
```

That attribute prepares the XmlFormatter to accept the XML for a DerivedData object whenever it is expecting the XML for an instance of any type from which the DerivedData class derives. So, by virtue of that attribute being added to the definition of the service's contract, when the XmlFormatter encounters XML for a DerivedData object when it is expecting XML for a Data object, it is able to deserialize that XML into an instance of the DerivedData class. It follows that if one was to define an operation in this way,

```
[OperationContract]
void DoSomething(object[] inputArray);
```

then one should add to the service contract a KnownType attribute for each of the types that might actually be included in the input parameter array.

That the KnownType attribute has to be added in order for the DerivedData objects to be successfully deserialized shows that one should avoid using inheritance as a way of versioning data contracts. If a base type is expected, but a derived type is received, serialization of the derived type will fail unless the code is modified with the addition of the KnownType attribute to anticipate the derived type.

The Windows Communication Foundation uses the XmlFormatter invisibly. So these remaining lines of client code in the sample simply show that it can be used separately from the rest of the Windows Communication Foundation for serializing data to XML:

```
MemoryStream stream = new MemoryStream();
XmlFormatter formatter = new XmlFormatter();
formatter.Serialize(stream, calculation);
Console.WriteLine(
  UnicodeEncoding.UTF8.GetChars(stream.GetBuffer()));
```

Exception Handling

Data contracts also assist in being able to notify clients of exceptions that may occur in a service. Too see how that works, follow these steps:

1. Add this class to the Program.cs module of the Serialization project referred to previously:

```
public class SomeError
{
  public string Content;
}
```

2. Create a data contract from that class using the DataContract and DataMember attributes:

```
[DataContract]
public class SomeError
{
  [DataMember]
  public string Content;
}
```

This yields a data contract that specifies the format of a simple error message that the service might send to the client.

3. Add an operation to the IServiceViewOfService interface that defines the service's version of the service's contract:

```
[OperationContract(Name="Faulty")]
decimal DivideByZero(decimal input);
```

4. Add a fault contract to the operation, informing clients that they should anticipate that, instead of returning the expected result, the service may return an error message of the form defined by the SomeError data contract:

```
[OperationContract(Name="Faulty")]
[FaultContract(typeof(SomeError))]
decimal DivideByZero(decimal input);
```

5. Add an implementation of the `DivideByZero()` method to the `DerivativesCalculator` class, which is the service type that implements the `DerivativesCalculator` service contract defined by the `IServiceViewOfService` interface:

```
public class DerivativesCalculator : IServiceViewOfService
{
  [...]
  public decimal DivideByZero(decimal input)
  {
    try
    {
      decimal denominator = 0;
      return input / denominator;
    }
    catch (Exception exception)
    {
      SomeError error = new SomeError();
      error.Content = exception.Message;
      throw new FaultException<SomeError>(error);
    }
  }
}
```

By virtue of this code, when the service traps an exception in the `DivideByZero()` method, it creates an instance of the `SomeError` class to convey selected information about the exception to the caller. That information is then sent to the caller using the Windows Communication Foundation's generic, `FaultException<T>`.

6. Because of the `FaultContract` attribute on the `DivideByZero()` method, if the metadata for the service was to be downloaded, and client code generated from it using the Service Metadata Tool, the client's version of the contract would automatically include the definition of the `DivideByZero()` method, and its associated fault contract. However, in this case, simply add the method and the fault contract to the client's version of the contract, which is in the `IClientViewOfService` interface:

```
[ServiceContract(Name="DerivativesCalculator")]
[KnownType(typeof(DerivedData))]
public interface IClientViewOfService
{
  [...]
  [OperationContract(Name = "Faulty")]
  [FaultContract(typeof(SomeError))]
  decimal DivideByZero(decimal input);
}
```

7. Now have the client use the `Faulty` operation by adding code to the static `Main()` method of the `Program` class, as shown in Listing 3.4.

LISTING 3.4   Anticipating a Fault

```
public class Program
{
  public static void Main(string[] args)
  {
    using (ServiceHost host = new ServiceHost(
      typeof(DerivativesCalculator),
        new Uri[] {
          new Uri("http://localhost:8000/Derivatives") }))
    {
      host.AddServiceEndpoint(
        typeof(IServiceViewOfService),
        new BasicHttpBinding(),
        "Calculator");
      host.Open();

      Console.WriteLine("The service is available.");

      string address =
        "http://localhost:8000/Derivatives/Calculator";

      ChannelFactory<IClientViewOfService> factory =
        new ChannelFactory<IClientViewOfService>(
          new BasicHttpBinding(),
          new EndpointAddress(
            new Uri(address)));
      IClientViewOfService proxy =
        factory.CreateChannel();

      [...]

      try
      {
        Decimal quotient = proxy.DivideByZero(9);
      }
      catch (FaultException<SomeError> error)
      {
        Console.WriteLine("Error: {0}.", error.Detail.Content);
      }
```

LISTING 3.4   Continued

```
      [...]

    }
  }
}
```

Because receiving an error message from an attempt to use the operation should be antici-
pated, as the FaultContract for the operation indicates, the client code is written to
handle that possibility. That is accomplished using the Windows Communication
Foundation's FaultException<T> generic, which was also used in the code for the service
to convey information about an exception to the client. The Detail property of the
FaultException<T> generic provides access to an instance of T, which, in this case, is an
instance of the SomeError class that the client can interrogate for information about the
error that occurred.

This approach to handling exceptions provided by the Windows Communication
Foundation has multiple virtues. It allows the developers of services to easily define the
structure of the error messages that they want to transmit to client programmers. It also
allows them to advertise to client programmers which operations of their services might
return particular error messages instead of the results they would otherwise expect. The
service programmers are able to easily formulate and transmit error messages to clients,
and client programmers have a simple syntax, almost exactly like ordinary exception-
handling syntax, for receiving and examining error messages. Most important, service
programmers get to decide exactly what information about errors that occur in their
services they want to have conveyed to clients.

However, the design of the Windows Communication Foundation does anticipate the
utility, solely in the process of debugging a service, of being able to return to a client
complete information about any unanticipated exceptions that might occur within a
service. That can be accomplished using the ReturnUnknownExceptionsAsFaults behavior.

Behaviors are mechanisms internal to Windows Communication Foundation services or
clients. They may be controlled by programmers or administrators.

Those behaviors that programmers are expected to want to control are manipulated using
attributes. For example, if a programmer knows that a service is thread-safe, the programmer can permit the Windows Communication Foundation to allow multiple threads to
access the service concurrently by adding the ServiceBehavior attribute to the service's
service type class, and setting the value of the ConcurrencyMode parameter of that
attribute to the Multiple value of the ConcurrencyMode enumeration:

```
[ServiceBehavior(ConcurrencyMode=ConcurrencyMode.Multiple)]
public class DerivativesCalculator : IServiceViewOfService
```

Behaviors that administrators are expected to want to control can be manipulated in the
configuration of a service or client. The ReturnUnknownExceptionsAsFaults behavior is

one of those. This configuration of a service will result in any unhandled exceptions being transmitted to the client:

```xml
<?xml version="1.0" encoding="utf-8" ?>
<configuration>
    <system.serviceModel>
        <services>
          <service type=
"DerivativesCalculator.DerivativesCalculatorServiceType,
DerivativesCalculatorService"
             behaviorConfiguration="DerivativesCalculatorBehavior">
                <endpoint
                    address=""
                    binding="basicHttpBinding"
                    contract=
"DerivativesCalculator.IDerivativesCalculator,DerivativesCalculatorService"
                />
            </service>
        </services>
        <behaviors>
            <behavior name="DerivativesCalculatorBehavior"
              returnUnknownExceptionsAsFaults="true"/>
        </behaviors>
    </system.serviceModel>
</configuration>
```

To reiterate, this configuration may be very useful for diagnosis in the process of debugging a service, but it is dangerous in debugging, because transmitting all the information about an exception to a client may expose information about the service that could be used to compromise it.

Summary

Data being sent from a Windows Communication Foundation client to a service is serialized to XML within the client, and data received from clients by Windows Communication Foundation services is deserialized from XML within the service. There are two XML serializers that the Windows Communication Foundation can use to accomplish the serialization to XML and deserialization from XML. One is the XmlSerializer class that has been a part of the .NET Framework class library from the outset. The other is the XmlFormatter class that is new with the Windows Communication Foundation. Whereas the XmlSerializer provides precise control over how data is represented as XML, the XmlFormatter provides very little control over that in order to make the serialization process very predictable, and, thereby, easier to optimize. As a result, the XmlFormatter outperforms the XmlSerializer.

Allowing the XmlFormatter to serialize one's custom types is very simple. One merely adds a DataContract attribute to the definition of the type, and DataMember attributes to each of the type's members that are to be serialized.

Implementing the IUnknownSerializationData interface in any type that is to be serialized using the XmlFormatter is wise. It allows for different versions of the same way of representing the data in XML to evolve independently of one another, yet still be usable together.

References

Ballinger, Keith. 2003. *.NET Web Services: Architecture and Implementation*. Reading, MA: Addison-Wesley.

Freud, Sigmund. 1977. *Three Essays on Sexuality*. In *On Sexuality: Three Essays on Sexuality and Other Works*, ed. Angela Richards. The Pelican Freud Library, ed. James Strachey, no. 7. London, UK: Penguin.

3

Security

Chapter 2, "The Fundamentals," which covered the fundamentals of the Windows Communication Foundation, showed that the technology makes security simple. Just opting to use the WSHttpBinding in configuring a service ensures not only that communications with the service are kept confidential, but also that the identities of the users of the clients are conveyed to the service so that the service can evaluate whether to grant the clients access to its resources.

More generally, by configuring the binding of a service, one can select how clients of the service are to be authenticated and how communications with the service are to be kept confidential. The built-in options for how a client may be authenticated are by a username and password combination, by its user's Windows identity, and by an X.509 certificate. However, one can also define custom tokens for authenticating clients. Communications with a service can be kept confidential either by using a secure transport protocol or by having messages encrypted before being transported.

All of these security facilities of the Windows Communication Foundation are well documented by the samples in the Microsoft Windows Software Development Kit (SDK) referred to in the Introduction. So those facilities are not covered in detail here. The auditing of security events is covered in Chapter 12, "Manageability." What this chapter focuses on is the Extensible Security Infrastructure (XSI) that the Windows Communication Foundation incorporates, which promises to greatly simplify the automation of business processes that extend across organizations.

Background

Organizations interact with one another. They do so a lot. In fact, many organizations exist solely for the purpose of interacting with other organizations. Only particular types of organizations, such as retailers, schools, hospitals, social service agencies, and some government departments, focus on dealing with individuals. Among those organizations, a recent trend has been to reduce their activity to the ownership of their brand, relying on other organizations for manufacturing, logistics, and customer service (Means and Schneider 2000, 1-18). That trend is evident even in government departments outsourcing their activities to private enterprises.

Yet, despite the fact that their processes involve other organizations, the automation of those processes has mostly been kept stubbornly internal (Daly 2000). Organizations tend to design their automation to suit their own requirements, and make only the most rudimentary accommodation for their automated systems working together with those of other organizations.

This problem is especially evident in how information about the users of systems is managed. If the users of the systems of one organization are to be able to use them to access the systems of another organization, some information about those users must be shared for use in authorizing access to the other organization's facilities. However, not only is information about users seldom organized for access by multiple organizations, but it is also often not properly organized within any single organization. It is very typical for individual systems to be designed to have their own store of information about their users, so as people join or leave an organization, their information has to be added to, or removed from, each system's repository of user data.

As long ago as 1988, the organization that is now known as the International Telecommunication Union, and the International Organization for Standardization, released a standard for directory services called X.500. In the mid-1990s, the Internet Engineering Task Force began to publish a slimmer version of X.500 exclusively designed for TCP/IP environments, which is called the *Lightweight Directory Access Protocol*, or *LDAP*. The directory services defined by those standards are meant to serve as the central repository for every asset and user in an organization, and also provide a language and an application programming interface for querying that repository.

Microsoft Active Directory, which was initially released as part of Microsoft Windows 2000 Server, was Microsoft's LDAP-compliant directory service offering. In accordance with its corporate strategy at the time, Microsoft made Active Directory not only LDAP-compliant, but COM-compliant as well.

However, the adoption of directory services like Microsoft Active Directory tends to have been limited to managing access to network resources: to computer desktops, shared folders, printers, and electronic mail. It seldom extends to managing access to software applications, yet less to particular features of those applications or to the items of information they manage.

So anyone designing a software application today can be certain only of these articles of uncertainty:

- Although the users of the system may initially be a quite restricted group, perhaps including the members of only a particular department within an organization, if the application is useful, the community of users may expand, quite possibly to include users from other organizations.

- What may be known about those users in order to assess their privileges within the application could be quite unpredictable. Some users might be listed in a directory service, but others might not be.

- What the application may need to do in order to determine the privileges for which a user is eligible not only may be quite specific to that application, but also may need to change over time. Although it would be ideal for the application to simply query a directory service to determine a user's privileges, that seldom suffices.

Consequently, to secure an application today, one would like to have a technology by which access can be readily expanded to include a wider community of legitimate users with diverse ways of identifying themselves. One would also like to have flexibility in how one determines the privileges to which users of the application are entitled. XSI is intended to be just such a technology: a flexible and easily customizable way of controlling access to the resources of a software application.

XSI

XSI consists of the set of classes in the `System.Security.Authorization` namespace of the `System.Security.Authorization` assembly. That assembly is another of the constituent assemblies of the Windows Communication Foundation, others being the `System.ServiceModel` and `System.Runtime.Serialization` assemblies discussed in the previous chapters.

XSI provides a way of controlling access to resources based on *claims*. To understand how it works, consider this scenario. A man walks into a bar, places his driver's license and a small sum of money on the bar, and asks the bartender for a beer. The bartender looks at the driver's license, takes the money, and serves the man a beer.

In this scenario, the bar represents a service. The serving of beer is an operation. The beer is a protected resource. To access it, a person must be of legal drinking age, and must pay a sum of money for it.

The driver's license and the money both represent claim sets. A *claim set* is a number of claims provided by the same issuer. In the case of the driver's license, the issuer is a government department that licenses drivers, and in the case of the money, the issuer is a country's central bank. However, those issuers are themselves present merely as sets of claims: as logos, signatures, and images on the driver's license and the money.

Claims consist of a type, a right, and a value. One of the claims in the set of claims represented by the driver's license is the driver's date of birth. The type of that claim is *date of birth*, and the value of that claim is the driver's birth date. The right that a claim confers on the bearer specifies what the bearer can do with the claim's value. In the case of the claim of the driver's date of birth, the right is simply possession. The driver possesses that date of birth but cannot, for example, alter it.

In examining the driver's license and the money, the bartender translates the claim about the bearer's date of birth provided by the driver's license into a claim about the bearer's age. The bartender also translates the value of each of the proffered items of money on the bar into a claim about the total sum of money being offered. The rules by which the bartender performs these translations from an input claim set to an output claim set constitute the bartender's authorization policy. The input claim set of an authorization policy is referred to as the *evaluation context*, and the output claim set is referred to as the *authorization context*. A set of authorization policies constitute an authorization domain.

In taking the money and serving the beer, the bartender compares the claim about the age of the person asking for a beer to the minimum drinking age, and compares the total sum of money being offered to the price of the requested beer. In that process, the bartender is comparing the authorization context claim set yielded by the authorization policy, to the access requirements for the operation of serving a beer. It so happened that the authorization context claim set of the age of the man asking for the beer, and the total sum of money being offered, satisfied the access requirements for the operation, so the bartender served the man a beer.

To summarize, in XSI, access to an operation on a protected resource is authorized based on claims. Claims have a type, a right, and a value. A claim set is a number of claims provided by the same issuer. The issuer of a claim set is itself a claim set. Authorization based on claims is accomplished in two steps. First, an authorization policy is executed, which takes an evaluation context claim set as input and translates that into an authorization context claim set that it outputs. Then the claims in the authorization context claim set are compared to the access requirements of the operation, and, depending on the outcome of that comparison, access to the operation is denied or granted.

Claims-based Authorization Versus Role-based Authorization

How does this claims-based approach to authorization compare to role-based authorization, which is a fairly common approach to controlling what users can do with software applications? A definition of role-based authorization would be helpful in answering that question.

"Role-based authorization is a mechanism that uses roles to assign users suitable rights for performing system tasks and permissions for accessing resources" (Tulloch 2003, 281). A role is a "symbolic category that collects together users who share the same levels of security privileges" (Tulloch 2003, 281).

Role-based authorization requires first identifying the user, then ascertaining the roles to which the user is assigned, and finally comparing those roles to the roles that are authorized to access a resource. Thus, in the role-based authorization system provided by Microsoft .NET role-based security, for example, the most important element is the principal object, which incorporates a user's identity and any roles to which the user belongs (*.NET Framework Class Library* 2006; Freeman and Jones 2003, 249).

By contrast, if one recalls what the bartender did in deciding whether to serve a beer to the man requesting one in the previous scenario, it is noteworthy that identifying the man was not important. Certainly, the proffered driver's license could also be used to establish the man's identity, because driver's licenses do typically make claims about the bearer's identity, but those claims were not important to the bartender; the bartender was only interested in the license's claim about the date of birth of the bearer. If the man proceeded to rob the bartender, then no doubt identifying him would become important.

In general, claims-based authorization subsumes role-based authorization. To be precise, roles membership is determined based on identity, identity is just one sort of right to the value of a claim, the right of using the value of the claim to identify oneself. A birth date is not a value of a claim that one has the right to use to identify oneself, because many people share the same birth date, whereas a photographic portrait is a value of a claim that one has the right to use identify oneself. Also, a role is just one type of claim.

Claims-based Authorization Versus Access Control Lists

How does the claims-based approach to authorization provided by XSI compare to controlling the use of resources with access control lists (ACLs), an approach that is common in administering access to network resources? Once again, having a definition of ACLs would be useful in answering the question.

"ACLs are composed of a series of Access Control Entries (ACEs) that specify which operations [a user or group] can perform on [a resource]" (Tulloch 2003, 7). An ACE consists of a security identifier (SID) identifying a user or group, and a set of access rights defining which operations the user or group is allowed or not allowed to perform on the resource (Tulloch 2003, 7).

ACLs "are used on Microsoft Windows platforms to control access to securable [resources] such as files, processes, services, shares, [and] printers" (Tulloch 2003, 7). Specifically, "[w]hen a user account is created on a Microsoft Windows platform, it is assigned a [SID] that uniquely identifies the account to the operating system" (Tulloch 2003, 7). When the user logs on using that account, an access token is created that contains the SID for that account and the SIDs of the groups to which the account belongs. That token "is then copied to all processes and threads owned by the account" (Tulloch 2003, 7). When the user tries to access a resource secured using an ACL, the SIDs in the token are compared with the SIDs in each ACE of the ACL, until a match is found, and access is either granted or denied (Tulloch 2003, 7).

Once again, claims-based authorization subsumes access control lists as a special case. The credentials by which a user logs on to an operating system, and the SIDs contained in the access token, are both claim sets. The process by which the operating system exchanges the credentials by which the user logs on for the SIDs in the access token that it issues is simply one case of the execution of an authorization policy. Comparing the SIDs in an access token with the SIDs in an ACL is merely an instance of comparing the claims in an authorization context claim set to the access requirements of whatever operation the user wants to perform on the resource secured by the ACL.

However, the more general model provided by XSI works far better than ACLs to accommodate the requirements of authorizing access to a distributed system. There are three reasons.

First, access tokens were never designed to be exchanged across platforms. Claims, by contrast, can be readily expressed in standard, interoperable formats like the one defined by the Security Assertion Markup Language (SAML).

Second, access tokens are issued by operating systems. Claims, however, can be issued by any source.

Third, and most important, the SIDs in access tokens and ACLs are generally useful only within the scope of the operating system issuing the access tokens. If that operating system is a domain controller, the utility of its SIDs will extend as far as the domain does. In contrast, a claim can be meaningful wherever the issuer of the claim is trusted.

Adopting Claims-based Authorization

However, despite these advantages of claims-based authorization over role-based authorization and access control lists, one should not necessarily eschew role-based authorization and access control lists in favor of claims-based authorization. The use of role-based authorization and access control lists is supported by a vast number of powerful tools. Many such tools are built into Microsoft Windows and their use is customary among network administrators. Support for claims-based authorization is mostly limited to XSI.

So instead of seeing claims-based authorization as a superior alternative to role-based authorization and access control lists, a wiser approach would be to use them together, leveraging their respective strengths where it is most appropriate to do so. Claims-based authorization is especially effective for controlling access to resources across platforms and between organizations. Therefore, in cases in which the users of one organization need to access resources managed by the systems of another organization, have them exchange their access tokens for claims that the other organization can use to decide whether to grant the users access.

How exactly might such a solution be implemented? Well, the Web Services Trust Language (WS-Trust) is a standard language for requesting and issuing claim sets. A system that issues claim sets in accordance with that language is called a *security token service* (STS) (Gudgin and Nadalin 2005, 7; Cabrera and Kurt 2005, 24-27). An organization whose users need to access the facilities of another organization's systems could provide their users with an STS from which they could request claim sets that the other organization's systems would understand. That STS would take the claims constituted by the SIDs in the users' access tokens and apply an authorization policy that would yield claims with types, rights, and values agreed on with the other organization. That other organization would provide a second STS to accept those claims and apply an authorization policy of its own to yield claims that the other systems within that organization could then use to decide whether to grant a user access to their resources. This solution is depicted in Figure 4.1. The approach has several important virtues.

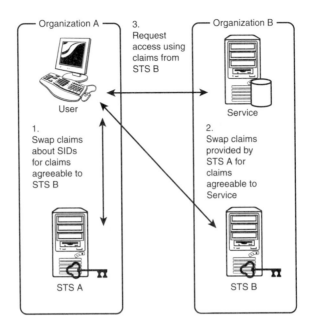

FIGURE 4.1   Cross-organization claims-based authorization.

First, trust relationships are minimized and the management of them is centralized. Specifically, the services with resources to protect need to trust the claims from only a single issuer, namely, their own organization's STS. That STS can be configured to trust claims issued by any number of other organizations' STSs. Configuring an STS to trust claims issued by another organization's STS is simply a matter of giving it access to the other organization's public key.

Second, the claims that one organization makes about its users attempting to access another organization's services are also hidden from the services by the authorization policy of the STS they trust. That STS applies the authorization policy to translate the claims made by the other organizations into claims that are familiar to the services. That process of translating the diverse sorts of claims that various organizations might make into the sorts of claims that are familiar to a suite of services is commonly referred to as *claims normalization.*

Third, the administration of access to services is truly federated. Federation is the formation of a unity in which the participants retain control over their internal affairs (*Oxford Dictionary of Current English* 2001), thereby minimizing the cost of maintaining the unity. In this case, the addition or removal of users and the elevation or reduction in users' privileges by the system administrators in one organization will determine their rights to access the services of the other organization, without the system administrators of that other organization needing to be involved. This benefit will be vividly demonstrated in the following exercise.

Using XSI

The exercise begins with a Windows Communication Foundation solution in which access to an Intranet resource is controlled using role-based authorization. That solution will show how the securing of Windows Communication Foundation applications simply leverages existing, familiar facilities of Microsoft Windows and Microsoft .NET, saving system administrators from having to learn new concepts and tools and saving software developers from having to learn new concepts and class libraries.

The exercise then proceeds to show how, with XSI, the same resource can be accessed from the same client deployed in a separate, federated organization, with the access being authorized based on claims. What should be impressive is that neither the code of the client nor the code of the service managing the resource will need to be altered to accomplish a fundamental change in how access to the resource is controlled. That should serve as yet another eloquent demonstration of the power of the software factory template for software communications that the Windows Communication Foundation provides, allowing one to fundamentally alter the behavior of an application by making some changes to a model while leaving its code intact.

Authorizing Access to an Intranet Resource Using Windows Identity

This first step will demonstrate a Windows Communication Foundation solution in which access to an Intranet resource is controlled using role-based authorization. The role-based authorization is accomplished using .NET Role-Based Security, the ASP.NET 2.0 AuthorizationStoreRoleProvider and the Windows Server 2003 Authorization Manager.

Readers using Windows XP Service Pack 2 can install the Windows Server 2003 Authorization Manager onto their systems by installing the Windows Server 2003 Service Pack 1 Administration Tools Pack. That can be obtained by searching for "Windows Server 2003 SP1 Administration Tools Pack" from the Microsoft Downloads Center.

Follow these instructions to get started:

1. Copy the code associated with this chapter that you downloaded from www.samspublishing.com to the folder C:\WCFHandsOn. The code is all in a folder called Security, and it contains a single Visual Studio solution with the same name. After the code has been unzipped, there should be a folder that looks like the one shown in Figure 4.2.

2. Open the solution, C:\WCFHandsOn\Security\Security.sln, in Visual Studio 2005.

3. Confirm that the startup project property of the solution is configured as shown in Figure 4.3.

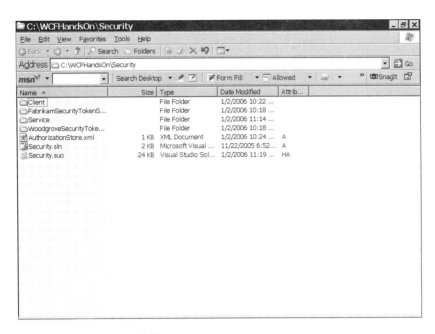

FIGURE 4.2   Security solution folder.

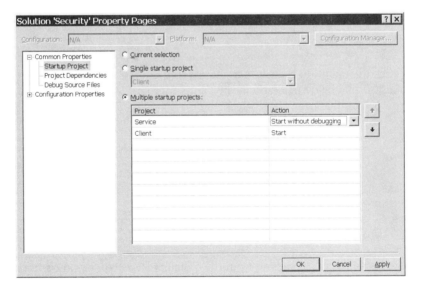

FIGURE 4.3   Security solution startup project property.

4. Start debugging the solution. The console application of the service should appear, as well as the user interface of the Resource Access client application, which is shown in Figure 4.4. That user interface has two large buttons. The button on the

left has a picture of coal on its face, and the one on the right has a picture of a more valuable resource, a diamond, on its face.

FIGURE 4.4   The Resource Access client user interface.

5. After the console application of the service has shown some activity, click the coal button. A message box should appear confirming that the less valuable resource, coal, has been accessed, as shown in Figure 4.5.

Figure 4.5   Successfully accessing coal.

6. Now click the diamond button. Alas, access to the more valuable resource of a diamond should be denied. Specifically, a message box like the one shown in Figure 4.6 should appear.

FIGURE 4.6   Unsuccessfully attempting to access a diamond.

7. Choose Debug, Stop Debugging from the Visual Studio 2005 menus, and close the console of the service.

The next few steps will explain why the coal was accessible but the diamond was not. Begin by following these instructions to open the Windows Server 2003 Authorization Manager user interface:

1. Open the Microsoft Management Console by choosing Run from the Windows Start menu, and entering this command in the Run dialog box:

   mmc

2. Select File, Add/Remove Snap-in from the Microsoft Management Console's menus.

3. Click the Add button on the Add/Remove Snap-in dialog.

4. Select Authorization Manager from the Add Standalone Snap-in dialog; click the Add button, and then the Close button.

5. Back on the Add/Remove Snap-in dialog, click the OK button.

   Now the Windows Server 2003 Authorization Manager user interface should be open, as shown in Figure 4.7. Proceed to examine the authorization store used to control access to the service's resources.

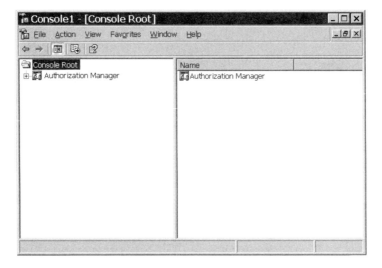

FIGURE 4.7   The Windows Server 2003 Authorization Manager user interface.

6. In the tree in the left pane of the Authorization Manager user interface in the Microsoft Management Console, right-click on Authorization Manager, and choose Open Authorization Store from the context menu.

7. Click Browse in the Open Authorization Store dialog shown in Figure 4.8, browse to the file C:\WCFHandsOn\Security\AuthorizationStore.xml in the file dialog that appears, and click on the Open button.

8. Expand the Authorization Manager tree in the left pane as shown in Figure 4.9. Select the StaffMember node in the tree on the left, and observe, in the pane on the right, that the users in the Everyone group are assigned to the StaffMember role.

FIGURE 4.8   Opening an authorization store.

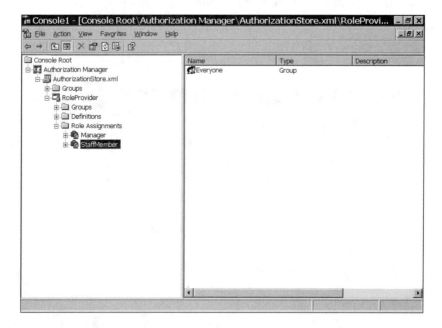

FIGURE 4.9   Role assignments.

9. Select the Manager node and see that no user is assigned to the Manager role.

10. Right-click on the Manager node, and select Assign Windows Users and Groups from the context menu. Enter the username of the currently logged-on user in the Select Users and Groups dialog, and click OK.

11. Start debugging the application again.

12. When the console of the service shows some activity, click on the diamond button in the Resource Access client user interface. The message shown in Figure 4.10 should confirm that diamonds are now accessible.

13. Choose Debug, Stop Debugging from the Visual Studio 2005 menus, and close the console of the service.

FIGURE 4.10   Successfully accessing diamonds.

14. Return to the authorization store console, and select the Manager node under Role Assignments. Right-click on the Administrator entry in the panel on the right, and choose Delete from the context menu to restore the access of the currently logged-on user to its original state.

Evidently, access to resources managed by the Windows Communication Foundation service is being controlled based on the roles to which the user of the client application is assigned within the Windows Server 2003 Authorization Manager authorization store, C:\WCFHandsOn\Security\AuthorizationStore.xml. The next few steps will reveal how that is possible:

1. In the Security solution in Visual Studio 2005, open the ResourceAccessServiceType.cs code module of the Service project. The content of the module is shown in Listing 4.1. There it is apparent that access to the operations of the service by which resources are made available is controlled by .NET Role-Based Security PrincipalPermission attributes that specify that only users assigned to the role of Manager can access the more valuable resource of diamonds.

LISTING 4.1   Using PrincipalPermission Attributes

```
using System;
using System.Collections;
using System.Collections.Generic;
using System.Security.Permissions;
using System.Runtime.Serialization;
using System.ServiceModel;
using System.Text;
using System.Web;
using System.Web.Security;


namespace Service
{
    public class ResourceAccessServiceType: IResourceAccessContract
    {
        #region IResourceAccessContract Members

        [PrincipalPermission(SecurityAction.Demand, Role = "StaffMember")]
        [PrincipalPermission(SecurityAction.Demand, Role = "Manager")]
```

LISTING 4.1   Continued

```
        string IResourceAccessContract.AccessCoal()
        {
            return "Here is your coal!";
        }


        [PrincipalPermission(SecurityAction.Demand, Role = "Manager")]
        string IResourceAccessContract.AccessDiamond()
        {
            return "Here is your diamond!";
        }


        #endregion

    }
}
```

2. Open the App.config file in the Service project, the contents of which are shown in Listing 4.2.

LISTING 4.2   Role-Based Authorization Configuration

```xml
<?xml version="1.0" encoding="utf-8" ?>
<configuration>


    <!-- Application Settings -->
  <appSettings>
    <add key="BaseAddress" value="http://localhost:8000/Woodgrove"/>
  </appSettings>


    <!-- Service Configuration -->
  <system.serviceModel>
    <services>
      <service type="Service.ResourceAccessServiceType"
               behaviorConfiguration="ServiceBehavior">
        <endpoint
            address="ResourceAccessService"
            binding="wsHttpBinding"
            contract="Service.IResourceAccessContract"/>
      </service>
    </services>
    <behaviors>
      <behavior name="ServiceBehavior"
       returnUnknownExceptionsAsFaults="true">
        <serviceAuthorization
            principalPermissionMode="UseAspNetRoles"  />
```

LISTING 4.2   Continued

```
            </behavior>
        </behaviors>
    </system.serviceModel>

        <!-- Role Provider Configuration -->
    <system.web>
        <roleManager defaultProvider="AuthorizationStoreRoleProvider"
                     enabled="true"
                     cacheRolesInCookie="true"
                     cookieName=".ASPROLES"
                     cookieTimeout="30"
                     cookiePath="/"
                     cookieRequireSSL="false"
                     cookieSlidingExpiration="true"
                     cookieProtection="All"  >
            <providers>
                <clear />
                <add
                  name="AuthorizationStoreRoleProvider"
                  type="System.Web.Security.AuthorizationStoreRoleProvider"
                  connectionStringName="AuthorizationServices"
                  applicationName="RoleProvider" />
            </providers>
        </roleManager>
    </system.web>
        <!-- Connection Strings -->
    <connectionStrings>
        <add
            name="AuthorizationServices"
connectionString="msxml://C:\WCFHandsOn\Security\AuthorizationStore.xml" />
    </connectionStrings>
</configuration>
```

The binding for the Windows Communication Foundation service that has the resources is the WSHttpBinding. By default, that binding uses the Windows access tokens of the users of client applications to identify those users to the service.

Behaviors were introduced in the preceding chapter. Here the ServiceAuthorization behavior is configured with UseAspNetRoles for its principal permission mode. That configuration specifies that .NET Role-Based Security PrincipalPermission attributes will be evaluated based on output from an ASP.NET 2.0 Role Provider, taking the Windows access token of the users of client applications as input.

The ASP.NET Role Provider is configured lower down in the App.config file. The configuration of the role provider is such that it uses Authorization Manager to determine the roles of users, via the `AuthorizationStoreRoleProvider`, and the particular authorization store that is being used by Authorization Manager for that purpose is the store `C:\WCFHandsOn\Security\AuthorizationStore.xml`.

So access to the resources of the Windows Communication Foundation service is being controlled by Role-Based Authorization using .NET Role-Based Security and an ASP.NET 2.0 Role Provider. This way of authorizing access to the service's resources has several benefits.

First, the Windows Communication Foundation is simply configured to delegate authorization to other technologies, to .NET Role-Based Security, an ASP.NET 2.0 Role Provider, and the Windows Server 2003 Authorization Manager. Consequently, the use of the Windows Communication Foundation is not imposing any requirement on software developers or network administrators to learn or adopt new technologies for authorization. Instead, existing technologies that should already be familiar to them are being used.

Second, access to the resources of the service can be administered using the Windows Server 2003 Authorization Manager's user interface. That user interface, which is very easy for system administrators to use, is built into Windows Server 2003, saving one from having to build a user interface for administering authorization. More information about the Windows Server 2003 Authorization Manager is provided in Dave McPherson's article "Role-Based Access Control for Multi-tier Applications Using Authorization Manager" (2005).

Third, the selection of where the authorization information for the service is stored, and how it is administered, is controlled through the configuration of the ASP.NET 2.0 Role Provider. The particular Windows Server 2003 Authorization Manager authorization store being used is specified by the connection string so that it can be altered without changing any code. More important, the fact that a Windows Server 2003 Authorization Manager authorization store is being used at all is determined by the selection of the AuthorizationStoreRoleProvider. A different role provider that used a different kind of store for authorization information could be selected in the configuration file, thereby completely altering how access to the application is administered, but, again, without altering any code whatsoever.

Improving the Initial Solution

One shortcoming of the existing solution is that the use of the .NET Role-Based Security `PrincipalPermission` attributes to control access to the service has the effect of winding the code for authenticating users into code of the service itself. The Windows Communication Foundation Service Model allows one to do better by isolating the code authorizing access to the operations of a service into a separate class that is identified by the configuration of the service. The following steps demonstrate how to accomplish that task:

1. Open the `ResourceAccessServiceType.cs` code module of the Service project, and comment out the `PrincipalPermission` attributes, as shown in Listing 4.3.

LISTING 4.3   Foregoing PrincipalPermission Attributes

```
using System;
using System.Collections;
using System.Collections.Generic;
using System.Security.Permissions;
using System.Runtime.Serialization;
using System.ServiceModel;
using System.Text;
using System.Web;
using System.Web.Security;


namespace Service
{
    public class ResourceAccessServiceType: IResourceAccessContract
    {
        #region IResourceAccessContract Members

        //[PrincipalPermission(SecurityAction.Demand, Role = "StaffMember")]
        //[PrincipalPermission(SecurityAction.Demand, Role = "Manager")]
        string IResourceAccessContract.AccessCoal()
        {
            return "Here is your coal!";
        }

        //[PrincipalPermission(SecurityAction.Demand, Role = "Manager")]
        string IResourceAccessContract.AccessDiamond()
        {
            return "Here is your diamond!";
        }

        #endregion
    }
}
```

2. Modify the App.config file of the Service project to look like the configuration in Listing 4.4. To save one from having to make the changes manually, a copy of the configuration is in the file App.Config1.txt in the C:\WCFHandsOn\Security\Service folder.

LISTING 4.4   OperationRequirementType Configuration

```
<?xml version="1.0" encoding="utf-8" ?>
<configuration>
    <configSections>
        <section name="operationRequirements"
```

LISTING 4.4   Continued

```
            type="Service.OperationRequirementsConfigurationSection, Service" />
</configSections>

<!-- Operation Requirements -->
<operationRequirements>
    <operation
    identifier="http://tempuri.org/IResourceAccessContract/AccessCoal">
        <role name="Manager"/>
        <role name="StaffMember"/>
    </operation>
    <operation
    identifier="http://tempuri.org/IResourceAccessContract/AccessDiamond">
        <role name="Manager"/>
    </operation>
</operationRequirements>

<!-- Application Settings -->
<appSettings>
    <add key="BaseAddress" value="http://localhost:8000/Woodgrove"/>
</appSettings>

<!-- Service Configuration -->
<system.serviceModel>
    <services>
        <service type="Service.ResourceAccessServiceType"
                behaviorConfiguration="ServiceBehavior">
            <endpoint
                address="ResourceAccessService"
                binding="wsHttpBinding"
                contract="Service.IResourceAccessContract"/>
        </service>
    </services>
    <behaviors>
        <behavior name="ServiceBehavior"
         returnUnknownExceptionsAsFaults="true">
            <serviceAuthorization
                principalPermissionMode="None"
                operationRequirementType="Service.AccessChecker, Service">
            </serviceAuthorization>
        </behavior>
    </behaviors>
</system.serviceModel>
```

LISTING 4.4   Continued

```
<!-- Role Provider Configuration -->
<system.web>
    <roleManager defaultProvider="AuthorizationStoreRoleProvider"
                 enabled="true"
                 cacheRolesInCookie="true"
                 cookieName=".ASPROLES"
                 cookieTimeout="30"
                 cookiePath="/"
                 cookieRequireSSL="false"
                 cookieSlidingExpiration="true"
                 cookieProtection="All"  >
        <providers>
           <clear />
           <add
             name="AuthorizationStoreRoleProvider"
             type="System.Web.Security.AuthorizationStoreRoleProvider"
             connectionStringName="AuthorizationServices"
             applicationName="RoleProvider" />
        </providers>
    </roleManager>
</system.web>

<!-- Connection Strings -->
<connectionStrings>
    <add
        name="AuthorizationServices"
connectionString="msxml://C:\WCFHandsOn\Security\AuthorizationStore.xml" />
</connectionStrings>

</configuration>
```

The configuration contains this custom section:

```
<operationRequirements>
        <operation
        identifier="http://tempuri.org/IResourceAccessContract/AccessCoal">
            <role name="Manager"/>
            <role name="StaffMember"/>
        </operation>
        <operation
        identifier="http://tempuri.org/IResourceAccessContract/AccessDiamond">
            <role name="Manager"/>
        </operation>
</operationRequirements>
```

That section names the roles authorized to access each operation of the service, those operations being identified by their URIs.

The modified configuration also changes how the `ServiceAuthorization` behavior is configured:

```
<behaviors>
  <behavior name="ServiceBehavior"
    returnUnknownExceptionsAsFaults="true">
    <serviceAuthorization
      principalPermissionMode="None"
    operationRequirementType="Service.AccessChecker, Service">
    </serviceAuthorization>
  </behavior>
</behaviors>
```

The new configuration signifies that authorization to access the facilities of the service will now be controlled by a class called `AccessChecker`. That class, which must derive from the abstract `Sysem.ServiceModel.OperationRequirement` class, is defined in the next steps.

3. Add the class module named `OperationRequirementsConfigurationSection.cs` in the `C:\WCFHandsOn\Security\Service` folder to the Service project of the Security solution. That class module contains classes for deserializing the information in the custom section of the configuration file that identifies the roles authorized to access the service's operations.

4. Add a class module named `AccessChecker.cs` to the Service project in the Security solution.

5. Replace the contents of that module with the code in Listing 4.5. A copy of the code should be found in the `AccessChecker1.txt` file in the `C:\WCFHandsOn\Security\Service` folder.

LISTING 4.5   An `OperationRequirement` Type

```
using System;
using System.Collections.Generic;
using System.Configuration;
using System.IO;
using System.Security.Authorization;
using System.ServiceModel;
using System.Web;
using System.Web.Security;

namespace Service
{
```

LISTING 4.5   Continued

```
public class AccessChecker : OperationRequirement
{
    private Dictionary<string, string[]> accessRequirements = null;

    public AccessChecker()
    {
        this.accessRequirements = new Dictionary<string, string[]>();

        OperationRequirementsConfigurationSection
            operationRequirementsConfigurationSection
            = ConfigurationManager.GetSection("operationRequirements")
            as OperationRequirementsConfigurationSection;

        OperationRequirementsCollection requirements =
            operationRequirementsConfigurationSection.OperationRequirements;
        List<string> roles = null;
        foreach (OperationElement operationElement in requirements)
        {
            roles = new List<string>(operationElement.Roles.Count);
            foreach (RoleElement roleElement in operationElement.Roles)
            {
                roles.Add(roleElement.Name);
            }

            this.accessRequirements.Add(
                operationElement.Identifier,
                roles.ToArray());
        }

    }

    public override bool AccessCheck(OperationContext operationContext)
    {
        string header =
            operationContext.RequestContext.RequestMessage.Headers.Action;
        string[] requiredRoles = null;
        if (!(this.accessRequirements.TryGetValue(header, out requiredRoles)))
        {
            return false;
        }

        string userName =
OperationContext.Current.ServiceSecurityContext.WindowsIdentity.Name;
        foreach (string requiredRole in requiredRoles)
```

```
        {
            if (Roles.Provider.IsUserInRole(userName,requiredRole))
            {
                return true;
            }
        }
        return false;
    }
  }
}
```

Because the `ServiceAuthorization` behavior has been configured to use this `AccessChecker` class to control access to the service, an instance of the `AccessChecker` class will be created along with the service's host. When that instance of the `AccessChecker` class is created, its constructor will execute.

That constructor reads the information from the configuration file that identifies the roles permitted to access the operations of the service. It populates a hash table that associates the names of the roles authorized to use each operation of the service with the URI of that operation.

When an attempt is made to use any one of the service's operations, the `AccessChecker` class's override of the `AccessCheck()` method of the abstract `OperationRequirement` class will be invoked. That method retrieves the URI of the operation to be used, as well as the identity of the user on whose behalf the attempt to use the operation is being made. Both the URI of the operation and the identity of the user are provided by the Windows Communication Foundation Service Model's `OperationContext` class, which was introduced in Chapter 2. The code uses the URI of the operation to retrieve the names of the roles permitted to access that operation from the hash table created by the constructor. Then it uses the ASP.NET 2.0 `Roles` class to check whether the user is assigned to any of the roles permitted to access the operation. If the user is assigned to any of those roles, the user is permitted to use the operation.

Test the modified solution by following these instructions:

1. Start debugging the application once again.

2. When the console of the service shows some activity, click on the coal button in the Resource Access client user interface. The message confirming access to the coal should appear, as before.

3. Click on the diamond button of the Resource Access client user interface. The message denying access to the diamonds should appear.

4. Choose Debug, Stop Debugging from the Visual Studio 2005 menus, and close the console of the service.

By virtue of these modifications to the original application facilitated by the Windows Communication Foundation, permissions for the users—in particular, roles to access the operations of the service—are no longer entangled with the code of the service itself. The configuration of the application identifies a separate class that is responsible for managing access to the service's operations.

Adding STSs as the Foundation for Federation

Now assume that the intranet service used in the preceding steps is deployed within an organization called Woodgrove. In the following steps, attempts to use that service will be made from within a partner organization called Fabrikam.

That feat will be accomplished in accordance with the architecture depicted in Figure 4.1. Both Fabrikam and Woodgrove will provide an STS. The Woodgrove STS will be configured to trust claims about users issued by the Fabrikam STS, and the Woodgrove service will be configured to trust claims about the users made by the Woodgrove STS.

When a user of the Resource Access client application within Fabrikam uses that application to access an operation provided by the Woodgrove service, the application will request a set of claims from the Fabrikam STS. That STS will execute an authorization policy to determine the claims it should issue for the user. That authorization policy identifies the user by the user's Windows access token and determines the roles to which the user is assigned using the ASP.NET 2.0 AuthorizationStoreRoleProvider and the Windows Server 2003 Authorization Manager. Based on the roles to which the user is assigned, the Fabrikam STS issues a set of claims about the user's roles to the Resource Access client application.

The Resource Access client application will submit the claim set obtained from the Fabrikam STS to the Woodgrove STS, which trusts claims issued by the Fabrikam STS. The Woodgrove STS will execute an authorization policy to translate the claims about the user's role made by the Fabrikam STS into a set of claims about the user's roles with which Woodgrove's service is familiar.

The Resource Access client application will submit the set of claims about the user's roles issued by the Woodgrove STS to the Woodgrove service, which trusts claims issued by that STS. The Woodgrove service will compare the Woodgrove STS's claims about the user's roles with the roles that are permitted access to the operation that the user is attempting to employ via the Resource Access client. By doing so, it will be able to determine whether the user should be granted access to the operation:

1. Install the certificates that the STSs will use to identify themselves by executing the batch file C:\WCFHandsOn\Security\SetUp.bat. That batch file assumes that the tools included with the version of the Microsoft Windows SDK for use with WinFX are installed in the folder C:\Program Files\Microsoft SDKs\Windows\v1.0\Bin. If they are not installed there, modify the batch file accordingly. If their location is unknown, search the hard disks for the tool CertKeyFileTool.exe; the other tools should be in the same location. A second batch file, C:\WCFHandsOn\Security\CleanUp.bat, is provided for removing the certificates after the exercise has been completed.

2. Add the Fabrikam STS to the solution. Do so by adding the project C:\WCFHandsOn\ Security\FabrikamSecurityTokenService\FabrikamSecurityTokenService.csproj to the Security solution. One does not risk building STSs from scratch, but rather uses STSs that are widely known to function correctly. Consequently, prebuilt STSs have been provided for use in this exercise. Those happen to have been programmed by Martin Gudgin, one of the two editors of the WS-Trust specification by which STSs are defined, so those STSs could hardly have a finer lineage. The behavior of this particular STS will be customized in a later step.

3. Open the ISecurityTokenService.cs file of the FabrikamSecurityTokenService project in the Security solution, and examine the ISecurityTokenService service contract that the Fabrikam STS implements. It is shown in Listing 4.6.

LISTING 4.6   STS Service Contract

```
using System;
using System.ServiceModel;

namespace SecurityTokenService
{
    [ServiceContract]
    public interface ISecurityTokenService
    {
        [OperationContract(
            Action =
            "http://schemas.xmlsoap.org/ws/2005/02/trust/RST/Issue",
            ReplyAction =
            "http://schemas.xmlsoap.org/ws/2005/02/trust/RSTR/Issue")]
        Message Issue(Message request);
        [OperationContract(
            Action =
            "http://schemas.xmlsoap.org/ws/2005/02/trust/RSTR/Issue",
            ReplyAction =
            "http://schemas.xmlsoap.org/ws/2005/02/trust/RSTR/Issue")]
        Message IssueChallenge(Message challenge);
        [OperationContract(
            Action =
            "http://schemas.xmlsoap.org/ws/2005/02/trust/RST/Renew",
            ReplyAction =
            "http://schemas.xmlsoap.org/ws/2005/02/trust/RSTR/Renew")]
        Message Renew(Message request);
        [OperationContract(
            Action =
            "http://schemas.xmlsoap.org/ws/2005/02/trust/RSTR/Renew",
            ReplyAction =
            "http://schemas.xmlsoap.org/ws/2005/02/trust/RSTR/Renew")]
        Message RenewChallenge(Message request);
```

LISTING 4.6   Continued

```
    [OperationContract(
        Action =
        "http://schemas.xmlsoap.org/ws/2005/02/trust/RST/Cancel",
        ReplyAction =
        "http://schemas.xmlsoap.org/ws/2005/02/trust/RSTR/Cancel")]
    Message Cancel(Message request);
    [OperationContract(
        Action =
        "http://schemas.xmlsoap.org/ws/2005/02/trust/RST/Validate",
        ReplyAction =
        "http://schemas.xmlsoap.org/ws/2005/02/trust/RSTR/Validate")]
    Message Validate(Message request);
    }
}
```

In this service contract, each operation is defined as receiving and returning instances of the Windows Communication Foundation's Message class. That class represents a SOAP message. So the operations are defined as simply receiving and returning SOAP messages.

The OperationContract attributes have Action and ReplyAction parameters. What do those signify?

The Action parameter of an OperationContract provides a URI as the address of an operation. Incoming messages that have that URI as the value of a Web Service Addressing (WS-Addressing) action header will be routed to the operation for processing by the Windows Communication Foundation Dispatcher.

The ReplyAction parameter specifies the URI that will be the value of the WS-Addressing action header of the response messages emitted by an operation. That value will allow the proxy code of a client using the operation to identify those messages that are the output of that particular operation from among any other messages emitted by the service.

Thus, the values of the Action and ReplyAction parameters of OperationContract attributes are for correlating messages with operations. The Windows Communication Foundation usually provides default values for those parameters. In the case of the ISecurityTokenService contract, specific values have been provided in accordance with the WS-Trust protocol, which specifies the WS-Addressing action headers for SOAP messages exchanged with an STS.

Consequently, the service contract defines a number of operations that receive and return SOAP messages with the WS-Addressing action headers defined by the WS-Trust protocol for messages exchanged with an STS. Hence, the service contract is, in effect, describing the interface of an STS as defined by the specification of the WS-Trust protocol.

4. Open the `App.config` file of the FabrikamSecurityTokenService project in the Security solution to see how the Fabrikam STS is configured:

<system.serviceModel>
 <services>
  <service
   type=
 "SecurityTokenService.SecurityTokenService, FabrikamSecurityTokenService"
    behaviorConfiguration="SecurityTokenServiceBehaviors">
    <endpoint address="SecurityTokenService"
     binding="wsHttpBinding"
   contract=
 "SecurityTokenService.ISecurityTokenService, FabrikamSecurityTokenService" >
     </endpoint>
    </service>
   </services>
  </system.serviceModel>

Its binding is the predefined `WSHttpBinding`. By default, services configured with that binding identify users by their Windows access tokens.

5. Add the Woodgrove STS to the Security solution by adding the project `C:\WCFHandsOn\Security\WoodgroveSecurityTokenService\` `WoodgroveSecurityTokenService.csproj`.

6. Open the `App.config` file of the WoodgroveSecurityTokenService project in the Security solution to see how the Woodgrove STS is configured. The pertinent elements of the configuration are shown in Listing 4.7.

LISTING 4.7 Woodgrove STS Configuration

```
<system.serviceModel>
  <services>
    <service
      type=
"SecurityTokenService.SecurityTokenService, WoodgroveSecurityTokenService"
      behaviorConfiguration="SecurityTokenServiceBehaviors">
      <endpoint address="SecurityTokenService"
        binding="wsFederationBinding"
        bindingConfiguration="TrustFabrikamSecurityTokenService"
        contract=
"SecurityTokenService.ISecurityTokenService, WoodgroveSecurityTokenService" />
    </service>
  </services>
  <bindings>
    <wsFederationBinding>
      <binding name="TrustFabrikamSecurityTokenService">
```

LISTING 4.7   Continued

```
        <security mode='Message'>
          <message
            issuedTokenType=
"http://docs.oasis-open.org/wss/oasis-wss-saml-token-profile-1.1#SAMLV1.1">
              <issuer address=
"http://localhost:8001/Fabrikam/SecurityTokenService" />
              <issuerMetadata address=
"http://localhost:8001/Fabrikam/mex"/>
          </message>
        </security>
      </binding>
    </wsFederationBinding>
  </bindings>
</system.serviceModel>
```

The definition of the Woodgrove STSs endpoint selects the predefined WSFederationBinding as the binding:

```
<endpoint address="SecurityTokenService"
        binding="wsFederationBinding"
        bindingConfiguration="TrustFabrikamSecurityTokenService"
        contract=
"SecurityTokenService.ISecurityTokenService, WoodgroveSecurityTokenService" />
```

That choice of binding implies that users will be expected to present security tokens to identify themselves.

The bindingConfiguration attribute in the definition of the endpoint identifies a particular set of custom settings for the WSFederationBinding. Those custom settings identify the issuer of the security tokens that users must present. That issuer is identified by the URI of the Fabrikam STS, which was added to the solution in step 2:

```
<bindings>
  <wsFederationBinding>
    <binding name="TrustFabrikamSecurityTokenService">
      <security mode='Message'>
        <message
          issuedTokenType=
"http://docs.oasis-open.org/wss/oasis-wss-saml-token-profile-1.1#SAMLV1.1">
            <issuer address=
"http://localhost:8001/Fabrikam/SecurityTokenService" />
            <issuerMetadata address=
"http://localhost:8001/Fabrikam/mex"/>
        </message>
```

```
      </security>
     </binding>
    </wsFederationBinding>
   </bindings>
```

7. Now configure the Woodgrove service to demand a security token from the Woodgrove STS to authenticate the user. That can be done by replacing the `system.ServiceModel` section of the `App.config` file in the Service project of the Security solution with the configuration in Listing 4.8. The complete configuration is in the file `C:\WCFHandsOn\Security\Service\App.Config2.txt`.

LISTING 4.8   Service Configuration

```
<system.serviceModel>
  <services>
    <service
      type="Service.ResourceAccessServiceType,Service"
    behaviorConfiguration="ServiceBehaviors">
    <endpoint address="ResourceAccessService"
      binding="wsFederationBinding"
        bindingConfiguration="TrustWoodgroveSecurityTokenService"
      contract="Service.IResourceAccessContract,Service" >
      </endpoint>
    </service>
  </services>
  <behaviors>
    <behavior name="ServiceBehaviors"
    returnUnknownExceptionsAsFaults="true">
    <serviceSecurityAudit
      auditLogLocation="Application"
      messageAuthenticationAuditLevel="SuccessOrFailure"
      serviceAuthorizationAuditLevel="SuccessOrFailure"/>
    <serviceCredentials>
      <serviceCertificate
        storeLocation="LocalMachine"
        storeName="My"
        x509FindType="FindBySubjectName"
        findValue="Woodgrove" />
    </serviceCredentials>
      <serviceAuthorization
        principalPermissionMode="None"
        operationRequirementType="Service.AccessChecker, Service">
      </serviceAuthorization>
    </behavior>
  </behaviors>
```

LISTING 4.8   Continued

```
<bindings>
  <wsFederationBinding>
  <binding name="TrustWoodgroveSecurityTokenService">
    <security  mode="Message">
      <message>
        <issuerMetadata
          address="http://localhost:8002/Woodgrove/mex"/>
        </message>
      </security>
  </binding>
  </wsFederationBinding>
</bindings>
</system.serviceModel>
```

This definition of the service's endpoint in this revised configuration selects the pre-defined WSFederationBinding as the binding:

```
<endpoint address="ResourceAccessService"
  binding="wsFederationBinding"
  bindingConfiguration="TrustWoodgroveSecurityTokenService"
  contract="Service.IResourceAccessContract,Service" >
</endpoint>
```

As mentioned earlier, that choice of binding implies that users of the operations provided at that endpoint will be expected to present security tokens to identify themselves.

The bindingConfiguration attribute in the definition of the endpoint identifies custom settings for the WSFederationBinding, and those custom settings identify the issuer of the security tokens that users must present. That issuer is identified by the URI of the Woodgrove STS, which was added to the solution in step 5:

```
<bindings>
    <wsFederationBinding>
    <binding name="TrustWoodgroveSecurityTokenService">
      <security  mode="Message">
        <message>
          <issuerMetadata
            address="http://localhost:8002/Woodgrove/mex"/>
          </message>
        </security>
    </binding>
    </wsFederationBinding>
  </bindings>
```

So the Fabrikam STS identifies users by their Windows access tokens, while the Woodgrove STS demands that users identify themselves with security tokens issued by the Fabrikam STS, and the Woodgrove service requires that users identify themselves with security tokens issued by the Woodgrove STS. Now the Resource Access client application must be configured to reflect this arrangement:

1. Modify the startup project property of the solution as shown in Figure 4.11.

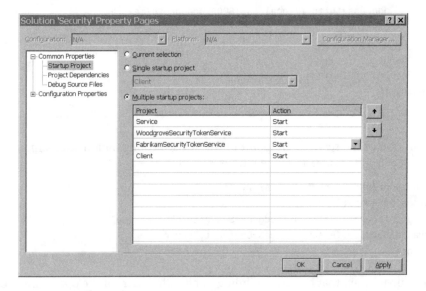

FIGURE 4.11   Security solution startup project property.

2. Start debugging the solution.

3. Open the Microsoft Windows Vista DEBUG Build Environment prompt by choosing All Programs, Microsoft Windows SDK, CMD Shell from the Windows Start menu.

4. Enter

   ```
   C:
   ```

   and then

   ```
   cd c:\WCFHandsOn\Security
   ```

   at that prompt to make the Security solution folder the current directory.

5. Enter this command to have the Windows Communication Foundation's Service Metadata Tool generate the necessary configuration for the client application:

   ```
   svcutil /config:app.config http://localhost:8000/Woodgrove
   ```

6. Stop debugging the solution.

7. Delete the existing configuration for the client by deleting the file `App.config` from the Client project of the Security solution.

8. Replace that configuration with the configuration file generated using the Service Metadata Tool by adding the file `C:\WCFHandsOn\Security\App.config` to the Client project of the Security solution.

9. Some modifications need to be made to the generated configuration file. So open the `App.config` file in the Client project of the Security solution, and modify the definition of the Woodgrove service's endpoint therein, providing a name for the endpoint, changing how the contract is identified, and specifying a behavior configuration, so that the endpoint configuration looks like this:

```
<client>
  <endpoint
    name="ResourceAccessService"
    address="http://localhost:8000/Woodgrove/ResourceAccessService"
    binding="customBinding"
    bindingConfiguration=
    "WSFederationBinding_IResourceAccessContract"
    contract="Client.IResourceAccessContract,Client"
    behaviorConfiguration="ResourceAccessClientBehavior">
    <identity>
      <dns value="Woodgrove" />
    </identity>
  </endpoint>
</client>
```

10. Add the behavior configuration named in the previous step as shown in Listing 4.9. The behaviors in this configuration specify that the client application will be relying on the STS to generate entropy to encrypt their conversation.

LISTING 4.9   Client Configuration

```
<client>
  <endpoint
    name="ResourceAccessService"
    address="http://localhost:8000/Woodgrove/ResourceAccessService"
    binding="customBinding"
    bindingConfiguration=
    "WSFederationBinding_IResourceAccessContract"
    contract="Client.IResourceAccessContract,Client"
    behaviorConfiguration="ResourceAccessClientBehavior">
    <identity>
      <dns value="Woodgrove" />
    </identity>
  </endpoint>
```

LISTING 4.9   Continued

```
</client>
<behaviors>
  <behavior name="ResourceAccessClientBehavior">
    <clientCredentials>
      <issuedToken keyEntropyMode ="ServerEntropy">
        <issuerChannelBehaviors>
          <add
          issuerAddress=
"http://localhost:8002/Woodgrove/SecurityTokenService"
            behaviorConfiguration=
"WoodgroveSecurityTokenServiceBehavior" />
          <add
            issuerAddress=
"http://localhost:8001/Fabrikam/SecurityTokenService"
        behaviorConfiguration=
"FabrikamSecurityTokenServiceBehavior" />
        </issuerChannelBehaviors>
    </issuedToken>
    </clientCredentials>
  </behavior>
  <behavior name="WoodgroveSecurityTokenServiceBehavior">
    <clientCredentials>
    <issuedToken keyEntropyMode ="ServerEntropy" />
    </clientCredentials>
  </behavior>
  <behavior name="FabrikamSecurityTokenServiceBehavior">
    <clientCredentials>
      <issuedToken keyEntropyMode ="ServerEntropy" />
    </clientCredentials>
  </behavior>
</behaviors>
<bindings>
[...]
```

To test the solution in its present state, follow these steps:

1. First, temporarily disable the authorization mechanism in the service. Open the
   AccessChecker class module of the Service project within the Security solution, and
   disable the authorization mechanism therein by modifying the AccessCheck()
   method in this way so that it immediately responds by permitting any authenticated user access to any operation:

   ```
   public override bool AccessCheck(OperationContext operationContext)
   {
     return true;
   ```

```
string header =
   operationContext.RequestContext.RequestMessage.Headers.Action;
string[] requiredRoles = null;
if (!(this.accessRequirements.TryGetValue(header, out requiredRoles)))
{
   return false;
}

string userName =
OperationContext.Current.ServiceSecurityContext.WindowsIdentity.Name;
   foreach (string requiredRole in requiredRoles)
   {
      if (Roles.Provider.IsUserInRole(userName,requiredRole))
      {
         return true;
      }
   }
   return false;
}
```

2. Start debugging the solution.

3. When the console of the service, the Woodgrove STS, and the Fabrikam STS all show some activity, click on the coal button in the Resource Access client user interface. After a moment, there should be more activity in the console of the Fabrikam STS, as shown in Figure 4.12, as it issues a security token for use in obtaining a second security token from the Woodgrove STS. Then there should be similar activity in the console of the Woodgrove STS as it issues a security token for accessing the Woodgrove service. Finally, a message should appear confirming access to the coal resource, because the Woodgrove service is configured to accept requests from any users that have security tokens issued by the Woodgrove STS.

FIGURE 4.12   Retrieving a security token from the Fabrikam STS.

4. Click on the diamond button of the Resource Access client user interface. A message should appear confirming access to the diamond resource. That is a temporary state of affairs due to the authorization mechanism of the service having been disabled, thereby permitting any authenticated user to access any resource.

5. Scroll through the output in the console of the Fabrikam STS, and output like that shown in Figure 4.13 should be visible. It shows details of the claims incorporated in the SAML security token issued by the Fabrikam STS. What that STS is currently doing is simply taking the claims implicit in the user's Windows access token and expressing those as User Principal Name and SID claims about the user.

FIGURE 4.13   Claims in the Fabrikam security token.

6. Stop debugging the solution.

In the next few steps, the Fabrikam STS will be modified with the addition of an XSI authorization policy. By virtue of that policy, instead of simply passing through the claims in the user's Windows access token, the Fabrikam STS will look up the user's roles in an Authorization Manager authorization store, and insert claims about the user's roles into the security token that it issues:

1. Open the app.config file of the FabrikamSecurityTokenService project in the Security solution.

2. Locate the elements of the configuration that specify the Windows Communication Foundation behaviors of the Fabrikam STS, and modify those by adding a serviceAuthorization element with an authorization policy like so:

```
<behaviors>
  <behavior
    name="SecurityTokenServiceBehaviors"
    returnUnknownExceptionsAsFaults="true">
    <serviceAuthorization>
      <authorizationPolicies>
      <add policyType=
```

```
"SecurityTokenService.AuthorizationPolicy, FabrikamSecurityTokenService" />
        </authorizationPolicies>
      </serviceAuthorization>
    </behavior>
  </behaviors>
```

The new element identifies the Fabrikam STS's XSI authorization policy module. That is the module in which claims presented by a user will be mapped to claims in the STS's authorization context, which will in turn be included in the security token issued to the user. It will be in a claim translation routine within that authorization policy module where the claims implicit in the user's Windows access token will be translated into claims about the user's role that Woodgrove's STS is expecting and will understand.

3. Add a new class module called `AuthorizationPolicy.cs` to the FabrikamSecurityTokenService project.

4. Alter the code therein to contain an `AuthorizationPolicy` class that implements XSI's `IAuthorizationPolicy` interface, as in Listing 4.10.

LISTING 4.10   An `AuthorizationPolicy` Class

```
using System;
using System.Collections.ObjectModel;
using System.Collections.Generic;
using System.Configuration;
using System.Runtime.Serialization;
using System.Security.Authorization;
using System.Security.Cryptography;
using System.Security.Cryptography.X509Certificates;
using System.ServiceModel;
using System.ServiceModel.Security;
using System.ServiceModel.Security.Protocols;
using System.ServiceModel.Security.Tokens;
using System.Text;
using System.Threading;
using System.Web.Security;
using System.Workflow.Runtime;
using System.Workflow.Runtime.Hosting;
using System.Xml;

namespace SecurityTokenService
{
    public class AuthorizationPolicy : IAuthorizationPolicy
    {
        public AuthorizationPolicy()
        {
        }
```

LISTING 4.10   Continued

```csharp
public ClaimSet Issuer
{
    get
    {
        return DefaultClaimSet.System.Issuer;
    }
}

#region IAuthorizationPolicy Members

bool IAuthorizationPolicy.Evaluate(
    EvaluationContext evaluationContext,
    ref object state)
{
    return true;
}
ClaimSet IAuthorizationPolicy.Issuer
{
    get
    {
        return this.Issuer;
    }
}


#endregion



#region IAuthorizationComponent Members

string IAuthorizationComponent.Id
{
    get
    {
        return Guid.NewGuid().ToString();
    }
}

#endregion
    }

}
```

5. Alter the IAuthorizationPolicy.Evaluate() method of the class as shown in Listing 4.11 so that it takes the claims incorporated in the user's Windows access token and maps those to claims about the user's role based on information in the Authorization Manager authorization store.

LISTING 4.11   AuthorizationPolicy Evaluate() Method

```
bool IAuthorizationPolicy.Evaluate(
        EvaluationContext evaluationContext,
        ref object state)
{
    List<Claim> claimsToAdd = new List<Claim>();
    ReadOnlyCollection<ClaimSet> inputClaims =
        evaluationContext.TargetClaimSets;
    for (int index = 0; index < inputClaims.Count; index++)
    {
        foreach (Claim claim in inputClaims[index].FindClaims(
            ClaimTypes.Upn, null))
        {
            string[] roles = Roles.Provider.GetRolesForUser(
                (string)claim.Resource);
            foreach (string role in roles)
            {
                claimsToAdd.Add(Claim.CreateRoleClaim(role));
            }
        }
    }

    if (claimsToAdd.Count > 0)
    {
        evaluationContext.AddToTarget(
            this, new DefaultClaimSet(
            this.Issuer, claimsToAdd));
    }

    return true;
}
```

In this code that implements the Evaluate() method of XSI's IAuthorizationPolicy interface, the information in the user's Windows access token is incorporated in the XSI EvaluationContext object. That object constitutes the claims that are input to the authorization policy. Based on information retrieved from the Windows Server 2003 Authorization Manager store, the code creates new XSI Claim objects representing claims about the user's roles. Those Claim objects are added to a context called the *target context* using the AddToTarget() method of the

EvaluationContract object. After the authorization policy has finished evaluating the input claims, that target context becomes the XSI authorization context, and the STS copies the claims therein into the security token that the STS issues for the user.

6. Configure the ASP.NET role provider to retrieve information about the user's roles from the same Authorization Manager authorization store used earlier. The necessary changes are shown in Listing 4.12, and are also in the file C:\WCFHandsOn\ Security\FabrikamSecurityTokenService\App.Config1.txt.

LISTING 4.12   Fabrikam STS Configuration

```
<?xml version="1.0" encoding="utf-8" ?>
<configuration>
    <appSettings>
        <add key="BaseAddress" value="http://localhost:8001/Fabrikam"/>
        <add key="IssuerName" value="Woodgrove"/>
    </appSettings>
    <connectionStrings>
        <add name="AuthorizationServices"
connectionString="msxml:// C:\WCFHandsOn\Security\AuthorizationStore.xml" />
    </connectionStrings>
    <system.web>
        <roleManager defaultProvider="AuthorizationStoreRoleProvider"
                     maxCachedResults="0"
                     enabled="true"
                     cacheRolesInCookie="false"
                     cookieName=".ASPROLES"
                     cookieTimeout="1"
                     cookiePath="/"
                     cookieRequireSSL="false"
                     cookieSlidingExpiration="true"
                     cookieProtection="All"  >
            <providers>
                <clear />
                <add
                  name="AuthorizationStoreRoleProvider"
                  type="System.Web.Security.AuthorizationStoreRoleProvider"
                  connectionStringName="AuthorizationServices"
                  cacheRefreshInterval="1"
                  applicationName="RoleProvider" />
            </providers>
        </roleManager>
    </system.web>
    <system.serviceModel>
        <services>
```

LISTING 4.12   Continued

```
        <service
            type="SecurityTokenService.SecurityTokenService,
FabrikamSecurityTokenService"
            behaviorConfiguration="SecurityTokenServiceBehaviors">
            <endpoint address="SecurityTokenService"
                binding="wsHttpBinding"
                contract="SecurityTokenService.ISecurityTokenService,
                        FabrikamSecurityTokenService" >
            </endpoint>
        </service>
    </services>
    <behaviors>
        <behavior
            name="SecurityTokenServiceBehaviors"
            returnUnknownExceptionsAsFaults="true">
            <serviceAuthorization>
                <authorizationPolicies>
                    <add policyType=
"SecurityTokenService.AuthorizationPolicy, FabrikamSecurityTokenService" />
                </authorizationPolicies>
            </serviceAuthorization>
        </behavior>
    </behaviors>
</system.serviceModel>
</configuration>
```

Now the Fabrikam STS has been configured, using XSI, to issue claims about the user's roles based on information retrieved from a Windows Server 2003 Authorization Manager store. To witness the effects of that, follow these instructions:

1. Start debugging the solution.

2. When the console of the service, the Woodgrove STS, and the Fabrikam STS all show some activity, click on the coal button in the Resource Access client user interface. Within a few moments, there should be more activity in the console of the Fabrikam STS as it issues a security token for use in obtaining a security token from the Woodgrove STS. Then there should be activity in the console of the Woodgrove STS as it issues a security token for accessing the Woodgrove service. A message should then appear confirming access to the coal resource.

3. Scroll through the output in the console of the Fabrikam STS, and output like that shown in Figure 4.14 should be visible, showing that, now, the SAML security token issued by the Fabrikam STS makes claims about the user's roles.

4. Leave the solution running.

FIGURE 4.14   Claims in the Fabrikam security token.

Using the Windows Workflow Foundation for Claims Normalization

Now the Woodgrove STS will be modified. It will be enhanced with the addition of an XSI authorization policy by which it will translate claims about a user's role in security tokens issued by the Fabrikam STS into claims about a user's role suitable for use with services internal to Woodgrove. Woodgrove may have agreed with Fabrikam that when Fabrikam makes claims about its users in its security tokens, Fabrikam may refer to roles called *StaffMember* and *Manager*. However, Woodgrove's internal services may not use the same language to decide whether to authorize access to their resources. Those services might only know about roles called *Executive* and *Other*, for example. So, the Woodgrove STS, in issuing Woodgrove security tokens for use with Woodgrove services, to Fabrikam users, in exchange for Fabrikam security tokens, will need to normalize the claims about roles in the Fabrikam tokens by translating them into claims that the Woodgrove services will understand.

There are many ways in which the Woodgrove STS could translate the claims in Fabrikam security tokens into claims that the services internal to Woodgrove can understand. The following steps use the Windows Workflow Foundation to provide a claims normalization mechanism that will be easy for a system administrator to configure.

Modifying the Authorization Mechanism of the Woodgrove Service to Use Woodgrove-Specific Claims

Follow these steps to modify the service to require claims specific to the Woodgrove organization:

1. Scroll through the output in the Woodgrove STS console. As shown in Figure 4.15, the Woodgrove STS is currently merely issuing a Woodgrove SAML security token that contains exactly the same claims that the security token issued by the Fabrikam STS contains. Specifically, the Woodgrove STS's token claims that the user is in the StaffMember role, just as the Fabrikam STS's token does.

2. Stop debugging the solution.

FIGURE 4.15   Claims in the Woodgrove security token.

3. Now reenable the authorization mechanism on the Woodgrove server. Do so by opening the `AccessChecker` class module of the Service project within the Security solution, and replacing the code in that module with the code in Listing 4.13. That code can also be found in the file `C:\WCFHandsOn\Security\Service\AccessChecker2.txt`.

LISTING 4.13   Reenabling the `OperationRequirement` Type

```
using System;
using System.Collections.Generic;
using System.Configuration;
using System.IO;
using System.Security.Authorization;
using System.ServiceModel;
using System.Web;
using System.Web.Security;

namespace Service
{

    public class AccessChecker : OperationRequirement
    {
        private Dictionary<string, Claim[]> accessRequirements = null;

        public AccessChecker()
        {
            this.accessRequirements = new Dictionary<string, Claim[]>();

            OperationRequirementsConfigurationSection
                operationRequirementsConfigurationSection
                = ConfigurationManager.GetSection("operationRequirements")
                as OperationRequirementsConfigurationSection;
```

LISTING 4.13   Continued

```
    OperationRequirementsCollection requirements =
        operationRequire1mentsConfigurationSection.OperationRequirements;
    List<Claim> roleClaims = null;
    foreach (OperationElement operationElement in requirements)
    {
        roleClaims = new List<Claim>(operationElement.Roles.Count);
        foreach (RoleElement roleElement in operationElement.Roles)
        {
            roleClaims.Add(
                new Claim(
            "http://schemas.microsoft.com/xsi/2005/05/ClaimType/:Role",
                    roleElement.Name,
                    Rights.PossessProperty));
        }

        this.accessRequirements.Add(
            operationElement.Identifier,
            roleClaims.ToArray());
    }

}

public override bool AccessCheck(OperationContext operationContext)
{
    string header =
        operationContext.RequestContext.RequestMessage.Headers.Action;
    Claim[] requiredClaims = null;
    if (!(accessRequirements.TryGetValue(header, out requiredClaims)))
    {
        return false;
    }

    AuthorizationContext authorizationContext =
        operationContext.ServiceSecurityContext.AuthorizationContext;

    foreach (Claim requiredClaim in requiredClaims)
    {
        for (
            int index = 0;
            index < authorizationContext.ClaimSets.Count;
            index++)
        {
            if (
                authorizationContext.ClaimSets[index].
                ContainsClaim(requiredClaim))
```

LISTING 4.13 Continued

```
                {
                    return true;
                }
            }
        }
        return false;
    }
}
```

The new code for the authorization module of the service compares the claims from the user's security token in the XSI authorization context with the claims required for accessing an operation. Note, in this code, the locution

```
new Claim(
"http://schemas.microsoft.com/xsi/2005/05/ClaimType/:Role",
    roleElement.Name,
    Rights.PossessProperty));
```

The reference to the URI `http://schemas.microsoft.com/xsi/2005/05/ClaimType/` `:Role` is to circumvent a defect in versions of the Windows Communication Foundation up to at least the February CTP version. Readers with later versions should instead use the locution

```
new Claim(
    ClaimTypes.Role,
    roleElement.Name,
    Rights.PossessProperty));
```

4. Now modify the configuration of the service so that it evaluates access to its diamond and coal resources based on whether the user is in the Executive role or the Other role, rather than based on whether the user is in the Manager role or the StaffMember role. Do that by opening the `App.config` file of the Server project within the Security solution and changing the `operationRequirements` element to look like this:

```
<operationRequirements>
    <operation
    identifier=
"http://tempuri.org/IResourceAccessContract/AccessCoal">
        <role name="Executive"/>
        <role name="Other"/>
    </operation>
    <operation
    identifier=
"http://tempuri.org/IResourceAccessContract/AccessDiamond">
```

```
            <role name="Executive"/>
        </operation>
    </operationRequirements>
```

5. Start debugging the solution.

6. When the console of the service, the Woodgrove STS, and the Fabrikam STS all show some activity, click on the coal button in the Resource Access client user interface. A message should appear, saying that access to the coal is denied. The reason is that the Fabrikam security token makes claims about whether the user is in the StaffMember or Manager roles, and the Woodgrove security token simply copies those claims; but the Woodgrove service is deciding whether to grant the user access based on whether the user is in the Executive or Other roles. To restore access to the coal resource, it will be necessary to enhance the Woodgrove STS with an XSI authorization policy to translate claims in the Fabrikam STS into claims that the Woodgrove service can understand.

Creating a Custom Windows Workflow Foundation Activity for Translating Fabrikam Claims into Woodgrove Claims

The constituents of Windows Workflow Foundation workflows are called *activities*. The next few instructions are for creating a custom activity for controlling the translation of claims in Fabrikam security tokens into the claims that the Woodgrove service expects:

1. Choose File, New, Project from the Visual Studio 2005 menus to add a Visual C# Workflow Activity Library project called ClaimMappingActivity to the Security solution, as shown in Figure 4.16.

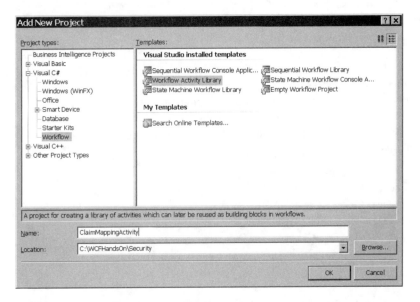

FIGURE 4.16   Adding a custom Workflow Activity Library project to the solution.

2. In the Solution Explorer in Visual Studio 2005, delete the class module `Activity 1.cs`.

3. Right-click on the ClaimMappingActivity project in the Solution Explorer, choose Properties from the context menu, and set the value of the Default Namespace property to `SecurityTokenService`.

4. Right-click on the ClaimMappingActivity project again, and choose Add, New Item from the context menu.

5. In the Add New Item dialog, select Activity, enter `ClaimMappingActivity.cs` in the Name box, and then click on the Add button.

6. Drag the Policy activity from the Windows Workflow tab in the toolbox onto the surface of the ClaimMappingActivity in the workflow designer.

7. The newly added Policy activity will have the name policyActivity1 by default. Right-click on the activity, choose Properties from the menu, and use the property editor to change the name of the activity to ClaimMappingPolicy.

8. Choose View, Code from the Visual Studio 2005 menus, and modify the definition of the `ClaimMappingActivity` class to look like this, adding a property to represent an input claim, and a property to represent the claim into which that input claim gets translated:

```
namespace SecurityTokenService
{
    public partial class ClaimMappingActivity: SequenceActivity
    {
      public string InputClaim = null;
      public string OutputClaim = null;

      public ClaimMappingActivity()
      {
        InitializeComponent();
      }
    }
}
```

9. Choose View, Designer from the Visual Studio 2005 menus, and select the ClaimMappingPolicy activity again.

10. Right-click and choose Properties from the menu, and use the property editor to enter the name `ClaimRuleSet` as the value of the `RuleSetReference` property.

11. Click on the ellipsis button next to the `RuleSetReference` property value to open the Select RuleSet dialog, as shown in Figure 4.17.

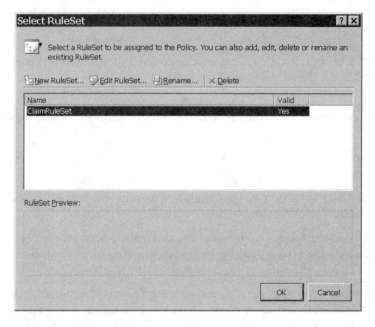

FIGURE 4.17   The Select RuleSet dialog.

12. Click on the Edit RuleSet button to open the Rule Set Editor shown in Figure 4.18.

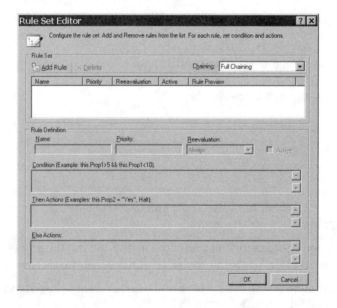

FIGURE 4.18   The Rule Set Editor.

13. Click on the Add Rule button and define a rule for mapping Fabrikam claims to Woodgrove claims, as shown in Figure 4.19.

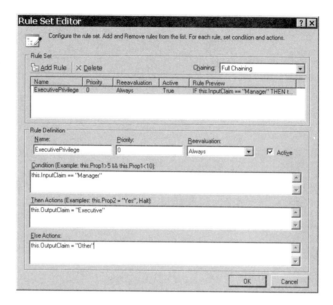

FIGURE 4.19   A rule for translating claims.

14. Choose Build, Build ClaimMappingActivity from the Visual Studio 2005 menus.

Creating a Workflow Incorporating the Policy for Translating Fabrikam Claims into Woodgrove Claims

Now a Windows Workflow Foundation activity has been created for translating Fabrikam claims into Woodgrove claims, and the rules it uses for the translation have been defined. Follow these steps to define a workflow to incorporate the policy activity, a workflow that the Woodgrove STS will execute to do the claims translation:

1. Add a Visual C# Sequential Workflow Library project to the Security solution, called ClaimMappingWorkflow, as shown in Figure 4.20.

2. In the Visual Studio 2005 Solution Explorer, delete the class module `Workflow1.cs`.

3. Right-click on the ClaimMappingActivity project in the Solution Explorer, choose Properties from the context menu, and set the value of the Default Namespace property to `SecurityTokenService`.

4. Right-click on the ClaimMappingActivity project in the Solution Explorer again, and choose Add, Sequential Workflow from the context menu.

5. Enter the name `ClaimMappingWorkflow.cs` in the Name box of the Add New Item dialog, and click on the Add button.

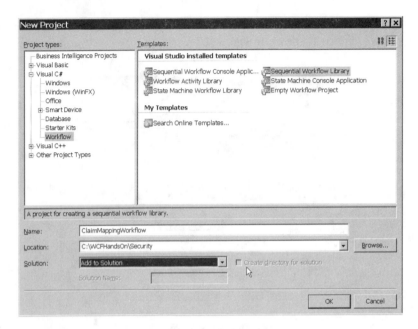

FIGURE 4.20   Adding a Sequential Workflow Library project.

6. Open ClaimMappingWorkflow.cs in the designer view, drag a Replicator activity from the Visual Studio Toolbox into the workflow represented in the designer, and set its Name property to ReplicationManager, as shown in Figure 4.21.

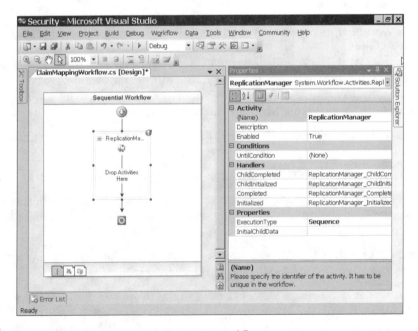

FIGURE 4.21   Adding a Replicator activity to a workflow.

The Windows Workflow Foundation's `Replicator` activity is for the purpose of executing another activity multiple times. It is required in this case, because there may be several claims about a user's role in the security tokens issued by the Fabrikam STS. Therefore, the claim-mapping policy that was created in the preceding set of steps will need to be executed for each of those claims so that all of them can be translated into the claims that the Woodgrove service is anticipating.

7. Drag a `ClaimMappingPolicy` activity from the Visual Studio Toolbox into the `Replicator` activity. That `ClaimMappingPolicy` activity is the activity that was built in the preceding set of steps. Set its `Name` property to `ClaimMappingActivity`, as shown in Figure 4.22.

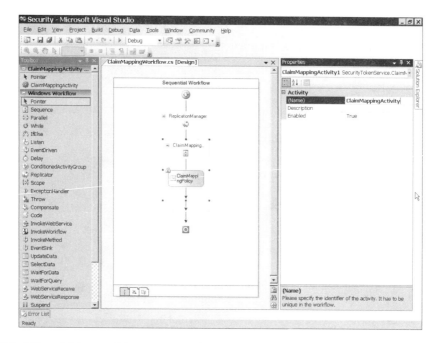

FIGURE 4.22   Adding a ClaimMappingPolicy to the Replicator activity.

8. Select the `Replicator` activity.

9. Right-click and choose Generate Handlers from the context menu. That should cause Visual Studio 2005 to switch to the code view of the `ClaimMappingWorkflow.cs` module to show the handlers it has generated for the events exposed by the `Replicator` activity.

10. Modify the code in the module to conform to Listing 4.14.

LISTING 4.14   ClaimMappingWorkflow

```
using System;
using System.ComponentModel;
using System.ComponentModel.Design;
using System.Collections;
using System.Collections.Generic;
using System.Drawing;
using System.Workflow.ComponentModel.Compiler;
using System.Workflow.ComponentModel.Serialization;
using System.Workflow.ComponentModel;
using System.Workflow.ComponentModel.Design;
using System.Workflow.Runtime;
using System.Workflow.Activities;
using System.Workflow.Activities.Rules;

namespace SecurityTokenService
{
    public sealed partial class ClaimMappingWorkflow : SequentialWorkflowActivity
    {
        private string requestIdentifier = null;
        private string[] inputClaims = null;
        private List<string> outputClaims = new List<string>();

        public ClaimMappingWorkflow()
        {
            InitializeComponent();
        }

        public string RequestIdentifier
        {
            get
            {
                return this.requestIdentifier;
            }

            set
            {
                this.requestIdentifier = value;
            }
        }

        public string[] InputClaims
        {
            get
```

LISTING 4.14 Continued

```
        {
            return this.inputClaims;
        }

        set
        {
            this.inputClaims = value;
        }
    }

    public string[] OutputClaims
    {
        get
        {
            return this.outputClaims.ToArray();
        }


    }

    private void ReplicationManager_ChildInitialized(object sender,
        ReplicatorChildEventArgs e)
    {
        ClaimMappingActivity child = (ClaimMappingActivity)e.Activity;
        child.InputClaim = (string)e.InstanceData;
    }

    private void ReplicationManager_Initialized(object sender, EventArgs e)
    {
        foreach (string inputClaim in this.InputClaims)
        {
            this.ReplicationManager.CurrentChildData.Add(inputClaim);
        }
    }

    private void ReplicationManager_Completed(object sender, EventArgs e)
    {

    }

    private void ReplicationManager_ChildCompleted(object sender,
        ReplicatorChildEventArgs e)
    {
        ClaimMappingActivity child = (ClaimMappingActivity)e.Activity;
```

LISTING 4.14   Continued

```
            this.outputClaims.Add((string)child.OutputClaim);
    }


}


}
```

The code in Listing 4.14 defines three properties for the workflow: the `InputClaims`, `OutputClaims`, and `RequestIdentifier` properties.

The `InputClaims` property is an array of strings to contain the claims in the Fabrikam security token. The `OutputClaims` property is an array of strings to contain the Woodgrove claims into which the Fabrikam claims are to be translated.

The `RequestIdentifier` property will be used to correlate inputs to the workflow with outputs from the workflow. Specifically, it will be used to correlate sets of Fabrikam claims input to the workflow with sets of Woodgrove claims output by the workflow.

The code in the handler of the `Replicator` activity's `Initialize` event loops through the input claims, and prepares to initialize an instance of the `ClaimMappingActivity` to translate each of those claims. The handler of the `Replicator` activity's `ChildInitialized` event passes an input claim to an instance of the `ClaimMappingActivity`. The code in the handler of the `Replicator` activity's `ChildCompleted` event copies a translated claim from the `ClaimMappingActivity` to the workflow's list of output claims so that it can be retrieved from the workflow's `OutputClaim` property.

11. Choose Build, Build ClaimMappingWorkflow from the Visual Studio 2005 menus.

Enhancing the Woodgrove Security Token Service to Use the Claim Mapping Workflow as Its Authorization Policy

These next steps have the Woodgrove STS use the claim-mapping workflow to translate Fabrikam claims into Woodgrove claims:

1. Add a reference to the ClaimMappingWorkflow project to the WoodgroveSecurityTokenService project in the Security solution.

2. Open the `AuthorizationPolicy.cs` module of the WoodgroveSecurityTokenService project. XSI authorization policy classes, by which incoming claims are translated into the claims to be included in a security token, should be quite familiar by now. Replace the code in that module with the code in Listing 4.15, which is also in the file `C:\WCFHandsOn\Security\WoodgroveSecurityTokenService\AuthorizationPolicy1.txt`.

LISTING 4.15   Woodgrove STS AuthorizationPolicy

```
using System;
using System.Collections.ObjectModel;
using System.Collections.Generic;
using System.Configuration;
using System.Runtime.Serialization;
using System.Security.Authorization;
using System.Security.Cryptography;
using System.Security.Cryptography.X509Certificates;
using System.ServiceModel;
using System.ServiceModel.Security;
using System.ServiceModel.Security.Protocols;
using System.ServiceModel.Security.Tokens;
using System.Text;
using System.Threading;
using System.Workflow.Runtime;
using System.Workflow.Runtime.Hosting;
using System.Xml;

namespace SecurityTokenService
{
    public class AuthorizationPolicy : IAuthorizationPolicy
    {
        private string claimMapLocation = null;
        private Dictionary<string, AutoResetEvent>
            waitHandles = new Dictionary<string, AutoResetEvent>();
        private Dictionary<string, string[]> outputClaims =
            new Dictionary<string, string[]>();
        private object waitHandlesLock = new object();
        private object outputClaimsLock = new object();

        public AuthorizationPolicy()
        {
            this.claimMapLocation =
                ConfigurationManager.AppSettings["ClaimMapLocation"];
        }


        public ClaimSet Issuer
        {
            get
            {
                return DefaultClaimSet.System.Issuer;
            }
        }
```

LISTING 4.15   Continued

```
public void ClaimMappingCompleted(object sender,
    WorkflowCompletedEventArgs e)
{
    string requestIdentifier =
        (string)e.OutputParameters[
        "RequestIdentifier"];
    string[] outputClaims = (
        string[])e.OutputParameters[
        "OutputClaims"];
    lock (this.outputClaimsLock)
    {
        this.outputClaims.Add(requestIdentifier, outputClaims);
    }
    AutoResetEvent waitHandle = null;
    lock (this.waitHandlesLock)
    {
        this.waitHandles.TryGetValue(requestIdentifier, out waitHandle);
        if (waitHandle != null)
        {
            waitHandle.Set();
        }
        this.waitHandles.Remove(requestIdentifier);
    }
}

private string[] MapClaims(string[] inputClaims)
{
    if (Thread.CurrentThread.Name == null)
    {
        Thread.CurrentThread.Name = Guid.NewGuid().ToString();
    }

    using (WorkflowRuntime workflowRuntime = new WorkflowRuntime())
    {
        workflowRuntime.StartRuntime();

        workflowRuntime.WorkflowCompleted += this.ClaimMappingCompleted;

        Type type = typeof(ClaimMappingWorkflow);

        Dictionary<string, object> parameters =
            new Dictionary<string, object>();
        parameters.Add(
            "RequestIdentifier",
```

LISTING 4.15   Continued

```
                    Thread.CurrentThread.Name);
            parameters.Add(
                "InputClaims",
                inputClaims);

            AutoResetEvent waitHandle = new AutoResetEvent(false);

            lock (this.waitHandlesLock)
            {
                this.waitHandles.Add(Thread.CurrentThread.Name, waitHandle);
            }

            workflowRuntime.CreateWorkflow(type, parameters).Start();

            waitHandle.WaitOne();

            workflowRuntime.StopRuntime();
        }

        string[] outputClaims = null;
        lock (this.outputClaimsLock)
        {
            this.outputClaims.TryGetValue(
                Thread.CurrentThread.Name,
                out outputClaims);
            this.outputClaims.Remove(
                Thread.CurrentThread.Name);
        }

        return outputClaims;
    }


    #region IAuthorizationPolicy Members

    bool IAuthorizationPolicy.Evaluate(EvaluationContext evaluationContext,
        ref object state)
    {

        List<Claim> claimsToAdd = new List<Claim>();

        List<string> inputClaims = new List<string>();

        AuthorizationContext context =
```

LISTING 4.15   Continued

```
OperationContext.Current.ServiceSecurityContext.AuthorizationContext;
        for (int index = 0; index < context.ClaimSets.Count; index++)
        {
            foreach (Claim claim in context.ClaimSets[index].FindClaims(
"http://schemas.microsoft.com/xsi/2005/05/ClaimType/:Role", null))
            {
                inputClaims.Add(claim.Resource.ToString());
            }
        }

        string[] roleClaims = this.MapClaims(inputClaims.ToArray());
        Claim targetClaim = null;
        foreach (string roleClaim in roleClaims)
        {
            targetClaim = new Claim(ClaimTypes.Role, roleClaim,
                Rights.PossessProperty);
            claimsToAdd.Add(targetClaim);
        }

        if (claimsToAdd.Count > 0)
        {
            evaluationContext.AddToTarget(this, new DefaultClaimSet(
                this.Issuer, claimsToAdd));
        }


        return true;
    }


    ClaimSet IAuthorizationPolicy.Issuer
    {
        get
        {
            return this.Issuer;
        }
    }


    #endregion



    #region IAuthorizationComponent Members
```

LISTING 4.15 Continued

```
    string IAuthorizationComponent.Id
    {
        get
        {
            return Guid.NewGuid().ToString();
        }
    }

    #endregion
}


}
```

This new code defines an XSI authorization policy for the Woodgrove STS by which it can translate claims in security tokens issued by the Fabrikam STS into the claims that are understood by the Woodgrove service. The code retrieves the location of the rule set defining how Fabrikam claims are to be translated into Woodgrove claims from the Woodgrove STS's configuration file. For each incoming request for a security token, the authorization policy sends the role claims in its evaluation context, which were read from the input security token, to an instance of the claim mapping workflow defined in the preceding steps, via the workflow's parameters. Then it retrieves the translated claims output by the workflow instance from the workflow's `OutputClaims` parameter. The claims emitted by the workflow instance are added to the target context, from which they will be copied by XSI to the authorization context. The claims in the authorization context will be incorporated into the security token issued by the Woodgrove Security Token Service.

This code again makes reference to the URI `http://schemas.microsoft.com/xsi/2005/05/ClaimType/:Role` to circumvent a defect in some prerelease versions of the Windows Communication Foundation. Readers with versions later than the February CTP version should instead use the expression

```
ClaimTypes.Role
```

in place of the URI.

Follow the next few instructions to see what has been accomplished:

1. Start debugging the solution.

2. When the console of the server shows some activity, click on the coal button in the Resource Access client user interface. Recall that access to the coal resource was denied on the last attempt. That was because the Woodgrove service was authorizing the user's access based on claims about the user's role membership in

Woodgrove terms, whereas the security token issued to the user for accessing the service made claims about the user's role membership in Fabrikam terms. This time access to the coal should be granted.

3. Click on the diamond button in the Resource Access client user interface. Access to the diamond resource should be denied. The reason is that the user is in the StaffMember role within Fabrikam, which maps to the Other role within Woodgrove, whereas one must be in a role that maps to the Executive role within Woodgrove in order to access the diamond resource.

4. Stop debugging the solution.

Experiencing the Power of Federated, Claims-based Identity with XSI

To witness the full benefit of the solution that has been built in this chapter, promote the current user within the Fabrikam organization and see that user instantly experience the benefit of enhanced access to resources within Woodgrove:

1. Promote the current user to the Manager role within Fabrikam. Do so by using the Windows Server 2003 Authorization Manager user interface to add the user to the Manager role in the Authorization Manager authorization store, according to the instructions for doing so provided earlier in this chapter.

2. Start debugging the solution.

3. When the console of the service, the Woodgrove STS, and the Fabrikam STS all show some activity, click on the diamond button in the Resource Access client user interface. Because the user has been promoted within Fabrikam, the user now has access to the more valuable diamond resource in Woodgrove that the user was previously prevented from accessing.

With that click on the diamond button in the Resource Access client user interface, the possibilities for commerce offered by XSI should have become vividly apparent. With not very much code at all, an application for secure messaging across organizations has been created that is, moreover, highly configurable. The authorization mechanisms in both organizations are available for modification by administrators using the Windows Server 2003 Authorization Manager user interface and the Windows Workflow Foundation Rule Set Editor.

Summary

The Extensible Security Infrastructure of the Windows Communication Foundation provides a flexible and easily customizable way of controlling access to the resources of a software application. It allows for access to resources to be controlled based on claims. Claims-based authorization subsumes both role-based authorization and authorization using access control lists.

The power of the Extensible Security Infrastructure was demonstrated by an exercise in which access to an intranet service controlled using role-based authorization was extended to permit controlled claims-based access by the users of another organization. That was accomplished by adding security token services built using the Extensible Security Infrastructure to the solution to serve as a foundation for federated identity. In the process, no changes had to be made to the code of either the client or the service, which is an eloquent demonstration of the power that the Windows Communication Foundation can bring to bear on complex business scenarios.

References

.NET Framework Class Library. 2006. S.v. "IPrincipal Interface." http://msdn.microsoft.com/library/default.asp?url=/library/en-us/cpref/html/frlrfsystemsecurityprincipaliprincipalclasstopic.asp. Accessed 1 January 2006.

Cabrera, Luis Felipe and Chris Kurt. 2005. *Web Services Architecture and Its Specifications: Essentials for Understanding WS-**. Redmond, WA: Microsoft.

Daly, Brenon. 2000. B-to-B's Fall into Discontent. *Business 2.0* (July). http://www.business2.com/b2/web/articles/0,17863,528021,00.html. Accessed December 31, 2005.

Freeman, Adam and Allen Jones. 2003. *Programming .NET Security*. Sebastopol, CA: Wiley.

Gudgin, Martin and Anthony Nadalin, eds. *Web Services Trust Language (WS-Trust)*. http://msdn.microsoft.com/library/en-us/dnglobspec/html/WS-trust.pdf. Accessed 1 January 2006.

McPherson, Dave. 2005. Role-Based Access Control for Multi-tier Applications Using Authorization Manager. http://www.microsoft.com/technet/prodtechnol/windowsserver2003/technologies/management/athmanwp.mspx. Accessed 2 January 2006.

Means, Grady and David Schneider. 2000. *Meta-Capitalism: The E-Business Revolution and the Design of 21st-Century Companies and Markets*. New York, NY: Wiley.

Oxford Dictionary of Current English. 2001 ed. S.v. "Federation."

Tulloch, Mitch. 2003. *Microsoft Encyclopedia of Security*. Redmond, WA: Microsoft.

CHAPTER **5**

Reliable Sessions, Transactions, and Queues

Reliability

When we build out systems and networks, we look at availability in 9s, as in 99.9xx. No one thinks it realistic that software, hardware, or the network will be available 100% of the time. Ironically, one of the key challenges of developing connected systems is connectivity itself.

In practical terms, sometimes this is the result of the network leaving us—network connectivity and hardware have temporary or extended outages. Other times, it's a case of us leaving the network—moving in and out of Wi-Fi coverage areas where we disconnect and reconnect silently behind the scenes.

When disruptions occur, there is an increased likelihood for the unpredictable. If the outage occurs during a multipart operation, the system we're communicating with may be left in an unstable state. Messages may be dropped. Messages may be delivered out of sequence. On restarting, messages may be duplicated.

These disruptions can introduce unplanned variables into the way an application was designed to run, rendering it potentially unreliable as a result. This is not acceptable for the connected systems being developed today.

Regardless of where they originate and why, these temporary losses of connectivity will occur, and your applications need to offset these impacts because they could make the system unreliable.

WS-Reliable Messaging (WS-RM)

The instigating outages are rarely predictable, so applications must be designed to adapt and compensate for these challenges. Fortunately, the problem of reliability has been addressed inside the firewall by a number of middleware vendors for a number of years.

While these solutions have had a number of recurring features in common, they have typically been tied to a particular OS platform or vendor(s) product(s). With the advent of services, it became critical to introduce a standard provided the ability to ensure reliability while being platform and product agnostic.

The industry recognized this and began work on a standard. In doing so, they consciously acknowledged that in a service-oriented world, it was very likely that in addition to being able to being agnostic to platform and product, it also needed the ability to survive multiple hops. Between endpoint A and endpoint B, a number of intermediaries could be used. Also recognized was that if this was also protocol agnostic, it would need to define the standard in such a way that reliability could be added to messaging that utilized unreliable transports as well.

The resulting standard, WS-Reliable Messaging, was put forth by major players in the industry, among them Microsoft, IBM, and Tibco. That specification defines the following reliability features:

- Guaranteed message delivery, or At-Least-Once delivery semantics

- Guaranteed message duplicate elimination, or At-Most-Once delivery semantics

- Guaranteed message delivery and duplicate elimination, or Exactly-Once delivery semantics

- Guaranteed message ordering for delivery within a group of messages

A number of vendors either have built implementations or have implementations under development. Table 5.1 identifies the status of WS-Reliable Messaging development by major companies in the industry, at the time of this writing.

TABLE 5.1   WS-RM Adoption Among Leading Vendors

Company	WS-RM Support
Microsoft WCF	Yes
IBM, ETTK—AlphaWorks	Yes
BEA, WebLogic 9.0	Yes
Cape Clear	Yes
Systinet	Yes
Blue Titan	Yes
Apache Axis 1.3 Sandesha	Yes
Sonic	In Development
Tibco	In Development

Reliability in WCF

In WCF, Reliability can be broken down into two distinct areas of functionality, Reliable Sessions and Queued Messaging. Each of these applies to scenarios with certain characteristics, which we will delve into in the next two sections of the chapter.

Reliable Sessions

In the world of TCP/IP, reliability and the issues discussed earlier in the chapter are handled by the protocol. WCF's Reliable Sessions provide that same functionality for SOAP messages.

Specifically, the reliable channel provides the capability to handle three of the potential scenarios that can lead to unreliability:

- Lost messages

- Duplicated messages

- Messages received out of order

Although WCF and TCP/IP may both handle these reliable messaging challenges, WCF goes about it in a different way. SOAP is defined to allow the use of multiple transports—some of which are not inherently reliable. In addition, between Endpoint A and Endpoint B, WCF messages can travel across multiple intermediaries and across multiple protocols. To accommodate all of this, WCF handles these issues at the message level.

In instances in which a client has gone silent in a session beyond a designated time, the server will free up resources associated with that session. Reliable Sessions will also help manage network congestion, adjusting the rate at which the server sends out messages.

Queued Messaging

The WS-Reliability specification contains specific guarantees that combine to form the requirements of reliable messaging. For those who have read the specification, you'll see that there is something noticeably absent from it, specifically rules around durability. More to the point, the WS-RM specification has no requirements for endpoints to place messages in a durable store at any point in the conversation.

The reality is that the specification as it stands today does not have any requirements in this area. Although the industry will possibly address this in a future iteration of the WS-* specs, this does not necessarily eliminate the need to provide durability in a number of scenarios.

In WCF v1.0 this can be accomplished using queues. Queues store messages from a sending application on behalf of a receiving application. The receiving application—at some point after the message has been placed on the queue—receives the message. Queues ensure reliable transfer of messages from sending applications to receiving applications. Queuing is supported in WCF through the use of Microsoft Message Queuing (MSMQ) transport.

Queued messaging can be done in scenarios in which WCF integrates with an existing non-WCF MSMQ application, as well as in situations in which client and server are using WCF for communications. This chapter focuses on the WCF-WCF scenario, and integration is handled in a later chapter.

When you remove the need for client and server to communicate in real-time and use a queue as a midpoint, a number of opportunities are provided.

This loose coupling helps avoid issues if the sender or receiver applications fail. When using services in real-time request-response patterns, if the receiver suffers a failure and is offline for a significant period, the client also is offline. New and existing work is stalled as a result. When using queues in this same scenario, the sender will happily send to his queue and business will continue to function. Once the receiver application is back online, she will begin processing messages again. This failure isolation provides increases in availability and reliability.

The same holds true for scenarios in which both the sender and the receiver are online, but network connectivity between the two becomes unavailable. There is no dependency on the server being available, allowing for applications to exist when no connectivity is present. After the connectivity is restored, the receiver happily receives the messages from the queue for processing.

In addition, because the application is not sending messages across the network, potential blocking that might result due to the speed and reliability of connectivity between sender and receiver are limited.

For the receiver, this helps avoid becoming overwhelmed, as a result of being forced to handle large spikes of message traffic. The use of queues provides the capability for the receiver to manage the rate at which it processes messages, regardless of the speed and volume of messages sent from the sender.

The use of queues also provides benefits in the production environment, as the management interface used is the standard MMC snap-in already used by MSMQ. From the perspective of the individuals who need to support a Queued Messaging scenario, this is ideal because it does not require new training and leverages any existing knowledge of MSMQ.

When to Use Reliable Sessions and When to Use Queued Messaging

Both Reliable Sessions and Queued Messaging have compelling features, and you may be wondering which one is right for your particular project. This varies on the requirements of the project, but the intent of this section is to provide some guidance on how to make that determination.

Reliable Sessions should be used in scenarios in which it is likely that client and server will be online and connected to the network at the same time. In that environment, Reliable Sessions provide the functionality to overcome failures at the transport level (that is, loss of network connectivity due to wireless, dial-up, or VPN) and the transport intermediary level (that is, the Web proxy), as well as the SOAP intermediary level (that is, SOAP router).

Queued Messaging really makes sense for those scenarios in which the business does not require real-time interaction with services and it is desirable to be able to work offline. Regarding Reliable Sessions, it was stated that they were ideal for scenarios in which both client and server are online at the same time. When there is no guarantee that the client and server will be online at the same time, and a more loosely coupled approach is desired, Queued Messaging is a good option for you.

Implementing Reliable Sessions

As you saw in Table 5.1, WCF does have support for WS-Reliable Messaging. The implementation of this functionality for scenarios in which both endpoints are online is referred to as Reliable Sessions.

Reliable Sessions provide end-to-end reliability between endpoints. Because the specification provides support at the message level, messages can reliably traverse multiple intermediaries on its way from endpoint A to endpoint B, and they may travel via various transport protocols.

Adding WCF SOAP Reliable Messaging to a WCF Project

Support for reliable messaging begins with creating an endpoint that supports a reliable session. WCF ships with six predefined bindings that support reliable messaging, as well as the capability to add reliability in custom bindings.

Of the out-of-the-box bindings that support reliable messaging, three of them—wsDualHttpBinding, NetNamedPipeBinding, and MsmqIntegrationBinding—have reliability enabled by default.

The complete list of bindings that support reliable messaging can be seen in Table 5.2.

TABLE 5.2   Reliability Support in WCF's Preconfigured Bindings

Binding	Supports Reliable Messaging	Reliability Enabled in Binding by Default
WSDualHttpBinding	X	X
NetNamedPipeBinding	X	X
MsmqIntegrationBinding	X	X
WSHttpBinding	X	
WSFederationBinding	X	
NetTcpBinding	X	

Creating a Banking Service and Client with Reliable Sessions

In this first exercise, we will showcase how to create code that utilizes Reliable Sessions.

Creating the Banking Service

1. Create a new WinFX Service project in C:\WCFHandsOn\Chapter5\PartI\Before\.

   Specify a name of ConsumerBankingService as the name of the project, and ReliableSessions as the name of the solution.

2. Within Visual Studio, add a new class and name it ConsumerBankingCore.cs.

3. Add a reference to System.ServiceModel.

4. Add using System.ServiceModel; to the top of the Program.cs file:

```
using System;
using System.Collections.Generic;
using System.Text;
using System.ServiceModel;
```

5. Next, create the service interface and service implementation. Specify that this Service Contract will use reliable sessions by specifying (Session=true):

```
namespace ConsumerBankingService
{
    [ServiceContract(Session=true)]
    public interface IConsumerBankingCore
    {
        [OperationContract]
        bool Deposit(int accountNumber, decimal amount);
        [OperationContract]
        bool Withdraw(int accountNumber, decimal amount);
        [OperationContract]
        decimal GetBalance(int accountNumber);
    }
    // This will share the information per a single session
    // [ServiceBehavior(InstanceContextMode=InstanceContextMode.PerSession)]
    // This will share the information in a single session, across multiple
    // clients
    // [ServiceBehavior(InstanceContextMode = InstanceContextMode.Shareable)]
    [ServiceBehavior(InstanceContextMode = InstanceContextMode.PerCall)]
    class ConsumerBankingCore : IConsumerBankingCore
    {
        private decimal _balance = default(decimal);

        public bool Deposit(int accountNumber, decimal amount)
        {
            _balance = _balance + amount;
            Console.WriteLine("Depositing {0} into Account {1}", amount,
    accountNumber);
```

```
            Console.WriteLine("Balance:" + _balance.ToString());
            return true; }
        public bool Withdraw(int accountNumber, decimal amount)
        {
            _balance = _balance - amount;
            Console.WriteLine("Withdrawing {0} from Account {1}", amount,
➥ accountNumber);
            Console.WriteLine("Balance:" + _balance.ToString());
            return true; }
        public decimal GetBalance(int accountNumber)
        { return _balance; }


    }
}
```

The next step is to create the host for the service.

1. Open Program.cs.

2. Add a reference to System.ServiceModel.

3. Add a reference to System.Configuration:

4. Modify Program.cs to use the ConsumerBankingService namespace and contain the
   following code:

```
using System;
using System.Collections.Generic;
using System.Text;
using System.ServiceModel;
using System.Configuration;
namespace ConsumerBankingService
{
    class Program
    {

        static void Main(string[] args)
        {

            // Get base address from app settings in configuration
            Uri baseAddressCore = new
➥Uri(ConfigurationManager.AppSettings["baseAddressCore"]);

            // Instantiate new ServiceHost
            ServiceHost CoreServiceHost = new ServiceHost(typeof
➥ (ConsumerBankingCore), baseAddressCore);
            CoreServiceHost.Open();
            Console.WriteLine("Consumer Banking Service is Online.");
```

```
                  Console.WriteLine("----------------------------------");


                  Console.WriteLine("Press any key to terminate service.");
                  Console.ReadKey();

                  CoreServiceHost.Close();



            }


         }
    }
```

The next step is to create the application configuration file for the banking service.

5. Within Visual Studio, add a new application configuration file named App.Config.

6. Using Solution Explorer, open the App.Config file and populate it to resemble the following code listing:

```
<?xml version="1.0" encoding="utf-8" ?>
<configuration>
  <appSettings>
  <!-- use appSetting to configure base address provided by host -->
  <add key="baseAddressCore"
➥ value="http://localhost:8080/ConsumerBankingService" />
  </appSettings>

<system.serviceModel>

   <services>
     <service
         type="ConsumerBankingService.ConsumerBankingCore">
       <!-- use base address provided by host -->
       <endpoint address=""
                 binding="wsHttpBinding"
                 contract="ConsumerBankingService.IConsumerBankingCore" />
     </service>
     <service
         type="ConsumerBankingService.ConsumerBankingBillPayment"
     >
       <!-- use base address provided by host -->
       <endpoint address=""
                 binding="wsHttpBinding"
                 contract=
```

```
➥ "ConsumerBankingService.IConsumerBankingBillPayment" />
    </service>
  </services>

</system.serviceModel>
</configuration>
```

Creating the Client for the Service

Having created the service, you will now create a client to interact with it.

1. In the open solution, add a new project.

2. Create a new Windows Forms application named ATMClient in `C:\WCFHandsOn\Chapter5\Before\PartI\`.

3. Create the proxy for the banking service.

4. Right-click on the ConsumerBankingService project, click Debug, and select Start New Instance.

   This will start the ConsumerBankingService, making it available for us to query it for metadata with the svcutil utility.

5. Enter the following at the command prompt:

   ```
   "C:\Program Files\Microsoft SDKs\Windows\v1.0\Bin\SvcUtil.exe "
   ➥http://localhost:8080/ConsumerBankingService
   ```

6. Stop the Debugger.

7. Open a Visual Studio command prompt and navigate to the directory `C:\WCFHandsOn\Chapter5\Before\PartI\`.

8. Using Solution Explorer, add `ConsumerBankingCoreProxy.cs` to the ATMClient project.

9. Using Solution Explorer, add `output.config` to the ATMClient project.

10. Rename `output.config` to `App.config`.

11. Open the `App.Config` file.

12. Modify the endpoint element to include the attribute name with a value of CoreBanking:

    ```
    <?xml version="1.0" encoding="utf-8"?>
    <configuration>
        <system.serviceModel>
            <client>
                <endpoint name="CoreBanking"
    ➥address="http://localhost:8080/ConsumerBankingService"
    ```

```
                    bindingConfiguration=
➥ "WSHttpBinding_IConsumerBankingCore"
                    binding="customBinding" contract="IConsumerBankingCore" />

        </client>
        <bindings>
            <customBinding>
                <binding name="Secure conversation bootstrap binding
➥ 5d58043f-7615-48c7-80e6-95668c8117f3">
                    <security defaultAlgorithmSuite="Default"
➥authenticationMode="SspiNegotiated"
                        defaultProtectionLevel="EncryptAndSign"
➥ requireDerivedKeys="true"
                        securityHeaderLayout="Strict" includeTimestamp="true"
➥  keyEntropyMode="CombinedEntropy"
                        messageProtectionOrder="SignBeforeEncrypt"
➥ protectTokens="false"
                        requireSecurityContextCancellation="true"
➥ securityVersion="WSSecurityXXX2005"
                        requireSignatureConfirmation="false">
                        <localClientSettings cacheCookies="true"
➥ detectReplays="true"
                            replayCacheSize="900000" maxClockSkew="00:05:00"
➥ maxCookieCachingTime="10675199.02:48:05.4775807"
                            replayWindow="00:05:00"
➥ sessionKeyRenewalInterval="10:00:00"
                            sessionKeyRolloverInterval="00:05:00"
➥ reconnectTransportOnFailure="true"
                            timestampValidityDuration="00:05:00"
➥ cookieRenewalThresholdPercentage="90" />
                        <localServiceSettings detectReplays="true"
➥ issuedCookieLifetime="10:00:00"
                            maxStatefulNegotiations="1024" replayCacheSize=
➥ "900000" MaxClockSkew="00:05:00"
                            negotiationTimeout="00:02:00"
➥ replayWindow="00:05:00" inactivityTimeout="01:00:00"
                            sessionKeyRenewalInterval="15:00:00"
➥ sessionKeyRolloverInterval="00:05:00"
                            reconnectTransportOnFailure="true"
➥ maxConcurrentSessions="1000"
                            timestampValidityDuration="00:05:00" />
                    </security>
                    <textMessageEncoding maxReadPoolSize="64"
➥ maxWritePoolSize="16"
                        messageVersion="Default" writeEncoding="utf-8" />
```

```
                          </binding>
                          <binding name="WSHttpBinding_IConsumerBankingCore">
                              <security defaultAlgorithmSuite="Default"
➡   authenticationMode="SecureConversation"
                                  bootstrapBindingConfiguration="Secure conversation
➡   bootstrap binding 5d58043f-7615-48c7-80e6-95668c8117f3"
                                  bootstrapBindingSectionName="customBinding"
➡ defaultProtectionLevel="EncryptAndSign"
                                  requireDerivedKeys="true"
➡ securityHeaderLayout="Strict"
➡ includeTimestamp="true"
                                  keyEntropyMode="CombinedEntropy"
➡ messageProtectionOrder="SignBeforeEncrypt"
                                  protectTokens="false"
➡ requireSecurityContextCancellation="true"
                                  securityVersion="WSSecurityXXX2005"
➡ requireSignatureConfirmation="false">
                                  <localClientSettings cacheCookies="true"
➡ detectReplays="true"
                                      replayCacheSize="900000" maxClockSkew="00:05:00"
➡ maxCookieCachingTime="10675199.02:48:05.4775807"
                                      replayWindow="00:05:00"
➡ sessionKeyRenewalInterval="10:00:00"
                                      sessionKeyRolloverInterval="00:05:00"
➡ reconnectTransportOnFailure="true"
                                      timestampValidityDuration="00:05:00"
➡ cookieRenewalThresholdPercentage="90" />
                                  <localServiceSettings detectReplays="true"
issuedCookieLifetime="10:00:00"
                                      maxStatefulNegotiations="1024"
➡ replayCacheSize="900000" maxClockSkew="00:05:00"
                                      negotiationTimeout="00:02:00"
➡ replayWindow="00:05:00" inactivityTimeout="01:00:00"
                                      sessionKeyRenewalInterval="15:00:00"
➡ sessionKeyRolloverInterval="00:05:00"
                                      reconnectTransportOnFailure="true"
➡ maxConcurrentSessions="1000"
                                      timestampValidityDuration="00:05:00" />
                              </security>
                              <textMessageEncoding maxReadPoolSize="64"
➡ maxWritePoolSize="16"
                                  messageVersion="Default" writeEncoding="utf-8" />
                              <httpTransport manualAddressing="false"
➡ maxBufferPoolSize="524288"
                                  maxMessageSize="65536" allowCookies="false"
```

```
➥ authenticationScheme="Anonymous"
                        bypassProxyOnLocal="false"
➥ hostNameComparisonMode="StrongWildcard"
                        mapAddressingHeadersToHttpHeaders="false"
➥ proxyAuthenticationScheme="Anonymous"
                        realm="" transferMode="Buffered"
➥ unsafeConnectionNtlmAuthentication="false"
                        useDefaultWebProxy="true" />
                </binding>
                <binding name="Secure conversation bootstrap binding
➥ d58973a4-c474-42f2-8fb8-f2a64bc07c96">
                    <security defaultAlgorithmSuite="Default"
➥ authenticationMode="SspiNegotiated"
                        defaultProtectionLevel="EncryptAndSign"
➥ requireDerivedKeys="true"
                        securityHeaderLayout="Strict" includeTimestamp="true"
➥ keyEntropyMode="CombinedEntropy"
                        messageProtectionOrder="SignBeforeEncrypt"
➥ protectTokens="false"
                        requireSecurityContextCancellation="true"
➥ securityVersion="WSSecurityXXX2005"
                        requireSignatureConfirmation="false">
                    <localClientSettings cacheCookies="true"
➥ detectReplays="true"
                        replayCacheSize="900000" maxClockSkew="00:05:00"
➥ maxCookieCachingTime="10675199.02:48:05.4775807"
                        replayWindow="00:05:00" sessionKeyRenewalInterval=
➥ "10:00:00"
                        sessionKeyRolloverInterval="00:05:00"
➥ reconnectTransportOnFailure="true"
                        timestampValidityDuration="00:05:00"
➥ cookieRenewalThresholdPercentage="90" />
                    <localServiceSettings detectReplays="true"
➥ issuedCookieLifetime="10:00:00"
                        maxStatefulNegotiations="1024" replayCacheSize="900000"
➥ maxClockSkew="00:05:00"
                        negotiationTimeout="00:02:00" replayWindow="00:05:00"
➥ inactivityTimeout="01:00:00"
                        sessionKeyRenewalInterval="15:00:00"
➥ sessionKeyRolloverInterval="00:05:00"
                        reconnectTransportOnFailure="true"
➥ maxConcurrentSessions="1000"
                        timestampValidityDuration="00:05:00" />
                </security>
                <textMessageEncoding maxReadPoolSize="64"
➥ maxWritePoolSize="16"
```

```
                messageVersion="Default" writeEncoding="utf-8" />
        </binding>




            </customBinding>
        </bindings>
    </system.serviceModel>
</configuration>
```

13. Next, open the code view for Form1.cs.

14. Add the line ConsumerBankingCoreProxy proxy = new
    ConsumerBankingCoreProxy("CoreBanking"); to the Form1 class:

```
public partial class Form1 : Form
    {
        ConsumerBankingCoreProxy proxy = new
➥   ConsumerBankingCoreProxy("CoreBanking");


        public Form1()
        {
            InitializeComponent();
        }
```

Next, design the Windows Form that will comprise the user interface.

15. Double-click on Form1.cs in Solution Explorer to modify the form in the designer.

16. Add a label named lblBankAccountNumber.

17. Set the text property for this label to "Bank Account Number".

18. Add a label named lblAmount.

19. Set the text property for this label to "Amount".

20. Add a textbox named tbAccountNumber.

21. Set the text property for this textbox to "12345".

22. Add a textbox named tbAmount.

23. Set the text property for this textbox to "25.00".

24. Add a label named lblBankBalance.

25. Set the text property for this label to "Current Bank Balance".

26. Add a label named lblBalance.

27. Set the text property for this label to "0".

28. Add a button named "btnDeposit".

29. Set the text property for this button to "Deposit".

30. Add a button named "btnWithdraw".

31. Set the text property for this button to "Withdrawal".

32. Add a button named "btnSonWithdraw".

33. Set the text property for this button to "Son Withdrawal".

34. Arrange these controls to resemble what's shown in Figure 5.1.

FIGURE 5.1   The designed form.

Now add the code to execute a deposit.

35. In the Windows Form designer double-click on the btnDeposit control.

36. This will open the code view. Add the following code to the btnDeposit_Click event:

```
private void btnDeposit_Click(object sender, EventArgs e)
        {
            bool success = proxy.Deposit
➥ (Convert.ToInt32(tbAccountNumber.Text),
➥ Convert.ToDecimal(tbAmount.Text));
            decimal balance = proxy.GetBalance(Convert.ToInt32(
➥ tbAccountNumber.Text));



            if (success)
            {
```

```
        lblBalance.Text = balance.ToString();
    }
    else
    {
        System.Windows.Forms.MessageBox.Show("Unable to make deposit");
    }


}
```

37. In the Windows Form designer, double-click on the btnWithdraw control.

38. This will open the code view. Add the following code to the btnWithdraw_Click event:

```
private void btnWithdraw_Click(object sender, EventArgs e)
    {
        bool success = proxy.Withdraw(Convert.ToInt32(
➥ tbAccountNumber.Text), Convert.ToDecimal(tbAmount.Text));
        decimal balance = proxy.GetBalance(Convert.ToInt32(
➥ tbAccountNumber.Text));


        if (success)
        {
            lblBalance.Text = balance.ToString();
        }
        else
        {
            System.Windows.Forms.MessageBox.Show(
➥ "Unable to make withdrawal");
        }


    }
```

You will now add the code that uses a second proxy that uses that same session:

39. In the Windows Form designer, double-click on the btnSonWithdraw control.

    This will open the code view.

40. Add the following code to the btnSonWithdraw_Click event:

```
private void btnSonWithdraw_Click(object sender, EventArgs e)
    {
        using (ConsumerBankingCoreProxy proxySon = new
ConsumerBankingCoreProxy("CoreBanking"))
```

```
            {

                    System.ServiceModel.EndpointAddress proxyAddress =
➡ proxy.InnerChannel.ResolveInstance();
                    proxySon.Endpoint.Address = proxyAddress;
                    bool success =
➡ proxySon.Withdraw(Convert.ToInt32(tbAccountNumber.Text),25);
                    decimal balance =
➡ proxySon.GetBalance(Convert.ToInt32(tbAccountNumber.Text));



                    if (success)
                    {
                        lblBalance.Text = balance.ToString();
                    }
                    else
                    {
                        System.Windows.Forms.MessageBox.Show(
➡ "Unable to make withdrawal");
                    }

            }
        }
```

You are now ready to test the application.

Test #1—No Sessions Enabled—Per Call Instancing

In this first test, we will run the client and service without the benefit of sessions.

1. Run the Service.

2. Run the Client.

3. Click the Deposit and Withdraw buttons.

You will notice that there is no information being shared between calls. Each call starts with no shared state of the prior actions. There is no session. The expected outcome of this test is shown in Figure 5.2.

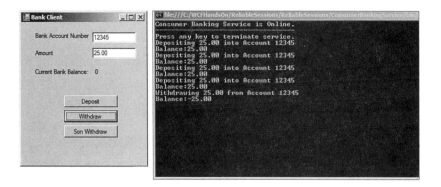

FIGURE 5.2   Screenshot of the resulting test.

Test #2—Sessions Enabled—PerSession Instancing

In this next test, we will enable sessions. This will be done by modifying the InstanceContextMode of the Service Behavior.

1. Stop the client and service.

2. Modify the service contract, commenting out the ServiceBehavior that specifies the InstanceContextMode of PerCall and uncommenting out the code for a ServiceBehavior of PerSession:

```
// This will share the information per a single session
[ServiceBehavior(InstanceContextMode=InstanceContextMode.PerSession)]
// This will share the information in a single session, across multiple
// clients
// [ServiceBehavior(InstanceContextMode = InstanceContextMode.Shareable)]
// [ServiceBehavior(InstanceContextMode = InstanceContextMode.PerCall)]
```

3. Run the Service.

4. Run the Client.

5. Click the Deposit and Withdraw buttons.

Note that when you perform deposits and withdrawals now, there is obvious knowledge of prior states.

The expected outcome of this test is shown in Figure 5.3.

FIGURE 5.3   Screenshot of the resulting test.

Test #3—Sessions Enabled—Sharable Instancing

There will be scenarios where you wish to share the same session among multiple clients. As in the last test, this can be done by modifying the InstanceContextMode.

1. Stop the client and service.

2. Modify the service contract, commenting out the ServiceBehavior that specifies the InstanceContextMode of PerSession and uncommenting out the code for a ServiceBehavior of Sharable:

```
// This will share the information per a single session
// [ServiceBehavior(InstanceContextMode=InstanceContextMode.PerSession)]
// This will share the information in a single session, across multiple
// clients
[ServiceBehavior(InstanceContextMode = InstanceContextMode.Shareable)]
// [ServiceBehavior(InstanceContextMode = InstanceContextMode.PerCall)]
```

In this test, you will see that you can have multiple proxies that can share the same session:

1. Run the Service.

2. Run the Client.

3. Click the Deposit and Withdraw buttons.

4. Click the Son Withdraw button.

The code for the click event of the Son Withdraw button resolves the address of the first proxy. It creates an EndpointAddress object and assigns that to the second proxy:

```
            System.ServiceModel.EndpointAddress proxyAddress =
➡ proxy.InnerChannel.ResolveInstance();
            proxySon.Endpoint.Address = proxyAddress;
```

That proxy, SonProxy, can now share the same session as the main proxy. Both proxies can interact with the shared state information.

Implementing Queued Messaging

Queued Messaging in Windows Communication Foundation enables clients and services to send and receive messages without requiring both applications to be running at the same time. The programming model for using queues basically consists of choosing the appropriate predefined binding or configuring your own custom binding.

Before we dive into Queued Messaging, it's important to review MSMQ and queuing in general.

Queued Messaging

If you were to call John Smith's office and ask a question, you would be engaging in synchronous messaging with John. You would be making a request and John would be providing a response in real-time.

If you were to call John Smith's office before he arrived, you would leave a voice-mail message with the question. When John Smith arrived at his office, he would see a blinking light to indicate that he had new voice-mail messages. From there, he would dial his voice-mail system and retrieve that message. He would then send a response with the answer by either phone or email.

Your message is being placed in a durable store, John Smith is notified that there are messages available, and he connects to the system to retrieve them.

Queuing is analogous to the voice-mail scenario. Conceptually, a sender initiates a communication by sending a message. Instead of going to voice mail, this message goes to a queue, where it is stored. A receiver application monitors that queue and receives messages at some point after they were delivered.

An MSMQ Primer

Microsoft Message Queue (MSMQ) is the technology Microsoft has provided to support queued messaging on the windows platform. Although MSMQ is not a new feature being introduced with WCF, it may be new to some readers. As such, this next section provides a primer.

We've given an overview of what queued messaging is; now we will begin to look at how queued messaging is done with MSMQ. To begin with, know that there are actually multiple types of queues within MSMQ. They can be placed into one of two buckets—user-created queues and system queues.

User-Created Queues

There are several types of user-created queues. Public queues are queues that are visible on the network and listed in Active Directory. Private queues are local to the computer on which they are created. Because their information is not published, an application must know the full path or label of the private queue to access it.

In addition to private and public queues, there are two other types of user-created queues: Administration Queues and Response Queues. Administration queues contain the acknowledgment messages for messages sent within a network. Response queues contain response messages. Response messages are returned to the sender by the receiver, after a message is received.

System Queues

Systems queues have several types as well: journal, dead-letter, report, and private system queues.

Journal queues can be set up to store copies of messages sent and retrieved from a queue. Separate journals exist on both the client and the server. On the client, there is a single journal queue that logs messages sent to/from that computer. On the server side, a separate journal queue is created for each individual queue, and it tracks only those messages attached to that queue.

When messages are undeliverable or have expired, they are placed in another type of system queue, a dead-letter queue. Dead letters are stored on the computer on which the message expired. When a transactional message dies, it is placed in a variant of dead-letter queue called a transaction dead-letter queue.

Report queues contain messages that identify the route a message took to its destination. In addition, it can also contain test messages. There is one report queue per computer.

The last type is private system queues. These queues store administrative and notification messages needed by the system to process messaging actions.

Dead-Letter Queues and WCF

The dead-letter queue was discussed earlier in the chapter, and it is essentially the queue where expired or otherwise undeliverable messages are sent.

Messages can end up in the dead-letter queue for a number of reasons. This can happen if a queue quota is exceeded, if there is an authorization failure, or if a message expires.

Message delivery can be time sensitive, and the content within messages may have a set lifetime. In these cases, after the expected lifetime, the message should no longer be considered valid. The lifetime of the message can be specified in the binding, specifically the TimeToLive value.

After the TimeToLive has passed, the message is considered expired and sent to the dead-letter queue.

On Windows Vista, WCF v1.0 moves away from a traditional shared dead-letter queue across all applications, providing instead a dead-letter queue for each sending application. By moving away from a traditional shared dead-letter queue, these application-specific dead-letter queues provide a level of isolation between applications and the processing of dead letters targeted for those applications.

Poison Messages

When a message exceeds the maximum number of delivery attempts to the receiving application, it is called a poison message.

This situation can arise, for example, when applications that read messages from a queue cannot process the message immediately because of errors. Aborting the transaction in which the queued message was received leaves the message in the queue so that the message is retried under a new transaction. If the problem that is causing the abort is not corrected, the receiving application can get stuck in an infinite loop, receiving and aborting the same message until the maximum number of delivery attempts has been exceeded and a poison message results.

Handling Poison Messages in WCF

Poison message handling in WCF provides a way for the receiving application to handle poison messages. Poison message handling is configured via the bindings for an endpoint.

The binding exposes four properties that can be set: `MaxRetries`, `MaxRetryCycles`, `RetryCycleDelay`, and `RejectAfterLastRetry`.

`MaxRetries` determines the number of times redelivery of a message from the main queue to the application should be attempted. This is typically sufficient if there is a temporary situation that will resolve itself between the initial and final attempts. A common example cited here is a point-in-time deadlock on SQL Server.

`MaxRetryCycles` identifies the maximum number of retry cycles. A retry cycle consists of putting a message back into the application queue from the retry queue to attempt delivery again.

`RetryCycleDelay` determines the delay between retry cycles. The combination of the retry cycle and the retry cycle delay provides a way to handle issues in which a longer delay between retries resolves the issue. The delay, which defaults to 10 minutes, provides the capability to compensate for scenarios in which periodic outages interrupting message delivery can be handled smoothly.

`RejectAfterLastRetry` specifies how to react when the last attempt fails to deliver the message. When true, a negative acknowledgment will be sent to the sender. When false, the message will be sent to the poison queue.

If the message is sent to the poison queue, it can be processed by a separate WCF Queued Message service.

> **NOTE**
>
> WCF support for handling poison messages is supported only on Windows Vista.

WCF's Bindings for MSMQ

WCF has two bindings for use with MSMQ as a transport: `NetProfileMsmqBinding` and `MsmqIntegrationBinding`. The criteria for selecting the appropriate binding concern the type of application used by the client and service, in particular whether they are WCF or MSMQ applications.

In a scenario in which both the client and the server will be using WCF to communicate, the NetProfileMsmqBinding should be used. If either the sender or the receiver is not using WCF for communications, the MsmqIntegrationBinding should be used. This binding maps messages to/from WCF to MSMQ messages based on the direction of the integration (sending or receiving).

Using MSMQ in an integration scenario is covered in Chapter 6, "Legacy Integration."

Creating a WCF Application Using Queued Messaging

Imagine that the bank wanted to provide a value-added service to its customers in the form of bill payment. In this particular scenario, the electric company is one of the payees that the bank would like to support.

This next example is the code used by the bank to implement bill payments using queues:

1. Open Visual Studio and create a new project. Create a new Windows Console application in C:\WCFHandsOn\Chapter5\Before\PartII.

   Name the project Service and name the solution Queues.

2. Add a reference to System.ServiceModel.

3. Add a reference to System.messaging.

4. Add a reference to System.Configuration.

5. Add a reference to System.Transactions.

6. Rename Program.cs to service.cs.

7. Open service.cs and add using statements such that the top of the file resembles the following:

```
using System;
using System.Configuration;
using System.Messaging;
using System.ServiceModel;
```

8. Define the service contract for IBillPayment. We have one operation, PayBill, and it is defined as a one-way operation:

```
{
    // Define a service contract.
    [ServiceContract]
    public interface IBillPayment
    {
        [OperationContract(IsOneWay=true)]
```

```
    void PayBill(int AccountNbr, int ElectricAccountNbr, double Amount);

    }
```

9. Define the implementation of the class, and insert code for the `PayBill` operation. Here we will write out the information that is received to the console.

> **NOTE**
>
> Note that this service is using queues, but the interface is the same as we've seen for other transports. WCF interacts with the queues behind the scenes, and allows us to focus on writing implementation code for our business logic.
>
> In the future, if we choose to use the `wsHttpBinding` rather than queuing, it can be done in the configuration file with no changes to the code. This underscores the power of the declarative model within WCF that provides you the ability to change the underlying protocols and bindings for transport totally outside the actual application logic.

```
    // Service class which implements the service contract.
    // Added code to write output to the console window
    public class BillPaymentService : IBillPayment
    {
        [OperationBehavior]
        public void PayBill(int AccountNbr, int ElectricAccountNbr,
    ➥ double Amount)
        {

            Console.WriteLine("Received Request to Pay Electric
    ➥ Company Account {0}  the amount of {1} from local account {2}",
    ➥ ElectricAccountNbr, Amount.ToString(), AccountNbr);
        }
```

10. In the `service.cs` file, add the code to host the service.

> **NOTE**
>
> Note that we use `System.Messaging` solely for the purpose of creating queues; we do not use `System.Messaging` for anything related to the actual service:

```
    // Host the service within this EXE console application.
    public static void Main()
    {
      // Get MSMQ queue name from app settings in configuration
      string queueName = ConfigurationManager.AppSettings["queueName"];
```

```
// Create the transacted MSMQ queue if necessary.
if (!MessageQueue.Exists(queueName))
  MessageQueue.Create(queueName, true);

// Get the base addresses.
// Including an Http base address for
// WS-MetaDataExchange requests is
// useful to generate a proxy for the client
string httpBaseAddress =
  ConfigurationManager.AppSettings["httpBaseAddress"];
string queueBaseAddress =
  ConfigurationManager.AppSettings["queueBaseAddress"];

// Create a ServiceHost for the BillPayment type.
using (ServiceHost serviceHost =
    new ServiceHost(
      typeof(BillPaymentService),
      new Uri[]{
        new Uri(httpBaseAddress),
        new Uri(queueBaseAddress)}))
{
  serviceHost.Open();
  Console.WriteLine("The Bill Payment Service is online.");
  Console.WriteLine("Press <ENTER> to terminate service.");
  Console.WriteLine();
  Console.ReadLine();

  // Close the ServiceHostBase to shut down the service.
  serviceHost.Close();
}
}
```

11. Create a new application configuration file and populate the file with the following configuration settings.

Note that we provide an http endpoint for the base address. This is used to expose metadata for our service using http, whereas the service itself uses MSMQ and the netMsmqBinding:

```
<?xml version="1.0" encoding="utf-8" ?>
<configuration>
  <appSettings>
    <add key="queueName" value=".\private$\BillPay" />
    <add key ="httpBaseAddress"
      value="http://localhost:8000/BillPay"/>
    <add key ="queueBaseAddress"
```

```
          value="net.msmq://localhost/private/"/>
      </appSettings>
      <system.serviceModel>
        <services>
          <service
            type="WCFHandsOn.BillPaymentService">
            <endpoint address="BillPay"
              binding="netMsmqBinding"
              bindingConfiguration="DefaultMsmqBinding"
              contract="WCFHandsOn.IBillPayment" />
          </service>
        </services>
        <bindings>
          <netMsmqBinding>
            <binding name="DefaultMsmqBinding" />
          </netMsmqBinding>
        </bindings>
      </system.serviceModel>
    </configuration>
```

Creating the Client for the Service

It is now time to create the client to interact with our service.

1. Add a new project to the solution.

2. Create a new Windows Console application in C:\WCFHandsOn\Chapter5\
   Before\PartII.

3. Name the project Client.

4. Add a reference to System.ServiceModel.

5. Add a reference to System.Messaging.

6. Add a reference to System.Configuration.

7. Add a reference to System.Transactions.

8. Rename Program.cs to client.cs.

9. Start the Service application.

   Because the metadata for the service is exposed using http, you can query it using
   SvcUtil.exe.

   Run SvcUtil.exe against the endpoint specified in the services App.Config file. This
   will query the metadata for the service and generate a proxy class for the service.

10. From the command prompt, execute the following:

```
"C:\Program Files\Microsoft SDKs\Windows\v1.0\Bin\SvcUtil.exe "
➥ http://localhost:8000/BillPay
```

This will generate two files, `BillPaymentService.cs` and `Output.config`.

11. Add both files to the Client project.

12. Rename `Output.config` to `App.Config`.

With the proxy for the service created, you can now write the code to call the queued service.

13. In the main method of `client.cs`, add the following lines of code:

```
static void Main()
{
  // Create a proxy
  using (BillPaymentProxy proxy = new BillPaymentProxy())
  {
    //Create a transaction scope.
    using (TransactionScope scope =
      new TransactionScope(TransactionScopeOption.Required))
    {

      proxy.PayBill(12345,67890,50);
      Console.WriteLine("Paying $50 towards acount 67890");

      proxy.PayBill(22345, 77890, 100);
      Console.WriteLine("Paying $100 towards account 77890");

      // Complete the transaction.
      scope.Complete();
    }

  }

  Console.WriteLine();
  Console.WriteLine("Press <ENTER> to terminate client.");
  Console.ReadLine();
}
```

You are now ready to test your queued messaging solution.

Test #1—Client and Service Online

The first test will show how the solution will respond in an ideal scenario where both client and service are online at the same time.

1. Start the Service.

2. Start the Client.

The client will call the service, which will utilize queues behind the scenes. The service will pick up the messages from the queue and write out that the bill payments have occurred.

The expected outcome is shown in Figure 5.4.

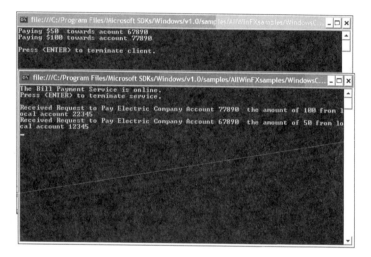

FIGURE 5.4   Screenshot of the resulting test.

Test #2—Service Offline When Message Sent, Online Later

In this test, we will simulate a disconnected scenario.

1. Start the client.

2. The client will call the service, which again utilizes queues behind the scenes.

3. Stop the client.

4. Start the service.

Notice that the service comes online, detects the messages, and processes the messages the client sent earlier.

This is because the messages were placed on the queue by the client, and the service retrieved the messages from the queue when it went online.

Transactions

If you go to a bank and transfer $100 from your savings account to your checking account, you are engaging in a transaction. There are two actions that need to occur—a withdrawal from your savings account and a deposit to your checking account.

If for some reason one of those actions were to succeed and the other were to fail, there would be a problem. If the transfer from the withdrawal from your savings account was successful, and the deposit failed, your $100 would disappear. This is not a desirable outcome for you.

If the withdrawal from your savings account failed, but the deposit to the checking account for that amount was successful, you would essentially have gained $100 in funds at the expense of the bank. Although this would possibly be a nice situation for you, this is a less-than-ideal situation for the bank.

For this transaction to reach a satisfactory conclusion for all parties involved, the activities need to complete as expected. If one of them fails, any changes that have occurred need to be "rolled back" to a state where they were before the transaction occurred.

Atomic, Consistent, Isolated, and Durable (ACID)

Transactions have four key characteristics. Transactions must be Atomic, Consistent, Isolated, and Durable (ACID). Definitions of each of these characteristics are listed in the text that follows.

Atomic

For a transaction to be atomic, either all the actions must be successfully committed, or any state that has been affected must be rolled back to values that existed prior to the actions occurring.

In our example, this would mean that the money would be successfully withdrawn from the savings account and deposited into the checking account, or the funds would remain as they were at the start of the transaction.

Consistent

Consistency guarantees a predictable transformation of state. In our example, the account being debited by $100 and $100 being deducted from the account is consistent with our expectation.

Isolated

Whereas atomic was defined essentially as an all-or-nothing application of the actions within a transaction, isolated ensures that the transaction, and the changes being made within it, are opaque to the outside world.

When the work and state changes made within the transaction are isolated, the world outside the transaction continues to work with a state that is valid.

Assume, in our example, that the accounts in question were joint accounts shared with a spouse. If John Smith was in the middle of making a fund transfer and Jane Smith was making a withdrawal from an ATM, both transactions would be invisible to the other. The transactions would become visible after they were committed (that is, after the transfer was completed or the funds were dispensed).

Durable

For a transaction to be durable, committed updates must survive failures.

In our example, this would mean that if a power outage occurred after the transaction had committed, when the power was restored the state changes resulting from the withdrawal and deposit must remain.

Transactions on Windows

As mentioned in Chapter 1, "Prerequisites—Generics and Transactions," Version 2.0 of the .NET framework introduced new additions for transactional programming. The System.Transactions namespace was introduced, as were two transaction managers (the Lightweight Transaction Manager [LTM] and the OleTx Transaction Manager). These were added to provide .NET developers the ability to develop more agile and performant transactional applications.

The Lightweight Transaction Manager provides support for transactions that exist in a single app domain; that have at most one durable store, for example SQL Server; and that do not require writes to the Transaction Log. For those transactions that involve multiple durable stores or cross app domains, the OleTx Transaction Manager would be used.

Through the System.Transactions namespace, .NET removes the need for the developer to make an upfront determination of which of these transaction managers to choose. System.Transactions provides the capability to promote transactions as required. By default, all transactions will utilize the Lightweight Transaction Manager and then be promoted to use the OleTx Transaction Manager in scenarios in which multiple durable stores are part of the transaction, or the transaction crosses multiple app domains.

Transactions and transactional behavior can be specified either declaratively using attributes or explicitly in .NET code. Examples of both can be seen here:

```
[Transaction(TransactionOption.Required)]
public class WireTransfer : ServicedComponent
{
    [AutoComplete]
    public double Transfer(
      int sourceAccountNbr,
      int targetAccountNbr,
      double amount);
    {
      ...
    }
}
```

```
public double Transfer(
   int sourceAccountNbr,
   int targetAccountNbr,
   double amount)
{
   TransactionOptions options = new TransactionOptions();
   options.IsolationLevel = IsolationLevel.ReadCommitted;
   using (TransactionScope scope =
     new TransactionScope(
       TransactionScopeOption.Required,
       options))
   {
       //Code that will be part of the transaction
   }
}
```

WS-Atomic Transaction

As with security and reliability, the industry grew tired of patchwork solutions that were only relatively interoperable and went to work on standards in the area of transactions as well.

The most implemented of these standards is WS-Atomic Transaction (WS-AT). WS-AT defines a specific set of protocols for implementing two-phase atomic transactions.

WS-AT allows you to leverage existing software investments when moving toward a service-oriented enterprise. WS-AT incorporates transactions at the message level, providing the capability to implement all-or-nothing transactions with closely coupled systems that may span platforms.

Transaction Support in WCF

WCF provides the capability to flow transactions from a client to a service. In a Windows-only environment, WCF provides the capability to use the transactional capability inherent in .NET and the Windows platform. For cross-platform scenarios, it provides the capability to utilize WS-Atomic Transactions.

> **NOTE**
>
> WCF provides an implementation of WS-AT that is built into the Microsoft Distributed Transaction Coordinator (MSDTC). It supports authentication using Windows identities, and, for cross-platform interoperability, authentication using certificates. For the latter case, a trusted certificate must be installed into the machine's certificate store, and communication must be via HTTPS with client certificate authentication.

WCF uses policy assertions to control transaction flow. These assertions can be found in the service's policy document, which clients can access using HTTP GET or WS-MEX. With the document, clients and/or tools can determine how to interact with a service.

The assertions within the document are the result of a combination of information specified in attributes, contracts, and the configuration file.

TransactionFlow **Attribute**

With the `TransactionFlow` attribute, WCF provides the capability to associate transaction flow assertions with a specific operation.

Through this attribute, you can specify whether individual operations may support transactions (`Allowed`), must require transactions (`Mandatory`), or do not allow transactions (`NotAllowed`):

```
[TransactionFlow(TransactionFlowOption.Mandatory)]
    bool PayBill(int account, decimal amount);
```

The enumeration `TransactionFlowOption` is used for this, and the default value is `NotAllowed`.

> **NOTE**
>
> If the attribute is defined to either allow or require a transaction flow, the affected operations are required not to be specified as one-way.

Specifying Transactional Behaviors

Behaviors provide a way to declaratively specify how the service should behave, in this case in respect to transactions. Here you can specify whether an operation auto-completes on successful execution, and specify whether a transaction scope is required:

```
[ServiceContract]
    public interface IElectricBillPay
    {
        [OperationContract]
        [OperationBehavior(TransactionAutoComplete=true,
➥ TransactionScopeRequired=true)]
        bool PayBill(int account, decimal amount);

        [OperationContract]
        decimal GetBalance(int account);

    }
```

Specifying the Transaction Protocol in Configuration

The protocol to use for transaction flow is specified in the configuration file. WCF provides three protocol options: OleTx, Wsat, or TxNego.

As you might imagine based on the text from earlier in the chapter, OleTx would be used for transactions that will occur only on the Microsoft platform, whereas Wsat is for support of transactions across platforms using WS-Atomic transactions. The third option, TxNego, actually provides the capability to let the service expose both. Reading the resulting policy file, services could determine the protocol they want to support.

As is noted in the documentation, the choice of protocol influences two separate factors:

- The format of the SOAP headers used to flow the transaction from client to server

- The protocol used between the client's transaction manager and the server's transaction to resolve the outcome of the transaction

Transaction Protocol for Preconfigured Bindings   For the out-of-the-box bindings provided with WCF, some default to OleTx protocol, whereas others default to WS-AT. The choice of transaction protocol within a binding can also be influenced programmatically.

TABLE 5.3   Default Support for Transactions in WCF's Preconfigured Bindings

Binding	Transaction Support	Default Protocol
BasicHttpBinding	No	N/A
WSHttpBinding	Yes	WS-AT
WSDualHttpBinding	Yes	WS-AT
WSFederationBinding	Yes	WS-AT
NetTcpBinding	Yes	OleTx
NetNamedPipeBinding	Yes	OleTx
NetMsmqBinding	Yes	OleTx
NetPeerTcpBinding	No	N/A
MsmqIntegrationBinding	Yes	OleTx

When creating the configuration file for services that use one of the preconfigured bindings, within the bindings section, you will add the `transactionFlow` attribute to the binding element and provide the value `true`:

```
<system.serviceModel>
  <services>
    <service
        type="GenericElectricCompany.ElectricBillPay"
    >
      <!-- use base address provided by host -->
      <endpoint address=""
                binding="wsHttpBinding"
                bindingConfiguration="transactionBinding"
                contract="GenericElectricCompany.IElectricBillPay" />
    </service>
  </services>
  <bindings>
    <wsHttpBinding>
      <binding name="transactionBinding" transactionFlow="true" />
    </wsHttpBinding>
```

```
    </bindings>
</system.serviceModel>
```

In many cases, only one protocol is supported; in that case the `transactionFlow` attribute is all that is required. In the case of several bindings, such as the `netTcpBinding` and the `netNamedPipeBinding`, a specific protocol can be specified. Here, you would add the `transactionProtocol` attribute and identify the preferred protocol, OleTx, Wsat, or TxNego:

```
    <bindings>
        <netTcpBinding>
            <binding name="test"
                closeTimeout="00:00:10"
                openTimeout="00:00:20"
                receiveTimeout="00:00:30"
                sendTimeout="00:00:40"
                transactionFlow="true"
                transactionProtocol="TxNego"
                hostNameComparisonMode="WeakWildcard"
                maxBufferSize="1001"
                maxConnections="123"
                maxMessageSize="1000"
                portSharingEnabled="true">
                <reliableSession ordered="false"
                    inactivityTimeout="00:02:00"
                    enabled="true" />
                <security mode="Message">
                    <message clientCredentialType="Windows" />
                </security>
            </binding>
        </netTcpBinding>
    </bindings>
</system.ServiceModel>
```

Transaction Protocol for Custom Bindings   When developing your own custom bindings, you will create a `transactionFlow` element for the binding and specify the transaction protocol using the `transactionProtocol` attribute:

```
<customBinding>
        <binding name="WCFHandsOnTxBinding">
          <transactionFlow transactionProtocol="Wsat"/>
        </binding>
    </customBinding>
```

ENABLING WS-ATOMIC TRANSACTIONS

WS-Atomic Transaction support is not turned on by default. The `xws_reg.exe` utility can be used to turn on WS-AT support from the command line.

Open the Visual Studio command prompt (select Start, All Programs, Microsoft Visual Studio 2005, Visual Studio Tools, Visual Studio command prompt).

Execute the utility with the following command-line parameter:

```
xws_reg -v -wsat+
```

Adding Transactions to the Solution

In this exercise, you will create a solution that consists of an ATM Client, a Web Service for a Bank, and a Bill Payment Web Service for the Electric Company.

In this scenario you will enable customers to pay their electric bill through the ATM. The ATM will connect to the Banking Web Service, which in turn creates a transaction when connecting to the Electric Company.

In this example the Banking Service is a client to a service at the Electric Company, and the transaction occurs between the Bank and the Electric Company.

Creating the Electric Company Service

The electric company would like to be able to enable banks to connect to their bill payment service. Because many of the electric company's customers are also customers of the bank, this will make it easier for those customers to pay their bills.

To facilitate this task, we will now create the Electric Company Service:

1. Open Visual Studio and create a new project. Create a new Windows Console application in `C:\WCFHandsOn\Chapter5\Before\PartIII`.

    Name the project GenericElectricCompany and name the solution Transactions.

2. Add a reference to `System.Workflow`.

3. Add a reference to `System.Transactions`.

4. Add a reference to `System.Configuration`.

5. Add a new class named `ElectricBillPay.cs`.

6. Modify the content of the `App.Config` file to resemble the following:

    ```
    using System;
    using System.Collections.Generic;
    using System.Text;
    using System.ServiceModel;
    using System.Transactions;
    ```

```
namespace GenericElectricCompany
{
    [ServiceContract]
    public interface IElectricBillPay
    {
        [OperationContract]
        [TransactionFlow(TransactionFlowOption.Required)]
➡ //Added for Transaction Support
        bool PayBill(int account, decimal amount);

        [OperationContract]
        decimal GetBalance(int account);

    }

    //Added for Sessions
    [ServiceBehavior(InstanceContextMode = InstanceContextMode.PerSession)]

    class ElectricBillPay : IElectricBillPay
    {
        public bool PayBill(int account, decimal amount)
        {

            Console.WriteLine("Paying {0} towards bill on Account {1}",
➡ amount, account);

            return true;
        }
        public decimal GetBalance(int account)
        {

            return 0;
        }

    }
}
```

NOTE

Note that in the code you've entered, you've placed an attribute on the PayBill operation that states that TransactionFlowOption is required.

7. Add a new application configuration file to the project named App.Config.

8. Modify the content of the `App.Config` file to resemble the following:

```xml
<?xml version="1.0" encoding="utf-8" ?>
<configuration><appSettings>
  <!-- use appSetting to configure base address provided by host -->
  <add key="baseAddress"
 value="http://localhost:8080/GenericElectricBillPayService" />
</appSettings>

<system.serviceModel>
  <services>
    <service
        type="GenericElectricCompany.ElectricBillPay"
    >
      <!-- use base address provided by host -->
      <endpoint address=""
                binding="wsHttpBinding"
                bindingConfiguration="transactionBinding"
                contract="GenericElectricCompany.IElectricBillPay" />
    </service>
  </services>
  <bindings>
    <wsHttpBinding>
      <binding name="transactionBinding" transactionFlow="true" />
    </wsHttpBinding>
  </bindings>


</system.serviceModel>
</configuration>
```

Note that the configuration file includes a binding to flow transactions.

Transactions will be used when paying a bill with this service. Because we're using the wsHttpBinding, we will be using WS-AT.

> **NOTE**
>
> If you've not already enabled WS-AT, you should do so using the instructions provided earlier in the chapter.

9. Modify the content of the `Program.cs` file to resemble the following:

```csharp
using System;
using System.Collections.Generic;
using System.Text;
using System.Configuration;
```

```
using System.ServiceModel;

namespace GenericElectricCompany
{
    class Program
    {

        static void Main(string[] args)
        {
            // Get base address from app settings in configuration
            Uri baseAddressBillPay =
➥new Uri(ConfigurationManager.AppSettings["baseAddress"]);


            // Instantiate new ServiceHost
            ServiceHost BillPayHost = new ServiceHost(typeof(ElectricBillPay),
➥ baseAddressBillPay);
            BillPayHost.Open();
            Console.WriteLine("Generic Electric Bill Payment Service
➥ is Online.");
            Console.WriteLine("----------------------------------");


            Console.WriteLine("Press any key to terminate service.");
            Console.ReadKey();

            BillPayHost.Close();

        }
    }
}
```

Creating the Banking Service

Next, you will consume the Electric Bill Payment Service at the bank, which will then expose that functionality to ATM customers.

1. Create a proxy for the Bill Pay Service.

2. Start the Generic Electric Bill Payment Service.

3. Open a Visual Studio command prompt and navigate to the directory
   C:\WCFHandsOn\Chapter5\Before\PartIII\.

4. Enter the following at the command prompt:

```
"C:\Program Files\Microsoft SDKs\Windows\v1.0\Bin\SvcUtil.exe "
➥http://localhost:8080/GenericElectricBillPayService
➥/out:GenericElectricBillPay.cs
```

SvcUtil.exe will generate two files, GenericElectricBillPay.cs and output.config.

GenericElectricBillPay.cs will contain a generated proxy class for the Bill Pay service. Output.config contains the configuration information for the service that can be renamed to App.Config.

5. Open Visual Studio, and create a new project in the current solution. Create a new Windows Console application in C:\WCFHandsOn\Chapter5\Before\PartIII.

Name the project ConsumerBankingService.

6. Add a reference to System.ServiceModel.

7. Add a reference to System.Transactions.

8. Add a reference to System.Runtime.Serialization.

Open the GenericElectricBillPay.cs and note that the proxy specifies that TransactionFlow is required:

```
[System.ServiceModel.OperationContractAttribute
➥ (Action="http://tempuri.org/IElectricBillPay/PayBill",
➥ReplyAction="http://tempuri.org/IElectricBillPay/PayBillResponse")]
[System.ServiceModel.TransactionFlowAttribute(
➥ System.ServiceModel.TransactionFlowOption.Required)]
bool PayBill(int account, decimal amount);
```

9. Add a new class file named ConsumerBankingCore.cs. Modify the class to contain the following code:

```
using System;
using System.Collections.Generic;
using System.Text;
using System.ServiceModel;

namespace ConsumerBankingService
{
    [ServiceContract]
    public interface IConsumerBankingCore
    {
        [OperationContract]
        bool Deposit(int accountNumber, decimal amount);
        [OperationContract]
```

```
        bool Withdraw(int accountNumber, decimal amount);
        [OperationContract]
        decimal GetBalance(int accountNumber);
    }


    class ConsumerBankingCore : IConsumerBankingCore
    {

        public bool Deposit(int accountNumber, decimal amount)
        {
            Console.WriteLine("Depositing {0} into Account {1}", amount,
➥ accountNumber);

            return true; }
        public bool Withdraw(int accountNumber, decimal amount)
        {
            Console.WriteLine("Withdrawing {0} from Account {1}", amount,
➥ accountNumber);
            return true; }
        public decimal GetBalance(int accountNumber)
        { return 0; }


    }
}
```

10. Add a new class file named `ConsumerBankingBillPayment.cs`.

11. Modify the class to contain the following code:

```
using System;
using System.Collections.Generic;
using System.Text;
using System.ServiceModel;

namespace ConsumerBankingService
{
    [ServiceContract]
    public interface IConsumerBankingBillPayment
    {
        [OperationContract]
        bool PayBill(int accountNumber, int accountNumberToPay,
➥ decimal amount);
```

```
        [OperationContract]
        string GetRegisteredBills(int accountNumber);
    }



    class ConsumerBankingBillPayment : IConsumerBankingBillPayment
    {

        public bool PayBill(int accountNumber, int accountNumberToPay,
➥ decimal amount)
        {
            bool success = false;

            ConsumerBankingCore banking = new ConsumerBankingCore();
            success = banking.Withdraw(accountNumber,amount);

            ElectricBillPayProxy proxy = new ElectricBillPayProxy("BillPay");
            success = success && proxy.PayBill(accountNumberToPay, amount);
            Console.WriteLine("Paying {0} from Account {1} towards
➥ GenericElectric account {2}", amount, accountNumber,accountNumberToPay);

            return success; }

        public string GetRegisteredBills(int accountNumber)
        { return "result"; }



    }
}
```

12. Modify the content of the `Program.cs` file to resemble the following:

```
using System;
using System.Collections.Generic;
using System.Text;
using System.ServiceModel;
using System.Configuration;

namespace ConsumerBankingService
{
    class Program
    {

        static void Main(string[] args)
        {
```

```
        // Get base address from app settings in configuration
        Uri baseAddressCore = new Uri(ConfigurationManager.AppSettings
➥ ["baseAddressCore"]);
        Uri baseAddressBillPay = new Uri
➥(ConfigurationManager.AppSettings["baseAddressBillPay"]);

        // Instantiate new ServiceHost
        ServiceHost CoreServiceHost = new ServiceHost(typeof(
➥ ConsumerBankingCore), baseAddressCore);
        CoreServiceHost.Open();
        Console.WriteLine("Consumer Banking Service is Online.");
        Console.WriteLine("---------------------------------");

        ServiceHost BillPayServiceHost = new
➥ ServiceHost(typeof(ConsumerBankingBillPayment), baseAddressBillPay);
        BillPayServiceHost.Open();
        Console.WriteLine("Consumer Bill Pay Service is Online.");
        Console.WriteLine("---------------------------------");

        Console.WriteLine("Press any key to terminate service.");
        Console.ReadKey();

        CoreServiceHost.Close();
        BillPayServiceHost.Close();

    }

  }
}
```

13. Open the App.Config file.

    The configuration file contains the configuration information to be a client for the Generic Electric Company Bill Payment Service.

14. Modify the file to include references to the base addresses, and service endpoints.

Your App.config file should resemble the following:

```
<?xml version="1.0" encoding="utf-8" ?>
<configuration>
<appSettings>
  <!-- use appSetting to configure base address provided by host -->
  <add key="baseAddressCore"
➥ value="http://localhost:8080/ConsumerBankingService" />
  <add key="baseAddressBillPay" value="http://localhost:8080/
➥ ConsumerBankingService/BillPay" />
</appSettings>
```

```
<system.serviceModel>

    <client>
      <endpoint name="BillPay"
➥ address="http://localhost:8080/GenericElectricBillPayService"
          bindingConfiguration="WSHttpBinding_IElectricBillPay"
➥ binding="customBinding"
          contract="IElectricBillPay" />
    </client>


  <services>
    <service
        type="ConsumerBankingService.ConsumerBankingCore"
    >
      <!-- use base address provided by host -->
      <endpoint address=""
              binding="wsHttpBinding"
              contract="ConsumerBankingService.IConsumerBankingCore" />
    </service>
    <service
        type="ConsumerBankingService.ConsumerBankingBillPayment"
    >
      <!-- use base address provided by host -->
      <endpoint address=""
                binding="wsHttpBinding"
                contract=
➥ "ConsumerBankingService.IConsumerBankingBillPayment" />
    </service>
  </services>

  <bindings>
    <customBinding>
      <binding name="Secure conversation bootstrap binding
➥ 51a11de1-ed0b-47b4-9893-c880ceaf4e22">
        <security defaultAlgorithmSuite="Default"
➥ authenticationMode="SspiNegotiated"
            defaultProtectionLevel="EncryptAndSign" requireDerivedKeys="true"
            securityHeaderLayout="Strict" includeTimestamp="true"
➥  keyEntropyMode="CombinedEntropy"
            messageProtectionOrder="SignBeforeEncrypt" protectTokens="false"
            requireSecurityContextCancellation="true"
➥ securityVersion="WSSecurityXXX2005"
            requireSignatureConfirmation="false">
          <localClientSettings cacheCookies="true" detectReplays="true"
```

```
                    replayCacheSize="900000" maxClockSkew="00:05:00"
➡ maxCookieCachingTime="10675199.02:48:05.4775807"
                    replayWindow="00:05:00" sessionKeyRenewalInterval="10:00:00"
                    sessionKeyRolloverInterval="00:05:00"
➡ reconnectTransportOnFailure="true"
                    timestampValidityDuration="00:05:00"
➡ cookieRenewalThresholdPercentage="90" />
              <localServiceSettings detectReplays="true"
➡ issuedCookieLifetime="10:00:00"
                    maxStatefulNegotiations="1024" replayCacheSize="900000"
➡ maxClockSkew="00:05:00"
                    negotiationTimeout="00:02:00" replayWindow="00:05:00"
➡ inactivityTimeout="01:00:00"
                    sessionKeyRenewalInterval="15:00:00"
➡ sessionKeyRolloverInterval="00:05:00"
                    reconnectTransportOnFailure="true" maxConcurrentSessions="1000"
                    timestampValidityDuration="00:05:00" />
          </security>
          <textMessageEncoding maxReadPoolSize="64" maxWritePoolSize="16"
              messageVersion="Default" writeEncoding="utf-8" />
        </binding>
        <binding name="WSHttpBinding_IElectricBillPay">
          <security defaultAlgorithmSuite="Default"
➡ authenticationMode="SecureConversation"
                    bootstrapBindingConfiguration=
➡ "Secure conversation bootstrap binding
➡  51a11de1-ed0b-47b4-9893-c880ceaf4e22"
                    bootstrapBindingSectionName="customBinding"
➡ defaultProtectionLevel="EncryptAndSign"
                    requireDerivedKeys="true" securityHeaderLayout="Strict"
➡ includeTimestamp="true"
                    keyEntropyMode="CombinedEntropy"
➡ messageProtectionOrder="SignBeforeEncrypt"
                    protectTokens="false" requireSecurityContextCancellation="true"
                    securityVersion="WSSecurityXXX2005"
➡ requireSignatureConfirmation="false">
              <localClientSettings cacheCookies="true" detectReplays="true"
                    replayCacheSize="900000" maxClockSkew="00:05:00"
➡ maxCookieCachingTime="10675199.02:48:05.4775807"
                    replayWindow="00:05:00" sessionKeyRenewalInterval="10:00:00"
                    sessionKeyRolloverInterval="00:05:00"
➡ reconnectTransportOnFailure="true"
                    timestampValidityDuration="00:05:00"
➡ cookieRenewalThresholdPercentage="90" />
              <localServiceSettings detectReplays="true"
```

5

```
➥ issuedCookieLifetime="10:00:00"
              maxStatefulNegotiations="1024" replayCacheSize="900000"
➥ maxClockSkew="00:05:00"
              negotiationTimeout="00:02:00" replayWindow="00:05:00"
➥ inactivityTimeout="01:00:00"
              sessionKeyRenewalInterval="15:00:00"
➥ sessionKeyRolloverInterval="00:05:00"
              reconnectTransportOnFailure="true" maxConcurrentSessions="1000"
              timestampValidityDuration="00:05:00" />
         </security>
         <textMessageEncoding maxReadPoolSize="64" maxWritePoolSize="16"
            messageVersion="Default" writeEncoding="utf-8" />
         <httpTransport manualAddressing="false" maxBufferPoolSize="524288"
            maxMessageSize="65536" allowCookies="false"
➥ authenticationScheme="Anonymous"
              bypassProxyOnLocal="false"
➥ hostNameComparisonMode="StrongWildcard"
              mapAddressingHeadersToHttpHeaders="false"
➥ proxyAuthenticationScheme="Anonymous"
              realm="" transferMode="Buffered"
➥ unsafeConnectionNtlmAuthentication="false"
              useDefaultWebProxy="true" />
       </binding>
     </customBinding>
   </bindings>
</system.serviceModel>
</configuration>
```

Creating the ATM Client

Create a proxy for the Bill Pay Service.

1. Start the Generic Electric Bill Payment Service.

2. Start the Consumer Banking Service.

3. Open a Visual Studio command prompt and navigate to the directory
   `C:\WCFHandsOn\Chapter5\Before\PartIII\`.

4. Enter the following at the command prompt:

   ```
   "C:\Program Files\Microsoft SDKs\Windows\v1.0\Bin\SvcUtil.exe "
   ➥ http://localhost:8080/ConsumerBankingService/
   ➥ BillPay /out:ConsumerBankingBillPay.cs
   ```
   SvcUtil.exe will generate two files, `ConsumerBankingBillPay.cs` and
   `output.config`.

`ConsumerBankingBillPay.cs` will contain a generated proxy class for the Bill Pay service. `Output.config` contains the configuration information for your service; rename the file `app.config`.

5. Open Visual Studio, and create a new project in the current solution. Create a new Windows Forms application in `C:\WCFHandsOn\Chapter5\Before\PartIII`.

6. Name the project ATMClient.

7. Add a reference to `System.ServiceModel`.

8. Add a reference to `System.Transactions`.

9. Add a reference to `System.Runtime.Serialization`.

10. Add the file `ConsumerBankingBillPay.cs` to the project.

11. Add the file `App.Config` to the project.

12. Open Form 1, and add three text boxes, three labels, and a button.

13. The text boxes should be named `tbAccountNumber`, `tbElectricAccountNumber`, and `tbAmountToPay`.

14. One label should be to the left of each text box, identifying the type of information that should be entered: `Account Number`, `Electric Account Number`, and `Amount to Pay`.

15. The button should be named `btnPayBill` and have the caption `Pay Bill`.

16. Double-click on the button and modify the `btnPayBill_Click` method to resemble the following:

```
private void btnPayBill_Click(object sender, EventArgs e)
{
  ConsumerBankingBillPaymentProxy proxyBillPay =
    new ConsumerBankingBillPaymentProxy("BillPay");
    bool success = proxyBillPay.PayBill(
      Convert.ToInt32(tbAccountNumber.Text),
      Convert.ToInt32(tbElectricAccountNumber.Text),
      Convert.ToDecimal(tbAmountToPay.Text));

  if (success)
  {
    System.Windows.Forms.MessageBox.Show(
      "Bill payment successful!");

  }
  else
```

```
    {
      System.Windows.Forms.MessageBox.Show(
        "Bill payment failed!");
    }
  }
}
```

Testing the Solution

You are now ready to test your solution end-to-end.

1. Start the Electric Company Service.

2. Start the Banking Service.

3. Start the ATM Client.

4. Enter 12345 in the Bank Account Number field.

5. Enter 67890 in the Electric Account Number field.

6. Enter 50 in the Amount to Pay field.

7. Press the button. Your screen should resemble what's shown in Figure 5.5.

FIGURE 5.5　Screenshot of the resulting test.

Our consumer is at an ATM, requesting an action on the part of the bank, specifically to pay the consumer's electric bill.

The bank consumes a service from the electric company to perform the transaction.

Summary

The chapter was introduced with a discussion of reliability in the development of connected systems. Whether it's dealing with lost connections, lost messages, or interrupted transactions, it should be clear that reliability is critical for your distributed applications.

WCF clearly provides solutions to these issues through its Reliable Sessions, Queued Messaging, and Transaction-related functionality.

And as distributed applications often cross vendor OS boundaries, this chapter has shown how WCF provides support for reliability and transactions across all platforms that support the industry specifications.

5

Legacy Integration

The Windows Communication Foundation provides a unified messaging API that provides the capability to integrate with a number of legacy technologies. This chapter focuses on WCF's capability to integrate with COM+ and non-WCF–based MSMQ applications.

COM+ Integration

The Windows Communication Foundation provides a rich environment for creating distributed applications. If you have a substantial investment in component-based application logic hosted in COM+, you can use WCF to extend your existing logic rather than having to rewrite it. A common scenario is when you want to expose existing COM+ or Enterprise Services business logic through Web services.

When an interface on a COM+ component is exposed as a Web service, the specification and contract of those services are determined by an automatic mapping to be performed at application initialization time. The conceptual model for this mapping is as follows:

- There is one service for each exposed COM class.

- The contract for the service is derived directly from the selected component's interface definition.

- The operations in that contract are derived directly from the methods on the component's interface definition.

- The parameters for those operations are derived directly from the COM interoperability type corresponding to the component's method parameters.

- Default addresses and transport bindings for the service are provided in a service configuration file, but those can be reconfigured as required.

NOTE

The contracts for the generated WCF services are tied to the underlying COM+ application's interfaces and configuration.

Modifying the COM+ component methods automatically results in an updated service when the application is next started. However, a modification to the number of interfaces does *not* automatically update the available services. In the latter scenario you will need to rerun the COM+ Service Model Configuration tool (`ComSvcConfig.exe`).

The authentication and authorization requirements of the COM+ application and its components continue to be enforced when used as a Web service. If the caller initiates a Web service transaction, components marked as transactional enlist within that transaction scope.

The steps that are required to expose a COM+ component's interface as a Web service without modifying the component are as listed here:

1. Determine whether the COM+ component's interface can be exposed as a Web service.

2. Select an appropriate hosting mode.

3. Use the COM+ Service Model Configuration tool (`ComSvcConfig.exe`) to add a Web service for the interface.

Supported Interfaces

There are some restrictions on the type of interfaces that can be exposed as a Web service. Here's the list of restricted interface types:

- Interfaces that accept object references as parameters

- Interfaces that accept types that are not compatible with the .NET Framework COM Interop conversions

- Interfaces for applications that have application pooling enabled when hosted by COM+

- Interfaces of components that are marked as "private" to the application

- COM+ infrastructure interfaces

- Interfaces from the system application

- Interfaces from managed components that have not been added to the Global Assembly Cache

Selecting the Hosting Mode

As is stated in the documentation, COM+ can expose Web services in one of the following three hosting modes.

COM+-Hosted

The Web service is hosted within the application's dedicated COM+ server process (Dllhost.exe). This mode requires the application to be explicitly started before it can receive Web service requests. The COM+ options Run as an NT Service or Leave Running When Idle can be used to prevent idle shutdown of the application and its services. This mode has the benefit that it provides both Web service and DCOM access to the server application.

Web-Hosted

The Web service is hosted within a Web server worker process. This mode does not require the COM+ application to be active when the initial request is received. If the application is not active when this request is received, it is automatically activated before the request is processed. This mode also provides both Web service and DCOM access to the server application, but it incurs a process hop for Web service requests. This typically requires the client to enable impersonation. In WCF, this can be done with the SetSspiSettings method and the Impersonation enumeration value.

> **NOTE**
>
> Like other WCF services, the security settings for the exposed service are administered through roles and web host settings. COM+ application roles are enforced, whereas traditional DCOM security settings such as the DCOM machine-wide permissions settings are not.

Web-Hosted In-Process

The Web service and the COM+ application logic are hosted within the Web server worker process. This provides automatic activation of the web hosted mode, without incurring the process hop for Web service requests. The disadvantage is that the server application cannot be accessed through DCOM.

Using the COM+ Service Model Configuration Tool

The mechanism used to configure COM+ interfaces to be exposed as Web services is the COM+ Service Model Configuration command-line tool (ComSvcConfig.exe). This tool will be used in this exercise to expose a COM+ business object.

The calling convention and command-line switches for ComSvcConfig are as shown here:

```
ComSvcConfig.exe /install ¦ /list ¦ /uninstall [/application:<ApplicationID
➥ ¦ ApplicationName>] [/contract<ClassID ¦ ProgID ¦ *,InterfaceID ¦
➥ InterfaceName ¦ *>] [/hosting:<complus ¦ was>] [/webSite:<WebsiteName>]
➥ [/webDirectory:<WebDirectoryName>] [/mex] [/id] [/nologo] [/verbose] [/help]
```

> **NOTE**
>
> You must be an administrator on the local computer to use ComSvcConfig.exe.

Table 6.1 describes the modes that can be used with `ComSvcConfig.exe`.

TABLE 6.1 Modes That Can Be Used with `ComSvcConfig.exe`

Option	Description
/install	Configures a COM+ interface for Service Model integration. Short form /i.
/uninstall	Removes a COM+ interface from Service Model integration. Short form /u.
/list	Queries for information about COM+ applications and components that have interfaces that are configured for Service Model integration. Short form /l.

Table 6.2 describes the options that can be used with `ComSvcConfig.exe`.

TABLE 6.2 Flags That Can Be Used with `ComSvcConfig.exe`

Option	Description
/application:< *ApplicationID* ¦ *ApplicationName* >	Specifies the COM+ application to configure. Short form /a. Specifies the COM+ component and interface to configure as a service contract.
/contract:< *ClassID* ¦ *ProgID* ¦ *, *InterfaceID* ¦ *InterfaceName* ¦ * >	Short form /c. Although the wildcard character (*) can be used when you specify the component and interface names, we recommend that you do not use it, because you may expose interfaces you did not intend to. Specifies whether to use the COM+ hosting mode or the Short form /h.
/hosting:< *complus* ¦ *was* > web hosting mode.	Using the COM+ hosting mode requires explicit activation of the COM+ application. Using the web hosting mode allows the COM+ application to be automatically activated as required. If the COM+ application is a library application, it runs in the Internet Information Services (IIS) process. If the COM+ application is a server application, it runs in the D11host.exe process.
/webSite:< *WebsiteName* >	Specifies the website for hosting when web hosting mode is used (see the /hosting flag). Short form /w. If no website is specified, the default website is used.
/webDirectory:< *WebDirectoryName* >	Specifies the virtual directory for hosting when web hosting is used (see the /hosting flag). Short form /d.
/mex	Adds a Metadata Exchange (MEX) service endpoint to the default service configuration to support clients that want to retrieve a contract definition from the service. Short form /x.

TABLE 6.2   Continued

Option	Description
/id	Displays the application, component, and interface information as IDs. Short form /k.
/nologo	Prevents ComSvcConfig.exe from displaying its logo. Short form /n.
/verbose	Output additional tool progress information. Short form /v.
/help	Displays the usage message. Short form /?.

Exposing a COM+ Component as a WCF Web Service

For this series of exercises, we will focus on a scenario in which a school has an application for registering students. The business logic for this application resides within an Enterprise Service component hosted in COM+. It is desired to expose that component as a Web service that can be consumed both by the school's web-based management application and from a Windows Forms-based smart client application.

This exercise involves taking a legacy COM+ component and exposing it as a Windows Communication Foundation service that is consumed in the smart client application. To begin, let's examine the COM+ component to understand its functionality.

Open C:\WCFHandsOn\ExerciseFive\Before\ComPlus.sln.

Within the Student Management Application, open the Students.cs file.

Because this component is being placed within COM+, it contains several attributes. The ApplicationName attribute identifies the name of the COM+ application into which this class will be installed. Also note that the interface and the class are attributed with GUIDs, and the class is attributed with a ProgID. Even though this was written in .NET, the component will be living in COM+, with the attributes providing the information necessary for consistent interop registration (See Listing 6.1).

As you go through the file, you'll see that this class provides methods to the user interface for additions, updates, and retrieval of basic student information. For additions and updates, the changes are sent to an MSMQ using the System.Messaging libraries. In this exercise, we will be invoking only the Add method.

LISTING 6.1   The COM+ Code

```csharp
using System;
using System.Collections.Generic;
using System.Text;
using System.Messaging;
using System.Data;
using System.Data.SqlClient;
using System.EnterpriseServices;
using System.Runtime.InteropServices;


[assembly: ApplicationName("StudentManagement")]
[assembly: ApplicationID("2C9BFEA5-005D-4218-8C69-A03F6B9037BA")]
[assembly: ApplicationActivation(ActivationOption.Server)]
[assembly: ApplicationAccessControl(false, AccessChecksLevel =
➥ AccessChecksLevelOption.Application)]

namespace WCFHandsOn
{
    [Guid("1C5677EC-8046-4c5b-B361-BA354CFA3DB3")]
    public interface IStudents
    {
        string Add(string FirstName, string LastName, string PhoneNumber);
        bool Update(string ID, string FirstName, string LastName,
➥ string PhoneNumber);
        bool Delete(string ID);
        System.Collections.ArrayList GetAll();

    }

    [Guid("E4A5D9FD-3B5F-4598-9E42-EC8D1329EE9D")]
    [ProgId("StudentManagement.Students")]
    public class Students : ServicedComponent, IStudents
    {
        public Students() { }

        string qPath = @"FormatName:DIRECT=OS:w2k3ee\private$\school";
        public string Add(string FirstName, string LastName, string PhoneNumber)
        {
            //For any modifications to the data, we place the
            //request on a queue.

            //First we generate a System.Messaging.Message for the queue.
            try
            {
```

LISTING 6.1   Continued

```
            string ID = Guid.NewGuid().ToString();
            Student student = new Student(ID, FirstName, LastName,
➥ PhoneNumber);

            System.Messaging.Message msg = GenerateAddMessage(student);

            //Now we place it to the queue
            PlaceMessageOnQueue(msg);

            //This is a new student, return the GUID
            return ID;
        }
        catch (Exception e)
        {
            //Debug.WriteLine(e.ToString());
            throw e;
        }
    }
}
```

In this exercise, we would like to expose the IStudents interface from the COM+ application as a Web service using WCF. This provides the capability to take this legacy component and allow it to provide a WS-* compatible service that can be consumed on any platform.

Because the component is a legacy application, it is already in COM+. To expose this as a WCF service, the ComSvcConfig utility will be used.

Before using this utility, you will need to create a virtual directory in which to house the service:

1. Choose Start, Programs, Administrative Tools, Internet Information Services Manager.

2. Create a directory at C:\WCFHandsOn\ChapterFive\Before\ StudentManagementService.

3. Navigate to the Default Website and create a new Virtual Directory. The alias for the directory should be WCFHandsOn_StudentMgmt, and the path for the directory is C:\WCFHandsOn\ChapterFive\Before\StudentManagementService.

You are now ready to use the ComSvcConfig utility:

1. Open a Visual Studio command prompt.

2. Navigate to C:\ WCFHandsOn\ChapterFive\Before\.

3. Run the following script to register the COM+ Component:

```
C:\Windows\Microsoft.NET\Framework\v2.0.50727\ComSvcConfig.exe /i
➥ /application:StudentManagement
➥ /contract:StudentManagement.Students,Students* /hosting:was
➥  /webDirectory:WCFHandsOn_StudentMgmt /mex
```

Reviewing this script, you can see that you are configuring the IStudents interface on the component from the StudentManagement application, hosting using IIS (versus COM+) and will be placing the files in the virtual directory WCFHandsOn_StudentMgmt.

If you now navigate to the virtual directory created earlier, you'll find that a service—named after the interface—was generated and placed in this directory.

To test the service, open the service file in your web browser. Navigate to http://localhost/WCFHandsOn_StudentMgmt/Service.svc. If the service is functioning properly, a page is displayed that identifies the location of the WSDL and how to consume the service (see Figure 6.1).

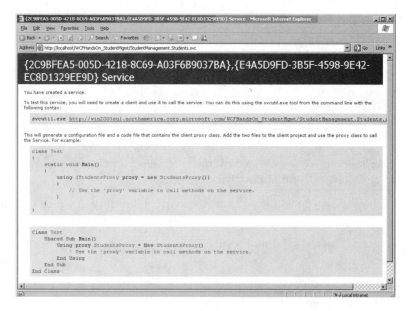

FIGURE 6.1   Web page generated from the metadata of your new service.

Record the address of the WSDL specified in the first box on this screen, because it is used in the next part of the exercise.

Referencing in the Client

The next step in the exercise is to connect the service to a Windows Forms client. It should be noted that although in this exercise you will be using a Windows Form client to consume the service, it is for the sake of simplicity. This service can be consumed in any application that can consume services:

1. Open a Visual Studio command prompt.

2. Run the following script to generate proxy code and a configuration file that can be used:

```
"C:\Program Files\Microsoft SDKs\Windows\v1.0\Bin\svcutil.exe "
➡ http://localhost/WCFHandsOn_StudentMgmt/StudentManagement.Students.svc
➡  /out:proxy.cs
```

This generates two files, `proxy.cs` and `output.config`.

3. Add both files to the Teacher Application project.

4. Rename the configuration file to `Web.Config` for the website and `App.Config` for the Windows Forms application.

The application provides an interface that provides the capability to add new students to the system.

5. Open the `Proxy.cs` file and note the name of the new proxy class that was created. This class will be referenced in your code to execute the service.

6 Modify the code for the button to add the students using the new Web service. This is done by adding the following code to the `btnUpdate_Click` method:

```
StudentsProxy proxy = new StudentsProxy("Students");
string result = proxy.Add(tbFirstName.Text,tbLastName.Text,tbPhone.Text);
MessageBox.Show("Student Added!");
proxy.Close();
```

7. Enter a first name, last name, and phone number into the application, and click Add to test it (see Figure 6.2). A message box will be displayed identifying that the student has been added.

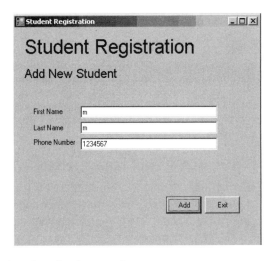

FIGURE 6.2   The user interface for the sample.

You've successfully integrated with a Legacy COM+ application, and established a plat-form-agnostic, WS-*–compliant service. You've also used the SvcUtil utility to generate proxies from this new service, and connected to a Windows Forms client.

Integrating with MSMQ

In this next exercise, we will be creating an MSMQ service. The service will send requests to a queue. A separate queue monitor application monitors this queue and retrieves the messages placed there by the service.

This scenario is not a "pure" Windows Communication Foundation scenario, meaning that one of the systems is using WCF and the other is using System.Messaging. In scenar-ios in which WCF will be used with native MSMQ applications, the MsmqIntegrationBinding is used.

The client application is a WCF application that uses the MsmqIntegrationBinding binding to send a durable, transactional message to the queue. The client application has a dummy contract to mimic invoking a service operation, but, in reality, the message is consumed by an MSMQ service.

The service contract is IStudents, which defines a one-way service that is suitable for use with queues. An MSMQ message does not have an Action header. It is not possible to map different MSMQ messages to operation contracts automatically. Therefore, there can be only one operation contract. If you want to define more than one operation contract for the service, the application must provide information as to which header in the MSMQ message (for example, the Label or correlationID) can be used to decide which opera-tion contract to dispatch.

The MSMQ message also does not contain information in itself as to which headers are mapped to the different parameters of the operation contract. So there can be only one parameter in the operation contract. The parameter is of type Generic MsmqMessage (MsmqMessage<T>) and contains the underlying MSMQ message. The type T in the generic MsmqMessage (MsmqMessage<T>) represents the data that is serialized into the MSMQ message body. In this exercise, a Student type is serialized into the MSMQ message body.

> **NOTE**
>
> If you want to map different headers of the MSMQ message (for example, Label or correlationID) to different parameters, the MessagePropertyAttribute attribute has to be used.

Creating a WCF Service That Integrates with MSMQ

In our scenario, we will be creating a Windows Communication Foundation service that provides the capability to update student records. We will begin by creating a struct that will contain the student information used when adding or updating a record. This will be followed by the creation of our service and client.

The resulting solution will yield in a WCF client that posts a message to MSMQ that is later received by a non-WCF application monitoring the queue. That receiver application would take the message and process it as appropriate.

Creating the Request

During this exercise, you will be sending requests to manipulate student information. A student is represented by four pieces of information, studentID, firstName, lastName, and phoneNumber. If we add or update a student, we will need to pass all of this information in the body of the message. You will create a new project that contains a struct containing this information, and this project will later be referenced by your service and client:

1. Create a new class library project named StudentManagementRequest in
   C:\Apps\WCFHandsOn\ExerciseThree\Before.

2. Delete Class1.cs.

3. Using Solution Explorer, add a new class named StudentManagementRequest.cs.

4. Populate the new class with the following code to create the struct:

```
using System;
using System.Collections.Generic;
using System.Text;

name
{
    [
    p                          ementRequest
    {
                               );
                               ;

                               er;
    }
}
```

Creating the Service

Now you will create the service for the scenario:

1. Create a new class library project named Service in C:\WCFHandsOn\ChapterFive\
   Before.

2. Delete Class1.cs.

3. Add a reference to System.Messaging.

4. Add a reference to System.Configuration.

5. Add a reference (project reference) to your project StudentManagementRequest.

6. Using Solution Explorer, add a new Application Configuration file.

   The configuration for our MSMQ Integration service is listed in the following code. In addition, the file also contains the name of our MSMQ queue. For this exercise, we're using a private queue on the local machine named school.

   Modify your App.Config file to resemble the following:

```
<?xml version="1.0" encoding="utf-8" ?>
<configuration>
    <appSettings>
        <!-- use appSetting to configure MSMQ queue name -->
        <add key="queueName" value=".\private$\school" />

</appSettings>
</configuration>
```

7. Using Solution Explorer, add a new class to the project named Program.cs.

   Open Program.cs, and the following namespaces to the top of the file:

```
using System;
using System.Collections.Generic;
using System.Text;
using System.Messaging;
using System.Configuration;
using System.Data;
using System.Data.SqlClient;
namespace WCFHandsOn
```

8. Next you will create the core of the service. Because this service is queue based, the code reads the queueName specified in the App.Config file and checks for its existence. If the queue does not exist, the queue is created. Note that the second parameter sent to MessageQueue.Create is true. This will create the queue as a transactional queue.

   The queue will be receiving messages at various times. To be notified of the arrival of a message, the code also assigns an event handler. The ProcessMessage method of this class will be called when new messages are received.

   The BeginReceive function is then called, and as its name implies, the MessageQueue object is monitoring for received messages.

   In Program.cs, enter the following code:

```
static void Main(string[] args)
{
    // Create a transaction queue using System.Messaging API
```

```
// You could also choose to not do this and instead create the
// queue using MSMQ MMC--make sure you create a transactional queue
if (!MessageQueue.Exists(ConfigurationManager.AppSettings["queueName"]))
  MessageQueue.Create(ConfigurationManager.AppSettings["queueName"], true);
//Connect to the queue
MessageQueue Queue = new
➥ MessageQueue(ConfigurationManager.AppSettings["queueName"]);

Queue.ReceiveCompleted += new ReceiveCompletedEventHandler(ProcessMessage);
Queue.BeginReceive();
Console.WriteLine("Message Processing Service is running");
Console.ReadLine();
}
```

The ProcessMessage method is called when the queue begins receiving a message. The message body is read and assigned to a StudentManagementRequest object and the message label inspected.

9. The server determines which action to take from the message label. Based on the text of the label, corresponding methods on the object are called.

Enter the following code:

```
public static void ProcessMessage(Object source,
    ReceiveCompletedEventArgs asyncResult)
{
    try
    {
        // Connect to the queue.
        MessageQueue Queue = (MessageQueue)source;

        // End the asynchronous receive operation.
        System.Messaging.Message msg =
➥ Queue.EndReceive(asyncResult.AsyncResult);

        msg.Formatter = new System.Messaging.XmlMessageFormatter(new
➥ Type[] { typeof(StudentManagementRequest) });

        StudentManagementRequest request =
➥ (StudentManagementRequest)msg.Body;
        switch (msg.Label)
        {
            case "Add":
                AddStudent(request);
                break;
            case "Update":
```

```
                                UpdateStudent(request);
                                break;
                        case "Delete":
                        DeleteStudent(request.studentID);
                                break;
                        default:
                        Console.WriteLine("The label of the message is of
    an unknown type or not set correctly.");
                                break;


                }

                Queue.BeginReceive();
            }
            catch (System.Exception ex)
            {
                Console.WriteLine(ex.Message);
            }
        }
}
```

10. The `ProcessMessage` function interprets the message and calls one of three methods: `UpdateStudent`, `AddStudent`, or `DeleteStudent`.

Enter the following code to process these requests:

```
private static void UpdateStudent(StudentManagementRequest s)
{
    Console.WriteLine("Just updated student {0} {1} with a phone number of
 {2}", s.firstName, s.lastName, s.phoneNumber);

}

private static void AddStudent(StudentManagementRequest s)
{
    Console.WriteLine("Just added student {0} {1} with a phone number of
 {2}", s.firstName, s.lastName, s.phoneNumber);
}

private static void DeleteStudent(string studentID)
{
    Console.WriteLine("Just deleted student with ID {0}", studentID);
}
```

Creating the Client

1. Open the Client application found at C:\WCFHandsOn\ChapterFive\Before.

2. Add a reference to System.ServiceModel.

3. Using Solution Explorer, add a reference to the StudentManagementRequest project.

4. Using Solution Explorer, add a new class called StudentManagementProxy.cs.

   This class will contain the service interface and proxy code we will use to communicate to MSMQ.

   Add the following code, taking note of several key pieces:

```
using System.ServiceModel;
using System.ServiceModel.Channels;

namespace WCFHandsOn
{

    [System.ServiceModel.ServiceContractAttribute(Namespace =
➡  "http://Microsoft.ServiceModel.Samples")]
    public interface IStudentManagement
    {

        [System.ServiceModel.OperationContractAttribute(IsOneWay = true,
➡ Action = "*")]
        void ProcessMessage(MsmqMessage<StudentManagementRequest> msg);
    }

    public interface IStudentManagementChannel : IStudentManagement,
➡  System.ServiceModel.IClientChannel
    {
    }

    public partial class StudentManagementProxy :
➡ System.ServiceModel.ClientBase<IStudentManagement>,
➡ IStudentManagement
    {

        public StudentManagementProxy()
        {
        }

        public StudentManagementProxy(string configurationName)
            :
                base(configurationName)
```

```
        {
        }

        public StudentManagementProxy(System.ServiceModel.Binding binding)
            :
                base(binding.Name.ToString())
        {
        }

        public StudentManagementProxy(System.ServiceModel.EndpointAddress
    address, System.ServiceModel.Binding binding)
            :
                base(address.Uri.ToString(), binding.Name.ToString())
        {
        }

        public void ProcessMessage(MsmqMessage<StudentManagementRequest> msg)
        {
            base.InnerProxy.ProcessMessage(msg);
        }
    }
}
```

The service interface provides only a single operation, `ProcessMessage`. This may seem odd, because you're aware that there are `Add`, `Update`, and `Delete` operations on the client. For MSMQ integration, you define a single operation that takes an MSMQ message of a particular type as a parameter. In this case, the parameter is the `StudentManagmentRequest` defined earlier.

It is not possible to map different MSMQ messages to operation contracts automatically. As a result, there can be only one operation contract. As seen earlier, the server determines which action to take based on the message label. Thus, as you will see with the `ProcessMessage` operation is called by the client, the `StudentManagementRequest` object will be populated and the operation to be performed will be identified by the `Label` property.

NOTE

It is possible to define more than one operation contract for the service; however, it requires additional effort because you must identify which header in the MSMQ message (`correlationID`, `Label`, and so on) can be used to dispatch.

5. Using Solution Explorer, add a new Application Configuration file.

   Populate the configuration file as shown in the following code:

```
<?xml version="1.0" encoding="utf-8" ?>
<configuration xmlns="http://schemas.microsoft.com/.NetConfiguration/v2.0">
```

```
<system.serviceModel>

    <client>
        <!-- Define NetProfileMsmqEndpoint -->
        < endpoint name="StudentManagementEndpoint"
          address="msmq.formatname:DIRECT=OS:.\private$\school"
          binding="msmqIntegrationBinding"
                    bindingConfiguration="Binding2"
                    contract="WCFHandsOn.IStudentManagement, Client">
        </endpoint>
    </client>

    <bindings>
        <msmqIntegrationBinding>
            <binding name="Binding2">
                <security mode="None" />
            </binding>
        </msmqIntegrationBinding>
    </bindings>

</system.serviceModel>

</configuration>
```

6. Modify the Program.cs file to include the following code:

```
static void Main(string[] args)
{
    AddStudent("Marc", "Mercuri", "123456789");

    Console.WriteLine();
    Console.WriteLine("Press <ENTER> to terminate client.");
    Console.ReadLine();
}

private static void AddStudent(string firstName, string lastName, string
➥ phoneNumber)
{
    using (StudentManagementProxy p = new
➥ StudentManagementProxy("StudentManagementEndpoint"))
      {

                using (TransactionScope tx = new
➥TransactionScope(TransactionScopeOption.Required))
                {
```

```
                StudentManagementRequest request = new
➡ StudentManagementRequest();

                MsmqMessage<StudentManagementRequest> msg = new
➡MsmqMessage<StudentManagementRequest>(request);

                request.firstName = firstName;
                request.lastName = lastName;
                request.phoneNumber = phoneNumber;
                request.studentID = System.Guid.NewGuid().ToString();
                msg.Label = "Add";
                msg.Body = request;
                p.ProcessMessage(msg);

                //Commit the transaction
                tx.Complete();

        }


    }


}
```

This code will generate a message and send it to the queue. Our service will extract the message and enter the data into the database.

Testing

With the code completed, it is time to test the application.

1. Using Solution Explorer, right-click on the Client project and select Debug, New Instance.

2. Using Solution Explorer, right-click on the Service project and select Debug, New Instance.

The client and server consoles will be displayed. The information entered in the client's Main method will send a message to the queue using WCF, which will be received by the waiting service using MSMQ.

To verify that the message was transferred, check the window of the Service application. The information provided should be displayed as in Figure 6.3.

FIGURE 6.3 Service output indicating that a student has been added.

Summary

Very few Enterprises are starting from scratch; they've evolved over time and have multiple legacy systems in place. Leveraging the information and business processes in these legacy applications is of keen interest to the Enterprise. In this chapter we reviewed how well WCF works with two of the most popular types of legacy applications, those that utilize COM+ and MSMQ.

CHAPTER **7**

Interoperability

The Windows Communication Foundation (WCF) provides a unified API for messaging. Chapter 6, "Legacy Integration," shows how to use the WCF to integrate with Microsoft technologies such as MSMQ and COM+. In addition to integration, the Windows Communication Foundation also provides significant benefits when it comes to interoperability. This chapter examines how to interoperate with other systems using Web services.

WCF is part of WinFX and has a dependency on the .NET Framework 2.0. For scenarios in which a client is running an earlier version of the framework, using a non-.NET language, and/or running on another platform, interoperability becomes critical.

This chapter demonstrates interoperability in several varieties seen in the real world. The first example involves creating a WCF client that connects to an existing ASMX Web service. Next, you will create a simple WCF service, and then create both a WCF client and an ASMX client to consume it.

An Overview of Interoperability

One of the key values of SOAP is that it is platform agnostic. Regardless of the platform a system may be on, there is potential to readily interoperate with others.

WS-I Basic Profile

Through the .NET Framework and the SOAP Toolkit, Microsoft provided the capability to create Web services hosted within Internet Information Server (IIS). The more common .NET Web services were stored in files with an extension of .ASMX and are commonly referred to as ASMX Web Services. Other software companies created their own

Web service implementations, and subtle differences among the implementations caused some challenges when they attempted to interoperate using other tools, languages, and/or platforms.

The Web Services Interoperability Organization (http://www.ws-i.org) creates, promotes, and supports generic protocols for the interoperable exchange of messages between Web services. The WS-I has published a profile of what must be supported for basic interoperability.

To facilitate interoperability, the WS-I established a working group for a basic profile that could be implemented to support interoperability across implementations and platforms. The Basic Profile 1.1 (BP1.1) consists of implementation guidelines recommending how a set of core Web services specifications should be used together to develop interoperable Web services. The guidelines address technologies that cover the following areas:

- **Messaging**—The exchange of protocol elements, usually over a network, to affect a Web service

- **Description**—The enumeration of the messages associated with a Web service, along with implementation details

- **Discovery**—Metadata that enables the advertisement of a Web service's capabilities

- **Security**—Mechanisms that provide integrity and privacy

BP 1.1 covers the following core Web services standards and provides constraints and clarifications to these base specifications, along with conventions about how to use them together, with the goal of promoting interoperability:

- SOAP 1.1
- WSDL 1.1
- UDDI 2.0
- XML 1.0 (Second Edition)
- XML Schema Part 1: Structures
- XML Schema Part 2: Data types
- RFC2246: The Transport Layer Security Protocol Version 1.0
- RFC2459: Internet X.509 Public Key Infrastructure Certificate and CRL Profile
- RFC2616: Hypertext Transfer Protocol 1.1
- RFC2818: HTTP over TLS Transport Layer Security
- RFC2965: HTTP State Management Mechanism
- The Secure Sockets Layer Protocol Version 3.0

To provide Basic Profile support in WCF is very straightforward, just specify the `basicHttpBinding`.

WS-*

Although having Basic Profile 1.1 is important, as the name implies, it is for basic interoperability. The functionality provided by the BP 1.1 does not address many of the needs critical to many real-world scenarios, particularly around security and reliability.

Much of what is supported by the Basic Profile is designed for services that have direct connections with their clients. In the emerging world of service-oriented Enterprises, messages no longer go strictly from a service at Point A to a client at Point B; instead a message may make multiple "hops" en route to its destination. This requires involvement not at the transport level, but at the message level.

When examining security in the Basic Profile, the channel between the server and its clients can be secured using SSL. Both server and client authenticity can be validated using certificates. This is typically acceptable when you're interacting in a scenario in which there is a 1:1 connection. But what about when you send a message, that message is then routed, and eventually it reaches its recipient? There could be any number of hops in between client and service, and the path is likely to vary based on various criteria (traffic, SLAs, and so on). Although setting up transport security with BP 1.1 could be done, this process now introduces a number of intermediaries and introduces the potential risk that messages could be modified en route. There was a need for standards around key areas in this space, with major focuses on security, transactions, and reliability. OASIS has been the leader in driving these standards.

OASIS (Organization for the Advancement of Structured Information Standards) is a not-for-profit, international consortium that drives the development, convergence, and adoption of e-business standards. Microsoft, IBM, SAP AG, Nokia, Oracle, and BEA Systems are among the 600 organizations that participate in OASIS.

The participants in OASIS have put forward a number of standards for advanced Web services, referred to collectively as the WS-* specifications. In WCF, WS-* interoperability includes platform-agnostic support of reliable sessions, transactions, transport security, and SOAP security.

To provide WS-* support to your services, use the `wsHttpBinding`.

Custom Bindings

In addition to the bindings provided with Windows Communication Foundation out of the box, WCF provides the capability to create custom bindings in the configuration file. This allows tremendous flexibility when interoperating with business partners, legacy systems, third-party products, and commercial Web services when the standard bindings provided do not meet the requirements of your service. Custom binding elements could be used, for example, to enable the use of new transports or encoders at a service endpoint. Custom bindings are used to define a binding from a set of binding elements.

Creating Proxy Code for Use in Client Applications

To facilitate the creation of client proxies, Windows Communication Foundation includes the Service MetaData Utility tool (`SvcUtil.exe`). This tool generates service model code from metadata documents and metadata documents from service model code.

In this chapter, we'll use the tool to generate proxy code to be used in interop scenarios. At least up until the February CPT release, it does not automatically map the preconfigured bindings by name. Instead, custom bindings will be created that map to the requirements of the service.

SvcUtil.exe is called using the command line and parameters found in Table 7.1.

Svcutil [*options*] [*metadataPath** ¦ *assemblyPath** ¦ *metadataUrl**]

TABLE 7.1   Parameters for SvcUtil.exe

Argument	Description
`metadataPath`	Path to metadata document that contains the contract to import into code (.wsdl, .xsd, .wspolicy, or .wsmex).
`AssemblyPaths`	Path to the assembly file that contains service contracts to export to metadata.
`metadataUrl`	URL to the running Web service that provides metadata for download through WS-Metadata Exchange or Http-Get.
Option	Description.
`/directory:<directory>`	Directory to create files in. Default: The current directory. Short form: `/d`.
`/out:<file>`	File name for the generated code. Default: Derived from the service name or target namespace of the schema document. Short form: `/o`.
`/target:[code ¦ metadata]`	Specifies the output to be generated by the tool. Default: Inferred from input. Short form: `/t`.
`/validate`	Instructs the tool to validate all service endpoints in associated config files. (A config file is loaded when an exe for the config file is passed to the tool.) Short form: `/w`.
`/config:<file1 [, file2]>`	Instructs the tool to generate a configuration file. If only one filename is given, that is the name of the output file. If two filenames are given, the first file is an input configuration file whose contents are merged with the generated configuration and written out into the second file.
`/noConfig`	Do not create a config file.
`/svcutilConfig:<file>`	Custom configuration file to use in place of the app config file. Allows the user to change metadata configuration without altering global app config settings.
`/language:<language>`	Specifies the programming language to use for code generation. Values: `c#`, `cs`, `csharp`, `vb`, `vbs`, `visualbasic`, `vbscript`, `js`, `jscript`, `javascript`, `vj#`, `vjs`, `vjsharp`, `c++`, `mc`, or `cpp`, or provide a fully qualified name for a class implementing `System.CodeDom.Compiler.CodeDomProvider`. Default: csharp. Short form: `/l`.

TABLE 7.1   Continued

Argument	Description
/compile	Compiles generated code into an assembly.
	Short form: /c.
/namespace:<"*schema*	Specifies the CLR namespace to associate with a schema target
namespace", "*CLR namespace*">	namespace.
	Default: Derived from the target namespace of the schema document.
	Short form: /n.
/reference:<*file path*>	References the specified assembly files.
	Short form: /r.
/nostdlib	Do not reference standard library (mscorlib.dll).
/referenceCollectionType:<*type list*>	Fully qualified or assembly-qualified type name to exclude from referenced types.
	Short form: /rct.
/excludeType:<*type*>	Fully qualified or assembly-qualified type name to exclude from referenced types.
	Short form: /et.
/async	Generate asynchronous method signatures.
	Short form: /a.
/internal	Generate classes marked internal (default: generate public classes).
	Short form: /i.
/typedMessages	Instructs the tool to generate code that uses typed messages.
	Short form: /tm.
/useXmlSerializer	Instructs the tool to generate code that uses XmlSerializer.
	Short form: /uxs.
/importXmlType	Import non-Data Contract types as IXmlSerializable.
	Short form: /ixt.
/enableDataBinding	Implement INotifyPropertyChanged interface on all XmlFormatter types to enable data binding.
	Short form: /edb.
/dataContractOnly	Instructs the tool to operate on Data Contract types only. Service Contracts will not be processed.
	Short form: /dconly.
/noLogo	Suppress the copyright and banner message.
/help	Displays command syntax and options for the tool.
	Short form: /?.

7

Creating a WCF Client for an ASMX Service with SvcUtil.exe

The following exercise creates a client for a very simple ASMX Web service with one web method, InteropHelloWorld. As you can see in the Listing 7.1, this method for that service receives a string parameter, Name, and returns a string value.

LISTING 7.1   ASMX Service Code

```
using System;
using System.Web;
using System.Web.Services;
using System.Web.Services.Protocols;

[WebService(Namespace = "http://tempuri.org/")]
[WebServiceBinding(ConformsTo = WsiProfiles.BasicProfile1_1)]
public class Service : System.Web.Services.WebService
{
    public Service () {

    }

    [WebMethod]
    public string InteropHelloWorld(string Name) {
        return "Hello " + Name + ", you've just interop'd.";
    }
}
```

This service was deployed using the setup script available at the publisher's website.

Validate that the service is online and create the proxy for the client:

1. Test that the service is online and available.

2. Open Internet Explorer, and navigate to the following URL:

   http://localhost/WCFHandsOn/InteropHelloWorld/Service.asmx

   This should display a page that lists the operations supported by this service. If this does not display, validate that the virtual directory exists and is pointing to C:\Apps\WCFHandsOn\Chapter7\PartI\After\InteropHelloWorld.

3. In the open solution, add a new project.

4. Create a new Windows Console application in C:\WCFHandsOn\Chapter7\Before\ PartI\WCFClient.

5. Add a reference to System.ServiceModel.

   Now you will create the proxy for the ASMX service.

6. Open a Visual Studio command prompt and navigate to the directory
   C:\WCFHandsOn\Chapter7\Before\PartI\WCFClient.

   Enter the following at the command prompt:

   ```
   "C:\Program Files\Microsoft SDKs\Windows\v1.0\Bin\SvcUtil.exe "
   ➥ http://localhost/WCFHandsOn/InteropHelloWorld/Service.asmx?wsdl
   ➥/out:proxy.cs
   ```

   SvcfUtil.exe generates two files, proxy.cs and output.config.

   Proxy.cs contains a generated proxy class for the ASMX Web service. Output.
   config contains the configuration information for the service that can be inserted
   into the application configuration file (App.config).

7. Within Visual Studio, add both of these files to the WCFClient project.

8. Rename output.config to App.config.

9. Using Solution Explorer, open the App.config file and examine its contents:

   ```xml
   <?xml version="1.0" encoding="utf-8"?>
   <configuration>
       <system.serviceModel>
           <client>
               <endpoint
   ➥ address="http://localhost/WCFHandsOn/InteropHelloWorld/Service.asmx"
                   bindingConfiguration="ServiceSoap" binding="customBinding"
                   name="ServiceSoap" contract="ServiceSoap" />
               <endpoint
   ➥address="http://localhost/WCFHandsOn/InteropHelloWorld/Service.asmx"
                   bindingConfiguration="ServiceSoap12" binding="customBinding"
                   name="ServiceSoap1" contract="ServiceSoap" />
           </client>
           <bindings>
               <customBinding>
                   <binding name="ServiceSoap">
                       <textMessageEncoding maxReadPoolSize="64"
   ➥maxWritePoolSize="16" messageVersion="Soap11Addressing1"
   ➥writeEncoding="utf-8" />
                       <httpTransport manualAddressing="false"
   ➥maxBufferPoolSize="524288" maxMessageSize="65536"
   ➥allowCookies="false" authenticationScheme="Anonymous"
   ➥bypassProxyOnLocal="false" ostNameComparisonMode="StrongWildcard"
   ➥mapAddressingHeadersToHttpHeaders="true"
   ➥proxyAuthenticationScheme="Anonymous" realm="" transferMode="Buffered"
   ➥unsafeConnectionNtlmAuthentication="false" useDefaultWebProxy="true" />
                   </binding>
                   <binding name="ServiceSoap12">
   ```

```
                        <textMessageEncoding maxReadPoolSize="64"
➥ maxWritePoolSize="16" messageVersion="Default"
➥writeEncoding="utf-8" />
                        <httpTransport manualAddressing="false"
➥maxBufferPoolSize="524288"maxMessageSize="65536"
➥allowCookies="false" authenticationScheme="Anonymous"
➥bypassProxyOnLocal="false" hostNameComparisonMode="StrongWildcard"
➥mapAddressingHeadersToHttpHeaders="true"
➥proxyAuthenticationScheme="Anonymous" realm=""
➥transferMode="Buffered" unsafeConnectionNtlmAuthentication="false"
➥useDefaultWebProxy="true" />
                </binding>
            </customBinding>
        </bindings>
    </system.serviceModel>
</configuration>
```

Notice that SvcUtil has created the two endpoints ServiceSoap and ServiceSoap1 for InteropHelloWorldService.

If you look at the WSDL document exposed by our ASMX service, you'll notice that these endpoints were created from the port information in that document:

```
<wsdl:service name="Service">
<wsdl:port name="ServiceSoap" binding="tns:ServiceSoap">
<soap:address location=
➥ "http://localhost:8000/WCFHandsOn/InteropHelloWorld/Service.asmx" />
</wsdl:port>
<wsdl:port name="ServiceSoap12" binding="tns:ServiceSoap12">
<soap12:address location=
➥ "http://localhost:8000/WCFHandsOn/InteropHelloWorld/Service.asmx" />
</wsdl:port>
</wsdl:service>
```

Also note that SvcUtil.exe creates custom bindings for each of these. Each of these displays a number of the configurable attributes that can be set, highlighting the flexibility available for interoperability.

10. From Solution Explorer, open proxy.cs.

This is the proxy class created by SvcUtil.exe. Notice that the ServiceSoap interface was defined, containing a single operation that was in our service.

In addition, a ServiceSoapProxy class was created. Note that in addition to several constructors for the class, the class also implements the ServiceSoap interface. When InteropHelloWorld is called on the proxy, it will call the operation on our ASMX service:

```
[System.ServiceModel.ServiceContractAttribute(Namespace=
➥"http://Samples.Microsoft.Com/")]
public interface ServiceSoap
{

    [System.ServiceModel.OperationContractAttribute(Action=
➥"http://Samples.Microsoft.Com/InteropHelloWorld",
➥ReplyAction="http://Samples.Microsoft.Com/InteropHelloWorld")]
    string InteropHelloWorld(string Name);
}

public interface ServiceSoapChannel : ServiceSoap,
➥System.ServiceModel.IClientChannel
{
}

public partial class ServiceSoapProxy :
➥System.ServiceModel.ClientBase<ServiceSoap>, ServiceSoap
{

    public ServiceSoapProxy()
    {
    }

    public ServiceSoapProxy(string endpointConfigurationName) :
            base(endpointConfigurationName)
    {
    }

    public ServiceSoapProxy(string endpointConfigurationName,
➥string remoteAddress) :
            base(endpointConfigurationName, remoteAddress)
    {
    }

    public ServiceSoapProxy(string endpointConfigurationName,
➥System.ServiceModel.EndpointAddress remoteAddress) :
            base(endpointConfigurationName, remoteAddress)
    {
    }

    public ServiceSoapProxy(System.ServiceModel.Binding binding,
➥System.ServiceModel.EndpointAddress remoteAddress) :
            base(binding, remoteAddress)
    {
```

7

```
    }

    public string InteropHelloWorld(string Name)
    {
        return base.InnerProxy.InteropHelloWorld(Name);
    }
}
```

Now that we have a proxy class and a configuration file, let's write the code to call the service.

11. Using Solution Explorer, open the file `Program.cs`.

12. Add using `System.ServiceModel;` to the top of the `Program.cs` file:

```
using System;
using System.Collections.Generic;
using System.Text;
using System.ServiceModel;
```

13. Modify the `Main` method in `Program.cs` to include the lines listed in bold in the following code:

```
static void Main(string[] args)
{
    ServiceSoapProxy proxy = new ServiceSoapProxy("ServiceSoap");
    Console.WriteLine("What's your name?");
    string name = Console.ReadLine().ToString();
    Console.WriteLine(proxy.InteropHelloWorld(name));

    Console.WriteLine("-----------------------");
    Console.WriteLine("Press Any Key To Exit");
    Console.ReadLine();

}
```

Note that we chose to reference the constructor that takes a `configurationName` as a parameter. At runtime, the name provided will be used to reference the appropriate endpoint, bindings, and contract in the `App.config` file.

14. Using Solution Explorer, right-click the WCFClient project and select Set as Startup Project.

15. From the Debug menu, select Start Debugging.

After you've entered your name at the prompt, the client will call out to the ASMX service and display the result.

Creating a WCF Service and WCF/ASMX Clients

In this next example, we'll look at interoperability from the other direction. Here we'll create a WCF service and then create ASMX and WCF clients that utilize it.

Creating the WCF Service

To create the new service project, follow these steps:

1. Open Visual Studio and add a new project. Create a new Windows Console application in C:\WCFHandsOn\Chapter7\Before\PartII\InteropHelloWorld2.

2. Add a Reference to System.ServiceModel.

3. Using Solution Explorer, open the file Program.cs.

4. Add using System.ServiceModel; to the top of the Program.cs file:

```
using System;
using System.Collections.Generic;
using System.Text;
using System.ServiceModel;
```

This service will expose one operation, InteropHelloWorld. First, add the interface IInteropHelloWorld to the Program.cs file.

5. Enter the following interface code:

```
namespace Samples.Microsoft.Com
{
   [ServiceContract]
   public interface IInteropHelloWorld
   {
     [OperationContract]
     string InteropHelloWorld(string Name);
   }
```

With the interface defined, we can now add the class for our service that implements it.

6. Enter the following code for the class:

```
public class InteropHelloWorld2 : IInteropHelloWorld
{

    public string InteropHelloWorld(string Name)
    {
       return "Hello " + Name + ", you've just interop'd.";
    }
}
```

For this exercise, the service will not be be hosted within IIS, but is instead hosted inside of a Windows Console application.

This requires the creation of a `ServiceHost` object to instantiate the service. When a new `ServiceHost` is being created, information regarding the service is provided in the constructor. In this case, we specify the `serviceType` that maps to the name of the class:

```
static void Main(string[] args)
{
    ServiceHost service =
      new ServiceHost(typeof(InteropHelloWorld2));
    service.Open();
    Console.WriteLine("Service is available.");
    Console.ReadLine();
}
```

Now we can create the `App.config` file and configure the service.

7. Add a new application configuration file to the project and accept the default name of `App.config`.

Open the configuration file and enter the information for the service's abc's (address, binding, contract) as seen here:

```
<?xml version="1.0" encoding="utf-8" ?>
<configuration>
  <appSettings>
    <!-- use appSetting to configure base address provided by host -->
    <add key="baseAddress" value=
➥"http://localhost:8080/WCFHandsOn/InteropHelloWorld2" />
  </appSettings>
  <system.serviceModel>
      <services>
          <service type="Samples.Microsoft.Com.InteropHelloWorld2">
              <endpoint address="" binding="basicHttpBinding"
➥contract="Samples.Microsoft.Com.IInteropHelloWorld"/>
          </service>
      </services>
  </system.serviceModel>
</configuration>
```

Our base address is specified in the `appSettings` setting, because we'll be setting this value inside of the code. Also note that the endpoint for this service is being made available on port 8000 of the local server. Because this is running in a console application and is not hosted within Internet Information Server, we've specified a separate port. Note that we are using the `basicHttpBinding`, and the service will be compliant with BP 1.0. Finally, note that the contract consists of the concatenation of the namespace and the interface for the service.

With the application configuration file populated, the project is now ready to be compiled.

8. Build the project.

9. Using Windows Explorer, navigate to the `InteropHelloWorld2.exe` just created and run the `InteropHelloWorld2` service. The full path to the file is `C:\WCFHandsOn\Chapter7\PartII\Before\InteropHelloWorld2\InteropHelloWorld2\bin\Debug\InteropHelloWorld2.exe`.

With the service now running, it is available for clients to query it for metadata and interact with it.

Creating a WCF Client

Creating the WCF client for our WCF service will be virtually identical to how we created the WCF client for the ASMX service in the initial example, using `SvcUtil.exe`:

1. Create a new Windows Console project in `C:\WCFHandsOn\Chapter7\PartII\Before\WCFClient\`.

2. Add a Reference to `System.ServiceModel`.

3. Open Visual Studio.NET Command Window.

4. Execute the `SvcUtil.exe` utility, pointing it at the WCF Service. This creates both a proxy and a configuration file to be used by the client:

   ```
   "c:\Program Files\Microsoft SDKs\Windows\v1.0\Bin\SvcUtil.exe "
   ➥http://localhost:8000/WCFHandsOn/InteropHelloWorld2 /out:proxy.cs
   ```

5. Using Solution Explorer, add `proxy.cs` to the WCFClient project.

6. Using Solution Explorer, add `output.config` to the WCFClient project.

7. Rename `output.config` to `App.config`.

8. Place the following code in the Main method in the `Program.cs` file:

   ```
   static void Main(string[] args)
   {
      Console.WriteLine("Please enter your name");
      string Name = Console.ReadLine();
      InteropHelloWorldProxy hello = new InteropHelloWorldProxy();
   ```

```
Console.WriteLine("This is the message from the WCF Web Service:");
Console.WriteLine(hello.InteropHelloWorld(Name));
Console.ReadLine();
}
```

9. In Solution Explorer, right-click the project and select Debug, Start New Instance.

The client will prompt you for your name. It will then call the `InteropHelloWorld` service and write the response to the console.

Creating an ASMX Client

There are very straightforward ways to enable ASMX clients to access your Windows Communication Foundation service. For projects in which clients will have both the .NET Framework 2.0 and WinFX installed, `SvcUtil.exe` can be used, as it was in the preceding example. In that environment, the `proxy.cs` and `output.config` files generated by `SvcUtil.exe` could be added to an ASMX Web service project without modification.

If your service consumers do not have WinFX installed and/or are unfamiliar with `SvcUtil.exe`, they can consume your BP 1.1 Web service as they would any other Web service, using the Add Web Reference functionality built into Visual Studio. The WCF service exposes both WSDL and MEX metadata, which can be used by programmers and development tools to consume the service on any platform.

This example looks at creating an ASMX client for the WCF Service created earlier.

Rather than using `SvcUtil.exe`, which requires the .NET Framework 2.0, as mentioned earlier, we'll use the Add Web Reference facility that's been available since the initial release of VisualStudio.NET. It is important to note that while WCF requires the .NET Framework 2.0, clients for BP 1.1 services can be created using earlier versions of the framework and Visual Studio.NET:

1. Within VisualStudio.NET, create a new website at `C:\WCFHandsOn\Chapter7\PartII\Before\`.

2. Name the website `ASMXClient`.

3. In Solution Explorer, add a web reference to the project.

   When prompted in the Add Web Reference dialog, enter the following URL:

   `http://localhost:8000/WCFHandsOn/InteropHelloWorld2?wsdl`

   With the web reference set, the ASMX client will now utilize the service within its own service. When the project was created, a file `Service.cs` was added to the project in the project's `App_Code` directory.

4. Open this file now and add the code for the `WebMethod`:

```
using System;
using System.Web;
```

```
using System.Web.Services;
using System.Web.Services.Protocols;

[WebService(Namespace = "http://Samples.Microsoft.Com/")]
[WebServiceBinding(ConformsTo = WsiProfiles.BasicProfile1_1)]
public class Service : System.Web.Services.WebService
{
    public Service () {

    }

    [WebMethod]
    public string HelloWorldAsmx(string Name) {
        localhost.InteropHelloWorld2 hello = new
➥localhost.InteropHelloWorld2();

        return "This is the message from the WCF Web Service" +
➥hello.InteropHelloWorld(Name); ;
    }

}
```

5. Using the Internet Information Services Manager, create a new virtual directory. The new directory should use the alias WCFHandsOn_ASMXClient and the local path for the virtual directory should point to the location of the project, C:\ WCFHandsOn\ Chapter7\PartII\Before\ASMXClient.

6. Using VisualStudio.NET, build the project.

7. Finally, test the "client" ASMX service by opening Internet Explorer and entering the URL for the service, http://localhost/WCFHandsOn/ASMXClient/Service.asmx.

Creating a WCF Client for a Lotus Notes Domino Server Web Service

Lotus Notes is a popular messaging and collaboration tool sold by IBM. Lotus Notes Domino is a Web server designed to publish information from the Notes data stores. Domino currently provides the capability to expose BP 1.1 services for use in client applications and scenarios such as B2B. Although Lotus does have client development tools, Enterprises that utilize notes and the consumers of Domino-published content may want to develop clients using Visual Studio.NET. This is particularly desirable for many companies looking to take advantage of technologies such as the Windows Presentation Foundation (WPF) for a rich user experience, the Workflow Foundation (WF) for workflow, and the Windows Communication Foundation (WCF) for secure, reliable, transacted services.

Fortunately, it's very easy to do this using the same `SvcUtil.exe` utility that we used in the preceding exercise.

Microsoft has a licensed copy of Domino Server running the site http://www.msdomino. net that is populated with content by our colleague Gary Devendorf. Gary is a Technical Evangelist at Microsoft, and he helps customers interoperate between Lotus and Microsoft technologies, or migrate over from Lotus to Microsoft solutions.

On this site, Gary has created a Web service for placing orders over the web that are deposited in a Lotus Notes database. This Web service provides operations that allow you to place an order, change the status of an order, and check the status of an order.

In this exercise, you will create a console application that places an order and immediately checks the status of that order. It then calls the service to change the status to Approved and check the status once more. As part of testing the service, we'll go to a Domino web page to validate that the order has been received and has been approved.

Creating the WCF client for our WCF service will be virtually identical to how we created the WCF client for the ASMX and WCF services in the earlier example, using `SvcUtil.exe`. In this case, we're using the same approach to interoperate with a non-Microsoft Web server:

1. Create a new Windows Console project in C:\WCFHandsOn\Chapter7\PartIII\ Before\DominoClient\.

2. Add a Reference to `System.ServiceModel`.

3. Add using `System.ServiceModel`; to the top of the `Program.cs` file:

   ```
   using System;
   using System.Collections.Generic;
   using System.Text;
   using System.ServiceModel;
   ```

4. Open Visual Studio.NET Command Window.

5. Execute the `SvcUtil.exe` utility with a reference to the service to create a proxy and configuration file to be used by the client.

   ```
   "c:\Program Files\Microsoft SDKs\Windows\v1.0\Bin\SvcUtil.exe "
   ➥http://www.msdomino.net/msorders.nsf/create_order?WSDL/out:proxy.cs
   ```

6. Using Solution Explorer, add `proxy.cs` to the DominoClient project.

7. Using Solution Explorer, add `output.config` to the DominoClient project.

8. Rename `output.config` to App.config.

9. Open the `App.config` file.

   In the client section, add a name for our endpoint that we will use when calling the service by adding the text name=`"DominoOrders"`:

```
<client>
    <endpoint name="DominoOrders" address=
➥http://www.msdomino.net:80/msorders.nsf/create_order?OpenWebService
➥bindingConfiguration="DominoSoapBinding" binding="customBinding"
➥contract="Update" />
</client>
```

You will now enter the core information for the client. Although there are sample values in the following code for the parameters (such as weight, shipAddress, shipCity), feel free to modify these.

10. Place the following code in the Main method in the Program.cs file:

```
static void Main(string[] args)
{
        using (UpdateProxy proxy = new UpdateProxy("DominoOrders"))
        {
            string customerID = "1";
            string orderDate = "10/25/2006";
            string weight = "50";
            string freight = "100";
            string shipAddress = "1 main street";
            string shipCity = "Redmond";
            string shipCountry = "USA";
            string amount = "500.00";

            //PLACE THE ORDER
            int orderID = proxy.NEWORDER(customerID,orderDate,amount,freight,
➥ weight, shipAddress, shipCity, shipCountry);
            System.Console.WriteLine("Your order was placed. Your order ID
➥for future reference is " + orderID.ToString());


            //CHECK THE STATUS OF THE ORDER
            System.Console.WriteLine("-------------------------------------
➥-------------------------------------");
            string status = proxy.CHECKSTATUS(orderID);
            System.Console.WriteLine();
            System.Console.WriteLine("Your order status is: " + status);

            //APPROVE THE ORDER
            System.Console.WriteLine("-------------------------------------
➥-------------------------------------");
            System.Console.WriteLine("Cancelling order#" +
orderID.ToString());
            proxy.CHANGESTATUS(orderID, "Approved");
```

```
                    // CHECK THE ORDER STATUS, TO SEE IF IT'S APPROVED
                    System.Console.WriteLine("-------------------------------------
➡-------------------------------------");
                    status = proxy.CHECKSTATUS(orderID);
                    System.Console.WriteLine();
                    System.Console.WriteLine("Your order status is: " + status);
                    System.Console.ReadLine();


            }
    }
```

11. In Solution Explorer, right-click the project and select Debug, Start New Instance.

    The client will then print out several messages in the console window, identifying that the order has been placed, the order ID assigned by the server, and that the order has been approved. Make a note of the order ID, because we will now validate that this was accepted on the server.

    Go to the page on Domino to view the results.

12. Open your web browser and navigate to http://www.msdomino.net/msorders.nsf.

    You should see a web page with several links on it, as shown in Figure 7.1.

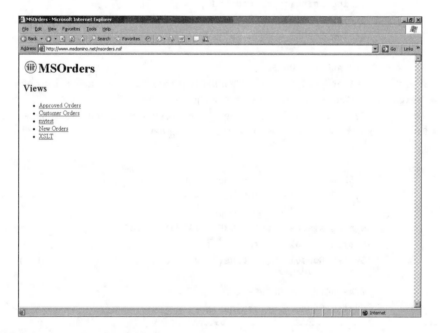

FIGURE 7.1 Lotus Domino Web server page.

13. Click on the Approved Orders link. This will display a list of all the orders that have been approved (see Figure 7.2).

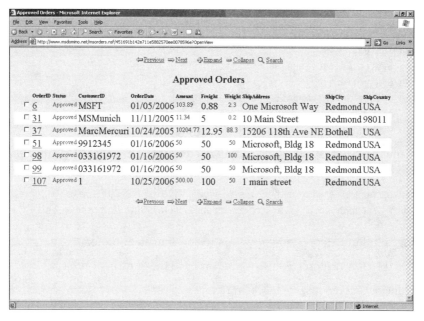

FIGURE 7.2   The Approved Orders page on the Lotus Domino Web server.

14. To complete the exercise, validate that your order ID is included in the list of approved orders.

Two for the Road

We've just done interop with a product from IBM; now let's continue down the path by creating test clients for two other major players, Oracle and Sun Microsystems. From a technology perspective, we'll be revisiting what we've done earlier in the chapter. So why include this in the book? To underscore the value that standards—and a tool such as WCF that is built on standards—provide to the Enterprise. The SvcUtil.exe utility reads platform-agnostic WSDL files, and we're up and interoperating in minutes.

Create a WCF Client to Test Interop with Sun Microsystems

Sun Microsystems has a public-facing Web service that can be used for interoperability testing. This service is provided solely for interoperability tests, so its operations are limited to "echoes." These operations will receive a value of a particular type, such as a string, and will return that same value to the caller:

1. Create a new Windows Console project in `C:\WCFHandsOn\Chapter7\PartIV\Before\SunClient\`.

2. Add a Reference to `System.ServiceModel`.

3. Add using `System.ServiceModel;` to the top of the `Program.cs` file:

```
using System;
using System.Collections.Generic;
using System.Text;
using System.ServiceModel;
```

4. Open Visual Studio.NET Command Window.

5. Execute the `SvcUtil.exe` utility with a reference to the service to create a proxy and configuration file to be used by the client.

```
"c:\Program Files\Microsoft SDKs\Windows\v1.0\Bin\SvcUtil.exe "
➥ http://soapinterop.java.sun.com/round2/base?WSDL /out:proxy.cs
```

6. Using Solution Explorer, add `proxy.cs` to the SunClient project.

7. Using Solution Explorer, add `output.config` to the SunClient project.

8. Rename `output.config` to `App.config`.

   Open `App.config` and add a name for the endpoint. Add the text `name="SunInterop"` to the endpoint element in the client section of the config file:

```
<client>
    <endpoint name="SunInterop" address=
➥"http://soapinterop.java.sun.com:80/round2/base"
        bindingConfiguration="RIBaseBinding" binding="customBinding"
        contract="RIBaseIF" />
</client>
```

9. Place the following code in the Main method in the `Program.cs` file:

```
static void Main(string[] args)
{
    RIBaseIFProxy proxy = new RIBaseIFProxy("SunInterop");
    System.Console.WriteLine("Enter in the phrase to tell Sun");
    String repeatText = System.Console.ReadLine();
    System.Console.WriteLine();
    System.Console.WriteLine("Sun - if you can understand me, repeat after me:"
➥ + repeatText);
    System.Console.WriteLine("Sun says:" + proxy.echoString(repeatText));
    System.Console.ReadKey();
}
```

10. In Solution Explorer, right-click the project and select Debug, Start New Instance.

The client will prompt you for some text to send to Sun. It will then contact the Sun Web service, which will return that same text.

Create a WCF Client to Test Interop with Oracle Application Server

Oracle has a public-facing website and services for its Oracle Application Server 10g. There is a public-facing Web service attached to the product. This service has several username and password controlled services; however, we're interested only in testing interop. In this exercise, we'll create a client that tests the `GetVersion` operation, which does not require a username or password:

1. Create a new Windows Console project in `C:\WCFHandsOn\Chapter7\PartIV\ Before\OracleClient\`.

2. Add a Reference to `System.ServiceModel`.

3. Add using `System.ServiceModel;` to the top of the `Program.cs` file:

   ```
   using System;
   using System.Collections.Generic;
   using System.Text;
   using System.ServiceModel;
   ```

4. Open Visual Studio.NET Command Window.

5. Execute the `SvcUtil.exe` utility with a reference to the service to create a proxy and configuration file to be used by the client.

   ```
   "C:\Program Files\Microsoft SDKs\Windows\v1.0\Bin\Svcutil.exe " /out:proxy.cs
   ➥http://messenger.oracle.com/xms/webservices?WSDL
   ```

6. Using Solution Explorer, add `proxy.cs` to the OracleClient project.

7. Using Solution Explorer, add `output.config` to the OracleClient project.

8. Rename `output.config` to `App.config`.

   Open `App.config` and add a name for the endpoint. Add the text name="OracleInterop" to the endpoint element in the client section of the config file:

   ```
   <client>
      <endpoint name="OracleInterop" address=
   ➥"http://notify.multimodeinc.com/xms/webservices"
         bindingConfiguration="XMSServerBinding" binding="customBinding"
         contract="XMSServerPortType" />
   </client>
   ```

9. Place the following code in the `Main` method in the `Program.cs` file:

```
static void Main(string[] args)
{
    //ORACLE
    XMSServerPortTypeProxy proxy = new
➥XMSServerPortTypeProxy("OracleInterop");
    string version = proxy.getVersion();
    System.Console.WriteLine("The version of Oracle currently running is:"
➥ + version);
    System.Console.ReadLine();
}
```

10. In Solution Explorer, right-click the project and select Debug, Start New Instance.

The client will connect to the Oracle service, return the current version, and display it in the console.

Summary

In this chapter we saw the power of Windows Communication Foundation to interoperate. WCF on the server provides the capability to interoperate with various systems, and this chapter showed how to interoperate with ASMX services in client and service scenarios. In addition, we saw examples for how to interoperate with existing technologies from Microsoft, Oracle, IBM, and Sun.

CHAPTER **8**

Custom Transports

The Windows Communication Foundation is highly extensible. A particularly important way in which it can be extended is by adding support for transport protocols that are not among the several it already accommodates. A *transport protocol* is any protocol that provides for the requirements of the Open Systems Interconnection reference model's Transport layer and all the layers below that one. Extensions to the Windows Communication Foundation to support additional transport protocols are all but invisible to developers using the Windows Communication Foundation to construct applications. They can continue to use the familiar Windows Communication Foundation programming model, yet have their applications communicate via the newly supported transport protocols. This chapter shows how to extend the Windows Communication Foundation by adding support for sending messages via Internet mail protocols.

The Windows Communication Foundation Channel Layer

In the Windows Communication Foundation, protocols are implemented as channels. Data passes through channels, and the channel arranges the data passing through it in accordance with the protocols that the channel implements:

```
public interface IChannel : ICommunicationObject,
IDisposable
{
    IChannelManager Manager { get; }
}
```

Channels are communication objects. Communication objects provide methods for being opened and closed:

```
public interface ICommunicationObject : IDisposable
{
    CommunicationState State { get; }
    event EventHandler Closed;
    event EventHandler Closing;
    event EventHandler Faulted;
    event EventHandler Opened;
    event EventHandler Opening;

    void Abort();
    IAsyncResult BeginClose(
        AsyncCallback callback, object state);
    IAsyncResult BeginClose(
        TimeSpan timeout, AsyncCallback callback, object state);
    IAsyncResult BeginOpen(
        AsyncCallback callback, object state);
    IAsyncResult BeginOpen(
        TimeSpan timeout, AsyncCallback callback, object state);
    void Close();
    void Close(TimeSpan timeout);
    void EndClose(IAsyncResult result);
    void EndOpen(IAsyncResult result);
    void Open();
    void Open(TimeSpan timeout);
}
```

The Windows Communication Foundation distinguishes between input channels and output channels. Output channels can send messages:

```
public interface IOutputChannel : IChannel, ICommunicationObject, IDisposable
{
    EndpointAddress RemoteAddress { get; }
    Uri Via { get; }

    IAsyncResult BeginSend(
        Message message,
        AsyncCallback callback,
        object state);
    IAsyncResult BeginSend(
        Message message,
        TimeSpan timeout,
        AsyncCallback callback,
        object state);
    void EndSend(IAsyncResult result);
```

```
    void Send(Message message);
    void Send(Message message, TimeSpan timeout);
}
```

Input channels provide methods for receiving messages from them:

```
public interface IInputChannel : IChannel, ICommunicationObject, IDisposable
{
    EndpointAddress LocalAddress { get; }

    IAsyncResult BeginReceive(AsyncCallback callback,
        object state);
    IAsyncResult BeginReceive(TimeSpan timeout,
        AsyncCallback callback,
        object state);
    IAsyncResult BeginTryReceive(TimeSpan timeout,
        AsyncCallback callback,
        object state);
    IAsyncResult BeginWaitForMessage(TimeSpan timeout,
        AsyncCallback callback,
        object state);
    Message EndReceive(IAsyncResult result);
    bool EndTryReceive(IAsyncResult result, out Message message);
    bool EndWaitForMessage(IAsyncResult result);
    Message Receive();
    Message Receive(TimeSpan timeout);
    bool TryReceive(TimeSpan timeout, out Message message);
    bool WaitForMessage(TimeSpan timeout);
}
```

Input channels are retrieved from listeners:

```
public interface IChannelListener<TChannel> :
        IChannelListener,
        IChannelManager,
        ICommunicationObject,
        IDisposable
            where TChannel : class, System.ServiceModel.IChannel
{
    TChannel AcceptChannel();
    TChannel AcceptChannel(TimeSpan timeout);
    IAsyncResult BeginAcceptChannel(AsyncCallback callback,
        object state);
    IAsyncResult BeginAcceptChannel(TimeSpan timeout,
        AsyncCallback callback, object state);
    TChannel EndAcceptChannel(IAsyncResult result);
}
```

Channels are created using channel factories:

```
public interface IChannelFactory<TChannel> :
    IChannelFactory, IChannelManager, ICommunicationObject, IDisposable
{
    TChannel CreateChannel(EndpointAddress to);
    TChannel CreateChannel(string address);
    TChannel CreateChannel(Uri address);
    TChannel CreateChannel(EndpointAddress to, Filter filter, int priority);
}
```

Channel factories are created by binding elements, which also create listeners:

```
public abstract class BindingElement
{
    protected BindingElement();
    protected BindingElement(BindingElement other);

    public virtual IChannelFactory BuildChannelFactory(
        ChannelBuildContext context);
    public virtual IChannelFactory<TChannel> BuildChannelFactory<TChannel>(
        ChannelBuildContext context);
    public virtual IChannelListener<TChannel> BuildChannelListener<TChannel> (
        ChannelBuildContext context
        ) where TChannel : IChannel
    public virtual bool CanBuildChannelFactory<TChannel>(
        ChannelBuildContext context);
    public virtual bool CanBuildChannelListener<TChannel> (
            ChannelBuildContext context
        ) where TChannel : IChannel
    public abstract BindingElement Clone();
    public virtual T GetCapabilities<T>(
        IList<BindingElement> lowerBindingElements
        ) where T : class;
    public abstract ChannelProtectionRequirements GetProtectionRequirements();
    public virtual ChannelProtectionRequirements GetProtectionRequirements(
        CustomBinding context);
}
```

Binding elements that can create transport protocol channels and transport protocol listeners are transport binding elements:

```
public interface ITransportBindingElement
{
    string Scheme { get; }
}
```

Transport protocol listeners use message encoders to assemble the streams of bytes they receive into messages:

```
public abstract class MessageEncoder
{
    protected MessageEncoder();

    public abstract string ContentType { get; }
    public abstract string MediaType { get; }
    public abstract MessageVersion MessageVersion { get; }

    public virtual bool IsContentTypeSupported(string contentType);
    public abstract Message ReadMessage(
        ArraySegment<byte> buffer, BufferManager bufferManager);
    public abstract Message ReadMessage(
        Stream stream, int maxSizeOfHeaders);
    public override string ToString();
    public abstract void WriteMessage(Message message, Stream stream);
    public ArraySegment<byte> WriteMessage(
        Message message, int maxMessageSize, BufferManager bufferManager);
    public abstract ArraySegment<byte> WriteMessage(
        Message message,
        int maxMessageSize,
        BufferManager bufferManager,
        int messageOffset);
}
```

Message encoders are created by message encoder factories:

```
public abstract class MessageEncoderFactory
{
    protected MessageEncoderFactory();

    public abstract MessageEncoder Encoder { get; }
    public abstract MessageVersion MessageVersion { get; }

    public virtual MessageEncoder CreateSessionEncoder();
}
```

Message encoder factories are created by binding elements that are message encoding binding elements:

```
public interface IMessageEncodingBindingElement
{
    AddressingVersion AddressingVersion { get; }

    MessageEncoderFactory CreateMessageEncoderFactory();
}
```

Bindings are composed of a collection of binding elements, exactly one of which must be a transport binding element, and one or more of which must be message encoding binding elements:

```
public class CustomBinding :
    Binding,
    ISecurityCapabilities,
    IBindingManualAddressing
{
    public CustomBinding();
    public CustomBinding(Binding binding);
    public CustomBinding(IEnumerable<BindingElement> bindingElements);
    public CustomBinding(params BindingElement[] bindingElements);
    public CustomBinding(string configurationName);
    public CustomBinding(
        string name,
        string ns,
        params BindingElement[] bindingElements);
    public BindingElementCollection Elements { get; }
    public override string Scheme { get; }

    public override BindingElementCollection CreateBindingElements();
    protected void Initialize();
    protected override void OnApplyConfiguration(string configurationName);
}
```

A service is made available by adding an endpoint for that service to a service host, an endpoint being a unique address, and a service contract together with a binding:

```
public class ServiceHost : ServiceHostBase
{
    protected ServiceHost();
    public ServiceHost(object serviceInstance, params Uri[] baseAddresses);
    public ServiceHost(Type serviceType, params Uri[] baseAddresses);

    public ServiceAuthorization Authorization { get; }
    public ServiceCredentials Credentials { get; }
    public virtual ServiceDescription Description { get; }
    public virtual ReflectedContractCollection ReflectedContracts { get; }
    public virtual Type ServiceType { get; }
    public virtual object SingletonInstance { get; }

    public ServiceEndpoint AddServiceEndpoint(
        Type implementedContract, Binding binding, string address);
    public ServiceEndpoint AddServiceEndpoint(
        Type implementedContract, Binding binding, Uri addressUri);
```

```
    protected void Initialize();
    protected virtual void OnApplyConfiguration(ServiceElement serviceSection);
    protected override void OnClose(TimeSpan timeout);
    protected virtual void OnCreateDescription();
    protected override void OnCreateListeners();
    protected override void OnEndClose(IAsyncResult result);
    protected void ReleasePerformanceCounters();
}
```

Service hosts are communication objects, which, as shown earlier, provide methods for being opened and closed:

```
public abstract class ServiceHostBase :
    CommunicationObject, IExtensibleObject<ServiceHostBase>
{
    protected ServiceHostBase(params Uri[] baseAddresses);
    protected ServiceHostBase(UriSchemeKeyedCollection baseAddresses);
    public UriSchemeKeyedCollection BaseAddresses { get; }
    public TimeSpan CloseTimeout { get; set; }
    protected override TimeSpan DefaultCloseTimeout { get; }
    protected override TimeSpan DefaultOpenTimeout { get; }
    public EndpointListenerCollection EndpointListeners { get; }
    public IExtensionCollection<ServiceHostBase> Extensions { get; }
    public TimeSpan OpenTimeout { get; set; }
    public event EventHandler<UnknownMessageReceivedEventArgs>
      UnknownMessageReceived;
    protected override void OnAbort();
    protected override IAsyncResult OnBeginClose(
        TimeSpan timeout, AsyncCallback callback, object state);
    protected override IAsyncResult OnBeginOpen(
    TimeSpan timeout, AsyncCallback callback, object state);
    protected override void OnClose(TimeSpan timeout);
    protected abstract void OnCreateListeners();
    protected override void OnEndClose(IAsyncResult result);
    protected override void OnEndOpen(IAsyncResult result);
    protected virtual void OnInitialize();
    protected override void OnOpen(TimeSpan timeout);
}
```

When the host of a service is opened, it uses the elements of each service's binding to create listeners. That process is actually undertaken on behalf of the service host by an element of the Windows Communication Foundation called the ServiceDescription, which creates, in effect, a description of the service from the specifications constituted by the address, the binding, and the contract. During the process, the characteristics of the contract are compared with the capabilities of the binding elements. For example, if the contract describes a message exchange pattern by which the service will be replying directly to requests from its clients, the communication protocols specified in the bindings must accommodate such a pattern. The binding elements' generic CanBuildChannelListener<TChannel>() method assists the ServiceDescription in comparing the capabilities of the listeners implied by the binding with the definition of the contract.

After the description of the service is complete, the Windows Communication Foundation's Dispatcher takes over. It calls the methods of the listener created from the first binding element's listener factory to retrieve an input channel, from which it will read messages that it will pass on to the code of the service. That listener in turn calls the methods of the listener created from the next binding element's listener factory to retrieve an input channel, and so on, until the request for an input channel reaches a listener that implements a transport protocol. That listener will listen for messages, typically using a socket. When a message arrives, the listener does two things. First, it uses the message encoder that must have been specified among the elements of the service's binding to assemble the bytes it has received from the socket into a coherent message. Then, it creates an input channel if it has not done so already, adds the message to that channel, and passes the input channel to the listener that requested it.

After some reflection on all of the foregoing, it should become apparent that adding support for an additional transport protocol to the Windows Communication Foundation really means adding a new transport binding element to the Channel Layer. That transport binding element would provide channel factories for creating transport channels that support the protocol. The new binding element would also provide listeners that support the protocol. With the new transport binding element, one could create a binding for a service endpoint that could send and receive messages via the transport protocol.

Adding Support for Additional Transport Protocols

The following steps show how to extend the Windows Communication Foundation by adding a transport binding element for sending and receiving messages via Internet mail protocols. The starting point is a simple application that uses TCP, a protocol that the Windows Communication Foundation already supports. After a binding element for the Internet mail protocols has been added to the Windows Communication Foundation's Channel Layer, the application will be modified to use those protocols instead.

Adding support for additional transports to the Windows Communication Foundation is made considerably easier by a sample that does just that, which is among the samples in the Microsoft Windows SDK referred to in the introduction. The sample adds support for the User Datagram Protocol (UDP).

See the Initial Solution Work

To see the solution work using one of the built-in transports, do the following:

1. Download the code for this book, and copy the code associated with this chapter to the folder C:\WCFHandsOn. The code is all in a folder called CustomTransport and

contains a single Visual Studio solution with the same name. After the code has
been copied, there should be a folder that looks like the one shown in Figure 8.1.

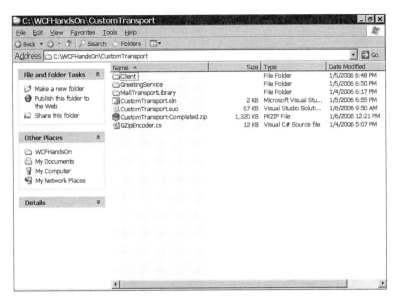

FIGURE 8.1   Custom transport solution folder.

2. Open the solution `C:\WCFHandsOn\CustomTransport\CustomTransport.sln` in Visual
   Studio 2005. The solution incorporates three projects. One project is for building a
   Greeting Service, which receives and displays a greeting from a client. A second
   project is for building a client of the Greeting Service. The third project, the
   MailTransportLibrary project, is currently empty. The Windows Communication
   Foundation extensions for communicating via Internet mail protocols will be added
   to that project.

3. Confirm that the startup project property of the solution is configured as shown in
   Figure 8.2.

4. Start debugging the solution. The console application of the Greeting Service should
   appear, followed by the console application of its client. When the console of the
   Greeting Service shows some activity, enter a keystroke into the console for the
   client. A message should appear in the console of the service, as shown in Figure 8.3.

5. Stop debugging the solution.

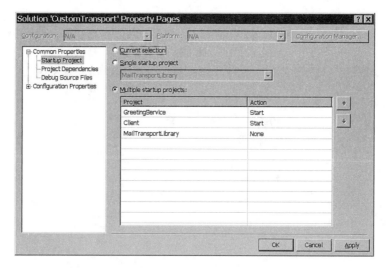

FIGURE 8.2   Custom transport solution startup project property.

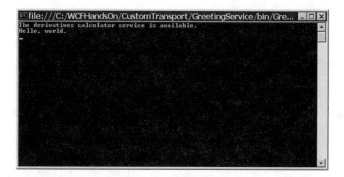

FIGURE 8.3   The Greeting Service.

Understand the Initial Solution

See how the initial solution works:

1. Open the file IGreeting.cs in the GreetingService project. It contains this simple service contract:

```
using System;
using System.Collections.Generic;
using System.ServiceModel;
using System.Text;

namespace CustomTransport
{
    [ServiceContract]
```

```
        public interface IGreeting
        {
            [OperationContract(IsOneWay=true)]
            void Greeting(
                string greeting);
        }
    }
```

2. Look in the file `GreetingService.cs` in the GreetingService project. It contains a service type that implements that contract:

```
using System;
using System.Collections.Generic;
using System.Text;

namespace CustomTransport
{
    public class GreetingServiceType: IGreeting
    {
        #region IGreeting Members

        void IGreeting.Greeting(
            string greeting)
        {
            Console.WriteLine(greeting);
        }

        #endregion
    }
}
```

3. Open the file `Program.cs` in the GreetingService project, which has code for hosting the service within an application domain. That code is shown Listing 8.1. In that code, the sole endpoint of the service is configured in the code using the `AddServiceEndpoint()` method of the `ServiceHost` class, rather than being configured via a configuration file.

LISTING 8.1   The Service Host

```
using System;
using System.Collections.Generic;
using System.Configuration;
using System.ServiceModel;
using System.Text;
```

LISTING 8.1   Continued

```
namespace CustomTransport
{
    public class Program
    {
        public static void Main(string[] args)
        {
            Type serviceType = typeof(GreetingServiceType);

            string tcpBaseAddress =
                ConfigurationManager.AppSettings["TCPBaseAddress"];
            Uri tcpBaseAddressURI = new Uri(tcpBaseAddress);
            Uri[] baseAdresses = new Uri[] {
                tcpBaseAddressURI};

            using(ServiceHost host = new ServiceHost(
                serviceType,
                baseAdresses))
            {
                host.AddServiceEndpoint(
                    typeof(IGreeting),
                    new NetTcpBinding(),
                    ConfigurationManager.AppSettings[
                    "GreetingEndpointAddress"]);
                host.Open();

                Console.WriteLine(
                    "The derivatives calculator service is available."
                );
                Console.ReadKey();

                host.Close();
            }
        }
    }
}
```

4. Look at the code for the client in the Program.cs file of the Client project. That code is reproduced in Listing 8.2. Here, too, the properties of the endpoint of the service are specified in code, rather than in a configuration file.

LISTING 8.2 The Client

```
using System;
using System.Collections.Generic;
using System.Configuration;
using System.ServiceModel;
using System.Text;

namespace CustomTransport
{
    public class Program
    {
        public static void Main(string[] args)
        {
            Console.WriteLine("Press any key when the service is ready.");
            Console.ReadKey();

            IGreeting proxy = new ChannelFactory<IGreeting>(
                new NetTcpBinding(),
                new EndpointAddress(
ConfigurationManager.AppSettings["GreetingServiceAddress"]))
                        .CreateChannel();
            proxy.Greeting(
                "Hello, world.");
            ((IChannel)proxy).Close();


            Console.WriteLine("Press any key to exit.");
            Console.ReadKey();


        }
    }
}
```

The Internet Mail Protocols

The Internet mail protocols are the Simple Mail Transfer Protocol (SMTP), which is for sending mail, and the Post Office Protocol Version 3 (POP3) (*Official Internet Protocol Standards* 2006). Therefore, to proceed through the instructions that follow for adding support for the Internet mail protocols to the Windows Communication Foundation, and to see the results, one needs to have access to an SMTP server and a POP3 server. Most Internet service providers offer access to an SMTP server and a POP3 server to their subscribers. Readers who are using a Windows server operating system may choose to install and configure the POP3 service provided with their operating system. Installing the POP3 service also provides support for SMTP.

Building an Internet Mail Transport Binding Element

Recall that adding support for an additional transport protocol to the Windows Communication Foundation really means adding a new transport binding element to the Channel Layer. Add a transport binding element for Internet mail to the solution now.

Getting Started

In adding support for additional transport protocols to the Windows Communication Foundation, one is advised to begin from a working sample. In this case, the aforementioned sample for UDP provided in the Windows SDK for use with the Windows Communication Foundation will be adapted to accommodate SMTP and POP3:

1. By default, the SDK installer places the UDP sample in the folder `C:\Program Files\Microsoft SDKs\Windows\v1.0\samples\Allsamples\ WindowsCommunicationFoundation\TechnologySamples\Extensibility\Transport\ Udp`. The parts of that sample that will be required in the following steps are in the subfolder `CS\UdpTransport`. Copy all the files in that subfolder with the extension `.cs` to the folder `C:\ C:\WCFHandsOn\CustomTransport\MailTransportLibrary`, except the file `UdpListenerFactory.cs`, which is not required. Add those files to the MailTransportLibrary project of the CustomTransport solution.

2. Build the MailTransportLibrary project to ensure that nothing has gone missing.

3. Rename each of the modules in the project that have `Udp` in their names, replacing `Udp` with `Mail`.

4. Open each of the modules that now has `Mail` in its name, and look for the name of each class in the class definitions contained in the module. Right-click on that name and choose Refactor and Rename from the context menu. Substitute `Mail` for `Udp` in the name of the class in the Rename dialog shown in Figure 8.4, clear the Preview Reference Changes option, and click OK. With the refactoring facility in Visual Studio 2005, it should take less than 5 minutes to change the names of all the classes and all the references to them. When the task is complete, build the project to confirm that no errors have been made.

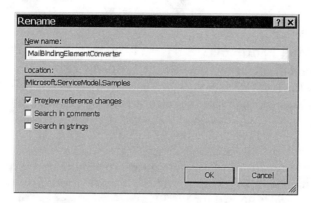

FIGURE 8.4   The Visual Studio Rename dialog.

Specifying a Scheme for the Internet Mail Transport Protocols

The initial part of a URI is called the *scheme*. In the URI `http://localhost:8000/Derivatives/Calculator` the scheme is `http`.

In the Windows Communication Foundation, schemes provide the link between the addresses and the bindings of endpoints. Thus, in

```
ServiceHost host = new ServiceHost(
    typeof(GreetingServiceType),
    new Uri[]{
        new Uri("http://localhost:8000/Service/"),
        new Uri("net.tcp://localhost:8010/Service/")
    });


host.AddServiceEndpoint(
    typeof(IGreeting),
    new NetTcpBinding(),
    "Greeting");
```

the base address of the `Greeting` endpoint is the second of the two base addresses of the service, `net.tcp://localhost:8010/Service/`, because the scheme of that base address is the scheme associated with the TCP transport protocol of the endpoint's `NetTcpBinding`.

So, in adding support for the Internet mail transport protocols to the Windows Communication Foundation, it is necessary to specify the scheme for the base addresses of any endpoints with Internet mail transport protocol bindings. The choice of the scheme is arbitrary. The scheme that will be used is `smtp.pop3`:

1. Open the module that should now be named `MailChannelHelpers` and modify the `Scheme` constant in the `MailConstants` class, replacing `soap.udp` with `smtp.pop3`, like so:

   ```
   static class MailConstants
   {
       internal const string EventLogSourceName
           = "Microsoft.ServiceModel.Samples";
       internal const string Scheme = "smtp.pop3";
       internal const string UdpBindingSectionName
           = "system.serviceModel/bindings/sampleProfileUdpBinding";
       internal const string UdpTransportSectionName = "udpTransport";
       internal const int WSAETIMEDOUT = 10060;
       [...]
   }
   ```

2. Use Visual Studio 2005's Find in Files command, which one accesses by choosing Edit, Find and Replace, Find in Files from the menus, and find all instances of the

expression `soap.udp` in the solution. That process should turn up this line of code in the `MailPolicyStrings` class,

```
public const string TransportAssertion = "soap.udp";
```

as well as this line in the `SampleProfileMailBinding` class, which represents a small imperfection in the sample:

```
public override string Scheme { get { return "soap.udp"; } }
```

3. Change them both like this:

```
public const string TransportAssertion = MailConstants.Scheme;
```

```
public override string Scheme { get { return MailConstants.Scheme; } }
```

The Listener

Recall, from the foregoing description of how protocols are implemented in the Windows Communication Foundation, that a listener typically does its work of listening for messages by listening on a socket. That should certainly be true of a UDP listener. What needs to be accomplished next in providing support for the Internet mail protocols is to modify the code in the UDP transport protocol sample by which the listener listens on a socket for messages conveyed via the UDP protocol, in such a way that the listener instead uses the socket to retrieve mail messages from a POP3 server.

If one was to search the code in the MailTransportLibrary project for references to the .NET Framework's Socket class, one would find that an instance of that class is instantiated in the `MailChannelListener` class, and that the work of listening for UDP messages on that socket gets underway in that class' `StartReceiving()` method, which is shown in Listing 8.3.

LISTING 8.3 The `StartReceiving()` Method

```
void StartReceiving(object state)
{
    Socket listenSocket = (Socket)state;
    IAsyncResult result = null;
    try
    {
        lock (ThisLock)
        {
            if (base.State == CommunicationState.Opened)
            {
                EndPoint dummy =
                    CreateDummyEndPoint(listenSocket);
                byte[] buffer =
                    this.bufferManager.TakeBuffer(maxMessageSize);
                result =
```

LISTING 8.3   Continued

```
                    listenSocket.BeginReceiveFrom(
                        buffer,
                        0,
                        buffer.Length,
                        SocketFlags.None,
                        ref dummy,
                        this.onReceive,
                        new SocketReceiveState(listenSocket, buffer));
            }
        }
        if (result != null && result.CompletedSynchronously)
        {
            ContinueReceiving(result, listenSocket);
        }
    }
    catch (Exception e)
    {
        Debug.WriteLine("Error in receiving from the socket.");
        Debug.WriteLine(e.ToString());
    }
}
```

Modify the method to receive messages via the POP3 Internet mail protocol:

1. Comment out the StartReceiving() method, and insert the alternative version in
   Listing 8.4, which is also provided in the file C:\WCFHandsOn\CustomTransport\
   StartReceiving.txt.

LISTING 8.4   The Revised StartReceiving() Method

```
private void StartReceiving(object state)
{
    try
    {
        while (base.State == CommunicationState.Opened)
        {
            lock (ThisLock)
            {
                if (this.listenSockets.Count == 0)
                {
                    IPHostEntry host = Dns.GetHostEntry(uri.Host);
                    IPAddress address = host.AddressList[0];
                    this.CreateListenSocket(address, this.uri.Port);
                }
```

LISTING 8.4   Continued

```
                this.POP3Reception();


        }
            Thread.Sleep(5000);
        }
    }
    catch (Exception exception)
    {
        Debug.WriteLine("Error in receiving from the socket.");
        Debug.WriteLine(exception.ToString());
    }
}


private void POP3Reception()
{
    const string LineTerminator = "\r\n";
    const string MessageTerminator = ".";

    StringBuilder messageBuffer = null;
    Regex regularExpression = new Regex(@"(^\+OK\s)(\d*)([\s])(\d*)");
    Match match = null;
    int messageCount;
    int mailDropSize;
    string mailMessage = null;
    Message message = null;
    byte[] buffer = null;
    this.LogIn();

    string response = null;
    response = this.Transmit("STAT", null);
    if (this.ErrorResponse(response))
    {
        throw new Exception("Error retrieving count of new messages.");
    }
    if (!(regularExpression.IsMatch(response)))
    {
        throw new Exception("Error parsing count of new messages.");
    }
    match = regularExpression.Match(response);
    messageCount = int.Parse(match.Groups[2].Value);
    mailDropSize = int.Parse(match.Groups[4].Value);
```

LISTING 8.4   Continued

```
for (int messageIndex = 1;
    messageIndex <= messageCount;
    messageIndex++)
{
    messageBuffer = new StringBuilder();
    while (true)
    {
        response = this.Transmit(
            string.Format("RETR {0}", messageIndex),
            mailDropSize);
        if (this.ErrorResponse(response))
        {
            throw new Exception("Error retrieving message.");
        }

        if (response.StartsWith(MessageTerminator))
        {
            if (!(response.EndsWith(
                MessageTerminator + LineTerminator)))
            {
                response = response.Substring(1);
            }
        }
        if (response.EndsWith(MessageTerminator + LineTerminator))
        {
            messageBuffer.Append(
                response.Substring(
                    0,
                    response.Length - LineTerminator.Length));
            break;
        }

        messageBuffer.Append(response);
    }
    mailMessage = messageBuffer.ToString();

    response = this.Transmit(
        string.Format("DELE {0}", messageIndex),
        null);
    if (this.ErrorResponse(response))
    {
        throw new Exception("Error deleting message.");
    }
```

8

LISTING 8.4   Continued

```
        buffer = Encoding.ASCII.GetBytes(mailMessage);
        message = messageEncoderFactory.Encoder.ReadMessage(
            new ArraySegment<byte>(buffer, 0, buffer.Length),
            bufferManager);
        if (message != null)
        {
            ThreadPool.QueueUserWorkItem(
                new WaitCallback(DispatchCallback), message);
        }
        else
        {
            EventLog.WriteEntry(
                MailConstants.EventLogSourceName,
"A message was dropped because it was not in the expected format.",
                EventLogEntryType.Warning);
        }
    }

    response = this.Transmit("QUIT", null);
    if (this.ErrorResponse(response))
    {
        throw new Exception("Error updating mailbox.");
    }

    this.CloseListenSockets(TimeSpan.Zero);
}

private bool ErrorResponse(string response)
{
    if (response.StartsWith("-ERR"))
    {
        return true;
    }
    return false;
}

private void LogIn()
{
    if (this.ErrorResponse(
        this.Transmit(string.Format("USER {0}", this.userName), null)))
    {
        throw new Exception("Username rejected.");
    }
    if (this.ErrorResponse(
```

LISTING 8.4 Continued

```
        this.Transmit(string.Format("PASS {0}", this.password), null)))
    {
        throw new Exception("Password rejected.");
    }
}

private string Transmit(string message, int? bufferSize)
{
    if (message != null)
    {
        this.listenSockets[0].Send(
            Encoding.ASCII.GetBytes(string.Concat(message, "\r\n")));
    }

    byte[] buffer = new byte[
        bufferSize != null ? bufferSize.Value + 512 : 512];
    int bytesRead = this.listenSockets[0].Receive(buffer);
    StringBuilder builder = new StringBuilder();
    builder.Append(Encoding.ASCII.GetChars(buffer), 0, bytesRead);
    return builder.ToString();
}
```

2. Add these C# using statements to those already in the module to incorporate the namespaces of some familiar .NET Framework classes to which we refer in our new StartReceiving() method:

```
using System.Text;
using System.Text.RegularExpressions;
```

The new StartReceiving() method works in the same way that Internet mail reader applications typically do. It connects to a POP3 server that it knows, logging in with credentials associated with an account that it knows. Then it queries the server for the number of new messages that have been received that were sent to the account, and retrieves each of those messages, instructing the server to delete each message after it has been retrieved. It then disconnects from the server, and goes to sleep for a time, after which it repeats the process.

Each message that is received gets sent on to the input channel that the Dispatcher is waiting for with this line of code:

```
ThreadPool.QueueUserWorkItem(new WaitCallback(DispatchCallback), message);
```

That line was simply taken from one of the methods that the original StartReceiving() process invoked, namely the ContinueReceiving() method, which is no longer used.

Reflecting on this process that is encoded in the new StartReceiving() method, one can identify all the other changes that have to be made in constructing the Internet mail protocol listenter. There are three such changes.

To begin with, the new code connects to the POP3 server and then disconnects on each cycle. Although that is characteristic of what Internet mail readers do, it is different from what the original code for the UDP listener did, which was to open a socket and simply wait for data to arrive. So one thing that has to be done is change how the connection is managed.

Also, credentials have to be provided to log on to the POP3 server. Hence, properties will need to be added to an Internet mail transport binding element by which users can supply credentials that the code can access and use to connect to the POP3 server. Providing custom properties is a common task when one is adding custom binding elements to the Windows Communication Foundation.

The third change that needs to be made concerns the format of the data retrieved from the POP3 server. The intention is for the messages that will be exchanged via Internet mail to be SOAP documents embedded in the bodies of Internet mail messages. Consequently, from among the bytes that are retrieved from the POP3 server representing each message, it will be necessary to extract the SOAP document and use that to yield a message, a message that will then be added to the input channel for the Dispatcher to retrieve and dispatch. Recall that, in the architecture of the Windows Communication Foundation's Channel Layer, transport protocol listeners use message encoders to assemble the streams of bytes they receive into messages. So it will be necessary to provide a message encoder that is familiar with the format of Internet mail messages and able to extract SOAP documents from within them.

Managing the Connection to the Server The original code for opening the UDP socket was invoked in the code shown in Listing 8.5.

LISTING 8.5 Opening the UDP Socket

```
protected override void OnOpen(TimeSpan timeout)
{
    if (uri == null)
    {
        throw new InvalidOperationException(
            "Uri must be set before ChannelListener is opened.");
    }

    base.OnOpen(timeout);
    if (this.listenSockets.Count == 0)
    {
        if (uri.HostNameType == UriHostNameType.IPv6 ||
            uri.HostNameType == UriHostNameType.IPv4)
        {
            listenSockets.Add(
```

LISTING 8.5   Continued

```
                CreateListenSocket(
                    IPAddress.Parse(uri.Host), uri.Port));
        }
        else
        {
            listenSockets.Add(
                CreateListenSocket(IPAddress.Any, uri.Port));
            if (Socket.OSSupportsIPv6)
            {
                listenSockets.Add(
                    CreateListenSocket(IPAddress.IPv6Any, uri.Port));
            }
        }
    }
}
```

Modify the original code in this way:

1. Comment out the code by which the UDP socket is opened, as shown in Listing 8.6.

LISTING 8.6   Removing the Code for Opening a UDP Socket

```
protected override void OnOpen(TimeSpan timeout)
{
    if (uri == null)
    {
        throw new InvalidOperationException(
            "Uri must be set before ChannelListener is opened.");
    }

    base.OnOpen(timeout);
    if (this.listenSockets.Count == 0)
    {
      /*
        if (uri.HostNameType == UriHostNameType.IPv6 ||
            uri.HostNameType == UriHostNameType.IPv4)
        {
            listenSockets.Add(
                CreateListenSocket(
                    IPAddress.Parse(uri.Host), uri.Port));
        }
        else
        {
            listenSockets.Add(
                CreateListenSocket(IPAddress.Any, uri.Port));
```

8

LISTING 8.6   Continued

```
            if (Socket.OSSupportsIPv6)
            {
                listenSockets.Add(
                    CreateListenSocket(IPAddress.IPv6Any, uri.Port));
            }
        }
        */
    }
}
```

2. Next, replace the original, lengthy CreateListenSocket() method with this simpler one that serves the more modest requirements of the new StartReceiving() method:

```
Socket CreateListenSocket(IPAddress address, int port)
{
    Socket listenSocket = new Socket(
        address.AddressFamily, SocketType.Stream, ProtocolType.Tcp);
    listenSocket.Connect(this.uri.Host, this.uri.Port);
    this.listenSockets.Add(listenSocket);
    if (this.ErrorResponse(this.Transmit(null, null)))
    {
        throw new Exception("Failure to connect.");
    }
    return listenSocket;
}
```

3. Finally, modify the OnOpened() method, omitting some statements that assumed that a socket would be kept open:

```
protected override void OnOpened()
{
    base.OnOpened();
    Socket[] socketsSnapshot = listenSockets.ToArray();
    WaitCallback startReceivingCallback = new WaitCallback(StartReceiving);
    ThreadPool.QueueUserWorkItem(startReceivingCallback);
}
```

Providing the Account Credentials   To provide credentials for logging on to the POP3 server, do as follows:

1. Look again at the LogIn() method that was added earlier, and that is used by the new version of the StartReceiving() method:

```
private void LogIn()
{
    if (this.ErrorResponse(
        this.Transmit(string.Format("USER {0}", this.userName), null)))
    {
        throw new Exception("Username rejected.");
    }
    if (this.ErrorResponse(
        this.Transmit(string.Format("PASS {0}", this.password), null)))
    {
        throw new Exception("Password rejected.");
    }
}
```

In supplying credentials to the POP3 server, the LogIn() method refers to the userName and password fields of the MailListenerFactory, which are, as yet, undeclared.

2. So add declarations of those fields to the MailListener factory now:

```
class MailChannelListener : ChannelListenerBase<IInputChannel>
{
    #region member_variables
    BufferManager bufferManager;

    //The UDP network sockets.
    List<Socket> listenSockets;

    int maxMessageSize;
    MessageEncoderFactory messageEncoderFactory;
    bool multicast;

    AsyncCallback onReceive;
    Uri uri;

    InputQueue<IInputChannel> channelQueue;

    //The channel associated with this listener.
    MailInputChannel currentChannel;

    object currentChannelLock;

    string userName = null;
    string password = null;

    #endregion
```

3. To see how values might be assigned to those fields, examine the constructor of the MailListenerFactory, which is shown in Listing 8.7.

LISTING 8.7   Original `MailListenerFactory` Constructor

```
internal MailChannelListener(
    MailTransportBindingElement bindingElement,
    ChannelBuildContext context)
            : base(context.Binding)
{

    #region populate_members_from_binding_element
    this.maxMessageSize = bindingElement.MaxMessageSize;
    this.multicast = bindingElement.Multicast;
    this.bufferManager = BufferManager.CreateBufferManager(
        bindingElement.MaxBufferPoolSize, bindingElement.MaxMessageSize);
    IMessageEncodingBindingElement messageEncoderBindingElement =
        context.UnhandledBindingElements.
            Remove<IMessageEncodingBindingElement>();
    if (messageEncoderBindingElement != null)
    {
        this.messageEncoderFactory =
            messageEncoderBindingElement.CreateMessageEncoderFactory();
    }
    else
    {
        this.messageEncoderFactory =
            MailConstants.DefaultMessageEncoderFactory;
    }
    this.channelQueue = new InputQueue<IInputChannel>();
    this.channelQueue.Open();
    this.currentChannelLock = new object();
    this.listenSockets = new List<Socket>(2);
    #endregion
}
```

The constructor receives, as a parameter, an instance of the binding element. If properties can be added to the binding element by which a user can provide a username and password for the POP3 server, those properties could be used to assign values to the userName and password fields of the MailListenerFactory.

4. Therefore, make the necessary amendments to the MailListenerFactory constructor, as shown in Listing 8.8.

LISTING 8.8   Revised `MailListenerFactory` Constructor

```
class MailChannelListener : ChannelListenerBase<IInputChannel>
{
    #region member_variables
    BufferManager bufferManager;

    //The UDP network sockets.
    List<Socket> listenSockets;

    int maxMessageSize;
    MessageEncoderFactory messageEncoderFactory;
    bool multicast;

    AsyncCallback onReceive;
    Uri uri;

    InputQueue<IInputChannel> channelQueue;

    //The channel associated with this listener.
    MailInputChannel currentChannel;

    object currentChannelLock;

    string userName = null;
    string password = null;

    #endregion
```

5. Then add the necessary properties to the `MailTransportBindingElement` class in the `MailTransportBindingElement.cs` module, as shown in Listing 8.9.

LISTING 8.9   `MailTransportBindingElement` Account Properties

```
#region CONFIGURATION_Properties
private string userName = null;
private string password = null;

public string UserName
{
    get
    {
        return this.userName;
    }

    set
```

LISTING 8.9   Continued

```
    {
        this.userName = value;
    }

}

public string Password
{
    get
    {
        return this.password;
    }

    set
    {
        this.password = value;
    }
}
```

6. Finally, modify the copy constructors of the `MailTransportBindingElement` class to ensure that when one instance of the class is constructed from another, the values of the newly added properties propagate properly:

```
protected MailTransportBindingElement(MailTransportBindingElement other)
    : base(other)
{
    this.maxBufferPoolSize = other.maxBufferPoolSize;
    this.maxMessageSize = other.maxMessageSize;
    this.multicast = other.multicast;

    this.userName = other.userName;
    this.password = other.password;
}
```

7. Compile the MailTransportLibrary project to ensure that no mistakes have been made up to this point.

Providing an Internet Mail Encoder   The new code for the listener has mail messages that are retrieved from the POP3 server transformed into Windows Communication Foundation messages by an Internet mail encoder. That is done with this line of code in the `POP3Reception()` method that is invoked by the new version of the `StartReceiving()` method:

```
message = messageEncoderFactory.Encoder.ReadMessage(
        new ArraySegment<byte>(buffer, 0, buffer.Length),
            bufferManager);
```

The next task is to develop that encoder. Developing an encoder for the Windows Communication Foundation is another task that is accelerated considerably by starting from a sample. The aforementioned SDK provided for use with the Windows Communication Foundation also has a sample of a custom encoder. It is an encoder for translating messages in and out of a compression format.

The compression encoder uses the standard Windows Communication Foundation text encoder internally, because the messages that are being compressed and decompressed are SOAP text messages. Specifically, incoming messages are translated out of the compression format into the SOAP text format, and then passed to the text encoder, which understands the SOAP text format, and translates the SOAP text into Windows Communication Foundation messages. Outgoing messages are translated into the SOAP text format by the standard text encoder, and then translated into the compression format.

This sample is perfectly suited for adaptation to the current task of working with Internet mail messages. Messages received in Internet mail format will have SOAP text messages incorporated within them. The Internet mail encoder can extract the SOAP text messages from the Internet mail messages, and pass the SOAP text message on to the standard Windows Communication Foundation text encoder to be made into Windows Communication Foundation messages. Conversely, for outgoing Windows Communication Foundation messages, the text encoder can be used to translate them into SOAP text documents, which the Internet mail encoder can then insert into the bodies of Internet mail messages:

1. The code for a sample compression encoder is provided in `C:\WCFHandsOn\CustomTransport\GZipEncoder.cs`. Add that module to the MailTransportLibrary project of the CustomTransport solution.

2. Change the name of the module to `MailEncoder.cs`.

3. Change the sole namespace declaration in the module to look like this:

   ```
   namespace Microsoft.ServiceModel.Samples
   ```

4. Use Visual Studio 2005's refactoring facility as before to replace any occurrence of compression in the name of a class in that module with `mail`, being careful to preserve the case of the original. Thus, the classes originally named `CompressionMessageEncoderFactory`, `CompressionMessageEncoder`, `CompressionMessageEncodingBindingElement`, and `CompressionMessageEncodingSection` will be renamed `MailMessageEncoderFactory`, `MailMessageEncoder`, `MailMessageEncodingBindingElement`, and `MailMessageEncodingSection`.

5. Locate these lines of code in what should now be called the `MailMessageEncoder` class:

```
public override string ContentType
{
    get { return compressionContentType; }
}

public override string MediaType
{
    get { return compressionContentType; }
}
```

6. Modify those lines of code so they read like this:

```
public override string ContentType
{
    get { return this.innerEncoder.ContentType; }
}

public override string MediaType
{
    get { return this.innerEncoder.MediaType; }
}
```

The core of a Windows Communication Foundation message encoder is its overrides of the abstract base `MessageEncoder` class' abstract `ReadMessage()` and `WriteMessage()` methods. In the next two steps, those overrides will be modified to produce Windows Communication Foundation messages from SOAP text messages extracted from incoming Internet mail messages, and to create SOAP text messages to be embedded in Internet mail messages from outgoing Windows Communication Foundation messages.

7. Change the override of the `ReadMessage()` method so that it looks like the code in Listing 8.10.

LISTING 8.10   The `MessageEncoder`'s `ReadMessage()` Method

```
public override Message ReadMessage(ArraySegment<byte> buffer,
    BufferManager bufferManager)
{
    string mailMessage =
        new StringBuilder().Append(
            Encoding.ASCII.GetChars(buffer.Array)).ToString();
    int position = mailMessage.IndexOf(@"<s:Envelope");
    if (position >= 0)
    {
```

LISTING 8.10   Continued

```
        string body = mailMessage.Substring(position);
        position = body.LastIndexOf("</s:Envelope>");
        if (position >= 0)
        {
            body = body.Substring(0, (position + "</s:Envelope>".Length));
        }
        byte[] soapBuffer = Encoding.ASCII.GetBytes(body);
        Message message =
            this.innerEncoder.ReadMessage(
                new ArraySegment<byte>(
                    soapBuffer,
                    0,
                    soapBuffer.Length),
                bufferManager);
        message.Properties.Encoder = this;
        return message;
    }
    return null;
}
```

That code extracts the portion of an incoming Internet mail message that contains a SOAP text document. It passes that to the standard text encoder, which yields a Windows Communication Foundation message from it.

8. Now change the override of the `WriteMessage()` method so that it looks like this:

```
public override ArraySegment<byte> WriteMessage(
    Message message,
    int maxMessageSize,
    BufferManager bufferManager,
    int messageOffset)
{
    ArraySegment<byte> buffer =
        innerEncoder.WriteMessage(
            message,
            maxMessageSize,
            bufferManager,
            messageOffset);
    return buffer;
}
```

This code takes an outgoing Windows Communication Foundation message and uses the standard text encoder to translate that into a SOAP text document ready to be incorporated into the body of an Internet mail message.

9. Build the MailLibraryProject of the CustomTransport solution to ensure that there are no errors.

The work on the Internet mail listener is now complete. There is now a custom Windows Communication Foundation listener that knows how to receive Internet mail messages. Thanks to the sample provided with the SDK, everything that had to be written had to do with communicating with a POP3 server and decoding the data retrieved from it, which is precisely what one would expect to have to do in adding support for Internet mail to the Windows Communication Foundation. It was not necessary to write any Windows Communication Foundation plumbing, and all that was required to write the code was some knowledge of the POP3 protocol. So, if one is a .NET developer, and has expertise, for instance, in developing solutions with International Business Machine's WebSphere MQ products, then one can expect, in extending the Windows Communication Foundation to support communicating via those products, that one's existing expertise will suffice for that task.

The Output Channel

All that remains to be done in adding support for Internet mail communications to the Windows Communication Foundation is to provide for the sending of messages via Internet mail. Recall from the explanation of how the Windows Communication Foundation implements protocols that messages are sent via the methods of output channels:

1. Locate the Send() method of the MailOutputChannel class in the MailOutputChannel.cs module of the MailTransportLibrary project. It is shown in Listing 8.11.

LISTING 8.11   The MailOutputChannel's Send() Method

```
public void Send(Message message)
{
    base.ThrowIfDisposedOrNotOpen();

    ArraySegment<byte> messageBuffer = EncodeMessage(message);

    try
    {
        int bytesSent = this.socket.SendTo(
            messageBuffer.Array,
            messageBuffer.Offset,
            messageBuffer.Count,
            SocketFlags.None,
            this.remoteEndPoint);

        if (bytesSent != messageBuffer.Count)
        {
```

LISTING 8.11   Continued

```
            throw new CommunicationException(
                string.Format(
                    CultureInfo.CurrentCulture,
                    "A Udp error occurred sending a message to {0}.",
                    this.remoteEndPoint));
        }
    }
    catch (SocketException socketException)
    {
        throw MailChannelHelpers.ConvertTransferException(socketException);
    }
    finally
    {
        // we need to make sure buffers
        // are always returned to the BufferManager
        parent.BufferManager.ReturnBuffer(messageBuffer.Array);
    }
}
```

2. Replace the code of that method with this code:

```
public void Send(Message message)
{
    base.ThrowIfDisposedOrNotOpen();
    ArraySegment<byte> messageBuffer = EncodeMessage(message);
    try
    {
        MailMessage mailMessage = new MailMessage();
        mailMessage.To =
            this.remoteAddress.Uri.LocalPath.TrimStart(new char[] { '/' });
        mailMessage.From = this.fromAddress;
        mailMessage.Subject = string.Empty;
        mailMessage.Priority = MailPriority.High;
        mailMessage.Body = new StringBuilder().Append(
            System.Text.Encoding.ASCII.GetChars(
                messageBuffer.Array)).ToString();
        SmtpMail.SmtpServer = this.remoteAddress.Uri.Host;
        SmtpMail.Send(mailMessage);
    }
    finally
    {
        parent.BufferManager.ReturnBuffer(messageBuffer.Array);
    }
}
```

8

3. Add a reference to the `System.Web` .NET assembly to the MailTransportLibrary project of the CustomTransportSolution.

4. Add this using clause to those already in the `MailOutputChannel.cs` module of that project to incorporate the classes in the `System.Web` namespace:

```
using System.Web.Mail;
```

The code added in the precediing few steps is a straightforward application of the familiar classes of the `System.Web.Mail` namespace to transmit an outgoing message via Internet mail. The only outstanding issue is that, in this line of code in the revised `Send()` method,

```
mailMessage.From = this.fromAddress;
```

it is assumed that the output channel has been supplied with an address to provide as the address from which the outgoing mail message originated. As in the case of the credentials that were needed to access the POP3 server to retrieve incoming messages, it would be desirable to retrieve that address from a property of the binding element that the user can configure. Getting the values of user-configurable properties of binding elements down to output channels is a common task in adding support for additional transport protocols to the Windows Communication Foundation.

5. To accomplish the task, begin by declaring the field that is being used to store the source address in the `MailOutputChannel` class:

```
class MailOutputChannel : ChannelBase, IOutputChannel
{
    #region member_variables
    EndpointAddress remoteAddress;
    Uri via;
    EndPoint remoteEndPoint;
    Socket socket;
    MessageEncoder encoder;
    MailChannelFactory parent;

    string fromAddress = null;
    #endregion
```

6. Modify the constructor of the `MailOutputChannel` class to initialize the field from a property of the channel factory:

```
internal MailOutputChannel(MailChannelFactory factory,
    EndpointAddress remoteAddress, Uri via, MessageEncoder encoder)
    : base(factory)
```

```
{
    #region ADDRESSING_validate_arguments
    this.fromAddress = factory.FromAddress;
```

7. Add the definition of the property to the `MailChannelFactory` class in
`MailChannelFactory.cs`:

```
#region simple_property_accessors
string fromAddress = null;

public string FromAddress
{
    get
    {
        return this.fromAddress;
    }

    set
    {
        this.fromAddress = value;
    }
}
```

8. Modify the constructor of the `MailChannelFactory` class so that the value of the
property is retrieved from a property of the binding element that is passed to the
`MailChannelFactory` constructor:

```
internal MailChannelFactory(
    MailTransportBindingElement bindingElement,
    ChannelBuildContext context)
    : base(context.Binding)
{
    #region populate_members_from_binding_element
    this.fromAddress = bindingElement.FromAddress;
```

9. Add the property to the properties of the `MailTransportBindingElement` class:

```
#region CONFIGURATION_Properties
private string userName = null;
private string password = null;
private string fromAddress = null;

public string FromAddress
{
    get
    {
```

```
            return this.fromAddress;
    }

    set
    {
        this.fromAddress = value;
    }
}
```

10. Modify the copy constructor of the `MailTransportBindingElement` as before to ensure that the value of the new property propagates correctly:

```
protected MailTransportBindingElement(MailTransportBindingElement other)
              : base(other)
{
    this.maxBufferPoolSize = other.maxBufferPoolSize;
    this.maxMessageSize = other.maxMessageSize;
    this.multicast = other.multicast;

    this.fromAddress = other.fromAddress;
    this.userName = other.userName;
    this.password = other.password;
}
```

The chain of information that needed to be constructed is now complete. The value that was required in the output channel is now retrieved from a property of the channel factory, that, in turn, is set by a property of the binding element that a user can configure.

11. Compile the MailTransportLibrary to ensure that no errors have been made.

Testing the New Internet Mail Protocol Binding Element

To test the new Internet mail protocol binding, modify the client and service applications of the initial solution to use the new binding. Follow these steps:

1. For the original code of the Greeting Service, in the `Program.cs` module of the GreetingService project, substitute the code in Listing 8.12. That code constructs a binding from the `MailMessageEncodingBindingElement` and the `MailTransportBindingElement`. The base address provided for the service is the URI of a POP3 server, with the scheme that was selected for the Internet mail protocol, smtp.pop3, as the prefix. The address of the endpoint that uses the Internet mail binding is an Internet mail account on the POP3 server.

LISTING 8.12   Internet Mail Service

```
using System;
using System.Collections.Generic;
using System.Configuration;
using System.ServiceModel;
using System.Text;

using Microsoft.ServiceModel.Samples;

namespace CustomTransport
{
    public class Program
    {
        public static void Main(string[] args)
        {
            Type serviceType = typeof(GreetingServiceType);

            string mailBaseAddress = "smtp.pop3://localhost:110/";
            Uri mailBaseAdressURI = new Uri(mailBaseAddress);
            Uri[] baseAdresses = new Uri[] {
                mailBaseAdressURI};

            MailTransportBindingElement transportBindingElement
                = new MailTransportBindingElement();
            transportBindingElement.UserName
                = "WCFHandsOnReader@WCFHandsOn.COM";
            transportBindingElement.Password
                = "pass@word1";

            MailMessageEncodingBindingElement encodingBindingElement
                = new MailMessageEncodingBindingElement();

            CustomBinding binding
                = new CustomBinding(new BindingElement[] {
                    encodingBindingElement,
                    transportBindingElement });

            using(ServiceHost host = new ServiceHost(
                serviceType,
                baseAdresses))
            {
                host.AddServiceEndpoint(
                    typeof(IGreeting),
                    binding,
                    "WCFHandsOnReader@WCFHandsOn.COM");
```

LISTING 8.12   Continued

```
        host.Open();

        Console.WriteLine(
            "The derivatives calculator service is available."
        );
        Console.ReadKey();

        host.Close();
      }
    }
  }
}
```

The value one should use in the server name portion of the URI provided as the base address of the service should be the name of the POP3 server of the reader's own Internet mail account. Similarly, the Internet mail account used as the address of the service's endpoint should also be the reader's own. Also, the values provided for the UserName and Password properties of the MailTransportBindingElement object should be the reader's credentials for the POP3 server of the reader's Internet mail account.

2. Replace the original code of the client application, in the Program.cs module of the Client project, with the code in Listing 8.13. Again, the values supplied for the UserName and Password properties of the MailTransportBindingElement object should be the reader's credentials for the reader's own Internet mail account. The value of the FromAddress should be the name of that account. The address of the service is given as smtp.pop3://localhost:110/WCFHandsOnReader@WCFHandsOn.COM in Listing 8.12. For localhost, the reader should substitute the name of the POP3 server of the reader's Internet mail account, and for WCFHandsOnReader@WCFHandsOn.COM, the reader should substitute the name of the reader's Internet mail account.

LISTING 8.13   Internet Mail Client

```
using System.Configuration;
using System.ServiceModel;
using System.Text;

using Microsoft.ServiceModel.Samples;

namespace CustomTransport
{
    public class Program
    {
        public static void Main(string[] args)
        {
```

LISTING 8.13   Continued

```
            Console.WriteLine("Press any key when the service is ready.");
            Console.ReadKey();

            MailTransportBindingElement transportBindingElement
                = new MailTransportBindingElement();
            transportBindingElement.UserName
                = "WCFHandsOnReader@WCFHandsOn.COM";
            transportBindingElement.Password
                = "pass@word1";
            transportBindingElement.FromAddress
                = "WCFHandsOnReader@WCFHandsOn.COM";

            MailMessageEncodingBindingElement encodingBindingElement
                = new MailMessageEncodingBindingElement();

            CustomBinding binding = new CustomBinding(new BindingElement[] {
                encodingBindingElement, transportBindingElement });

            IGreeting proxy = new ChannelFactory<IGreeting>(
                binding,
                new EndpointAddress(
"smtp.pop3://localhost:110/WCFHandsOnReader@WCFHandsOn.COM"))
                        .CreateChannel();
            proxy.Greeting(
                "Hello, world.");
            ((IChannel)proxy).Close();


            Console.WriteLine("Press any key to exit.");
            Console.ReadKey();

        }
    }
}
```

3. Start debugging the solution. The console application of the Greeting Service should appear, followed by the console application of its client. When the console of the Greeting Service shows some activity, enter a keystroke into the console for the client. After a short time, mostly depending on the speed at which messages are relayed by the SMTP and POP3 servers used, a message should appear in the console of the service, as it did in the original solution, as shown in Figure 8.3 earlier. However, in this case, the message will have been transmitted via the Internet mail protocols, rather than via TCP, as it had been before.

The custom Internet mail binding element is selected and configured in code in Listings 8.12 and 8.13, rather than being selected and configured using an application configuration file. Custom binding elements can be selected and configured using configuration files, though. How to provide for that option is covered in Chapter 13, "Representational State Transfer and Plain XML Services."

Summary

The Windows Communication Foundation can be extended to support additional transport protocols with remarkably little effort. A good approach is to start with the sample custom transport binding elements and message encoding binding elements provided with the SDK, and to modify those to use the transport and encoding protocols one would like to support. However the binding elements to support additional transport protocols are constructed, the genius of the Windows Communication Foundation is in hiding the implementation details away from programmers who use those binding elements to construct applications.

References

Official Internet Protocol Standards. 2006. http://www.rfc-editor.org/rfcxx00.html. Accessed 6 January 2006.

CHAPTER 9

Custom Behaviors

One of the best things about Windows Communication Foundation is how easy it is to customize it. This chapter focuses on one way of customizing the Windows Communication Foundation: adding one's own behaviors.

In the Windows Communication Foundation, behaviors are mechanisms internal to services and proxies that can be controlled. One example of a built-in behavior is the instancing behavior, which determines whether a Windows Communication Foundation server creates a new instance of a service type to process an incoming message or uses an existing one. The design of the Windows Communication Foundation makes it easy for developers to create custom behaviors by which administrators can control new internal mechanisms of Windows Communication Foundation proxies and services.

Understanding the Types of Behaviors

There are proxy behaviors and dispatch behaviors. Proxy behaviors, depicted in Figure 9.1, are the mechanisms by which proxies do their work of taking invocations of operations in the code for a client and translating those into messages to be transmitted to a service via the Channel Layer. Dispatch behaviors, depicted in Figure 9.2, are the mechanisms by which incoming messages, after having been processed by the Channel Layer, are translated into invocations of the methods of the service type by the Windows Communication Foundation's Dispatcher.

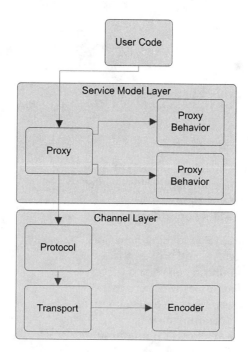

FIGURE 9.1   Proxy behaviors.

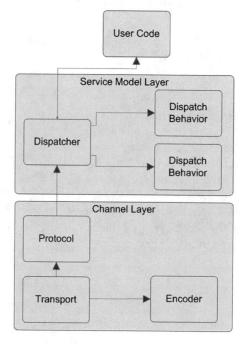

FIGURE 9.2   Dispatch behaviors.

There are five subtypes of proxy and dispatch behaviors:

- Channel behaviors are proxy behaviors that apply to all of the invocations of the methods of a proxy, such as the built-in ViaUri behavior.

- Service behaviors are dispatch behaviors that apply to all the messages to be processed by a service type, such as the built-in ServiceMetadata behavior.

- Endpoint behaviors are dispatch behaviors that apply to the messages arriving via a given endpoint, such as the built-in ListenUri behavior.

- Contract behaviors are proxy or dispatch behaviors specific to a given contract.

- Operation behaviors are proxy or dispatch behaviors specific to a given operation.

Configuring Behaviors

For behaviors to be used, they must be configured for use on the service or proxy. There are three possibilities for configuring behaviors: with attributes, in code, or via a configuration file.

Configuring Behaviors with Attributes

When an interface with attributes is first added to either a ChannelFactory or a Service Host, the Windows Communication Foundation identifies the set of attributes on the interface using reflection.

The following text gives an example of how to create an attribute and then an example of that attribute being applied.

The following code creates an attribute named Audit.

```
[AttributeUsage(AttributeTargets.Interface)]
public class AuditAttribute: Attribute, IChannelBehavior
{
    public void ApplyBehavior(
                        ChannelDescription description,
                        ProxyBehavior behavior,
                        BindingParameterCollection parameters)
    {
        ChannelFactory<IAudit> fact = new ChannelFactory<IAudit>("ClientAudit");
        IAudit prt = fact.CreateChannel();
```

```
ClientAuditMessageInspector insp = new ClientAuditMessageInspector(prt);

    behavior.MessageInspectors.Add(insp);
    }
}
```

The following shows the Audit attribute being applied to the IChat interface:

```
[System.ServiceModel.ServiceContractAttribute()]
[ClientAuditBehavior.Audit]
public interface IChat
```

Implementing behaviors as attributes is important for scenarios in which behaviors will always be required. It excludes the possibility of changes being made in the configuration that could lead to undesirable and/or unexpected results.

Configuring Behaviors in Code

You can configure behaviors in code by adding them to the appropriate Behaviors collection. The following example shows how to add a Service Behavior:

```
ServiceHost sh = new ServiceHost(typeof(Chat),baseServiceAddress);
   sh.Description.Behaviors.Add(new ServiceAuditBehavior.AuditAttribute());
sh.Open();
```

Configuring Behaviors in the Configuration File

To enable your own behaviors within the configuration file, you will need to add your behavior to the behaviorElementExtensions section. The following is an example of how this could be done with the behaviors created earlier in the chapter:

```
<system.serviceModel>
    <extensions>
        <behaviorElementExtensions>
            <add name="clientAuditBehavior" type="ClientAuditBehavior, Audit,
                Version=1.0.0.0, Culture=neutral, PublicKeyToken=null" />
        </behaviorElementExtensions>
    </extensions>
</system.serviceModel>
```

After the element and its configuration type are defined, the extension can be used, as is illustrated here:

```
<behaviors>
    <behavior configurationName="ClientBehavior">
        <clientAuditBehavior />
    </behavior>
</behaviors>
```

Creating a Behavior Extension

Placing behaviors in the configuration file provides more flexibility. This allows for adaptability and changes in deployment.

The following creates a behavior extension called `ServiceAuditBehavior` and adds the capability to configure it using a property named `Enabled`:

```
using System;
using System.Collections.Generic;
using System.Text;
using System.ServiceModel.Configuration;
namespace ServiceAuditBehavior
{
    class ServiceAuditBehaviorExtension: BehaviorExtensionSection
    {
        public override string ConfiguredSectionName
        {
            get { return "ServiceAuditBehavior"; }
        }
        [ConfigurationProperty("Enabled")]
        public string Enabled
        {
            get { return (string)base["Enabled"]; }
            set { base["Enabled"] = value; }
        }
        public override object CreateBehavior()
        {
            ServiceAuditBehavior behavior = new ServiceAuditBehavior();
            behavior.Enabled = Enabled;
            return behavior;
        }
    }
}
```

Creating a Behavior to Inspect Messages on the Server

The following sections contain several exercises that enable the creation and use of behaviors on both the client and the service side. These examples use what is likely the most common type of behavior, a type of behavior that inspects and interacts with the messages passing between client and service.

There are various scenarios in which it may be important for the content of a message to be inspected and/or altered. In these examples, there is a simple communication program in use, and the business requirements dictate that messages from both the client and the server must be audited by another service for storage.

Here we're using a simple chat/echo service, but the real world presents numerous places where auditing would be required. Those include the ever-growing auditing requirements of government/industry compliance in the private sector and the need to monitor the online interactions of children out of safety concerns in the household. And that is just in the context of monitoring the content of the messages for auditing; as you can imagine, with the capability to access the message itself, there are a number of other situations for which to use these custom behaviors.

In these exercises, you will also be introduced to the two interfaces used to incorporate the MessageInspector functionality. These are IStubMessageInspector on the service side and IProxyMessageInspector on the client side.

Creating the Auditing Service

Both the service and the client applications that will be created will report the messages they transmit to an auditing service. That auditing service is a simple one with a single operation, ProcessMessage. Follow these steps to create the auditing service:

1. Create a blank solution in Visual Studio called Custom Behaviors.

2. Add a C# Windows console project named AuditingService to the solution.

3. Add references to the System.ServiceModel and System.Configuration assemblies.

4. Add a new class module named Contracts.cs.

5. Define the contract for the chat application by replacing the code in the module with this code:

```
using System;
using System.Collections.Generic;
using System.Text;
using System.ServiceModel;

namespace AuditingService
{
   [ServiceContract]
    public interface IAudit
    {
        [OperationContract(IsOneWay = true)]
        void ProcessMessage(
                        string reportedFrom,
                        string messageType,
                        string message);
    }
}
```

6. Create the service type by adding a new class module named Audit.cs to the project and entering this code into that module:

```csharp
namespace AuditingService
{
    public class Auditor : IAudit
    {
        public void ProcessMessage(
                                   string reportedFrom,
                                   string messageType,
                                   string message)
        {
            Console.WriteLine("Received Message From:" + reportedFrom);
            Console.WriteLine("Processing Message of Type:" + messageType);
            Console.WriteLine("Message:");
            Console.WriteLine(message);
            Console.WriteLine("-----------------------------");
            return;
        }
    }
}
```

7. Provide a host for the service by replacing the code in the `Program.cs` module with this code:

```csharp
using System;
using System.Collections.Generic;
using System.Configuration;
using System.Text;
using System.ServiceModel;

namespace AuditingService
{
    class Program
    {
        static void Main(string[] args)
        {
            Uri baseServiceAddress =
                new Uri(
                    System.Configuration.ConfigurationManager.
                    AppSettings.Get("baseAddress"));
            using (ServiceHost sh = new ServiceHost(
                typeof(AuditingService.Auditor),
                new Uri[]{baseServiceAddress}))
            {
                sh.Open();
                Console.WriteLine("Auditing Service is now running.");
```

```
        Console.ReadLine();
    }
  }
}
```

8. Configure the auditing service by adding an Application Configuration file named
   App.Config to the project, and replacing its contents with the following:

```xml
<?xml version="1.0" encoding="utf-8" ?>
<configuration>
  <appSettings>
    <add key="baseAddress" value="http://localhost:8000/Auditor" />
  </appSettings>
  <system.serviceModel>
    <services>
      <service
                      type="AuditingService.Auditor" >
              <endpoint behaviorConfiguration="ServiceBehavior"
                        address=""
                        binding="basicHttpBinding"
                        contract ="AuditingService.IAudit" />
      </service>
    </services>
    <bindings>
      <basicHttpBinding>
      </basicHttpBinding>
    </bindings>
    <behaviors>

        <behavior
          name="ServiceBehavior"
          returnUnknownExceptionsAsFaults="True">
          <metadataPublishing
            enableGetWsdl="True"
            enableHelpPage="True"
            enableMetadataExchange="True"
              />
        </behavior>
    </behaviors>
  </system.serviceModel>
</configuration>
```

Creating the Dispatch Service Behavior

Follow these next steps to create the dispatch service behavior that will send copies of all
messages received by a service to the auditing service:

1. Add a new C# class library project to the solution and name it ServiceAuditBehavior.

2. Add references to the System.ServiceModel and System.Runtime.Serialization assemblies.

3. Add a version of the auditing service's contract to the service behavior project by adding a new class module called Contracts.cs, and replacing the code therein with this code:

```
using System;
using System.Collections.Generic;
using System.Text;
using System.ServiceModel;

namespace AuditingService
{
    [ServiceContract]
     public interface IAudit
     {
         [OperationContract(IsOneWay = true)]
         void ProcessMessage(
                         string reportedFrom,
                         string messageType,
                         string message);
     }
}
```

4. Define an attribute by which the service behavior can be attached to a service by adding a new class module called AuditAttribute.cs to the project, and replacing the default code in that module with this code:

```
using System;
using System.Collections.Generic;
using System.Text;
using System.ServiceModel;
using System.ServiceModel.Configuration;
using System.Collections.ObjectModel;

namespace ServiceAuditBehavior
{

    [AttributeUsage(AttributeTargets.Class)]
    public class AuditAttribute : Attribute, IServiceBehavior
    {
        public void ApplyBehavior(
                        ServiceDescription description,
                        ServiceHostBase shBase,
```

```
                        Collection<DispatchBehavior> behaviors,
                        Collection<BindingParameterCollection> parameters)
        {
            foreach (DispatchBehavior behavior in behaviors)
            {
                ChannelFactory<IAudit> fact =
                    new ChannelFactory<IAudit>("ServiceAudit");
                IAudit prt = fact.CreateChannel();
                ServiceAuditMessageInspector insp =
                    new ServiceAuditMessageInspector(prt);
                behavior.MessageInspectors.Add(insp);
            }


        }
    }
}
```

There are several points to note from this code. The class implements both the
Attribute and the ServiceBehavior interfaces. The implementation of the
ApplyBehavior() method of the ServiceBehavior interface is where the mechanism
of the custom behavior gets inserted into the dispatch operations of the service,
adding the custom behavior as an inspector of each incoming message that is to be
dispatched.

5. Begin creating the actual custom behavior by adding a new class named
   AuditMessageInspector.cs to the project, and replacing the default code in that
   module with this code:

```
using System;
using System.Collections.Generic;
using System.Text;
using System.Xml;
using System.IO;
using System.ServiceModel;


namespace ServiceAuditBehavior
{
    class ServiceAuditMessageInspector : IStubMessageInspector
    {
        private IAudit _proxy;

        public ServiceAuditMessageInspector(IAudit prx)
        {
            _proxy = prx;
        }
```

```csharp
        public object AfterReceiveRequest(
            ref Message request,
            IClientChannel channel,
            InstanceContext instanceContext)
        {

            _proxy.ProcessMessage("Server", request.Headers.Action,
➥request.ToString());

            return null;



        }

        public void BeforeSendReply(ref Message request,
➥object correlationState)
        {
            System.Console.WriteLine(request.Headers.MessageVersion.Envelope);
        }
    }
}
```

This code defines a class that implements the `IStubMessageInspector` interface.
That interface has two methods, `AfterReceiveRequest()` and `BeforeSendReply()`,
which provide the opportunity to inspect and interact with incoming and outgoing
messages. In this case, incoming messages are sent to the auditing service, and
outgoing messages are simply registered in output to the console.

Creating the Service

Now the service behavior has been programmed. Follow these next few steps to create a
simple chat/echo service to which that behavior will be applied:

1. Add a new C# console application project called Service to the solution.

2. Add references to the `System.Configuration`, `System.ServiceModel`, and
   `System.Runtime.Serialization` assemblies.

3. Add a reference to the ServiceAuditBehavior project.

4. Add a new class module, `Contracts.cs`, to the solution and replace the default code
   in that class with this code:

```csharp
using System;
using System.Collections.Generic;
using System.Text;
using System.ServiceModel;
```

```
namespace Service
{
    [ServiceContract]
    public interface IChat
    {
        [OperationContract]
        string Talk(string chatText);
    }
}
```

5. Replace the code in the Program.cs module with code for a service that implements the service contract defined in the preceding step:

```
using System;
using System.Collections.Generic;
using System.Text;
using System.ServiceModel;

namespace Service
{

    [ServiceAuditBehavior.Audit]
    public class Chat : IChat
    {
        static void Main(string[] args)
        {
            Uri baseServiceAddress = new Uri(
              System.Configuration.ConfigurationManager.AppSettings.Get(
                "baseAddress"));
            ServiceHost sh = new ServiceHost(typeof(Chat),baseServiceAddress);
            sh.Open();
            Console.WriteLine("Service is now running.");

            Console.ReadLine();

        }


        public string Talk(string chatText)
        {
            Console.WriteLine("Client said:" + chatText);
            return ("Did you say " + chatText + " ?");
        }
    }
}
```

This code defines a service type that implements the service contract defined in the preceding step. The custom audit behavior is added to the service type as an attribute.

6. Configure the service by adding an application configuration file to the project with this content. Replace the code in the Program.cs module with code for a service that implements the service contract defined in the preceding step:

```
<configuration>
  <appSettings>
    <add key="baseAddress" value="http://localhost:8000/Behaviors" />
  </appSettings>
  <system.serviceModel>
    <client>
      <endpoint
        name="ServiceAudit"
        address="http://localhost:8000/Auditor"
        binding="basicHttpBinding"
        contract ="ServiceAuditBehavior.IAudit" />
    </client>
    <services>
      <service type="Service.Chat">
        <endpoint behaviorConfiguration="ServiceBehavior"
          address=""
          contract="IChat"
          binding ="basicHttpBinding"/>
      </service>
    </services>
  </system.serviceModel>
</configuration>
```

This configuration includes the configuration of a client for the auditing service, because the custom behavior that has been added to the chat/echo service sends messages to the auditing service.

Creating a Behavior to Inspect Messages on the Client

What has been accomplished thus far is the creation of a dispatch service behavior to operate on messages directed at the chat/echo service. Now a proxy channel behavior will be constructed to operate on messages sent by a chat/echo client.

Creating the Proxy Channel Behavior

Execute these steps to create a proxy channel behavior that will send copies of all messages sent by a client to the auditing service:

1. Right-click on the solution and create a new C# class library project named ClientAuditBehavior.

2. Add references to the `System.Runtime.Serialization` and `System.ServiceModel` assemblies.

3. Provide a copy of the Auditing service's contract by creating a new class module named `Contract.cs` and replacing the default code in that module with this code:

```csharp
using System;
using System.Collections.Generic;
using System.Text;
using System.ServiceModel;

namespace AuditingService
{
    [ServiceContract]
    public interface IAudit
    {
        [OperationContract(IsOneWay = true)]
        void ProcessMessage(
                        string reportedFrom,
                        string messageType,
                        string message);
    }
}
```

4. Now provide the code for the proxy channel behavior by adding a new class module called `AuditMessageInspector.cs` to the ClientAuditBehavior project, and replacing the default code in that module with this code:

```csharp
using System;
using System.Collections.Generic;
using System.Text;
using System.ServiceModel;
using System.Xml;
using System.IO;

namespace ClientAuditBehavior
{
        class ClientAuditMessageInspector : IProxyMessageInspector
        {
          private IAudit _proxy;

          public ClientAuditMessageInspector(IAudit prx)
          {
```

```
    proxy = prx;
  }

  public object BeforeSendRequest(
    ref Message request,
    IClientChannel channel)
  {
    return null;
  }

  public void AfterReceiveReply(
    ref Message reply,
    object correlationState)
  {
    MessageBuffer buf = reply.CreateBufferedCopy(1000000);
    Message msg = buf.CreateMessage();

    TextWriter strWrt = new StringWriter();
    XmlTextWriter wrt = new XmlTextWriter(strWrt);
    msg.WriteBody(wrt);
    wrt.Flush();
    strWrt.Flush();
    String msgStr = strWrt.ToString();
    wrt.Close();
    strWrt.Close();

    _proxy.ProcessMessage("Client",msg.Headers.Action, msgStr);
    msg.Close();
    reply = buf.CreateMessage();
  }
 }
}
```

Note that the class defined in this code implements the IProxyMessageInspector interface of the Windows Communication Foundation. That interface defines a method called BeforeSendRequest() for operating on outgoing messages, and another called AfterReceiveReply() for operating on responses.

5. The next step is to define the attribute class by which the proxy channel behavior will be attached to a channel. Do so by adding a new class module called AuditAttribute.cs to the ClientAuditBehavior project, and replacing the default code in that module with this code:

```
using System;
using System.Collections.Generic;
```

```
using System.Text;
using System.ServiceModel;

namespace ClientAuditBehavior
{
    [AttributeUsage(AttributeTargets.Class)]
    public class AuditAttribute: Attribute, IChannelBehavior
    {
        public void ApplyBehavior(
          ChannelDescription description,
          ProxyBehavior behavior,
          BindingParameterCollection parameters)
        {
          ChannelFactory<IAudit> fact =
            new ChannelFactory<IAudit>("ClientAudit");
          IAudit prt = fact.CreateChannel();

          ClientAuditMessageInspector insp =
            new ClientAuditMessageInspector(prt);

          behavior.MessageInspectors.Add(insp);
        }
    }
}
```

Creating the Client

Follow these steps to create a client for the chat/echo service to which the proxy channel behavior will be applied:

1. Add a new C# Windows console project named Client to the solution.

2. Add a reference to the System.ServiceModel assembly to that new project.

3. Also add a reference to the ClientAuditBehavior project.

4. Add a reference to the System.ServiceModel assembly to that new project.

5. Right-click on the Service project in the solution and select Debug, and then Start New Instance from the content menu.

6. Open the Microsoft Windows Vista DEBUG Build Environment prompt, make the directory containing the Client project file the current directory, and enter this command:

    svcutil http://localhost:8000/Behaviors /out:proxy.cs /config:app.config

7. Stop debugging the solution and add the files `proxy.cs` and `app.config` output by the command in the preceding step to the Client project.

8. Replace the default code in the `Program.cs` module with this code that uses the generated proxy class in the `Proxy.cs` module, adding the proxy channel behavior to it first:

```
using System;
using System.Collections.Generic;
using System.Text;
using System.ServiceModel;
namespace Client
{
    class Program
    {
        static void Main(string[] args)
        {
            ChatProxy c = new ChatProxy();
            c.ChannelFactory.Description.Behaviors.Add(
              new ClientAuditBehavior.AuditAttribute());
            System.Console.WriteLine("Welcome to Chat");
            System.Console.WriteLine();
            System.Console.WriteLine("Enter text below and press ENTER to send");
            string cont = Console.ReadLine();
            while (cont != "q")
            {
                Console.WriteLine("Server Said:" + c.Talk(cont));
                cont = Console.ReadLine();
            }
        }
    }
}
```

9. Modify the `app.config` file of the Client project by adding this second `endpoint` subelement to the `client` element to define how the proxy channel auditing behavior is to communicate with the auditing service:

```
<endpoint
  name="ClientAudit"
  address="http://localhost:8000/Auditor"
  binding="basicHttpBinding"
  contract ="ClientAuditBehavior.IAudit" />
```

Testing the Solution

The solution is now complete. Execute these steps to see it in action:

1. Right-click on the solution and select Set Startup Projects from the menu.

2. Configure the Startup project properties as shown in Figure 9.3.

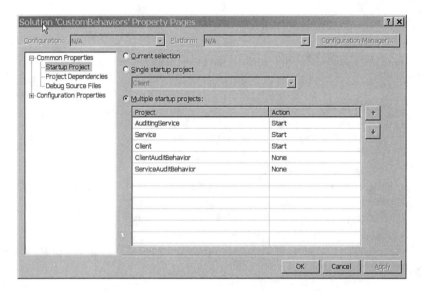

FIGURE 9.3 Startup project configuration.

3. Start debugging the solution. Three console windows will open: one for the audit service, one for the chat/echo service, and one for the client.

4. When there is activity in all three console windows, type some text into the client window and press the Enter key. The expected result is shown in Figure 9.4: The client sends a message to the service, the dispatch behavior on the service passes a copy of the message to the auditing service, and, when the service's response is received by the client, the proxy channel behavior on the client passes a copy of that response to the auditing service as well.

FIGURE 9.4   The solution in action.

Summary

This chapter introduced the various categories of behaviors in the Windows Communication Foundation. It also showed how to extend the Windows Communication Foundation's Service Model layer with the addition of custom behaviors.

CHAPTER 10

Publish/Subscribe Systems

In "publish/subscribe systems[...]processes can subscribe to messages containing information on specific subjects, while other processes produce (i.e. publish) such messages" (Tannenbaum and van Steen 2002, 701). Publish/subscribe systems are required in many scenarios. In the financial industry, subscriptions to prices are needed. Subscriptions to sensor data and to information about other equipment are required in manufacturing. In computer systems administration, the administrators need to subscribe to information about the security and states of the systems.

Web Services Eventing and Web Services Notification are competing protocols pertinent to publish/subscribe systems. Both specify formats for subscription messages and for publication messages. Neither format is likely to become very important until at least both International Business Machines (IBM) and Microsoft endorse just one of the protocols.

The Web Services Notification specification provides a handy description of some of the various ways in which publishers can provide updates to subscribers (Graham, Hull and Murray 2005, 24). In push-style notification, subscribers send subscription messages to publishers, who then send publication messages to the subscribers. In pull-style notification, subscribers send subscription messages to publishers, who send publication messages to a pull-point that is known to the subscribers, from which the subscribers retrieve the publication messages. In brokered notification, subscribers send subscription messages to brokers, who retrieve publication messages sent by publishers and make them available to the subscribers.

There are various ways of constructing publish/subscribe systems with the Windows Communication Foundation. This chapter describes several of them.

Publish/Subscribe Using Callback Contracts

A simple way of building a publish/subscribe system with the Windows Communication Foundation is to use callback contracts. This service contract, IPublisher,

```
[ServiceContract(Session=true,CallbackContract=typeof(ISubscriber))]
public interface IPublisher
{
    [OperationContract]
    KnownDataPoint[] GetKnownDataPoints();

    [OperationContract]
    void Subscribe(KnownDataPoint[] dataPoints, out bool subscriptionAccepted);
}
```

identifies a callback contract, ISubscriber, that clients of the service are required to implement:

```
[ServiceContract]
public interface ISubscriber
{
    [OperationContract(IsOneWay=true)]
    void Notify(Guid dataPointIdentifier, byte[] value);
}
```

Because all clients of a service that implements IPublisher must implement ISubscriber, which exposes a one-way operation called Notify(), the service can rely on being able to use the client's Notify() operation to publish data to the client. The callback contract can include any number of operations, but they must all be one-way operations.

Note that the IPublisher service contract also has the value of the Session parameter of the ServiceContract attribute set to true. That signifies that the messages exchanged between a client and a service for the duration of a connection between them will be grouped together by the Windows Communication Foundation into a session, and that the Windows Communication Foundation will maintain some information about the state of each session. Having the Windows Communication Foundation do that is a prerequisite for using callback contracts.

Using callback contracts requires not only the obvious task of specifying a callback contract for a service contract, but also the task of selecting a binding for the service by which the service can initiate transmissions to the client. For a binding to allow for that possibility, it must incorporate the composite duplex binding element, `CompositeDuplexBindingElement`. Two standard bindings that incorporate that binding element are `WSDualHttpBinding` and `NetTcpBinding`.

To use the operations of the callback contract implemented by the client, the service requires a proxy for communicating with the client. The service obtains that proxy by using the `GetCallbackChannel<T>()` generic method of the Windows Communication Foundation's `OperationContext` class, introduced in Chapter 2, "The Fundamentals":

```
ISubscriber proxy = OperationContext.Current.GetCallbackChannel<ISubscriber>();
proxy.Notify(...);
```

To see how to use the `ISubscriber` callback contracts in a publish/subscribe solution, follow these steps:

1. Copy the code associated with this chapter that you downloaded from www.s amspublishing.com to the folder `C:\WCFHandsOn`. The code is all in a folder called `PublishSubscribe`. After you have unzipped the code, there should be a folder that looks like the one shown in Figure 10.1.

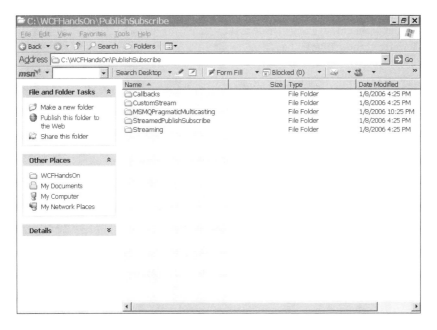

FIGURE 10.1   PublishSubscribe folder.

2. Open the solution `C:\WCFHandsOn\PublishSubscribe\Callbacks\ CallbackContract.sln`.

The solution consists of six projects:

- The RandomDataPoint project is for building a class library with a class called RandomDataPoint that represents the source of the information that subscribers want to receive.

- The RandomDataPoint class derives from the DataPoint class provided by the class library built from the DataPoint project.

- The PublisherService project is for building a class library incorporating the IPublisher service contract, which has ISubscriber as a callback contract. The class library also includes the PublisherService class, a service type that implements the IPublisher service contract.

- The PublisherServiceHost project provides a console application to serve as the host for the PublisherService service type.

- SubscriberOne and SubscriberTwo are both console applications with clients of PublisherService service that implement the ISubscriber callback contract.

3. Examine the IPublisher service contract in the IPublisher.cs module of the PublisherService project in the CallbackContract solution:

```
[ServiceContract(Session=true,CallbackContract=typeof(ISubscriber))]
public interface IPublisher
{
    [OperationContract]
    KnownDataPoint[] GetKnownDataPoints();

    [OperationContract]
    void Subscribe(KnownDataPoint[] dataPoints,
                      out bool subscriptionAccepted);
}
```

The IPublisher interface is a Windows Communication Foundation service contract that designates ISubscriber as its callback contract. The service contract provides the GetKnownDataPoints() operation for retrieving the identifiers of the data items about which a service that implements the contract can publish information. The Subscribe() operation is provided for clients to subscribe to information about one or more of those data items.

4. Look at the ISubscriber service contract in the ISubscriber.cs module of the PublisherService project:

```
[ServiceContract]
public interface ISubscriber
```

```
{
    [OperationContract(IsOneWay=true)]
    void Notify(Guid dataPointIdentifier, byte[] value);
}
```

ISubscriber is a service contract, all the operations of which are one-way operations. Actually, there is just one operation, called Notify(), by which the service can push the current values of a data item to the client.

5. Examine the PublisherService service type's implementation of the IPublisher contract's Subscribe() method, in the PublisherService.cs module of the PublisherService project:

```
void IPublisher.Subscribe(
    KnownDataPoint[] dataPoints, out bool subscriptionAccepted)
{
    Console.WriteLine("Received subscription request.");
    subscriptionAccepted = false;
    string dataPointIdentifier = null;
    if (dataPoints.Length == 1)
    {
        dataPointIdentifier = dataPoints[0].Identifier;
        this.ValidateDataPoint(dataPointIdentifier, out subscriptionAccepted);
    }

    if (subscriptionAccepted)
    {
        if (!(this.randomDataPoint.Active))
        {
            this.randomDataPoint.Active = true;
        }
        lock (this.subscribersLock)
        {
            this.subscribers.Add(
                OperationContext.Current.GetCallbackChannel<ISubscriber>());
        }
    }
}
```

After confirming that the subscription request is for information about a data item of which the service is aware, the method retrieves a proxy for communicating with the subscriber using the Windows Communication Foundation's OperationContext class. Then it adds that proxy to a list of subscriber proxies.

6. Study the NextValueHandler() method of the PublisherService service type, which is also in the PublisherService.cs module of the PublisherService project:

```
private void NextValueHandler(IDataPoint sender, byte[] newValue)
{
    lock(this.subscribersLock)
    {
        for(int index = this.subscribers.Count - 1; index >= 0; index--)
        {
            try
            {
                this.subscribers[index].Notify(sender.Identifier, newValue);
            }
            catch (Exception exception)
            {
                Console.WriteLine(
                    "Removing subscriber due to exception {0}.",
                    exception.ToString());
                this.subscribers.RemoveAt(index);
            }
            if (this.subscribers.Count <= 0)
            {
                this.randomDataPoint.Active = false;
            }
        }
    }
}
```

This method is the one by which the service type is notified of a change in the value of the data item about which it publishes information. The service type iterates through the list of subscriber proxies, using each proxy to publish a message concerning the fluctuation in the value of the data item to a subscriber.

7. Look at the subscribers' implementation of the Notify() operation of the ISubscriber callback contract, which is in the Subscriber.cs module of the SubscriberOne project of the CallbackContract solution. It simply outputs the content of messages published by the client to the console:

```
void ISubscriber.Notify(Guid dataPointIdentifier, byte[] value)
{
    Console.WriteLine(
        "Notified of value {0} of data point {1}.",
            BitConverter.ToInt32(value,0),
            dataPointIdentifier.ToString());
}
```

8. Start debugging the solution. Console windows for the PublisherServiceHost and for the two subscribers should appear.

9. When there is activity in the console of the PublisherServiceHost, enter a keystroke into the console windows of both subscribers' consoles.

   After a few moments, the service should begin publishing messages about fluctuations in the value of a data item to both of the subscribers, as shown in Figure 10.2. It may take a moment after the first published message is received by the first subscriber before the first published message is received by the second subscriber.

10. Stop debugging the solution.

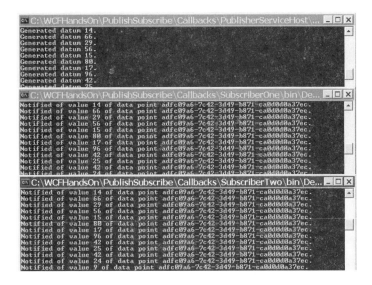

FIGURE 10.2   Publish/Subscribe using callback contracts.

Callback contracts provide a very easy way of implementing publish/subscribe with the Windows Communication Foundation. As is true of push-style notification solutions generally (Graham, Hull and Murray 2005, 24), the technique presupposes the network being configured to allow the publisher to transmit messages to the client.

Publish/Subscribe Using MSMQ Pragmatic Multicasting

Version 3 of Microsoft Message Queuing (MSMQ), a technology provided free of charge with Microsoft Windows operation systems, added support for the pragmatic multicasting (PGM) protocol. As shown in Figure 10.3, a nontransactional queue can be associated with a PGM address, and any number of queues can be associated with the same PGM address.

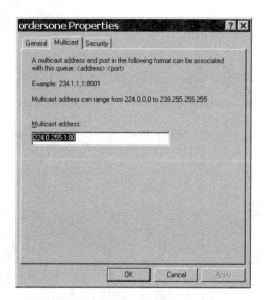

FIGURE 10.3   Associating a PGM address with an MSMQ queue.

As Anand Rajagopalan points out, this new facility of MSMQ provides a simple way of doing publish/subscribe with pull-style notification (Rajagopalan 2005). A publisher can direct publication messages to a PGM address via MSMQ, which will result in those messages being added to all the subscriber queues associated with that address. Subscribers can then pull the messages from their respective queues. Because, as Rajagopalan further points out, the Windows Communication Foundation provides the `MsmqIntegrationBinding` for exchanging messages with MSMQ applications, this way of doing publish/subscribe can also be implemented with the Windows Communication Foundation:

1. Open the solution `C:\WCFHandsOn\PublishSubscribe\MSMQPragmaticMulticasting\MSMQPragmaticMulticasting.sln`.

   The solution consists of four projects:

   - The Order project is for building a class library with a class called `PurchaseOrder`.

   - The Publisher project provides a console application that publishes information about incoming purchase orders to a PGM address via MSMQ, using the Windows Communication Foundation's `MsmqIntegrationBinding`.

   - SubscriberOne and SubscriberTwo are both console applications that subscribe to notifications of incoming purchase orders, using the Windows Communication Foundation's `MsmqIntegrationBinding` to pull the notifications from queues associated with the PGM address to which the Publisher sends the notifications.

2. Look at the PurchaseOrder class in the Order.cs module of the Order project in the MSMQPragmaticMulticasting project, reproduced in Listing 10.1. The class claims to be serializable by having the Serializable attribute. It overrides the ToString() method of the base class, Object, to provide an informative representation of itself as a string. It will be instances of this class that the publisher in this solution will be sending to the subscribers.

LISTING 10.1   Notification Class

```csharp
[Serializable]
public class PurchaseOrder
{
    public string orderIdentifier;
    public string customerIdentifier;
    public PurchaseOrderLineItem[] orderLineItems;
    private OrderStates orderStatus;

    public float TotalCost
    {
        get
        {
            float totalCost = 0;
            foreach (PurchaseOrderLineItem lineItem in orderLineItems)
                totalCost += lineItem.TotalCost;
            return totalCost;
        }
    }

    public OrderStates Status
    {
        get
        {
            return orderStatus;
        }
        set
        {
            orderStatus = value;
        }
    }

    public override string ToString()
    {
        StringBuilder buffer =
            new StringBuilder("Purchase Order: " + orderIdentifier + "\n");
        buffer.Append("\tCustomer: " + customerIdentifier + "\n");
        buffer.Append("\tOrderDetails\n");
```

10

LISTING 10.1   Continued

```
    foreach (PurchaseOrderLineItem lineItem in orderLineItems)
    {
        buffer.Append("\t\t" + lineItem.ToString());
    }

    buffer.Append("\tTotal cost of this order: $" + TotalCost + "\n");
    buffer.Append("\tOrder status: " + Status + "\n");
    return buffer.ToString();
    }
}
```

3. Examine the IOrderSubscriber interface in the Publisher.cs module of the
   Publisher project, and in the Subscriber.cs module of the SubscriberOne project:

```
[ServiceContract(Namespace = "http://Microsoft.ServiceModel.Samples")]
[KnownType(typeof(PurchaseOrder))]
public interface IOrderSubscriber
{
    [OperationContract(IsOneWay = true, Action = "*")]
    void Notify(MsmqMessage<PurchaseOrder> message);
}
```

This .NET interface is designated as a Windows Communication Foundation service
contract by the ServiceContract attribute. It includes a single operation, Notify(),
that accepts a single parameter of the type MsmqMessage<PurchaseOrder>.
MsmqMessage<T> is a generic type provided by the Windows Communication
Foundation for which any serializable type can serve as the type argument. It allows
data to be marshaled in and out of MSMQ messages sent or received via the MSMQ
integration binding.

In Chapter 4, " Security," it was explained that the value of the Action parameter of
the OperationContract attribute is used to correlate messages with operations. A
value usually does not have to be provided for that parameter, because the Windows
Communication Foundation automatically and invisibly supplies appropriate
default values.

However, the value "*" is provided for the Action parameter of the
OperationContract attribute on the IOrderSubscriber contract's Notify()
operation. Specifying Action="*" as the parameter to the OperationContract
attribute signifies that the operation with that attribute is the unmatched message
handler, which means that operation will be used to process all messages not
matched with another operation. All messages received via the MSMQ integration
binding are dispatched to the unmatched message handler of the receiving service.
In this case all such messages will be dispatched to the method by which the
IOrderSubscriber contract's Notify() operation is implemented.

4. Study the static `Main()` method of the `Publisher` class in the `Publisher.cs` module of the Publisher project:

```
static void Main(string[] args)
{
    [...]

    PurchaseOrder order = new PurchaseOrder();
    order.customerIdentifier = "somecustomer.com";
    order.orderIdentifier = Guid.NewGuid().ToString();

    PurchaseOrderLineItem firstLineItem = new PurchaseOrderLineItem();
    [...]

    PurchaseOrderLineItem secondLineItem = new PurchaseOrderLineItem();
    [...]

    order.orderLineItems =
        new PurchaseOrderLineItem[] {firstLineItem,    secondLineItem };

    IOrderSubscriber proxy =
        new ChannelFactory<IOrderSubscriber>(
            "OrderPullPoint").CreateChannel();

    proxy.Notify(new MsmqMessage<PurchaseOrder>(order));
    ((IChannel)proxy).Close();

    [...]
}
```

The method sends notification of a purchase order to the subscribers using a proxy that is obtained in a customary way, using the Windows Communication Foundation's `ChannelFactory<T>` generic. The Publisher code simply invokes the proxy's `Notify()` operation, passing an instance of `MsmqMessage<PurchaseOrder>` created from the purchase order about which it wants to notify the subscribers.

5. Look at the configuration of the Publisher in the `App.Config` file of the Publisher project to see the `OrderPullPoint` configuration referred to in the construction of the proxy:

```
<?xml version="1.0" encoding="utf-8" ?>
<configuration>
    <system.serviceModel>
        <client>
            <endpoint name="OrderPullPoint"
                    address="msmq.formatname:MULTICAST=224.0.255.1:80"
                    binding="msmqIntegrationBinding"
```

10

```
                          bindingConfiguration="OrderPublicationBinding"
                          contract
                ="Microsoft.ServiceModel.Samples.IOrderSubscriber">
               </endpoint>
          </client>
          <bindings>
              <msmqIntegrationBinding>
                  <binding name=" OrderPublicationBinding" exactlyOnce="false" >
                      <security mode="None" />
                  </binding>
              </msmqIntegrationBinding>
          </bindings>
      </system.serviceModel>
  </configuration>
```

That configuration selects the Windows Communication Foundation's standard
`MsmqIntegrationBinding` as the binding to use in publishing the service. The
settings of that standard binding are modified so as to not require the assurance of
messages being delivered exactly once. That assurance, which is provided by default
by the `MsmqIntegrationBinding`, is not possible in this case, because the destination
queues are not transactional queues. They are not transactional queues because
MSMQ queues associated with PGM addresses cannot be transactional.

The address provided as the destination of the messages is *msmq.formatname:*
MULTICAST=224.0.255.1:80. In that address, *msmq* is the scheme associated with the
MSMQ-integration transport protocol by the MSQM integration binding. The
expression *formatname:MULTICAST* signifies that the destination for messages is to be
identified by a PGM address. The PGM address given is `224.0.255.1`. The component *80* of the address is a port number.

6. Compare the configuration of the Publisher with the configuration of a subscriber,
   such as the configuration of the first subscriber, in the `App.Config` file of the
   SubscriberOne project:

```
<?xml version="1.0" encoding="utf-8" ?>
<configuration>
    <appSettings>
        <add key="orderQueueName" value=".\private$\WCFHandsOnOne" />
    </appSettings>
    <system.serviceModel>
    <services>
      <service
        type="Microsoft.ServiceModel.Samples.OrderSubscriber">
        <endpoint address="msmq.formatname:DIRECT=OS:.\private$\WCFHandsOnOne"
                  binding="msmqIntegrationBinding"
                  bindingConfiguration="OrderSubscriptionBinding"
                  contract="Microsoft.ServiceModel.Samples.IOrderSubscriber">
```

```
      </endpoint>
    </service>
  </services>
  <bindings>
    <msmqIntegrationBinding>
      <binding name="OrderSubscriptionBinding" exactlyOnce="false" >
        <security mode="None" />
      </binding>
    </msmqIntegrationBinding>
  </bindings>
  </system.serviceModel >
</configuration>
```

The subscriber configuration defines the configuration of a Windows Communication Foundation service that receives messages via MSMQ. The selection and
configuration of the binding corresponds exactly with the selection and configuration of the binding for the publisher. Whereas the address provided as the destination of the publisher's messages was a PGM address, the address provided as the
source of messages for the subscriber service is the name of an MSMQ queue associated with that PGM address.

7. Examine the static Main() method of the OrderSubscriber class of one of the
subscribers in the Subscriber.cs module of the SubscriberOne project:

```
public static void Main()
{
    string queueName = ConfigurationManager.AppSettings["orderQueueName"];

    if (!(MessageQueue.Exists(queueName)))
    {
        MessageQueue.Create(queueName);
        MessageQueue queue = new MessageQueue(queueName);
        queue.MulticastAddress =
            ConfigurationManager.AppSettings["multicastAddress"];
    }

    using (ServiceHost serviceHost = new ServiceHost(typeof(OrderSubscriber)))
    {
        serviceHost.Open();

        Console.WriteLine("The service is ready.");
        Console.WriteLine("Press any key to terminate the service.");
        Console.ReadLine();

        serviceHost.Close();
    }
}
```

The method creates the queue that serves as the subscriber's pull-point if it does not already exist. In creating the queue, it associates the queue with the PGM address to which the publisher directs its messages.

An instance of the OrderSubscriber class, which implements the IOrderSubscriber service contract, is then loaded into an application domain using an instance of the Windows Communication Foundation's ServiceHost class. Then the Open() method of the ServiceHost instance is invoked, whereupon the Windows Communication Foundation's channel layer will begin watching for messages delivered to the queue specified in the subscriber's configuration file. Such messages will be dispatched, by the Windows Communication Foundation, to the implementation of the unmatched message handler, the Notify() operation, of the IOrderSubscriber service contract.

8. Look at the OrderSubscriber class's implementation of the Notify() operation of the IOrderSubscriber contract:

```
public void Notify(MsmqMessage<PurchaseOrder> message)
{
    PurchaseOrder order = (PurchaseOrder)message.Body;
    Random statusIndexer = new Random();
    order.Status = (OrderStates)statusIndexer.Next(3);
    Console.WriteLine("Processing {0} ", order);
}
```

Recall that the Notify() operation is designated as the unmatched message handler of the IOrderSubscriber contract, and also that all messages received via the MSMQ integration binding are dispatched to the method that implements the unmatched message handler. In this case, that method is the Notify() method of the OrderSubscriber class. The received messages are dispatched to the Notify() method as instances of the MsmqMessage<PurchaseOrder> type, from which instances of the PurchaseOrder class are extracted with this simple statement:

```
PurchaseOrder order = (PurchaseOrder)message.Body;
```

9. Start debugging the MSMQPragmaticMulticastingSolution. Console windows for the two subscriber applications should appear, as well as the console window of the publisher.

10. When there is activity in both of the subscriber application's console windows, enter a keystroke into the console window of the publisher. The results should appear as shown in Figure 10.4. Notifications of incoming purchase orders are published to the subscriber's pull-points by the publisher, from which they are retrieved by the subscribers.

11. Stop debugging the application.

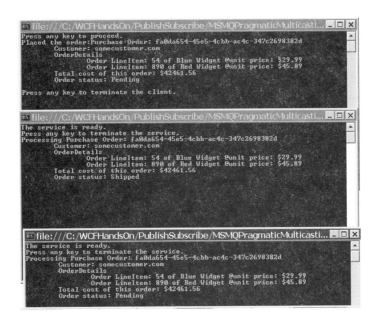

FIGURE 10.4 Publish/Subscribe using MSMQ PGM.

Generally, when Windows Communication Foundation applications send messages to other Windows Communication Foundation applications via MSMQ queues, one uses the Windows Communication Foundation's standard `NetMsmqBinding`, rather the `MsmqIntegrationBinding`. The `NetMsmqBinding` has the virtue of being more flexible, not requiring messages to be sent and received in the form of instances of `MsmqMessage<T>` types, and also allowing messages to be dispatched to operations other than the unmatched message handler. Usually, one must only resort to using the `MsmqIntegrationBinding` when a Windows Communication Foundation application must communicate with a non–Windows Communication Foundation application via MSMQ. In this case, however, all the applications communicating via MSMQ are Windows Communication Foundation applications, so what is the reason for using the `MsmqIntegrationBinding` rather than the `NetMsmqBinding`? The reason is that the implementation of the PGM protocol in MSMQ represents, in effect, a non–Windows Communication Foundation application interposed between the Windows Communication Foundation applications.

Publish/Subscribe Using Streaming

In using either callback contracts or MSMQ PGM to do publish/subscribe with the Windows Communication Foundation, there is the shortcoming of incurring the cost of sending an entire message with each notification from the publisher to the subscribers. That price is more acceptable when the size of the notification in proportion to the total size of the messages is larger, and when notifications are required less frequently. However, the requirement to publish frequent notifications of small items of information is commonplace. One can use the Windows Communication Foundation's streamed transfer mode to avoid having to create an entire message for each notification in such cases.

The Streamed Transfer Mode

The Windows Communication Foundation uses a buffered transfer mode by default. That means that the entire contents of an outgoing message must have been written into a buffer before the message is sent, and that the entire contents of an incoming message must be read from a buffer before the message is dispatched for processing. However, the Windows Communication Foundation provides the option of a streamed transfer mode by which the content of an incoming message may be dispatched for processing by the receiver even before the entire content of the message has been formulated by the source:

1. Open the solution C:\WCFHandsOn\PublishSubscribe\Streaming\Streaming.sln. It consists of two projects. The Client project is for building a Windows Forms application that displays an image retrieved from a Windows Communication Foundation service. That service is built using the other project in the solution, called Service.

2. Examine the interface IPictureServer in the Program.cs module of the Service project. It is designated as a Windows Communication Foundation service contract, of which the only notable feature is that its sole operation, GetPicture(), is defined as returning a Stream object:

```
[ServiceContract]
public interface IPictureServer
{
    [OperationContract]
    Stream GetPicture(string pictureName);
}
```

3. Look at the PictureServer class, which is a service type that implements the IPictureServer contract. It returns the image requested by a client as a FileStream object:

```
internal class PictureServer: IPictureServer
{
    Stream IPictureServer.GetPicture(string pictureName)
    {
        try
        {
            return new FileStream(pictureName, FileMode.Open);
        }
        catch (Exception)
        {
            return null;
        }
    }
}
```

4. See how the service is configured in the `App.Config` file of the PictureService project:

```xml
<?xml version="1.0" encoding="utf-8" ?>
<configuration>
    <system.serviceModel>
        <services>
            <service type="Server.PictureServer">
                <endpoint    address="http://localhost:8000/Picture/Server"
                             binding="basicHttpBinding"
                             bindingConfiguration="StreamedHttp"
                             contract="Server.IPictureServer,Server"/>
            </service>
        </services>
        <bindings>
            <basicHttpBinding>
                <binding
                    name="StreamedHttp"
                    transferMode="StreamedResponse"
                    maxMessageSize="9223372036854775807"/>
            </basicHttpBinding>
        </bindings>
    </system.serviceModel>
</configuration>
```

The standard Windows Communication Foundation `BasicHttpBinding` is selected for the service, but the value of the transfer mode property of that binding is set to `StreamedResponse`. Note that the value of the `maxMessageSize` property is set to a very large number, which happens to be the maximum value.

5. Examine the client application's use of the `GetPicture()` operation of the service in the `RetrievePicture()` method of the `MainForm.cs` module of the Client project:

```csharp
private void RetrievePicture(object state)
{
    if (this.InvokeRequired)
    {
        IPictureServer pictureServer =
            new ChannelFactory<IPictureServer>("PictureServer")
                .CreateChannel();
        Stream pictureStream =
            pictureServer.GetPicture(
                ConfigurationManager.AppSettings["PictureName"]);
        ((IChannel)pictureServer).Close();

        this.Invoke(
            new RetrievePictureDelegate(
```

10

```
                        this.RetrievePicture),new object[]{pictureStream});
    }
    else
    {
        Bitmap bitMap = new Bitmap((Stream)state);
        this.Picture.Image = bitMap;
    }
}
```

The `Stream` object retrieved from the service via the `GetPicture()` operation is marshaled onto the user interface thread. Then it is displayed in the `PictureBox` control of the client application's form.

6. Start debugging the application. The console window of the service should appear, along with the client application's form.

7. When there is activity in the console window of the service, click the Get the Picture! button on the client application's form. After a moment, a picture, retrieved from the service, should appear on the client application's form, as shown in Figure 10.5.

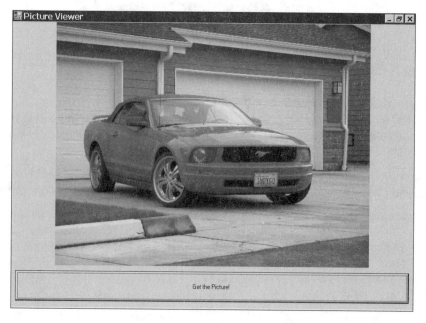

FIGURE 10.5   Retrieving a picture from a service using the streamed transfer mode.

8. Stop debugging the application.

9. Alter the `App.Config` file of the Service project as shown in Listing 10.2, thereby adding the mechanism introduced in Chapter 2 for logging the messages sent and received by the service.

LISTING 10.2   Streamed Transfer Configuration with Message Logging

```xml
<?xml version="1.0" encoding="utf-8" ?>
<configuration>
    <system.diagnostics>
        <sources>
            <source
                name="System.ServiceModel.MessageLogging"
                switchValue="Verbose">
                <listeners>
                    <add
                        name="xml"
                        type="System.Diagnostics.XmlWriterTraceListener"
initializeData="C:\WCFHandsOn\PublishSubscribe\Streaming\message.log" />
                </listeners>
            </source>
        </sources>
        <trace autoflush="true" />
    </system.diagnostics>
    <system.serviceModel>
        <diagnostics>
            <messageLogging logEntireMessage="true"
                            maxMessagesToLog="300"
                            logMessagesAtServiceLevel="false"
                            logMalformedMessages="true"
                            logMessagesAtTransportLevel="true" />
        </diagnostics>
        <services>
            <service type="Server.PictureServer">
                <endpoint    address="http://localhost:8000/Picture/Server"
                             binding="basicHttpBinding"
                             bindingConfiguration="StreamedHttp"
                             contract="Server.IPictureServer,Server"/>
            </service>
        </services>
        <bindings>
            <basicHttpBinding>
                <binding
                    name="StreamedHttp"
                    transferMode="StreamedResponse"
                    maxMessageSize="9223372036854775807"/>
            </basicHttpBinding>
        </bindings>
    </system.serviceModel>
</configuration>
```

10

10. Now repeat steps 6, 7, and 8.

11. Open the file C:\WCFHandsOn\PublishSubscribe\Streaming\Mesage.log.

    That file should contain the following record of the message by which the service
    replied to the client, showing that the stream object was incorporated in the body
    of a SOAP message:

```
<s:Envelope
    xmlns:a="http://schemas.xmlsoap.org/ws/2004/08/addressing"
    xmlns:s="http://schemas.xmlsoap.org/soap/envelope/">
    <s:Header>
        <a:Action s:mustUnderstand="1">
        http://tempuri.org/IPictureServer/GetPictureResponse</a:Action>
        <a:To s:mustUnderstand="1">
        http://schemas.xmlsoap.org/ws/2004/08/addressing/role/anonymous
        </a:To>
        </s:Header>
        <s:Body>... stream ...</s:Body>
</s:Envelope>
```

12. Alter the App.Config file of the Client project to omit the adjustment to the maxi-
    mum message size of the binding:

```
<?xml version="1.0" encoding="utf-8" ?>
<configuration>
        <appSettings>
            <add key="PictureName" value="Pony.jpg"/>
        </appSettings>
        <system.serviceModel>
        <client>
            <endpoint name="PictureServer"
                    address="http://localhost:8000/Picture/Server"
                    binding="basicHttpBinding"
                    bindingConfiguration="StreamedHttp"
                    contract="Client.IPictureServer,Client"/>
        </client>
        <bindings>
            <basicHttpBinding>
                <binding name="StreamedHttp"
                    transferMode="StreamedResponse"
                />
            </basicHttpBinding>
        </bindings>
    </system.serviceModel>
</configuration>
```

13. Repeat, once again, steps 6, 7, and 8.

On this occasion, the client application should throw an exception, as shown in Figure 10.6.

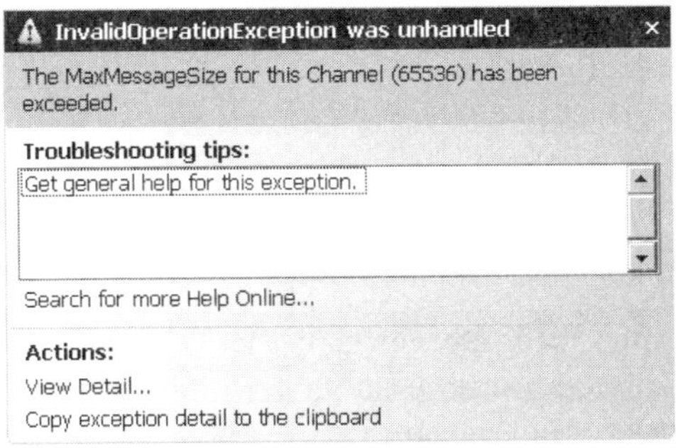

FIGURE 10.6   Exceeding the maximum message size.

This solution has demonstrated how to select the streamed transfer mode for the `BasicHttpBinding`. It has also shown that one can transmit a `Stream` object using the Windows Communication Foundation. By logging and examining the messages transmitted by the service, it became apparent that, by default, the Windows Communication Foundation sends streams embedded within SOAP messages. When the size of the stream causes the size of the message in which it is embedded to exceed the maximum message size of the binding, a trappable error is thrown.

However, the effect of the streamed transfer mode has remained mostly invisible. It has not yet been made apparent that the initial content of the stream was available to the client before the entire content of the stream was received.

Most important, this crucial line of code by which the service returned the stream to the client,

```
return new FileStream(pictureName, FileMode.Open);
```

does not reveal how individual data items can be sent progressively via a stream. That is what would be required in order to implement publish/subscribe using the Windows Communication Foundation's streamed transfer mode.

Transmitting a Custom Stream with the Streamed Transfer Mode

To see how individual data items can be fed through a stream, follow these steps:

1. Open the solution `C:\WCFHandsOn\PublishSubscribe\CustomStream\CustomStream.sln`. It consists of two projects. The Client project is for building a console application that retrieves an image from a Windows Communication Foundation service. The service is built using the other project in the solution, called Service.

2. Examine the interface IPictureServer in the Program.cs module of the Service
project. It represents the same service contract that was used previously, with a
single operation, GetPicture(), that returns a stream object:

```
[ServiceContract]
public interface IPictureServer
{
    [OperationContract]
    Stream GetPicture(string pictureName);
}
```

3. See, however, that the PictureServer class that implements the IPictureServer
contract is slightly altered from the earlier version. This time the stream that it
returns is an instance of the CustomStream() class:

```
internal class PictureServer: IPictureServer
{
    Stream IPictureServer.GetPicture(string pictureName)
    {
        try
        {
            CustomStream customStream = new CustomStream(pictureName);
            return customStream;

        }
        catch (Exception)
        {
            return null;
        }
    }
}
```

4. Study the definition of the CustomStream class in the CustomStream.cs module of
the Service project (see Listing 10.3).

LISTING 10.3   A Custom Stream Class

```
public class CustomStream: Stream
{
    private string backingStore = null;
    private FileStream backingStream = null;
    private bool initialRead = true;
    private DateTime startRead;
    private long totalBytes = 0;
```

LISTING 10.3   Continued

```
private CustomStream()
{
}

public CustomStream(string fileName)
{
    this.backingStore = fileName;
}

[...]

public override int Read(byte[] buffer, int offset, int count)
{
    TimeSpan duration;

    if (this.initialRead)
    {
        this.startRead = DateTime.Now;
        this.initialRead = false;
    }
    else
    {
        Thread.Sleep(100);
    }

    Console.WriteLine(string.Format(
        "Reading {0} bytes from backing store.", count));

    if (this.backingStream == null)
    {
        this.backingStream = new FileStream(
            this.backingStore,
            FileMode.Open);
    }

    int bytesRead = this.backingStream.Read(buffer, offset, count);

    if (bytesRead <= 0)
    {
        this.backingStream.Close();
    }
```

10

LISTING 10.3 Continued

```
        this.totalBytes += bytesRead;

        duration = (DateTime.Now - this.startRead);

        Console.WriteLine(
            "Sent {0} bytes in {1}:{2}.",
            this.totalBytes,
            duration.Seconds,
            duration.Milliseconds);

        return bytesRead;
    }

    [...]
}
```

The CustomStream class derives from the abstract Stream class. Although it is required to override all the latter's abstract methods, it really only provides a substantive override for the Read() method. What the CustomStream class's Read() method does is return a chunk of the image requested by the client application, the maximum size of the chunk being specified by a parameter passed to the Read() method.

5. Start debugging the application. The console window of the service application should appear, followed by the console window of the client application.

6. When there is activity in the console window of the service application, enter a keystroke into the console window of the client application. The results should be as shown in Figure 10.7: As chunks of the image requested by the client are still being retrieved from the CustomStream object within the service, the chunks already transmitted to the client are being retrieved from the CustomStream object within the client.

7. Stop debugging the solution.

This makes the effect of the streamed transfer mode vividly apparent. In response to a single request from a client, data is being transmitted to the client in chunks. The chunks received by the client are immediately available for processing, before all the chunks have been sent by the service.

FIGURE 10.7   Using the streamed transfer mode with a custom stream class.

In the service's implementation of the operation used by the client to retrieve the picture,

```
internal class PictureServer: IPictureServer
{
    Stream IPictureServer.GetPicture(string pictureName)
    {
        try
        {
            CustomStream customStream = new CustomStream(pictureName);
            return customStream;

        }
        catch (Exception)
        {
            return null;
        }
    }
}
```

this single line of code,

```
return customStream;
```

causes the Windows Communication Foundation to send the initial parts of the response message to the client,

```
<s:Envelope
    xmlns:a="http://schemas.xmlsoap.org/ws/2004/08/addressing"
    xmlns:s="http://schemas.xmlsoap.org/soap/envelope/">
    <s:Header>
        <a:Action s:mustUnderstand="1">
        http://tempuri.org/IPictureServer/GetPictureResponse</a:Action>
        <a:To s:mustUnderstand="1">
        http://schemas.xmlsoap.org/ws/2004/08/addressing/role/anonymous
        </a:To>
        </s:Header>
        <s:Body>
```

and then calls the Read() method of the stream iteratively, requesting up to one kilobyte of data from it on each iteration. Each chunk of data retrieved in that manner is transmitted to the client:

```
... stream ...
```

When the Read() method returns zero bytes, the Windows Communication Foundation closes the stream and transmits the remainder of the message:

```
        </s:Body>
</s:Envelope>
```

Implementing Publish/Subscribe Using the Streamed Transfer Mode and a Custom Stream

Now it should be evident how to use the Windows Communication Foundation's streamed transfer mode to implement publish/subscribe. When the data to be published consists of small data items, and the subscribers require notifications with minimal delay, the publisher can send a stream to each of its subscribers using the Windows Communication Foundation's streamed transfer mode. The streams should be custom streams. The Windows Communication Foundation will invoke the Read() methods of the custom streams iteratively, requesting kilobytes of data to transmit to the subscribers. If the custom stream objects have updates available, they can provide those to the Windows Communication Foundation to publish to the subscribers. If no updates are available, the Read() methods of the streams can sleep until updates occur, or until some configurable timeout expires. If the timeout expires, zero bytes can be returned to the Windows Communication Foundation, which will close the stream. The subscriber can then choose to renew the subscription. The publisher buffers updates pertinent to the subscriber for a configurable period so that if the subscription is renewed, updates that occurred between the closing of the initial stream and the renewal of the subscription can be sent to the subscriber immediately upon the renewal.

If updates continue to be available, so that the custom streams continue to make data available to the Windows Communication Foundation as it iteratively calls their Read()

method, the maximum sizes for the messages into which the Windows Communication Foundation is embedding the data retrieved from the custom streams will eventually be exceeded. So there should be logic in the custom streams that detects when the maximum message size is about to be exceeded. That logic will have the Windows Communication Foundation close the current stream and then immediately open a new stream to the subscriber.

All of these capabilities are implemented in a reusable library called StreamingPublicationSubscription that is included in the solution `C:\WCFHandsOn\PublishSubscribe\StreamedPublishSubscribe\StreamedPublishSubcribe.sln`. The key classes that it provides are the `BufferedSubscriptionManager` class and the `NotificationStreamWriter` class. The former is programmed to buffer data items to which subscriptions have been received for configurable periods, whereas the latter is programmed to retrieve data items from the `BufferedSubscriptionManager` and make them available to the Windows Communication Foundation. The `NotificationStreamReader` class is programmed to read the streams output by the `NotificationStreamWriter` class.

To see these classes in action, and to understand how to use them to implement publish/subscribe solutions, follow these steps:

1. Open the solution `C:\WCFHandsOn\PublishSubscribe\StreamedPublishSubscribe\StreamedPublishSubcribe.sln`. Besides the project for building the StreamingPublicationSubscription library, the solution also has the Subscriber project, for building a subscriber console application, and the PublisherServiceHost project, for building a console application to host the publisher built from the PublisherService project.

2. Examine the `ISubscriber` interface in the `ISubscriber.cs` module of the PublisherService project. That interface defines the service contract that all subscribers are expected to implement. It defines a single operation, `Notify()`, that takes a `Stream` object as a parameter:

```
[ServiceContract]
public interface ISubscriber
{
    [OperationContract(IsOneWay=true)]
    void Notify(Stream stream);
}
```

3. Look at the `Subscribe()` method of the `PublisherService` class in the PublisherService.cs module of the PublisherService project. That method, shown in Listing 10.4, executes when subscribers submit subscription requests. After validating the subscription and the subscriber, the method invokes the `Activate()` method of the `PublishingAgent` class on a background thread.

LISTING 10.4   Method for Processing Subscription Requests

```
void IPublisher.Subscribe(
  KnownDataPoint[] dataPoints,
  out bool subscriptionAccepted)
{
    subscriptionAccepted = false;
    string dataPointIdentifier = null;
    if (dataPoints.Length == 1)
    {
        dataPointIdentifier = dataPoints[0].Identifier;
        this.ValidateDataPoint(dataPointIdentifier, out subscriptionAccepted);
    }

    string configuration = null;
    if(subscriptionAccepted)
    {
        this.ValidateSubscriber(
        OperationContext.Current.ServiceSecurityContext.WindowsIdentity.Name,
            out subscriptionAccepted,
            out configuration);
    }

    if (subscriptionAccepted)
    {

        ThreadPool.QueueUserWorkItem(
            new WaitCallback(
                ((IPublishingAgent)new PublishingAgent(
                    configuration,
                    dataPointIdentifier)).Activate
                ),null);
    }
}
```

4. See what is done by the Activate() method of the PublishingAgent class, in the
   PublishingAgent.cs module of the PublisherService project. The method is reproduced in Listing 10.5.

LISTING 10.5   Activating a Publication Agent

```
void IPublishingAgent.Activate(object state)
{
    this.randomDataPoint.Active = true;

    NotificationStreamWriter writer = null;
```

LISTING 10.5 Continued

```
IBufferedSubscriptionManager bufferedDataSubscriptionManager
    = new BufferedSubscriptionManager(this.subscriberConfiguration, 100);
bufferedDataSubscriptionManager.AddSubscription(this.randomDataPoint);

while (true)
{
    using (SubscriberProxy subscriberProxy
        = new SubscriberProxy(this.subscriberConfiguration))
    {
        ISubscriber subscriber = (ISubscriber)subscriberProxy;
        writer = new NotificationStreamWriter(
            bufferedDataSubscriptionManager,
            long.Parse(ConfigurationManager.AppSettings["MessageCapacity"]),
            new TimeSpan(
                0,
                0,
                0,
int.Parse(
    ConfigurationManager.AppSettings["UpdateFrequencyInSeconds"]))),
            new TimeSpan(
                0,
                0,
                0,
                0,
int.Parse(
    ConfigurationManager.AppSettings["DataSourceTimeoutInMilliseconds"]))));
        subscriber.Notify(writer);
        subscriberProxy.Close();
        Console.WriteLine("Batch completed.");
    }
}
}
```

The method adds details of the subscription to an instance of the
BufferedDataSubscriptionManager class, which will begin buffering updates to the
values of the data point to which the subscription pertains. Then the method
invokes the subscriber's Notify() operation, passing an instance of a
NotificationStreamWriter, which will then proceed to read updates from the
BufferedDataSubscriptionManager and pass them to the Windows Communication
Foundation for transmission.

5. Start debugging the solution. The console windows of the Subscriber application
   and the PublisherServiceHost application should appear.

10

6. When there is activity in the console window of the PublisherServiceHost application, enter a keystroke into the console of the Subscriber application. After a moment, updates from the publisher will begin to be registered in the console window of the subscriber.

7. Watch for notification in the console window of the subscriber that the maximum size of a message incorporating a stream was about to be exceeded, resulting in that stream being closed and a new one automatically being provided by the publisher. This effect is shown in Figure 10.8.

FIGURE 10.8   Implementing publish/subscribe with the StreamingPublicationSubscription library.

8. Stop debugging the solution.

Summary

There are various ways of implementing publish/subscribe solutions with the Windows Communication Foundation. Callback contracts and MSMQ PGM are suitable for scenarios in which the size of notifications is larger and the required frequency for updates is lower. When the notifications are smaller and more frequent, one can use the streamed transfer mode with a custom stream class to stream the notifications to the subscribers.

References

Graham, Steve, David Hull, and Bryan Murray. 2005. *Web Services Base Notification 1.3 (WS-BaseNotification)*. Billerica, MA: OASIS.

Rajagopalan, Anand. 2005. *Building Pub-sub applications using MSMQ*. http://blogs.msdn.com/solutions/archive/2005/09/20/471615.aspx. Accessed 9 January 2006.

Tannenbaum, Andrew and Maarten van Steen. 2002. *Distributed Systems: Principles and Paradigms*. Upper Saddle River, NJ: Prentice Hall.

CHAPTER 11

Peer Communication

Introducing Peer Channel

As explained in Chapter 8, "Custom Transports," Windows Communication Foundation protocols are implemented as channels. A channel for multiparty, peer-to-peer communication is provided, called *Peer Channel*.

Peer Channel is a significant innovation of the Windows Communication Foundation that provides two very important benefits. First, it enables the construction of sophisticated peer-to-peer applications involving the exchange of structured data. More generally, though, Peer Channel provides simply the easiest way to leverage the new Windows Peer-to-Peer Networking facilities available in Windows XP Service Pack 2 and later Windows client operating systems.

Using Structured Data in Peer-to-Peer Applications

Today, on Windows XP and later Windows operating systems, the Windows application programming interface (API) incorporates a real-time communications client API. That API enables one to develop applications incorporating facilities for real-time human communications in a variety of forms: instant messaging, two-way voice and video, and application sharing. The various Microsoft instant messaging solutions are built using the real-time communications client API.

Although one can certainly construct powerful and interesting applications with that API, those applications rely on the human participants to structure the data that is being exchanged. When one is doing instant messaging or conversing verbally with someone via one's computer over a network, one relies on one's linguistic and verbal abilities to be understood. Yet there are many circumstances in which the computer could assist considerably in structuring the data that is being passed around. For example, in the species of file-sharing application exemplified by the original Napster, users provide some input every now and then, but the bulk of the activity is done by the application that accepts the user's input, puts it into a form meaningful to its peers, and then goes about getting what the user wanted. Here is another example. It is becoming increasingly common for technology companies to offer technical support via instant messaging. Users of those technical-support instant messaging applications do want to start exchanging free-form text messages with one another. However, before they reach that point, they must generally identify themselves, and describe their needs so that the appropriate support person can be engaged to assist them, which is a process in which structured data must be gathered from them, exchanged between applications, and processed. The Windows Communication Foundation's Peer Channel facility is the right technology to choose in any scenario like that, in which computer software applications need to exchange structured data with one another on behalf of their respective human users.

Leveraging the Windows Peer-to-Peer Networking Development Platform

Windows XP Service Pack 2 and later Windows client operating systems provide Windows Peer-to-Peer Networking as an optional Windows Networking Services Component. Windows Peer-to-Peer Networking is a developer platform for building secure, scalable, and autonomic peer-to-peer applications of any kind. Its key components are these:

- The Peer Name Resolution Protocol (PNRP) as a solution to the problem of resolving the name of network peers to network addresses in scenarios in which there is no central domain name server or in which the network addresses assigned to the peers change relatively frequently

- Teredo as an implementation of IPv6 NAT Traversal or NAT-T, a proposed standard solution to the problem of traversing Network Address Translators (NATs)

- Graphing, a mechanism for maintaining paths, ideally as short as possible, between every two peers in the network, and sustaining the graph as peers leave and join the network

- Facilities for securing the network: controlling which peers are permitted to communicate, and ensuring the confidentiality and integrity of the communication

Peer Channel is the very easiest way to leverage all the capabilities of Windows Peer-to-Peer Networking to build serverless applications.

Using Peer Channel

This chapter explains Peer Channel by showing how to use it to construct an application for conducting a quiz in a classroom. In the scenario, each pupil has a computer program that can receive the questions in the quiz from a software application that the teacher has. The pupils respond to the quiz questions using their program, and their responses are transmitted to the teacher, who can grade the pupils' answers as they come in, and transmit grades back to each individual class member. The teacher can also broadcast instructions to the entire class.

This scenario is not a good one in which to apply an instant messaging solution. Besides the tedium involved in the teacher having to type out each question, the pupils' application could do little more than simply show the pupil what the teacher typed. It would be better for the teacher's application to transmit structured data to the pupils' application, which could then meaningfully process the information that it received and display it accordingly. Of course, one could transmit strings of XML between the applications via an instant messaging API like the real-time communications client API, but then one would have to write code to parse the XML. As will soon become apparent, considerable effort will be saved when the Windows Communication Foundation's Peer Channel is used to implement the solution.

Be aware that to use Peer Channel, one's computer system must have a network connection. That is necessary even for communication among applications residing together on that system.

Envisaging the Solution

Figure 11.1 shows the user interface of the teacher's application. As the pupils start their applications, each pupil's application transmits the pupil's name and photograph to the teacher's application, which displays the photographs in the area at the top. When the teacher sees that all the pupils have started their applications, and are therefore ready to begin the quiz, the teacher clicks on the Start button to transmit the quiz questions to the students. There is a box for text entry along with a Send button for broadcasting announcements to the class. As the students answer the quiz questions, their responses are displayed in the box in the Grading section of the screen. The teacher can scroll backward and forward through the responses that have been received, and indicate, for each response, whether it is correct or incorrect. The teacher can then click the Grade button to send a message to the application of the pupil who submitted the response, indicating whether the pupil's response was correct.

The user interface of the pupils' application is shown in Figure 11.2. It has an area on the left to display a picture, an area at the top to display an instruction, and a set of radio buttons to show the possible answers, with a button to submit a selected answer. When the teacher has graded a particular answer, a check mark shows up next to the radio buttons if the answer is correct, and a cross shows up if the answer is incorrect. There are buttons to navigate back and forth through the questions.

Figure 11.3 depicts one possible sequence of messages that may be exchanged. There are really only two rules, though, governing the sequence of messages. The first rule is that the pupils' application must send the teacher's application a `Join` message before the teacher's application can begin transmitting `AddItem` messages to the pupil with the quiz questions. The second rule is that the pupils' application must send a `Response` message with the answer to a question before the teacher's application can send a `Response` message with the teacher's assessment of the answer.

FIGURE 11.1   The teacher's application.

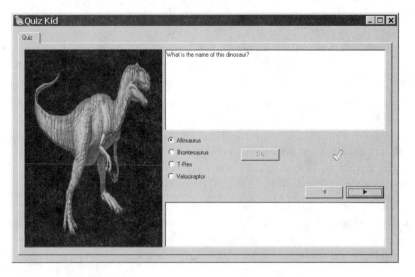

FIGURE 11.2   The pupil's application.

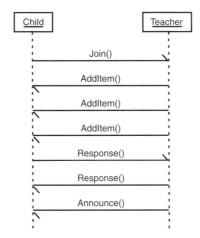

FIGURE 11.3   One possible sequence of messages.

Almost all the data exchanged between the teacher's application and the pupils' application via these messages is structured:

- The message that each pupil's application transmits to the teacher's application when it starts consists of a picture and a name. The teacher's application unpacks that message and displays the picture, while using the name, in the background, to open a private connection with that pupil's application.

- Each quiz question that the teacher's application transmits to the pupils' application consists of a picture, an instruction, and set of possible answers for the pupil to choose from. The pupils' application unpacks the messages containing the questions, and displays each element in the appropriate area of the pupils' user interface.

- When a pupil's application conveys an answer to a question to the teacher's application, the message consists of the pupil's name, the identifier of the question being answered, and the answer itself. The teacher's response to the pupil indicating whether the response was correct or incorrect conveys the identifier of the question that the pupil answered and whether the pupil's answer was correct. The pupil's application reads that message, identifies the quiz item to which it pertains, and updates it with the teacher's evaluation of the pupil's answer.

Only the announcements that the teacher broadcasts to the class during the quiz constitute unstructured data.

Designing the Messages and the Message Exchange Patterns

To translate this design of how the teacher's and pupils' applications will interact with one another into code, follow these steps:

1. Copy the code associated with this chapter that you downloaded from www.samspublishing.com to the folder C:\WCFHandsOn. The code is all in a folder

called PeerChannel. After the code has been unzipped, there should be a folder that looks like the one shown in Figure 11.4.

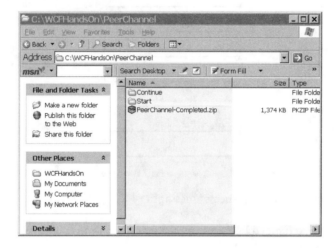

FIGURE 11.4   PeerChannel folder.

2. Open the solution C:\WCFHandsOn\PublishSubscribe\Start\PeerChanel.sln. It consists of two Windows projects: one called Child for building the pupils' application, and another called Teacher, for building the teacher's application.

3. Add a class module called Quiz.cs to the Teacher project. Modify its contents so that it looks like the code in Listing 11.1.

LISTING 11.1   Message Definitions

```
using System;
using System.Collections.Generic;
using System.Drawing;
using System.Runtime.Serialization;
using System.ServiceModel;
using System.Text;

namespace WindowsCommunicationFoundationHandsOn.School
{
    public struct Student
    {
        public string Name;
        public byte[] Image;
    }

    public struct QuizItem
    {
```

LISTING 11.1   Continued

```csharp
    public string Identifier;
    public byte[] ItemImage;
    public string Text;
    public QuizResponse[] Responses;

    public bool Submitted;

    public string ResponseText
    {
        get
        {
            foreach (QuizResponse response in Responses)
            {
                if (response.Submitted)
                {
                    return response.ResponseText;
                }
            }

            return null;
        }
    }

    public bool? Correct
    {
        get
        {
            foreach (QuizResponse response in Responses)
            {
                if (response.Submitted)
                {
                    return response.Correct;
                }
            }

            return null;
        }
    }
}

public struct QuizResponse
{
    public string ResponseIdentifier;
    public Student Responder;
```

LISTING 11.1   Continued

```
        public QuizItem Item;
        public string ResponseText;
        public bool? Correct;

        public bool Submitted;
    }


}
```

Thus we define structs to represent the messages to be exchanged between the teacher's application and the students' application. The Student struct represents the message, with the pupil's name and photograph, that the pupil's application will send to the teacher's application to signal that the pupil has started the application.

The QuizItem struct represents the message that the teacher's application will send to the pupils' application containing a quiz question. The Identifier, ItemImage, Text, and Responses members of that class represent the identifier of the quiz question, the picture to which the question pertains, the instruction, and various possible responses. The Submitted member will be used internally in the pupils' application to track whether the response to the question that the pupil selected has been submitted to the teacher.

The QuizResponse struct represents the message from the pupils' application to the teacher's application conveying the pupil's response, as well as the message from the teacher's application to the pupils' application with the teacher's assessment of the response. The Responder member identifies the pupil who is responding to the question. The Item member indicates which quiz question is being answered. The ResponseText member contains the pupil's answer. The Correct member contains the teacher's evaluation of the pupil's answer. The Submitted member will be used internally in the pupil's application to track whether the response is the pupil's chosen response, and by the teacher's application to track whether the teacher's assessment of the response has been transmitted to the pupil who submitted it.

4. Now add these definitions to the Quiz.cs module:

```
public interface IQuizManagement
{
    void Join(Student student);

    void Announce(string announcement);
}

public interface IQuizQuestion
{
    void AddItem(QuizItem item);
}
```

```
public interface IQuizResponse
{
    void SendResponse(QuizResponse response);
}
```

These interfaces define the simple message exchange patterns required for the solution. The IQuizManagement interface's Join() method represents the pupil's application sending a message to the teacher's application to announce that the pupil has started the application and is ready for the quiz. The Announce method of that interface represents the teacher broadcasting an announcement message to the pupil. The IQuizQuestion interface's sole AddItem method represents the teacher's application sending a quiz question to the pupil's application, and the IQuizResponse's sole SendResponse method represents the pupil's application sending one of the pupil's answers to the teacher's application, and the teacher sending an evaluation of that answer back to the pupil.

Now that the messages and the patterns for exchanging them have been defined, the Windows Communication Foundation's Peer Channel can be used to transmit the messages between the teacher's application and the pupils'.

5. Add DataContract attributes to the structs, and DataMember attributes to certain of their fields, as shown in Listing 11.2. The attributes indicate to the Windows Communication Foundation which members of which data types are to be incorporated in the messages that will be conveyed via the methods defined by the interfaces.

LISTING 11.2   Data Contract Definitions

```
[DataContract]
public struct Student
{
    [DataMember]
    public string Name;
    [DataMember]
    public byte[] Image;
}

[DataContract]
public struct QuizResponse
{
    [DataMember]
    public Student Responder;
    [DataMember]
    public QuizItem Item;
    [DataMember]
    public string ResponseText;
    [DataMember]
```

LISTING 11.2   Continued

```csharp
    public string ResponseIdentifier;
    [DataMember]
    public bool? Correct;

    public bool Submitted;
}

[DataContract]
public struct QuizItem
{
    [DataMember]
    public string Identifier;
    [DataMember]
    public byte[] ItemImage;
    [DataMember]
    public string Text;
    [DataMember]
    public QuizResponse[] Responses;
    public bool Submitted;

    public string ResponseText
    {
        get
        {
            foreach (QuizResponse response in Responses)
            {
                if (response.Submitted)
                {
                    return response.ResponseText;
                }
            }

            return null;
        }
    }

    public bool? Correct
    {
        get
        {
            foreach (QuizResponse response in Responses)
            {
                if (response.Submitted)
                {
```

```
                    return response.Correct;
                }
            }

            return null;
        }
    }
}
```

6. Modify the definitions of the interfaces in the `Quiz.cs` module in this way:

```
[ServiceContract(CallbackContract = typeof(IQuizQuestion))]
[PeerBehavior]
public interface IQuizQuestion
{
    [OperationContract(IsOneWay = true)]
    void AddItem(QuizItem item);
}

[ServiceContract(CallbackContract = typeof(IQuizResponse))]
[PeerBehavior]
public interface IQuizResponse
{
    [OperationContract(IsOneWay = true)]
    void SendResponse(QuizResponse response);
}

[ServiceContract(CallbackContract = typeof(IQuizManagement))]
[PeerBehavior]
public interface IQuizManagement
{
    [OperationContract(IsOneWay = true)]
    void Join(Student student);

    [OperationContract(IsOneWay = true)]
    void Announce(string announcement);
}
```

7. Add these interfaces, which derive from those already defined, to the `Quiz.cs` module:

```
public interface IQuizQuestionChannel : IQuizQuestion, IClientChannel
{
}

public interface IQuizResponseChannel : IQuizResponse, IClientChannel
```

```
    {
    }


    public interface IQuizManagementChannel : IQuizManagement, IClientChannel
    {
    }
```

ServiceContract and OperationContract attributes have now been added to the inter-faces and their methods. Those attributes signify that Windows Communication Foundation messages are to be transmitted by invoking the methods.

As explained in the preceding chapter, the CallbackContract parameter of the ServiceContract attribute designates an interface by which the receiver of a message can transmit messages back to the sender. When using Peer Channel, the CallbackContract parameter of a ServiceContract attribute must refer to the very interface to which the ServiceContract attribute applies. For instance, the CallbackContract parameter of the ServiceContract attribute on the IQuizResponse interface,

```
[ServiceContract(CallbackContract = typeof(IQuizResponse))]
[PeerBehavior]
public interface IQuizResponse
{
    [OperationContract(IsOneWay = true)]
    void SendResponse(QuizResponse response);
}
```

refers to the IQuizResponse interface. So to transmit messages via the IQuizResponse interface of the receiver, the sender must implement the IQuizResponse interface as well. In this particular case, the pupils' application is to send responses to quiz items to the teacher's application via the SendResponse() method of the interface, and the teacher's application is to send the teacher's evaluation of a response back to the pupil via the same method. That the OperationContract attribute on the method has its IsOneWay parameter set to true means that the pupils' application will not wait for a response from the teacher's application, and vice versa.

The PeerBehavior attribute on the service contract interfaces signals to the Windows Communication Foundation that the proxies it provides for communicating via that service contract must be capable of broadcasting and intercepting signals that peer proxies are coming online or going offline. For example, given the definition of IQuizResponse,

```
[ServiceContract(CallbackContract = typeof(IQuizResponse))]
[PeerBehavior]
public interface IQuizResponse
{
    [OperationContract(IsOneWay = true)]
    void SendResponse(QuizResponse response);
}
```

and the definition of IQuizResponseChannel,

```
public interface IQuizResponseChannel : IQuizResponse, IClientChannel
{
}
```

one can write a class like the one shown in Listing 11.3.

LISTING 11.3   Monitoring Peers

```
public class QuizApplication : IQuizResponse
{
    public static void Main()
    {
        InstanceContext instanceContext =
            new InstanceContext(new QuizApplication("Matt"));

        using (ChannelFactory<IQuizResponseChannel> factory =
            new ChannelFactory<IQuizResponseChannel>("QuizResponseEndpoint"))
        {
            using (IQuizResponseChannel participant =
                factory.CreateDuplexChannel(instanceContext))
            {
                PeerNode node = participant.Extensions.Find<PeerNode>();
                node.Online += new EventHandler(OnOnline);
                node.Offline += new EventHandler(OnOffline);

                participant.Open();

                [...]

            }
        }
    }

    static void OnOnline(object sender, EventArgs e)
    {
        Console.WriteLine("Participant came online");
    }

    static void OnOffline(object sender, EventArgs e)
    {
        Console.WriteLine("Participant went offline");
    }
}
```

That class obtains a proxy called participant for communicating via the
IQuizResponseChannel interface with these statements:

```
ChannelFactory<IQuizResponseChannel> factory =
            new ChannelFactory<IQuizResponseChannel>("QuizResponseEndpoint");
(IQuizResponseChannel participant =
            factory.CreateDuplexChannel(instanceContext);
```

Because IQuizResponseChannel derives from the IQuizResponse service contract, which
has the PeerChannel attribute, the class can retrieve an instance of the PeerNode class
from the proxy:

```
PeerNode node = participant.Extensions.Find<PeerNode>();
```

With the instance of the PeerNode class, it can receive notifications of other proxies for
the IQuizResponseChannel coming online or going offline:

```
node.Online += new EventHandler(OnOnline);
node.Offline += new EventHandler(OnOffline);
```

Also, the statement

```
participant.Open();
```

will broadcast notification that this proxy is online.

Unfortunately, this facility of Peer Channel is not very useful at this point in the
Windows Communication Foundation's development. The Online and Offline events
provided by the PeerNode class do not provide any information other than some proxy
coming online or going offline. So for the applications to be used by the teacher and the
pupils for the classroom quiz, the IQuizManagement interface is provided, with a Join()
method that can convey information about the pupil whose application is coming online:

```
[ServiceContract(CallbackContract = typeof(IQuizManagement))]
[PeerBehavior]
public interface IQuizManagement
{
    [OperationContract(IsOneWay = true)]
    void Join(Student student);

    [OperationContract(IsOneWay = true)]
    void Announce(string announcement);
}
```

Note that, elsewhere in the Windows Communication Foundation, it is preferred to apply
attributes that are behaviors to classes that implement service contract interfaces, rather
than to the service contract interfaces themselves. The PeerBehavior attribute is an exception to that rule: It can be applied only to an interface.

Implementing the Communication

Usually, in building solutions using the Windows Communication Foundation, after one has defined service contracts, the interfaces that describe how messages are to be exchanged, the next step is to write classes that implement those interfaces. The same procedure applies when using Peer Channel:

1. Add a class named QuizTeacher.cs to the Teacher application, and modify its contents to conform with Listing 11.4, which is also in the file C:\WCFHandsOn\ PeerChannel\Start\Teacher\QuizTeacher1.txt.

LISTING 11.4   Implementing the Communication

```
using System;
using System.Collections.Generic;
using System.Configuration;
using System.Drawing;
using System.Security.Cryptography;
using System.Security.Cryptography.Xml;
using System.Security.Cryptography.X509Certificates;
using System.ServiceModel;
using System.ServiceModel.Security.Tokens;
using System.Text;

namespace WindowsCommunicationFoundationHandsOn.School
{
    public class QuizTeacher :
        IQuizQuestion,
        IQuizResponse,
        IQuizManagement,
        IDisposable
    {
        private const string BaseAddressKey
            = "baseAddress";
        private const string QuizPortKey
            = @"quizPort";
        private const string MeshIdentifierKey
            = @"MeshIdentifier";
        private const string QuizQuestionEndpointKey
            = @"quizQuestionEndpoint";
        private const string QuizManagementEndpointKey
            = @"quizManagementEndpoint";
        private const string QuizResponseEndpointKey
            = @"quizResponseEndpoint";
        private const string PeerChannelAddressPrefix
            = @"net.p2p://";
        private const string CurrentUserCertificateStore
            = @"My";
```

LISTING 11.4   Continued

```
private const string CertificateSubjectName
    = @"Woodgrove";

private ServiceHost resolverService = null;
private IQuizQuestion questionProxy = null;
private IQuizManagement managementProxy = null;
private int port;
private string meshIdentifier = null;
private Resolver resolver = null;
private InstanceContext site = null;
private PeerSecurityBehavior peerSecurity;

private MainForm form = null;

private Dictionary<string, IQuizResponse> responseProxies
    = new Dictionary<string, IQuizResponse>();

public QuizTeacher(MainForm form)
{
    this.form = form;

    Uri baseAddress =
        new Uri(
            ConfigurationManager.AppSettings[
                QuizTeacher.BaseAddressKey]);
    this.resolver = new Resolver();
    this.resolverService = new ServiceHost(resolver, baseAddress);
    this.resolverService.Open();
}

private X509Certificate2 GetCertificate()
{
    X509Store store = new X509Store(
        QuizTeacher.CurrentUserCertificateStore,
        StoreLocation.LocalMachine);
    store.Open(OpenFlags.ReadOnly);
    X509CertificateCollection certificateCollection =
        store.Certificates.Find(
            X509FindType.FindBySubjectName,
            QuizTeacher.CertificateSubjectName,
            false);
    return (X509Certificate2)certificateCollection[0];
}
```

LISTING 11.4   Continued

```
#region IQuizQuestion Members

void IQuizQuestion.AddItem(QuizItem item)
{
}

#endregion

#region IQuizResponse Members

void IQuizResponse.SendResponse(QuizResponse response)
{
}


#endregion

#region IQuizManagement Members

void IQuizManagement.Join(Student student)
{
}

void IQuizManagement.Announce(string announcement)
{
}

#endregion

#region IDisposable Members

void IDisposable.Dispose()
{
}

#endregion
    }
}
```

Now there is a class, QuizTeacher, that implements the IQuizQuestion,
IQuizResponse, and IQuizManagement service contracts. The QuizTeacher class's
implementations of the methods of those interfaces are currently blank.

2. Provide content for one of the QuizTeacher's implementations of the methods of the service contracts by modifying the implementation of the SendResponse() method of the IQuizResponse interface in this way:

```
void IQuizResponse.SendResponse(QuizResponse response)
{
    this.form.AddResponse(response);
}
```

This code for the teacher's application accepts a response to a quiz question sent by the pupils' application and passes it to the main form of the teacher's application for display.

3. Switch to the MainForm.cs module, and examine the AddResponse() method, reproduced in Listing 11.5.

LISTING 11.5   Marshaling Messages onto the User Interface Thread

```
public void AddResponse(QuizResponse response)
{
    if (this.InvokeRequired)
    {
        AddResponseDelegate addResponseDelegate = new AddResponseDelegate(
            this.AddResponse);
        this.Invoke(
            addResponseDelegate,
            new object[] { response });
    }
    else
    {
        lock (this)
        {
            response.Submitted = false;
            List<QuizResponse> responses = new List<QuizResponse>(

            this.quiz.Responses);
            responses.Add(response);
            this.quiz.Responses = responses.ToArray();

            if (this.quiz.Responses.Length == 1)
            {
                this.currentResponse = 0;
                this.DisplayResponse();
            }

            this.EnableNavigationButtons();
        }
    }
}
```

That method does the necessary work of marshaling the data received from the pupils' application onto the user interface thread so that it can be displayed.

In Windows Communication Foundation applications, after a service contract interface has been implemented in a class, the next steps are to specify an address to which messages directed at that class can be sent, and a binding that defines how those messages must be transmitted. The procedure is no different when using Peer Channel.

4. Provide a method to return the binding by adding the `BuildBinding()` method to the `QuizTeacher` class:

```
private NetPeerTcpBinding BuildBinding(int port)
{
    NetPeerTcpBinding binding = new NetPeerTcpBinding();
    binding.MaxMessageSize = long.MaxValue;
    binding.PeerNodeAuthenticationMode = PeerAuthenticationMode.None;
    binding.MessageAuthentication = false;
    binding.Port = port;

    return binding;
}
```

The Windows Communication Foundation binding that is used in building Peer Channel applications is the `NetPeerTcpBinding`, so the `BuildBinding()` method returns an instance of that binding. As the name of the binding implies, Peer Channel transmissions use TCP. Peer Channel's reliance on TCP simply reflects that of Windows Peer-to-Peer Networking.

In making use of the `NetPeerTcpBinding`, one must specify the port one will be using. Hence, the `BuildBinding()` method accepts a port number as a parameter, and assigns that port number to the `Port` property of the binding:

```
binding.Port = port;
```

If the solution was to be deployed exclusively on machines running Windows XP Service Pack 2 and later Windows client operating systems that had Windows Peer-to-Peer Networking installed, the code for configuring the Peer Channel binding in the `BuildBinding()` method would be complete. As mentioned earlier, Windows Peer-to-Peer Networking provides an implementation of PNRP to resolve peer node names to network addresses. Windows Server 2003 does not support Windows Peer-to-Peer Networking and, consequently, does not have a PNRP implementation. That Windows Server 2003, which is designed to be a server operating system, is not optimized for peer-to-peer scenarios makes sense, of course. However, Peer Channel can still be used on Windows Server 2003, but to do so, one must provide one's own solution for resolving peer node names to network addresses. That is accomplished by providing a class that derives from the abstract `PeerResolver` class.

The PeerResolver class is defined in this way:

```
public abstract class PeerResolver
{
    protected PeerResolver();

    public abstract object Register(
        string meshId,
        PeerNodeAddress nodeAddress,
        TimeSpan timeout);
    public abstract ReadOnlyCollection<PeerNodeAddress> Resolve(
        string meshId,
        int maxAddresses,
        TimeSpan timeout);
    public abstract void Unregister(
        object registrationId,
        TimeSpan timeout);
    public abstract void Update(
        object registrationId,
        PeerNodeAddress updatedNodeAddress,
        TimeSpan timeout);
}
```

The Register method is for adding a node to the network of peer nodes, which, in the argot of Peer Channel, is referred to as a *mesh*. The Resolve method returns the network addresses of the peer nodes in a given mesh.

For the classroom quiz, the peer name resolution system works in the following way. The teacher's application incorporates a class that does peer name resolution, called Resolve. It also incorporates a class that derives from PeerResolver, called ResolverClient. ResolverClient delegates the peer name resolution work to the Resolver class. To service the peer name resolution requirements of the pupils' application, Resolver is exposed as a Windows Communication Foundation service. The pupils' application incorporates a ResolverClient class of its own that derives from PeerResolver, and that ResolverClient class invokes the methods of the remote peer name resolution service hosted by the teacher's application to do the peer name resolution work for it. This peer name resolution system is examined in detail in the next few steps.

5. Open the IPeerResolver.cs module in the Teacher project to see the declaration of the IPeerResolver interface that describes the facilities of a remote peer name resolution service that the pupils' application can use for peer name resolution:

```
public abstract class PeerResolver
{
    protected PeerResolver();
```

```
      public abstract object Register(
          string meshId,
          PeerNodeAddress nodeAddress,
          TimeSpan timeout);
      public abstract ReadOnlyCollection<PeerNodeAddress> Resolve(
          string meshId,
          int maxAddresses,
          TimeSpan timeout);
      public abstract void Unregister(
          object registrationId,
          TimeSpan timeout);
      public abstract void Update(
          object registrationId,
          PeerNodeAddress updatedNodeAddress,
          TimeSpan timeout);
  }
```

6. Next, open the ResolverService.cs module in the Teacher project, reproduced in Listing 11.6, and examine the definition of the Resolver class that implements the IPeerResolver interface and does the actual work of peer name resolution.

LISTING 11.6   Peer Name Resolution Service

```
public struct Peer
{
    public Guid identifier;
    public PeerNodeAddress nodeAddress;
    public TimeSpan timeout;
}

[ServiceBehavior(InstanceContextMode = InstanceContextMode.Single)]
public class Resolver: IPeerResolver
{
    private static Dictionary<string, Dictionary<Guid, Peer>> meshes
        = new Dictionary<string, Dictionary<Guid, Peer>>();

    public object Register(
        string meshIdentifier,
        PeerNodeAddress nodeAddress,
        TimeSpan timeout)
    {
        lock (this)
        {
            Dictionary<Guid, Peer> mesh = null;
            if (!(meshes.ContainsKey(meshIdentifier)))
            {
```

LISTING 11.6   Continued

```
                mesh = new Dictionary<Guid, Peer>();
                meshes.Add(meshIdentifier, mesh);
            }
            else
            {
                mesh = meshes[meshIdentifier];
            }

            Peer peer = new Peer();
            peer.identifier = Guid.NewGuid();
            peer.nodeAddress = nodeAddress;
            peer.timeout = timeout;
            mesh.Add(peer.identifier, peer);

            return peer.identifier;
        }
    }

    public PeerNodeAddress[] Resolve(
        string meshIdentifier,
        int maximumAddresses,
        TimeSpan timeout)
    {
        List<PeerNodeAddress> addresses = new List<PeerNodeAddress>();
        if (meshes.ContainsKey(meshIdentifier))
        {
            Dictionary<Guid, Peer> mesh = meshes[meshIdentifier];
            foreach (Peer peer in mesh.Values)
            {
                addresses.Add(peer.nodeAddress);
                if (addresses.Count >= maximumAddresses)
                {
                    break;
                }
            }
        }
        return addresses.ToArray();

    }

    public void Unregister(object registrationId, TimeSpan timeout)
    {
        lock (this)
```

LISTING 11.6   Continued

```csharp
    {
        foreach (Dictionary<Guid, Peer> mesh in meshes.Values)
        {
            if (mesh.ContainsKey((Guid)registrationId))
            {
                mesh.Remove((Guid)registrationId);
            }
        }
    }
}

public void Update(
    object registrationId,
    PeerNodeAddress updatedNodeAddress,
    TimeSpan timeout)
{
    lock (this)
    {
        Peer peer;
        foreach (Dictionary<Guid, Peer> mesh in meshes.Values)
        {
            if (mesh.ContainsKey((Guid)registrationId))
            {
                peer = mesh[(Guid)registrationId];
                peer.nodeAddress = updatedNodeAddress;
            }
        }
    }
}
}
```

7. Open the app.config file in the Teacher project. See that it specifies a Windows Communication Foundation address and binding for the remote peer name resolution service defined by the IPeerResolver interface:

```xml
<?xml version="1.0" encoding="utf-8" ?>
<configuration>
    <appSettings>
        <!-- use appSetting to configure base address provided by host -->
        <add key="baseAddress"
            value="net.tcp://localhost:8089/School/PeerResolverService" />
        <add key="meshIdentifier" value="Classroom_3A" />
        <add key="quizQuestionEndpoint" value="QuizQuestion" />
        <add key="quizResponseEndpoint" value="QuizResponse" />
```

```
            <add key="quizManagementEndpoint" value="QuizManagement" />
            <add key="quizPort" value="8090"/>
        </appSettings>
        <system.serviceModel>
            <services>
                <service
                    type="WindowsCommunicationFoundationHandsOn.School.Resolver">
                    <endpoint address=""
                            binding="netTcpBinding"
    contract="WindowsCommunicationFoundationHandsOn.School.IPeerResolver" />
                </service>
            </services>
        </system.serviceModel>
    </configuration>
```

8. Switch back to the `QuizTeacher.cs` module in the Teacher project, and look again at the constructor of the `QuizTeacher` class:

```
public QuizTeacher(MainForm form)
{
    this.form = form;

    Uri baseAddress =
        new Uri(
            ConfigurationManager.AppSettings[
                QuizTeacher.BaseAddressKey]);
    this.resolver = new Resolver();
    this.resolverService = new ServiceHost(resolver, baseAddress);
    this.resolverService.Open();
}
```

It uses the Windows Communication Foundation's `ServiceHost` class to provide for the peer name resolution service being hosted within the teacher's application.

9. Now modify the `BuildBinding()` method, added to the `QuizTeacher` class earlier, so that it looks like this:

```
private NetPeerTcpBinding BuildBinding(Resolver resolver, int port)
{
    NetPeerTcpBinding binding = new NetPeerTcpBinding();
    binding.MaxMessageSize = long.MaxValue
    binding.PeerNodeAuthenticationMode = PeerAuthenticationMode.None;
    binding.MessageAuthentication = false;
    binding.Port = port;
    binding.Resolver = new ResolverClient(resolver);

    return binding;
}
```

The modified code provides a peer name resolver for the teacher's application by assigning an instance of a class that derives from the abstract `PeerResolver` class to the `Resolver` property of the `NetPeerTcpBinding`.

10. Examine the `app.config` file in the Child project:

```xml
<?xml version="1.0" encoding="utf-8" ?>
<configuration>
    <appSettings>
        <!-- use appSetting to configure base address provided by host -->
        <add key="meshIdentifier" value="Classroom_3A" />
        <add key="quizQuestionEndpoint" value="QuizQuestion" />
        <add key="quizResponseEndpoint" value="QuizResponse" />
        <add key="quizManagementEndpoint" value="QuizManagement" />
    </appSettings>
    <system.serviceModel>
        <client>
            <endpoint name="PeerResolverService"
address="net.tcp://localhost:8089/School/PeerResolverService"
binding="netTcpBinding"
contract="WindowsCommunicationFoundationHandsOn.School.IPeerResolver, Child"/>
        </client>
    </system.serviceModel>
</configuration>
```

It configures the pupils' application as a Windows Communication Foundation client of the peer name resolution service hosted by the teacher's application.

11. Look at the `ResolverClient` class in the `ResolverClient.cs` module of the Child project, reproduced in Listing 11.7. The class derives from the abstract `PeerResolver` class, and, in its implementation of that class's methods, delegates the actual work of `PeerName` resolution to the remote peer name resolution service hosted by the teacher's application.

LISTING 11.7   Peer Name Resolution Client

```csharp
using System;
using System.Collections.Generic;
using System.Collections.ObjectModel;
using System.ServiceModel;
using System.Text;

namespace WindowsCommunicationFoundationHandsOn.School
{
    public class ResolverClient : PeerResolver
    {
        private const string PeerResolverServiceConfiguration
            = "PeerResolverService";
```

LISTING 11.7   Continued

```
public override object Register(
    string meshId,
    PeerNodeAddress nodeAddress,
    TimeSpan timeout)
{

    IPeerResolver proxy = null;
    try
    {
        proxy = new ChannelFactory<IPeerResolver>(
            ResolverClient.PeerResolverServiceConfiguration).
                CreateChannel();
        object registrationId =
            proxy.Register(
                meshId,
                nodeAddress,
                timeout);
        return registrationId;
    }
    catch (Exception)
    {
        return null;
    }
    finally
    {
        IChannel channel = (IChannel)proxy;
        if (channel.State == CommunicationState.Opened)
        {
            channel.Close();
        }
    }
}

public override ReadOnlyCollection<PeerNodeAddress> Resolve(
    string meshId,
    int maxAddresses,
    TimeSpan timeout)
{

    IPeerResolver proxy = null;
    try
    {
        ReadOnlyCollection<PeerNodeAddress> addresses = null;
        proxy = new ChannelFactory<IPeerResolver>(
            ResolverClient.PeerResolverServiceConfiguration).
                CreateChannel();
```

LISTING 11.7   Continued

```
            PeerNodeAddress[] addressArray
                = proxy.Resolve(
                    meshId,
                    maxAddresses,
                    timeout);
            addresses =
                new System.Collections.ObjectModel.
                    ReadOnlyCollection<PeerNodeAddress>(
                        addressArray);
            return addresses;
        }
        catch (Exception)
        {
            return null;
        }
        finally
        {
            IChannel channel = (IChannel)proxy;
            if (channel.State == CommunicationState.Opened)
            {
                channel.Close();
            }
        }
    }

    public override void Unregister(object registrationId, TimeSpan timeout)
    {
        IPeerResolver proxy = null;
        try
        {
            proxy = new ChannelFactory<IPeerResolver>(
                ResolverClient.
                PeerResolverServiceConfiguration).
                CreateChannel();
            proxy.Unregister(registrationId, timeout);
        }
        catch (Exception)
        {
        }
        finally
        {
            IChannel channel = (IChannel)proxy;
            if (channel.State == CommunicationState.Opened)
            {
```

LISTING 11.7   Continued

```
                    channel.Close();
                }
            }
        }

    public override void Update(
        object registrationId,
        PeerNodeAddress updatedNodeAddress,
        TimeSpan timeout)
    {
        IPeerResolver proxy = null;
        try
        {
            proxy =
                new ChannelFactory<IPeerResolver>(
                ResolverClient.
                PeerResolverServiceConfiguration).
                CreateChannel();
            proxy.Update(registrationId, updatedNodeAddress, timeout);
        }
        catch (Exception)
        {
        }
        finally
        {
            IChannel channel = (IChannel)proxy;
            if (channel.State == CommunicationState.Opened)
            {
                channel.Close();
            }


        }
    }
}
}
```

12. Open the `QuizChild.cs` module of the `Pupil` class, and locate the `BuildBinding()` method of the `QuizChild` class therein:

```
private NetPeerTcpBinding BuildBinding(int port)
{
    NetPeerTcpBinding binding = new NetPeerTcpBinding();
    binding.MaxMessageSize = long.MaxValue;
    binding.PeerNodeAuthenticationMode = PeerAuthenticationMode.None;
```

```
        binding.Port = port;
        binding.MessageAuthentication = false;
        binding.Resolver = new ResolverClient();

        return binding;
    }
```

This method is the counterpart, in the pupils' application, to the BuildBinding()
method that was added to the teacher's application. It instantiates an instance of
Peer Channel's NetPeerTcpBinding class for the pupils' application to use in transmitting messages to the network of peers within the classroom.

13. Switch back to the Teacher project, and the QuizTeacher.cs module once again,
    and modify the constructor of the QuizTeacher class so that it looks as it does in
    Listing 11.8.

LISTING 11.8   Defining Endpoints

```
public QuizTeacher(MainForm form)
{
    this.form = form;

    Uri baseAddress =
        new Uri(
            ConfigurationManager.AppSettings[
                QuizTeacher.BaseAddressKey]);
    this.resolver = new Resolver();
    this.resolverService = new ServiceHost(resolver, baseAddress);
    this.resolverService.Open();

    this.site = new InstanceContext(this);
    this.port =
        int.Parse(
        ConfigurationManager.AppSettings[QuizTeacher.QuizPortKey]);
    EndpointAddress address = null;

    address =
        new EndpointAddress(
            @"net.p2p://Classroom_3A/QuizManagement");
    NetPeerTcpBinding binding =
        this.BuildBinding(this.resolver,this.port);
    ChannelFactory<IQuizManagementChannel> managementChannelFactory =
        new ChannelFactory<IQuizManagementChannel>(
            this.site,
            binding,
            address);
```

LISTING 11.8   Continued

```
managementChannelFactory.Open();
managementProxy =
    (IQuizManagementChannel)managementChannelFactory.
        CreateDuplexChannel();
((IChannel)managementProxy).Open();
}
```

The additional code defines an address for messages directed at the IQuizManagement interface within the network of peers, the address net.p2p://Classroom_3A/ QuizManagement. In that address, net.p2p is the scheme that signifies an address associated with a NetPeerTcpBinding binding. The next part of the address, Classroom_3A, is referred to as the *mesh identifier*, a mesh being, as mentioned previously, a particular network of peer nodes. The final part of the address, QuizManagement, is an arbitrary pathname chosen for the IQuizManagement endpoint.

After the address for the IQuizManagement interface has been defined, the BuildBinding() provided earlier is used to create an instance of the NetPeerTcpBinding. Then the address and the instance of the NetPeerTcpBinding are used together with regular Windows Communication Foundation client code to open a duplex communication channel, a channel by which messages can be sent from either end.

When the statement

```
((IChannel)managementProxy).Open();
```

executes, two things will happen:

- The managementProxy object will become available as a means to transmit messages defined by the IQuizManagement interface.

- Any messages from nodes in the mesh directed at the IQuizManagement interface will be received by the instance of the QuizTeacher class that is being constructed.

The latter is by virtue of the statement

```
this.site = new InstanceContext(this);
```

together with the subsequent reference to this.site in the statement

```
ChannelFactory<IQuizManagementChannel> managementChannelFactory =
    new ChannelFactory<IQuizManagementChannel>(
        this.site,
        binding,
        address);
```

14. Now that the `managementProxy` object is available as a means for transmitting `IQuizManagement` messages, add this method to the `QuizTeacher` class in the `QuizTeacher.cs` module of the QuizTeacher project:

```
public void SendAnnouncement(string announcement)
{
    managementProxy.Announce(announcement);
}
```

This method uses the `managementProxy` object to broadcast the teacher's announcements to the instances of the pupils' application.

15. Switch to the code view of the `MainForm.cs` module of the QuizTeacher project, and locate the `SendButton_Click()` method of the `MainForm` class, which serves as the handler of the `Click` event of the button that the teacher uses for dispatching announcements:

```
private void SendButton_Click(object sender, EventArgs e)
{
    this.quizService.SendAnnouncement(this.AnnouncementBox.Text);
    this.AnnouncementBox.Text = string.Empty;
}
```

It uses the `SendAnnouncements()` method that has just been added for broadcasting the teacher's announcements.

16. Go to the Child project, open the `QuizChild.cs` module, and examine the constructor of the `QuizChild` class. It contains this code, which is very similar to that used to open the channel for `IQuizManagement` messages in the code of the teacher's application:

```
//Management
endpoint =
    ConfigurationManager.
    AppSettings[QuizChild.QuizManagementEndpointKey];
address = new EndpointAddress(
    "net.p2p://Classroom_3A/QuizManagement");
ChannelFactory<IQuizManagementChannel> managementChannelFactory =
    new ChannelFactory<IQuizManagementChannel>(
        site,
        this.BuildBinding(port),
        address);
managementChannelFactory.Open();
managementProxy =
    (IQuizManagementChannel)managementChannelFactory.
    CreateDuplexChannel();
((IChannel)managementProxy).Open();
```

This is the code by which the pupils' application can send and receive messages defined by the IQuizManagment interface and directed at the peers within the Classroom_3A mesh.

Recall how the IQuizManagement interface is defined:

```
public interface IQuizManagement
{
    void Join(Student student);

    void Announce(string announcement);
}
```

Also recall that the pupils' application is to send the Join message in order to signal to the teacher that the pupil is ready to participate in the quiz, and the teacher's application is to send the Announce message to the pupils' application when the teacher has an announcement to make to the students. Now, in fact, when a pupil's application sends the Join message, Peer Channel will deliver that message to all the peer nodes in the Classroom_3A mesh listening for messages directed at the QuizManagement path. Consequently, not only will the teacher's application receive a Join message sent by a pupil's application, but so will all the other instances of the pupils' application.

17. Open the QuizChild.cs module of the Child project and see that, although the QuizChild class implements the IQuizManagement interface, the implementation of that interfaces Join() is blank:

```
public class QuizChild :
    IQuizQuestion,
    IQuizResponse,
    IQuizManagement,
    IDisposable
{
    /* ... */

    void IQuizManagement.Join(Student student)
    {
    }

    void IQuizManagement.Announce(string announcement)
    {
        this.form.DisplayAnnouncement(announcement);
    }
}
```

So, although every instance of the pupils' application will receive the Join messages sent by every other instance of that application, the pupils' application simply ignores those messages.

18. See how the proxy for the IResponse service contract is obtained in the constructor of the QuizChild class in the same QuizChild.cs module of the Child project:

```
//Response
endpoint =
    ConfigurationManager.
        AppSettings[QuizChild.QuizResponseEndpointKey];
address = new EndpointAddress(
    string.Concat("net.p2p://Classroom_3A/QuizResponse", "_",
    this.student.Name));
ChannelFactory<IQuizResponseChannel> responseChannelFactory =
    new ChannelFactory<IQuizResponseChannel>(
        site,
        this.BuildBinding(port),
        address);
responseChannelFactory.Open();
responseProxy =
    (IQuizResponseChannel)responseChannelFactory
    .CreateDuplexChannel();
((IChannel)responseProxy).Open();
```

The address given for the IQuizResponse address includes the name of the pupil. For example, if the name of the pupil is Matt, the address for the channel for IQuizResponse messages for that pupil's instance of the pupils' application will be net.p2p://Classroom_3A/QuizResponse_Matt. Then, assuming that the name Matt is unique in the class, the teacher's application will be able to send messages containing the teacher's evaluation of Matt's answers to that address, over the network of peers, and have those messages received exclusively by Matt's instance of the pupils' application.

19. To facilitate that on the teacher's side of the exchange, go back to the QuizTeacher.cs module of the Teacher project, and complete the implementation of the Join() method of the IQuizManagement interface as shown in Listing 11.9.

LISTING 11.9 Joining a "Private" Mesh

```
void IQuizManagement.Join(Student student)
{
    if (!(this.responseProxies.ContainsKey(student.Name)))
    {
        string endpoint =
            ConfigurationManager.
            AppSettings[QuizTeacher.QuizResponseEndpointKey];
        EndpointAddress address = new EndpointAddress(
            string.Concat(
                "net.p2p://Classroom_3A/QuizResponse", "_",
```

LISTING 11.9   Continued

```
                this.student.Name));
        NetPeerTcpBinding binding =
            this.BuildBinding(this.resolver, this.port);
        ChannelFactory<IQuizResponseChannel> responseChannelFactory =
            new ChannelFactory<IQuizResponseChannel>(
                this.site,
                binding,
                address);
        responseChannelFactory.Open();
        IQuizResponseChannel responseProxy =
            (IQuizResponseChannel)responseChannelFactory.
            CreateDuplexChannel();
        ((IChannel)responseProxy).Open();
        this.responseProxies.Add(student.Name, responseProxy);

        this.form.UpdateStudents(student.Image);
    }
}
```

This code for the teacher's application receives IQuizManagement Join messages from the pupils' application. It creates a channel for sending the teacher's evaluation of a pupil's responses to the quiz questions directly to that pupil's application within the Peer Channel mesh. It does that by formulating an address incorporating the pupil's name in the same way that the pupil's application formulated an address in opening a channel to receive those messages from the teacher's application. The code then goes on to dispatch the image of the pupil, also included in the message received from the pupils' application, to the user interface for display.

Notice how the message is already structured when it arrives, so that it is possible to access the name of the pupil contained in the message by writing student.Name in the code, and to access the image of the pupil that is also contained in the message by writing student.Image. This facility is commonplace in programming with the Windows Communication Foundation, but it is novel in the context of peer-to-peer programming. Before, to send structured messages among peers, one had to resort to laborious measures, such as composing an XML document, storing that in a string, and passing the string as a parameter to the SendMessage() method of the Session class in the real-time communications client API.

See the Peer Channel Solution in Action

Follow these steps to witness Peer Channel at work:

1. Close the solution and open another version of it, C:\WCFHandsOn\PeerChannel\ Continue\PeerChannel.sln. This version of the solution simply accelerates progress by having a completed version of the QuizTeacher class in the QuizTeacher.cs of the Teacher project.

2. Open that module and examine the implementation of the `Dispose()` method:

```
void IDisposable.Dispose()
{
    if (this.resolverService.State == CommunicationState.Opened)
    {
        this.resolverService.Close();
    }

    this.CloseChannel((IChannel)this.questionProxy);
    this.CloseChannel((IChannel)this.managementProxy);
    foreach (IQuizResponse responseProxy in this.responseProxies.Values)
    {
        this.CloseChannel((IChannel)responseProxy);
    }
}
```

This code simply follows good practice in closing the peer name resolution service and all the channels for peer-to-peer communication that have been opened, when the application is shutting down. This `Dispose()` method is called from the handler of the `FormClosed` event of the application's main form.

3. Right-click on the Teacher project in the Visual Studio Solution Explorer, and choose Debug, Start New Instance from the context menu that appears. The teacher's application should appear, as shown in Figure 11.5.

4. Right-click on the Child project in the Visual Studio Solution Explorer, and choose Debug, Start New Instance from the context menu that appears. The pupil's application should appear, as shown in Figure 11.6.

5. Switch back to the main form of the teacher's application. At the top of that form, there should be the picture of a pupil transmitted by the pupil's application as that application started, as shown previously in Figure 11.1.

6. Click on the Start button on the main form of the teacher's application, and switch to the main form of the pupil's application. The pupil's application should now have received a quiz question from the teacher's application. In fact, if you were to use the buttons labeled with arrows to navigate forward and backward through the quiz questions, you should find that several quiz questions have been received by the pupil's application.

7. Select an answer for any one of the questions, and click on the OK button.

8. Switch back to the teacher's application, and, in the Grading section, the response chosen in the pupil's application should be shown in the teacher's application.

9. Choose whether the answer is correct, and click on the Grade button.

10. Switch to the pupil's application, and a checkmark or a cross will have appeared to signify whether the answer to the question was judged to be correct or incorrect.

11. Stop debugging the applications.

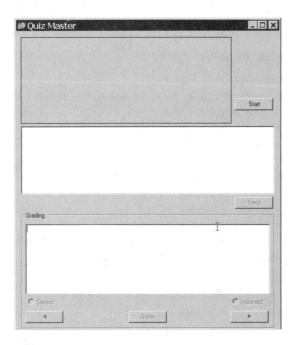

FIGURE 11.5   Teacher's application.

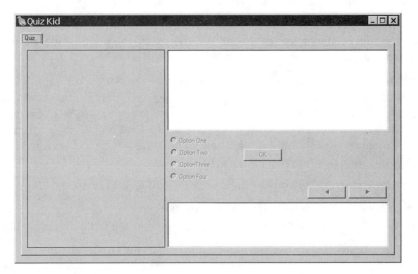

FIGURE 11.6   Pupils' application.

Securing the Peer Channel Solution

Follow these steps to secure the peer communication:

1. Open the `QuizTeacher.cs` module of the Teacher project. Locate the `BuildBinding()` method of the `QuizTeacher` class, and modify that method to read as shown here:

```
private NetPeerTcpBinding BuildBinding(Resolver resolver, int port)
{
    NetPeerTcpBinding binding = new NetPeerTcpBinding();
    binding.MaxMessageSize = long.MaxValue;
    binding.PeerNodeAuthenticationMode =
        PeerAuthenticationMode.MutualCertificate;
    binding.MessageAuthentication = true;
    binding.Port = port;
    binding.Resolver = new ResolverClient(resolver);

    return binding;
}
```

This enables the authentication of the sources of messages within the network of peers, as well as the digital signing of the messages to ensure that any tampering with the contents of the messages en route will be detected. The mode of authentication that we have selected requires that messages be signed with the private key of an X.509 certificate, the public key of which is trusted by the recipient.

2. Locate the definition of the `ServiceValidator` class in the same `QuizTeacher.cs` module, and modify it as shown here:

```
public override void Validate(X509Certificate2 certificate)
{
    if (certificate.SubjectName.Name != "CN=Woodgrove")
    {
        throw new Exception("We don't trust you!");
    }
}
```

The `ServiceValidator` class derives from the abstract `X509CertificateValidator` class. In the implementation of that abstract class' sole `Validate()` method, one does the work of deciding whether to accept the X.509 certificate passed as a parameter to the method.

3. Now go to the constructor of the `QuizTeacher` class in the same module, and modify it as shown in Listing 11.10.

LISTING 11.10   Using the PeerSecurityBehavior in the Teacher's Application

```
public QuizTeacher(MainForm form)
{
    this.form = form;

    Uri baseAddress = new Uri(
        ConfigurationManager.AppSettings[QuizTeacher.BaseAddressKey]);
    this.resolver = new Resolver();
    this.resolverService = new ServiceHost(resolver, baseAddress);
    this.resolverService.Open();

    site = new InstanceContext(this);
    this.port = int.Parse(
        ConfigurationManager.AppSettings[QuizTeacher.QuizPortKey]);
    this.meshIdentifier =
        ConfigurationManager.
        AppSettings[QuizTeacher.MeshIdentifierKey];
    string endpoint = null;
    EndpointAddress address = null;

    SecurityValidator validator = new SecurityValidator();
    peerSecurity = new PeerSecurityBehavior();
    peerSecurity.SetSelfCertificate(this.GetCertificate());
    peerSecurity.SetPeerNodeX509Authentication(validator);
    peerSecurity.SetMessageX509Authentication(validator);

    endpoint =
        ConfigurationManager.
        AppSettings[QuizTeacher.QuizManagementEndpointKey];
    address = new EndpointAddress(
        string.Concat(
            QuizTeacher.PeerChannelAddressPrefix,
            this.meshIdentifier,
            "/",
            endpoint));
    ChannelFactory<IQuizManagementChannel> managementChannelFactory =
        new ChannelFactory<IQuizManagementChannel>(
            this.BuildBinding(
                this.resolver,
                this.port),
            address);
    managementChannelFactory.Description.Behaviors.Add(peerSecurity);
    managementChannelFactory.Open();
    managementProxy =
        (IQuizManagementChannel)managementChannelFactory.
```

LISTING 11.10   Continued

```
        CreateDuplexChannel(
            this.site);
    ((IChannel)managementProxy).Open();

    endpoint =
        ConfigurationManager.
        AppSettings[QuizTeacher.QuizQuestionEndpointKey];
    address =
        new EndpointAddress(
            string.Concat(
                QuizTeacher.PeerChannelAddressPrefix,
                this.meshIdentifier,
                "/",
                endpoint));
    ChannelFactory<IQuizQuestionChannel> questionChannelFactory =
        new ChannelFactory<IQuizQuestionChannel>(
            this.BuildBinding(
                this.resolver,
                this.port),
            address);
    questionChannelFactory.Description.Behaviors.Add(peerSecurity);
    questionChannelFactory.Open();
    questionProxy =
        (IQuizQuestionChannel)questionChannelFactory.
        CreateDuplexChannel(this.site);
    ((IChannel)questionProxy).Open();
}
```

The newly-added code instantiates an instance of the SecurityValidator class;
then it creates an instance of the PeerSecurityBehavior class, and passes the
instance of the SecurityValidator class to the SetPeerNodeX509Authentication()
and SetMessageX509Authentication() methods. That configures the
PeerSecurityBehavior object so that, as messages arrive, the sources thereof, as well
as the digital signatures certifying the integrity of the messages, are validated by the
SecurityValidator class defined earlier.

The line

```
peerSecurity.SetSelfCertificate(this.GetCertificate());
```

tells the PeerSecurityBehavior which X.509 certificate our application should use
to sign its messages and authenticate itself to other nodes in the peer network.
The lines

```
managementChannelFactory.Description.Behaviors.Add(peerSecurity);
```

and

```
questionChannelFactory.Description.Behaviors.Add(peerSecurity);
```

apply the `PeerSecurityObject` that we have configured to the channels that we use for communicating with the pupils' application.

4. Add a similar line to the implementation of the `IQuizManagement` interface's `Join()` method in the `QuizTeacher` class, as shown in Listing 11.11.

LISTING 11.11   Securing the "Private" Meshes

```
void IQuizManagement.Join(Student student)
{
    if (!(this.responseProxies.ContainsKey(student.Name)))
    {
        string endpoint =
            ConfigurationManager.
            AppSettings[QuizTeacher.QuizResponseEndpointKey];
        EndpointAddress address =
            new EndpointAddress(
                string.Concat(
                    QuizTeacher.PeerChannelAddressPrefix,
                    this.meshIdentifier,
                    "/",
                    endpoint,
                    "_",
                    student.Name));
        ChannelFactory<IQuizResponseChannel> responseChannelFactory =
            new ChannelFactory<IQuizResponseChannel>(
                this.BuildBinding(
                    this.resolver,
                    this.port),
                address);
        responseChannelFactory.Description.Behaviors.Add(this.peerSecurity);
        responseChannelFactory.Open();
        IQuizResponseChannel responseProxy =
            (IQuizResponseChannel)responseChannelFactory.CreateDuplexChannel(
                this.site);
        ((IChannel)responseProxy).Open();
        this.responseProxies.Add(student.Name, responseProxy);

        this.form.UpdateStudents(student.Image);
    }
}
```

5. Now open the `QuizChild.cs` module of the Child project, and modify the
   `BuildBinding()` method of the `QuizChild` class therein so that the security configuration of the binding used by the pupils' application matches that of the teacher's
   application:

```csharp
private NetPeerTcpBinding BuildBinding(int port)
{
    NetPeerTcpBinding binding = new NetPeerTcpBinding();
    binding.MaxMessageSize = long.MaxValue;
    binding.PeerNodeAuthenticationMode =
➥PeerAuthenticationMode.MutualCertificate;
    binding.Port = port;
    binding.MessageAuthentication = true;
    binding.Resolver = new ResolverClient();

    return binding;
}
```

6. Amend the constructor of the `QuizChild` class as shown in Listing 11.12.

LISTING 11.12   Using the PeerSecurityBehavior in the Pupils' Application

```csharp
public QuizChild(MainForm form, string[] parameters)
{
    this.form = form;

    this.student.Name = parameters[0];
    int port = int.Parse(parameters[1]);

    InstanceContext site = new InstanceContext(this);

    string endpoint = null;
    EndpointAddress address = null;
    string meshIdentifier =
        ConfigurationManager.AppSettings[QuizChild.MeshIdentifierKey];

    SecurityValidator validator = new SecurityValidator();
    peerSecurity = new PeerSecurityBehavior();
    peerSecurity.SetSelfCertificate(this.GetCertificate());
    peerSecurity.SetPeerNodeX509Authentication(validator);
    peerSecurity.SetMessageX509Authentication(validator);

    //Management
    endpoint =
        ConfigurationManager.
        AppSettings[QuizChild.QuizManagementEndpointKey];
```

LISTING 11.12   Continued

```
address = new EndpointAddress(
    string.Concat(
        QuizChild.PeerChannelAddressPrefix,
        meshIdentifier,
        "/",
        endpoint));
ChannelFactory<IQuizManagementChannel> managementChannelFactory =
    new ChannelFactory<IQuizManagementChannel>(
        this.BuildBinding(port),address);
managementChannelFactory.Description.Behaviors.Add(peerSecurity);
managementChannelFactory.Open();
managementProxy =
    (IQuizManagementChannel)managementChannelFactory.CreateDuplexChannel(
        site);
((IChannel)managementProxy).Open();

//Question
endpoint =
    ConfigurationManager.
    AppSettings[QuizChild.QuizQuestionEndpointKey];
address =
    new EndpointAddress(
        string.Concat(
            QuizChild.PeerChannelAddressPrefix,
            meshIdentifier,
            "/",
            endpoint));
ChannelFactory<IQuizQuestionChannel> questionChannelFactory =
    new ChannelFactory<IQuizQuestionChannel>(
        this.BuildBinding(port),
        address);
questionChannelFactory.Description.Behaviors.Add(peerSecurity);
questionChannelFactory.Open();
questionProxy =
    (IQuizQuestionChannel)questionChannelFactory.CreateDuplexChannel(
        site);
((IChannel)questionProxy).Open();

//Response
endpoint =
    ConfigurationManager.
    AppSettings[QuizChild.QuizResponseEndpointKey];
address =
    new EndpointAddress(
```

LISTING 11.12   Continued

```
            string.Concat(
                QuizChild.PeerChannelAddressPrefix,
                meshIdentifier,
                "/",
                endpoint,
                "_",
                this.student.Name));
    ChannelFactory<IQuizResponseChannel> responseChannelFactory =
        new ChannelFactory<IQuizResponseChannel>(
                this.BuildBinding(port),
                address);
    responseChannelFactory.Description.Behaviors.Add(peerSecurity);
    responseChannelFactory.Open();
    responseProxy =
        (IQuizResponseChannel)responseChannelFactory.CreateDuplexChannel(site);
    ((IChannel)responseProxy).Open();

    //Announce student to teacher:
    this.Join();
}
```

7. Install the certificate used to secure the exchange of messages by executing the batch file C:\WCFHandsOn\PeerChannel\SetUp.bat. The Setup.bat batch file assumes that the tools included with the version of the Microsoft Windows SDK for use with WinFX are installed in the folder C:\Program Files\Microsoft SDKs\Windows\v1.0\Bin. If they are not installed there, modify the batch file accordingly. If their location is unknown, search the hard disks for the tool CertKeyFileTool.exe; the other tools should be in the same location. A second batch file, C:\WCFHandsOn\CleanUp.bat, is provided for removing the certificate after the exercise has been completed.

8. Start testing the newly secured solution by right-clicking on the Teacher project in the Visual Studio Solution Explorer, and choosing Debug, Start New Instance from the context menu that appears. The teacher's application should appear.

9. Right-click on the Child project in the Visual Studio Solution Explorer, and choose Debug, Start New Instance from the context menu that appears. The pupil's application should appear.

10. Switch back to the main form of the teacher's application. At the top of that form, there should be the picture of a pupil transmitted by the pupil's application as that application started, confirming that the pupil's application can still transmit messages to the teacher's application.

11. Click on the Start button on the main form of the teacher's application, and switch to the main form of the pupil's application. The pupil's application should now have received a quiz question from the teacher's application, confirming that the teacher's application can still send messages to the pupil's application.

12. Stop debugging the applications.

Defense in Depth

The Windows Peer-to-Peer Networking infrastructure that underlies Peer Channel provides for securing the exchange of messages among peers using a shared secret, either a password or an X.509 certificate. In the foregoing steps, a shared X.509 certificate was used.

Note, however, that depending on how the binding of the peer name resolution service is configured, the participants must also authenticate themselves to that service in order to access the network of peers. In the application used in this chapter, the configuration file of the teacher's application set the binding to be the NetTcpBinding, which, by default, authenticates users by their Windows access tokens:

```
<?xml version="1.0" encoding="utf-8" ?>
<configuration>
    [...]
    <system.serviceModel>
        <services>
            <service
                type="WindowsCommunicationFoundationHandsOn.School.Resolver">
                <endpoint address=""
                        binding="netTcpBinding"
contract="WindowsCommunicationFoundationHandsOn.School.IPeerResolver" />
            </service>
        </services>
    </system.serviceModel>
</configuration>
```

However, the authentication and authorization of users of the peer name resolution service can be configured in any of the myriad ways that are supported by the Windows Communication Foundation. That provides an important, initial layer of security for peer-to-peer communications.

Style

In the foregoing steps, Windows Communication Foundation channels were created and configured using code rather than a configuration file. If it was not necessary to add security to the channels, they might have been defined using a configuration file in this way:

```
<system.serviceModel>
    <client>
        <endpoint configurationName="PeerResolverService"
            address="net.tcp://localhost:8089/School/PeerResolverService"
```

```
            binding="netTcpBinding"
            contract=
"WindowsCommunicationFoundationHandsOn.School.School.IPeerResolver, Pupil"/>
        <endpoint configurationName="QuizQuestion"
            address="net.p2p://Classroom_3A/QuizQuestion"
            binding="netPeerTcpBinding"
            bindingConfiguration="PeerBinding"
            contract=
"WindowsCommunicationFoundationHandsOn.School.School.IQuizQuestion, Pupil"/>
    </client>

    <bindings>
        <netPeerTcpBinding>
            <binding configurationName="PeerBinding"
                port="8091"
                maxMessageSize="4194304"
                messageAuthentication="true"
                peerNodeAuthenticationMode="mutualCertificate"
            />
        </netPeerTcpBinding>
    </bindings>
</system.serviceModel>
```

Then one could simply write

```
ChannelFactory<IQuizQuestion> questionChannelFactory =
    new ChannelFactory<IQuizQuestion>(site,"QuizQuestion");
questionChannelFactory.Open();
questionProxy = (IQuizQuestion)questionChannelFactory.CreateDuplexChannel();
((IChannel)questionProxy).Open();
```

rather than

```
endpoint =
    ConfigurationManager.
    AppSettings[QuizTeacher.QuizQuestionEndpointKey];
address =
    new EndpointAddress(
        string.Concat(
            QuizTeacher.PeerChannelAddressPrefix,
            this.meshIdentifier,
            "/",
            endpoint));
ChannelFactory<IQuizQuestionChannel> questionChannelFactory =
    new ChannelFactory<IQuizQuestionChannel>(
        this.BuildBinding(
```

```
        this.resolver,
        this.port),
    address);
questionChannelFactory.Description.Behaviors.Add(peerSecurity);
questionChannelFactory.Open();
questionProxy =
    (IQuizQuestionChannel)questionChannelFactory.
    CreateDuplexChannel(this.site);
((IChannel)questionProxy).Open();
```

However, the `PeerSecurityBehavior` class used in the exercise can be defined only using code, not configuration. So all the definition of the channels was done in code rather than in configuration.

Summary

The Windows Communication Foundation's Peer Channel makes it easy to use the facilities of the Windows Peer-to-Peer Networking infrastructure to construct applications involving the exchange of structured data among peers. Peer Channel applications, like any Windows Communication Foundation applications, are defined by an address, a binding, and a contract. The addresses must have netP2P as the scheme. The binding is the `NetPeerTcpBinding`. The contracts must be defined with themselves as their callback contracts. A behavior, `PeerBehavior`, is provided for publishing and subscribing to the events of coming online and going offline. On Windows XP SP2, and other operating systems with the Windows Peer-to-Peer Networking infrastructure, peer name resolution can be left to that infrastructure. On other operating systems, such as Windows Server 2003, it is necessary to provide a peer name resolution service, which is easy to build as an implementation of the abstract `PeerResolver` class. While the exchange of messages via Peer Channel may be secured using a symmetric secret, access to the peer name resolution service can be controlled in a wider variety of ways, providing an additional layer of defense for sensitive peer-to-peer applications.

CHAPTER 12

Manageability

In their book *Understanding SOA with Web Services*, Eric Newcomer and Greg Lomow present a vision of "the service-oriented enterprise": "Driven by the convergence of key technologies and the universal adoption of Web services, the service-oriented enterprise promises to significantly improve corporate agility, speed time-to-market for new products and services, reduce IT costs, and improve operational efficiency" (Newcomer and Lomow 2005, 2).

This is precisely the vision being used to sell business decision-makers on the idea of adopting service orientation. Yet service orientation is merely a way of making software, developing it in the form of classes that implement WSDL interfaces. So what is the magic by which a particular approach to developing software yields significant improvements in corporate agility and time-to-market, reduced information technology costs, and operational efficiency? Well, service-oriented software is assumed to be readily composable units of which not only the functionality but also the costs and other operational characteristics are well-known. Thus, a business equipped with service-oriented software is presumed to be able to adjust to its market by quickly reassembling its information systems appropriately from various service-oriented components, "deriving the information system design from the business design [to] more easily drive changes into the information system at the rate and pace of change in the business design" (High, Kinder and Graham 2005, 7). For that to be possible, it is not sufficient only to know what a software service can do and how it communicates, which is all that WSDL can say. It is also necessary for its cost of ownership to be measurable and monitored so that the financial feasibility of a given assembly of services can be readily and continually assessed, and it must be easy to deploy and administer. Only then can one hope to be able to "tun[e] the operational environment to meet the business objectives...and measur[e] success or failure to meet those objectives" (High, Kinder and Graham 2005, 23). Software services, then, are supposed to be manageable, both as software entities by systems administrators and as components of a business enterprise, as budget line items.

Yet, although an important impetus for the adoption of service orientation is the prospect of an information services infrastructure composed of readily manageable units, the manageability of services has been quite neglected in the various facilities for developing software services that have been available up to this point. Microsoft .NET Web Services and the Web Services Enhancements for Microsoft .NET provide no management features specifically for software services, although AmberPoint Express, which provides for monitoring the performance of services and diagnosing errors in them, is freely available for use with certain versions of Microsoft Visual Studio 2005. IBM's Emerging Technologies Toolkit for Web Services and Autonomic Computing only provides classes for developing implementations of the WS-Resource Framework specification. That specification defines a language by which a service can identify properties it can monitor and manipulate, and by which clients can retrieve and modify property values. IBM also offers for sale the Tivoli Application Manager for SOA, which, similar to AmberPoint's free Express product, allows one to monitor and remedy the performance of software services.

In stark contrast to its predecessors, the Windows Communication Foundation is deliberately designed to meet the requirement for manageable software services. It does so in two ways. First, it provides a rich variety of tools for systems administrators to use to manage Windows Communication Foundation solutions. Second, it allows software developers to easily augment those tools for systems administrators, and also to add facilities that will be unique to each business enterprise, by which business administrators can monitor costs, risks, and returns.

In preparation for exploring these tools, follow these steps:

1. Copy the code associated with this chapter that you downloaded from www.samspublishing.com to the folder C:\WCFHandsOn. The code is all in a folder called Management. After the code has been unzipped, there should be a folder that looks like the one shown in Figure 12.1.

2. Open the solution C:\WCFHandsOn\Management\TradingService.sln.

3. Install Microsoft Message Queuing (MSMQ), if it is not already installed.

Also complete these next few steps if support for the WS-AtomicTransactions protocol in the Microsoft Distributed Transactions Coordinator has not already been enabled:

1. Open the Microsoft Windows Vista DEBUG Build Environment prompt, which, assuming a complete and normal installation of the Microsoft Windows SDK for the December 2005 WinFX CTP, should be accessible from the Windows Start menu by choosing All Programs, Microsoft Windows SDK, CMD Shell.

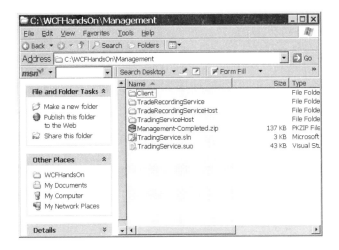

FIGURE 12.1   The Management folder.

2. Enter this command:

   xws_reg –wsat+

3. Then enter this one:

   exit

The solution is for building a derivatives trading system. Derivatives were introduced in Chapter 2, "The Fundamentals," and the derivatives trading system manages the risk in buying them. The TradingService project in the solution builds a trading service for pricing and purchasing derivatives, and the TradingServiceHost project constructs the host for that service. The TradeRecordingService project builds a trade recording service that the trading service uses to execute the purchase of derivatives, and the TradeRecordingServiceHost project constructs the host of the recording service. The client project in the solution is for building a risk management system. That risk management system uses the trading service to price and execute two derivatives purchases at a time: a primary purchase, and another one that is intended as a hedge against the possibility of losses on the first purchase. Depending on the difference in the prices of the primary and hedge purchases, the risk management system will commit either to both purchases together or to neither. If the risk management system chooses not to commit to the purchases, the records of those purchases in the recording service are erased; otherwise, those records are kept.

Administration Facilities

The Windows Communication Foundation provides these tools for administering software services:

- A configuration system for deployment and for post-deployment control and tuning
- A configuration editor

- Configurable auditing of security events

- Message logging

- The tracing of internal activities and of sequences of activities across nodes

- A Trace Viewer designed for following sequences of activities across nodes

- Performance counters for key operational, security, reliability, and transaction statistics for services; the various endpoints of a service; and the individual operations of an endpoint

- A Windows Management Instrumentation (WMI) provider for querying and modifying the properties of running services

The Configuration System

Windows Communication Foundation services are defined by an address that specifies where they are located, a binding that specifies how to communicate with them, and a contract that specifies what they can do. The internal operations of Windows Communication Foundation services and clients can be controlled through properties called *behaviors*.

Although one can write code to specify the addresses, bindings, and contracts of services, and to modify the behaviors of services and clients, the Windows Communication Foundation allows one to instead specify addresses, bindings, and contracts and to modify behaviors in configuration files. That allows system administrators to control how services behave without requiring programming modifications. Indeed, using configuration files to specify addresses, bindings, and contracts is preferred to using code.

The Windows Communication Foundation's configuration system simply extends that of Microsoft .NET. Therefore, it should be familiar to any administrator of .NET applications. The language of the Windows Communication Foundation's configuration system is defined in the file \Program Files\Microsoft Visual Studio 8\Xml\Schemas\ DotNetConfig.xsd, on the disc where Visual Studio 2005 resides, after the Visual Studio 2005 Extensions for WinFX have been installed.

The Configuration Editor

A configuration editor is provided to ease, and give guidance for, the task of editing configuration files. This tool is one of the most rapidly evolving components of the Windows Communication Foundation. The Windows Communication Foundation's Service Model had to be completed before coding of the tools for using it could proceed in earnest, and after initial versions of the tools were released, refinements to them have followed quickly. Indeed, the configuration editor is being superseded by a configuration wizard, a prototype of which was being shown internally at Microsoft in early January

2006. Consequently, details on the use of the tools in these pages are very likely to have been made obsolete by changes in how the tools work in subsequent releases. So do not read these details to see exactly how to use the tools, but rather to see that even in early versions, the tools are intuitive to use and they work. Because future versions will be even more intuitive to use, adapting the details that follow to those subsequent versions should be quite straightforward.

The Configuration Editor is `SvcConfigEditor.exe`. It should be found in the folder `\Program Files\Microsoft SDKs\Windows\v1.0\Bin`, assuming a complete and normal installation of the Microsoft Windows SDK for the December 2005 WinFX CTP.

Configuring the Trade Recording Service with the Configuration Editor

Recall that the trade recording service of the trading service solution is a service for recording the purchase of derivatives. That service is not currently in a working state. To confirm that, do the following:

1. Right-click on the trade recording service host project of the trading service solution in Visual Studio 2005, and choose Debug, Start New Instance from the context menu.

   An exception should be thrown with this error message: "Service has zero application (non-infrastructure) endpoints, [which] might be because no configuration file was found for your application, or because there was a problem with the type in the configuration file." The message is quite accurate: The service cannot start because no endpoints have been defined for it. There is indeed no configuration file with endpoint definitions.

2. Stop debugging.

Follow these steps to use the Configuration Editor to configure an endpoint for the trade recording service:

1. Execute `\Program Files\Microsoft SDKs\Windows\v1.0\Bin\SvcConfigEditor.exe`.

2. Choose File, Open, Executable from the menus, as shown in Figure 12.2.

3. Select the trade recording service's host assembly `C:\WCFHandsOn\Management\TradeRecordingServiceHost\bin\Debug\TradeRecordingServiceHost.exe`, as shown in Figure 12.3.

4. On the Services tab, click on the New button shown in Figure 12.4.

5. A service is configured by identifying the service type and defining its endpoints. To select the service type from the General tab of the Service Editor, shown in Figure 12.5, click on the ellipsis button opposite the ServiceType label.

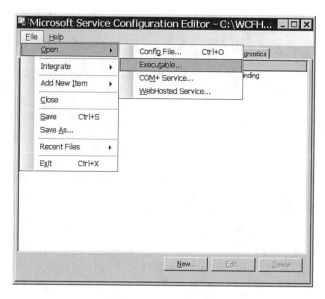

FIGURE 12.2   Selecting an executable.

FIGURE 12.3   Selecting the trade recording service's host assembly.

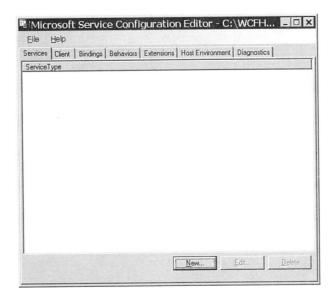

FIGURE 12.4   The Services tab.

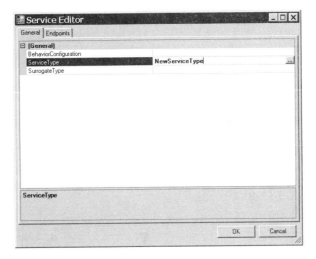

FIGURE 12.5   The General tab of the Service Editor.

6. The service type of the trade recording service is in the assembly built from the trade recording service project: `C:\WCFHandsOn\Management\ TradeRecordingServiceHost\bin\Debug\TradeRecordingService.dll`. Select that assembly, as shown in Figure 12.6, and click on the Open button.

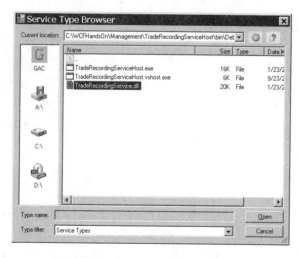

FIGURE 12.6   Selecting an assembly.

7. Choose the Fabrikam.TradingRecorder service type from within the assembly, as shown in Figure 12.7, and click on the Open button.

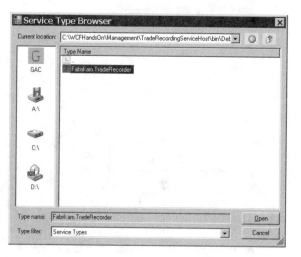

FIGURE 12.7   The Service Type Browser.

8. The General tab of the Service Editor should now show Fabrikam.TradeRecorder as the service type, as shown in Figure 12.8. Click OK to return to the main screen of the Configuration Editor, which should now appear as shown in Figure 12.9.

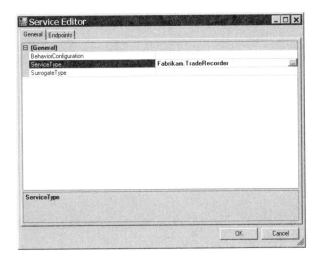

FIGURE 12.8   The selected service type.

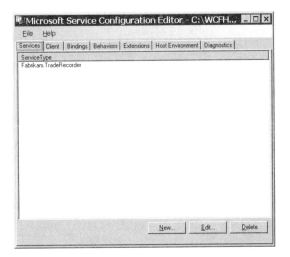

FIGURE 12.9   Service configured with a service type.

9. Select the Bindings tab, and then choose netMsmqBinding from the list of binding types as shown in Figure 12.10.

10. Click on the New button, and then configure a netMsmqBinding with the name QueuedBinding, as shown in Figure 12.11.

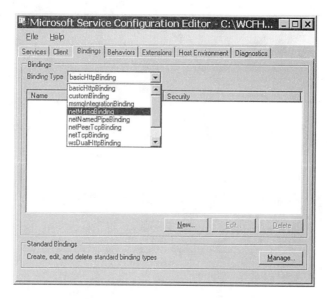

FIGURE 12.10   Selecting a binding.

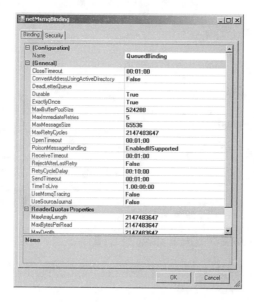

FIGURE 12.11   Configuring a binding.

11. Select the Security tab, and select None from the list of security modes, as shown in Figure 12.12.

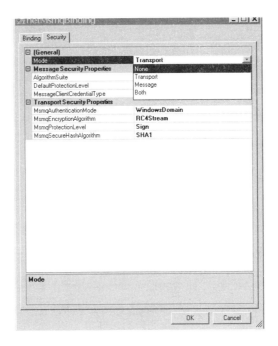

FIGURE 12.12   Configuring the security of a binding.

12. Click OK, and the Bindings tab should appear as shown in Figure 12.13.

FIGURE 12.13   A configured binding.

13. Now that a suitable binding configuration has been created, an endpoint with that binding can be added to the service. Select the Services tab again, and click on the Edit button, depicted in Figure 12.14.

FIGURE 12.14   Preparing to configure the endpoints of a service.

14. Select the Endpoints tab of the Service Editor represented in Figure 12.15.

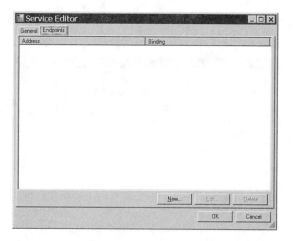

FIGURE 12.15   The Endpoints tab of the Service Editor.

15. Specify the address of the endpoint as shown in Figure 12.16.

16. Select netMsmqBinding from the list of bindings, as shown in Figure 12.17.

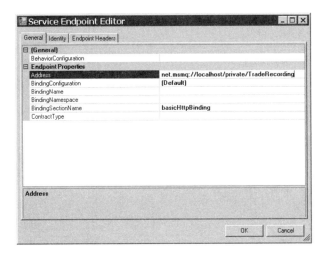

FIGURE 12.16   Specifying the address of an endpoint.

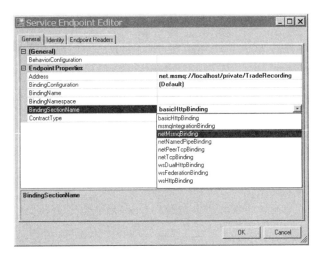

FIGURE 12.17   Specifying the binding of an endpoint.

17. Select the QueuedBinding binding configuration, which was defined in the preceding steps, from the list of available binding configurations, as shown in Figure 12.18.

18. To identify the contract exposed at the endpoint, click on the ContractType ellipsis button shown in Figure 12.19.

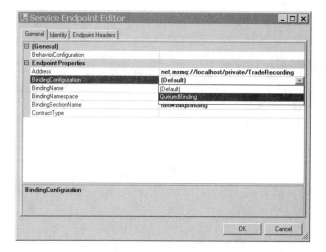

FIGURE 12.18   Configuring the binding of an endpoint.

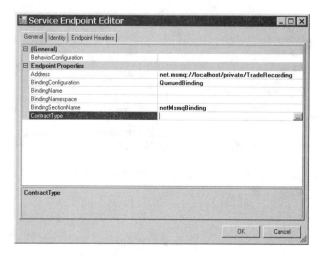

FIGURE 12.19   Preparing to identify the contract of an endpoint.

19. Select the Fabrikam.ITradeRecorder service contract in the assembly `C:\WCFHandsOn\Management\TradeRecordingServiceHost\bin\Debug\TradeRecordingService.dll`, as shown in Figure 12.20, and click on the Open button.

20. The endpoint configuration should now appear as shown in Figure 12.21. Click on the OK button to return to the Endpoints tab of the Service Editor.

FIGURE 12.20   Identifying the contract of an endpoint.

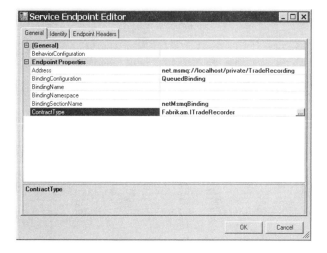

FIGURE 12.21   The endpoint configuration in the Service Endpoint Editor.

21. The Endpoints tab of the Service Editor should now appear as depicted in Figure 12.22, showing the address and the binding of the endpoint. Click on the OK button to return to the main screen of the Configuration Editor.

22. Choose File, Save from the Configuration Editor menus, as shown in Figure 12.23.

Confirm that whereas the trade recording service was not initially in a working state, it now is able to work because it has been properly configured using the Windows Communication Foundation's configuration editor:

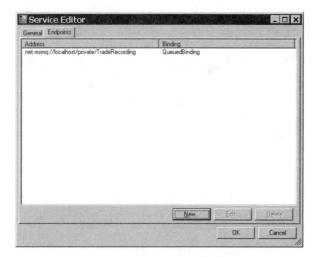

FIGURE 12.22   The endpoint configuration in the Service Editor.

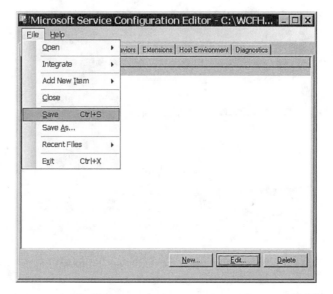

FIGURE 12.23   Saving the service configuration.

1. Right-click on the trade recording service host project of the trading service solution in Visual Studio 2005, and choose Debug, Start New Instance from the context menu. After a few seconds, the console application window of the trade recording service host should appear, confirming that the service is available.

2. Stop debugging.

Configuring a Client Application with the Configuration Editor

Follow these steps to configure the client risk management application to communicate with the trading service, which, in turn, uses the trade recording service to record derivatives purchases. The trading service has an endpoint at the address http://localhost:8000/TradingService. That endpoint uses the Windows Communication Foundation's standard WSHttpBinding. The WSHttpBinding is customized to include information about the state of transactions within messages, and to ensure that the messages are delivered exactly once, and in order:

1. Choose File, Open, Executable from the Configuration Editor's menus, as shown in Figure 12.24.

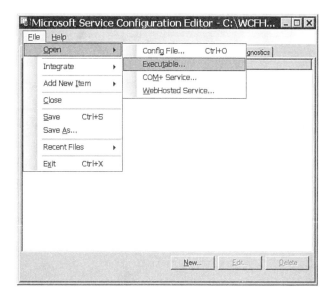

FIGURE 12.24   Selecting an executable.

2. Select C:\WCFHandsOn\Management\Client\bin\Debug\Client.exe, as shown in Figure 12.25.

3. Select the Bindings tab, as shown in Figure 12.26.

4. Select wsHttpBinding from the list of bindings, and then click on the New button to create a new configuration of that standard binding, as shown in Figure 12.27.

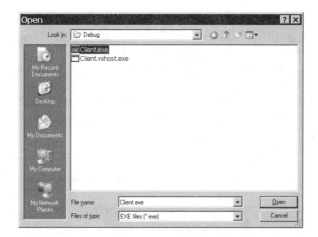

FIGURE 12.25 Selecting the client executable.

FIGURE 12.26 The Bindings tab.

5. As shown in Figure 12.28, give the binding configuration the name
    ReliableHttpBinding, set the value of the TransactionFlow property to True, and,
    under the ReliableSession Properties heading, set the values of the Enabled and
    Ordered properties to True.

FIGURE 12.27   Selecting the binding.

FIGURE 12.28   Configuring the binding.

6. Click OK, and the Bindings tab should appear as shown in Figure 12.29.

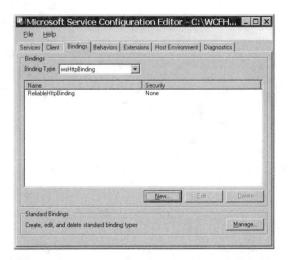

FIGURE 12.29   A configured binding.

7. Now that a suitable binding configuration has been created, the service endpoint to be addressed by the client application can be defined. Select the Client tab, and click on the Edit button, depicted in Figure 12.30.

FIGURE 12.30   The Client tab.

8. Enter TradingService as the name of the endpoint configuration, and http://localhost:8000/TradingService as the address of the service endpoint, as shown in Figure 12.31.

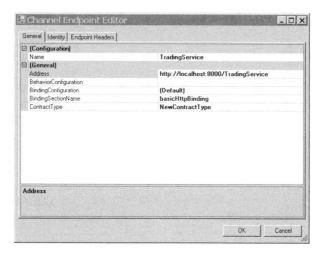

FIGURE 12.31   Specifying an endpoint address.

9. Choose wsHttpBinding from the list of bindings, as indicated in Figure 12.32.

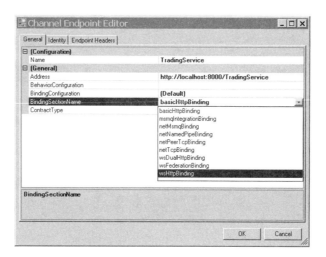

FIGURE 12.32   Selecting a binding.

10. Select ReliableHttpBinding from the list of binding configurations, as indicated in Figure 12.33.

11. To identify the contract exposed at the endpoint, click on the ContractType ellipsis button shown in Figure 12.34.

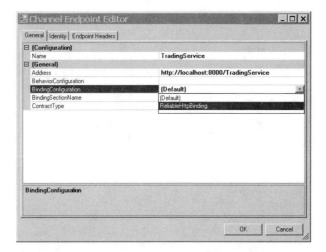

FIGURE 12.33   Configuring a binding.

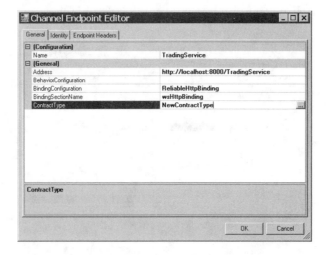

FIGURE 12.34   Preparing to identify the contract of an endpoint.

12. The contract is defined in the client assembly, so select the `C:\WCFHandsOn\`
`Management\Client\bin\Debug\Client.exe` assembly, as shown in Figure 12.35, and
click on the Open button.

13. Select the `Client.ITradingService` service contract as shown in Figure 12.36, and
click on the Open button.

FIGURE 12.35   Selecting the assembly containing the contract.

FIGURE 12.36   Selecting a service contract.

14. The endpoint configuration should now appear as shown in Figure 12.37. Select the Identity tab.

15. Enter the current user's principal name in the format *domain\name* as the value of the UserPrincipalName property, as shown in Figure 12.38, but substituting the current user's principal name for the name shown. Click on the OK button to return to the Client tab of the Service Editor.

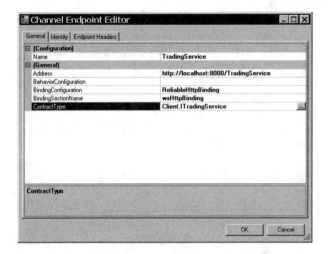

FIGURE 12.37   The endpoint configuration in the Channel Endpoint Editor.

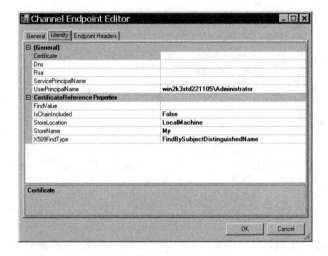

FIGURE 12.38   Setting the UserPrincipalName property of the identity.

16. The client configuration should now appear as shown in Figure 12.39. Choose File, Save from the Configuration Editor's menus, as shown in Figure 12.40.

17. Choose File, Exit from the menus to close the Configuration Editor.

FIGURE 12.39   The client configuration.

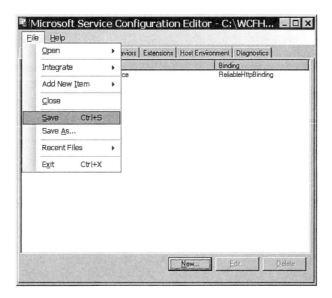

FIGURE 12.40   Saving the client configuration.

Test the newly configured solution by following these steps:

1. In Visual Studio 2005, right-click on the solution at the top of the tree in the Solution Explorer, and choose Set Startup Projects from the context menu. Confirm that the Startup Project properties are configured as shown in Figure 12.41

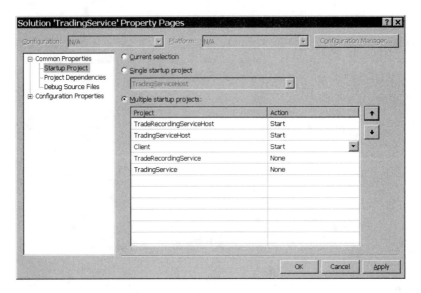

FIGURE 12.41   Startup Project properties.

2. Choose Debug, Start Debugging from the menus.

3. When there is activity in the console application windows of the trade recording service host and the trading service host, confirming that the services they host are ready, enter a keystroke into the console application window of the client application.

   After a few moments, activity should start to appear in the console application window of the trading service host, as the client risk management system begins pricing and purchasing a derivative. There may be a pause as the trading service loads the Microsoft Distributed Transactions Coordinator for the first time. Then the pricing and purchasing of primary and hedging derivatives purchases should proceed.

4. Stop debugging.

Configurable Auditing of Security Events

The Windows Communication Foundation records security events in the Windows event log. That facility is one of the Windows Communication Foundation's many behaviors, and it is configurable. To see how to configure it, follow these steps:

1. Execute \Program Files\Microsoft SDKs\Windows\v1.0\Bin\SvcConfigEditor.exe.

2. Choose File, Open, Executable from the menus, as shown in Figure 12.42, and open the assembly C:\WCFHandsOn\Management\TradingServiceHost\bin\Debug\ TradingServiceHost.exe.

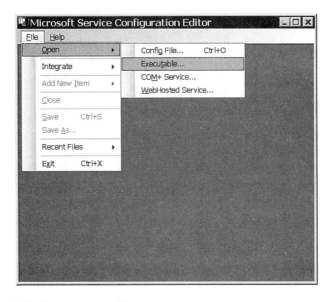

FIGURE 12.42   Selecting an executable.

3. Select the Behaviors tab, and click on the New button, as shown in Figure 12.43.

FIGURE 12.43   The Behaviors tab.

4. In the Behavior Editor, provide the name TradingService for the behavior, as shown in Figure 12.44.

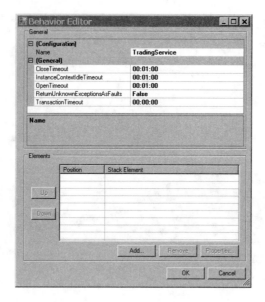

FIGURE 12.44   The Behavior Editor.

5. Click on the Add button in the Elements section.

6. Select serviceSecurityAudit from the list of behaviors meant to be configured by an administrator, as shown in Figure 12.45. The ServiceSecurityAudit behavior is the behavior by which the Windows Communication Foundation's auditing of security events can be controlled.

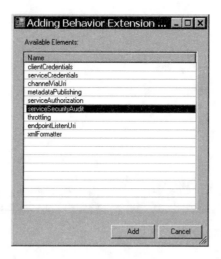

FIGURE 12.45   Selecting the ServiceSecurityAudit behavior.

7. Click on the Add button.

8. Back in the main screen of the Behavior Editor, select serviceSecurityAudit, which now appears in the list in the Elements section, as shown in Figure 12.46, and click on the Properties button.

FIGURE 12.46 Preparing to configure the ServiceSecurityAudit behavior.

9. In the property editor for the ServiceSecurityAudit behavior, select Application as the AuditLogLocation, as shown in Figure 12.47.

10. Choose SuccessOrFailure as the value for the MessageAuthenticationAuditLevel, as shown in Figure 12.48.

11. Choose SuccessOrFailure as the value for the ServiceAuthenticationAuditLevel, as shown in Figure 12.49.

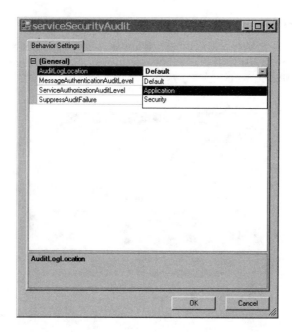

FIGURE 12.47   Selecting the audit log location.

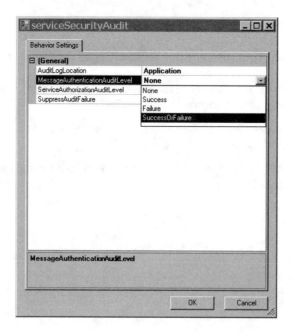

FIGURE 12.48   Setting the message authentication audit level.

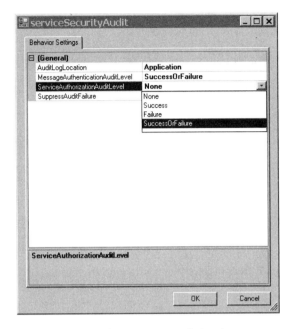

FIGURE 12.49   Setting the service authentication audit level.

12. Click on the OK button to return to the Behavior Editor.

13. Click OK to return to the main screen of the Configuration Editor.

Now a behavior configuration including the ServiceSecurityAuditBehavior has been created. That behavior configuration will now be associated with the trading service.

14. Select the Services tab, and select Fabrikam.TradingSystem in the list of services, as shown in Figure 12.50, and click on the Edit button.

15. Select the TradingService behavior configuration from the list of behavior configurations, as shown in Figure 12.51.

16. Click the OK button to return to the main screen of the Configuration Editor.

17. Choose File, Save from the menus, as shown in Figure 12.52.

18. Select File, Exit from the menus to close the Configuration Editor.

FIGURE 12.50   Preparing to configure the service with the behavior.

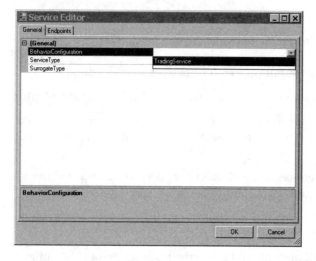

FIGURE 12.51   Applying a behavior configuration to a service.

FIGURE 12.52   Saving a configuration.

Follow these steps to test the new configuration of the security auditing behavior:

1. In Visual Studio 2005, in the trading service solution, Choose Debug, Start Debugging from the menus.

2. When there is activity in the console application windows of the trade recording service host and the trading service host, confirming that the services they host are ready, enter a keystroke into the console application window of the client application.

3. After seeing activity in the console application windows of the trading service host and the client as they price and purchase derivatives, stop debugging.

4. Open the Windows Event viewer.

5. Refresh the application log.

6. Locate and examine events with the source `ServiceModel Audit`. Those are the Windows Communication Foundation's security audit events. They should look like the event shown in Figure 12.53.

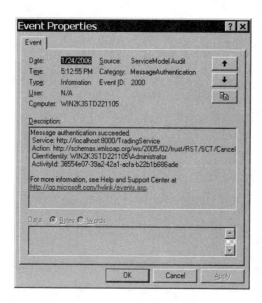

FIGURE 12.53   Windows Communication Foundation security audit event.

Message Logging

Windows Communication Foundation applications can be configured to log incoming and outgoing messages. Messages can be logged not only at the point at which they are transported, but also as they proceed through the Channel Layer.

The message logging facility is implemented using the trace listening mechanism already incorporated in .NET, in the System.Diagnostics namespace. A *trace listener* is a class that knows how to output diagnostic information to a particular destination, such as an event log, or file of a particular format. When particular categories of diagnostic information are directed to a trace listener, the information in that category is dispatched to the destination to which the trace listener sends its output. The same diagnostic information can be recorded in various ways when information is directed to multiple trace listeners.

Message logging is a particular type of diagnostic information that can be sent to a trace listener for recording. By providing message logging via trace listeners, the Windows Communication Foundation not only uses a mechanism with which .NET developers will already be familiar, but also allows developers, enterprises, and other software vendors that may have developed custom trace listeners to use those for logging messages. To see how to log messages, follow these steps:

1. Execute \Program Files\Microsoft SDKs\Windows\v1.0\Bin\SvcConfigEditor.exe.

2. Start the Configuration Editor; choose File, Open, Executable from the menus, and open the assembly C:\WCFHandsOn\Management\TradingServiceHost\bin\Debug\TradingServiceHost.exe.

3. Select the Diagnostics tab as shown in Figure 12.54.

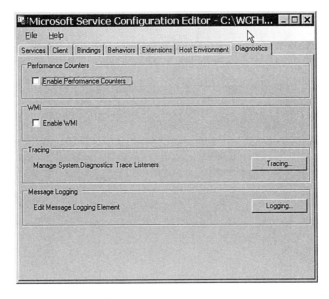

FIGURE 12.54   The Diagnostics tab.

4. Click on the Logging button to access the Message Logging Editor shown in Figure 12.55.

FIGURE 12.55   The Message Logging Editor.

5. Select the Logging tab, shown in Figure 12.56, and set the values of the
   `LogEntireMessage`, `LogMessagesAtServiceLevel`, and `LogMessagesAtTransportLevel`
   properties to `True`.

FIGURE 12.56   The Logging tab.

6. Select the Listeners tab, shown in Figure 12.57, and click on the Create button.
   Doing that serves to direct the message logs to a custom trace listener.

FIGURE 12.57   The Listeners tab.

7. Use the Save Log As dialog, shown in Figure 12.58, to specify that the trace listener is to record the message log in the file `C:\WCFHandsOn\Management\TradingServiceHost_messages.e2e`.

FIGURE 12.58   Selecting a message logging location.

8. The Message Logging Editor should now appear as shown in Figure 12.59. Click on the OK button.

FIGURE 12.59   The message logging configuration.

9. Choose File, Save from the Configuration Editor menus to save the configuration, as shown in Figure 12.60.

FIGURE 12.60   Saving the configuration.

10. Select File, Exit from the menus to close the Configuration Editor.

To see messages being logged, do the following:

1. In Visual Studio 2005, in the trading service solution, choose Debug, Start Debugging from the menus.

2. When there is activity in the console application windows of the trade recording service host and the trading service host, confirming that the services they host are ready, enter a keystroke into the console application window of the client application.

3. Wait until the console application window of the client application confirms that it is done pricing and purchasing derivatives.

4. Enter a keystroke into each console application window.

5. Execute the Windows Communication Foundation's Trace Viewer, which is SvcTraceViewer.exe. It should be found at C:\Program Files\Microsoft SDKs\ Windows\v1.0\Bin, assuming a complete and normal installation of the Microsoft Windows SDK for the December 2005 WinFX CTP. The Trace Viewer is shown in Figure 12.61.

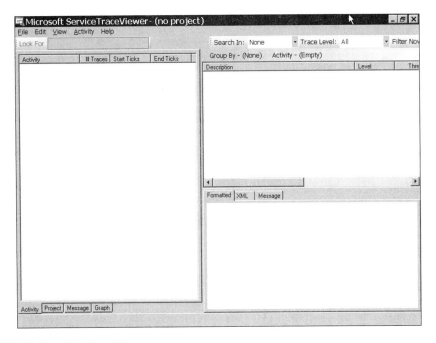

FIGURE 12.61   The Trace Viewer.

6. Choose File, Open from the menus, and open the file
   `C:\WCFHandsOn\Management\TradingServiceHost_messages.e2e`, which is the file in
   which the trace listener was to record the message logs.

7. Select the first entry in the activity list on the left of the Trace Viewer; then select
   the XML tab on the lower right, and scroll through the entry on that tab. It
   contains a record of a message, as shown in Figure 12.62.

Traces

Wikipedia defines a trace as "a detailed record of the steps a computer program executes
during its execution, used as an aid in debugging" (Wikipedia 2006). The Windows
Communication Foundation generates traces for internal processing milestones, events,
exceptions, and warnings. The traces are intended to enable administrators to see how an
application is behaving and understand why it may be misbehaving without having to
resort to using a debugger. In fact, the members of the Windows Communication
Foundation development team are encouraged to diagnose unexpected conditions they
might encounter using the traces rather than a debugger, and to file a bug report demand-
ing additional traces if the existing traces are not sufficient to allow them to render a
diagnosis.

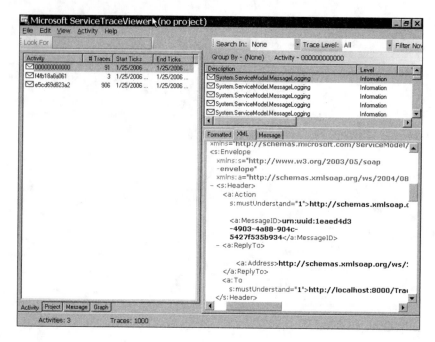

FIGURE 12.62   A logged message.

The Microsoft .NET Framework Class Library 2.0 provides an enhanced tracing infrastructure in the form of classes that have been added to the `System.Diagnostics` namespace, and the Windows Communication Foundation leverages those new classes. The most important of them is the `TraceSource` class that allows one to generate traces associated with a named source:

```
private static TraceSource source = new TraceSource("ANamedSource");
source.TraceEvent(TraceEventType.Error,1,"Trace error message.");
```

Given a named source of traces, one can configure trace listeners to listen for traces from that particular source:

```
<configuration>
  <system.diagnostics>
    <sources>
      <source name="ANamedSource"
        switchValue="Warning"
        <listeners>
          <add name="AListener"/>
          <remove name="Default"/>
        </listeners>
      </source>
    </sources>
    <sharedListeners>
```

```
    <add name="AListener"
      type="System.Diagnostics.TextWriterTraceListener"
      initializeData="myListener.log">
      <filter type="System.Diagnostics.EventTypeFilter"
        initializeData="Error"/>
    </add>
  </sharedListeners>
 </system.diagnostics>
</configuration>
```

The name of the source of traces emitted by the Windows Communication Foundation's Service Model is System.ServiceModel. Thus, one might configure a trace listener to listen for traces emitted by the Service Model in this way:

```
<configuration>
  <system.diagnostics>
    <sources>
      <source name="System.ServiceModel"
        switchValue="Verbose"
        <listeners>
          <add name="xml"
            type="System.Diagnostics.XmlWriterTraceListener"
            initializeData="ClientTraces.e2e"
          />
        </listeners>
      </source>
    </sources>
  </system.diagnostics>
</configuration>
```

Traces emitted by the Windows Communication Foundation's own XML serializer, XmlFormatter, originate from a source named System.Runtime.Serialization, whereas traces from XSI have a source with the name System.SecurityAuthorization.

Trace sources have a Switch property for filtering traces emanating from that source according to their level of importance. Traces emitted by the Windows Communication Foundation can be filtered by six levels of importance, as shown, in descending order, in Table 12.1. Filtering a source for traces with a given level of importance will exclude traces with a lower level of importance, and include any traces of which the level of importance is the specified level or higher.

TABLE 12.1   Windows Communication Foundation Trace Levels

Level	Description
Critical	Traces of catastrophic errors that cause an application to cease functioning
Error	Traces of exceptions
Warning	Traces of conditions that may subsequently cause an exception, such as a limit having been reached or credentials having been rejected

TABLE 12.1   Continued

Level	Description
Information	Traces of milestones significant for monitoring and diagnosis
Verbose	Traces of processing milestones interesting to developers for diagnosis and optimization
ActivityTracing	Traces of activity boundaries

The Windows Communication Foundation does not emit traces by default. Activating tracing is easily done using the Configuration Editor:

1. From the Diagnostics pane, click on the Tracing button shown in Figure 12.63.

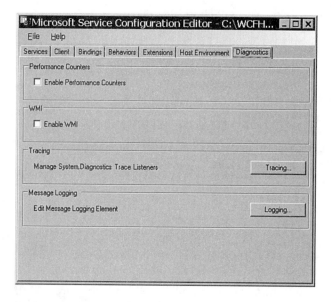

FIGURE 12.63   The Tracing button.

2. In the Diagnostics Tracing dialog, shown in Figure 12.64, click on the Create button to configure a trace listener.

3. Specify where the tracing information is to be written, as shown in Figure 12.65.

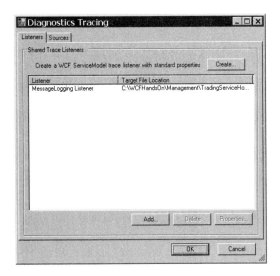

FIGURE 12.64   The Diagnostics Tracing dialog.

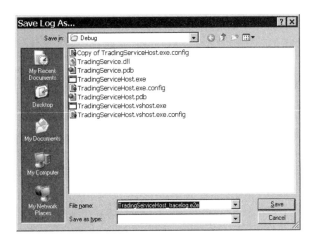

FIGURE 12.65   Specifying a destination for traces.

After traces have been recorded, they can be examined using the Trace Viewer, `C:\Program Files\Microsoft SDKs\Windows\v1.0\Bin\SvcTraceViewer.exe`. An example of what might be seen is displayed in Figure 12.66.

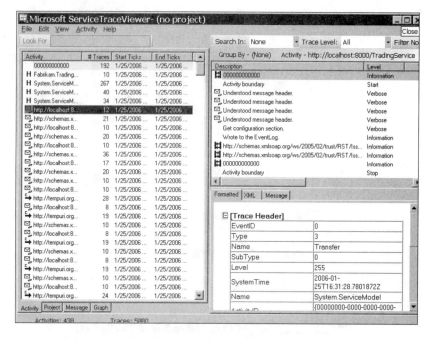

FIGURE 12.66   Viewing traces.

The Trace Viewer

The Windows Communication Foundation's Trace Viewer has already been introduced. As can be seen in Figure 12.66, the Trace Viewer displays a list of activities in a pane on the left, and all the traces pertaining to a selected activity in the pane on the upper right. The lower-right pane shows the details of a particular trace. As shown in Figure 12.62, the Trace Viewer can also be used to view logs of messages.

The most impressive capability of the Trace Viewer, though, is in allowing one to examine the flow of an activity across network nodes. Windows Communication Foundation traces have a globally unique identifier, and whenever a Windows Communication Foundation application is configured to emit traces, the activity identifiers are included in any messages it sends. To see the significance of that, follow these steps:

1. Open the Trace Viewer, `C:\Program Files\Microsoft SDKs\Windows\v1.0\Bin\ SvcTraceViewer.exe`.

2. Choose File, Open from the menus, as shown in Figure 12.67.

3. In the File Open dialog, select all the trace files in the folder `C:\WCFHandsOn\ Management\Traces`, as shown in Figure 12.68, and click on the Open button.

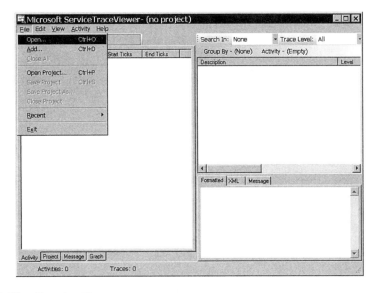

FIGURE 12.67   Opening Traces.

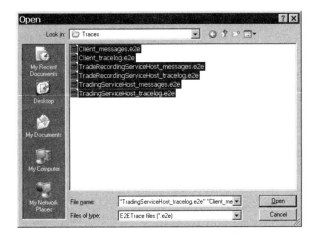

FIGURE 12.68   Selecting trace files.

4. Click the OK button on the File Partial Loading dialog shown in Figure 12.69.

5. Select an activity from the list in the pane on the left, as shown in Figure 12.70.

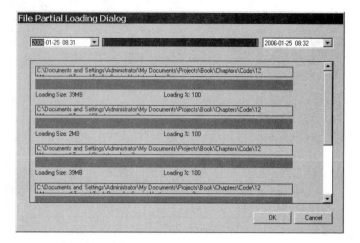

FIGURE 12.69 File Partial Loading dialog.

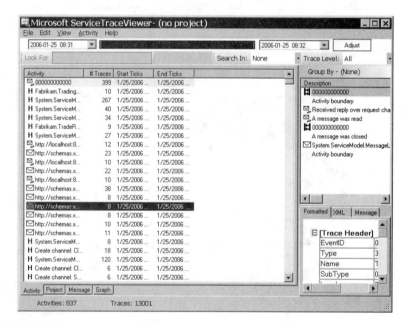

FIGURE 12.70 Selecting an activity.

6. Select the Graph tab, shown in Figure 12.71.

The Trace Viewer is able to show transfers of activity between the endpoints of a system! That feature allows one to follow an activity from a client to a service and back. For instance, one can select any step in the sequence depicted in the graphical view to see details of the traces emitted in that step in the panes on the right.

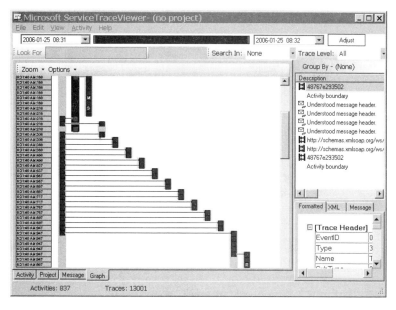

FIGURE 12.71 The Graph tab.

Performance Counters

The Windows Communication Foundation provides a rich variety of performance counters for the monitoring, diagnosis, and optimization of applications. There are performance counters for monitoring services, the individual endpoints of a service, and the individual operations exposed at an endpoint. To examine the performance counters, follow these steps:

1. Start the Configuration Editor, and choose File, Open, Executable from the menus, and open the assembly `C:\WCFHandsOn\Management\TradingRecordingServiceHost\bin\Debug\TradingRecordingServiceHost.exe`.

2. Select the Diagnostics tab.

3. Check the box labeled Enable Performance Counters, as shown in Figure 12.72.

4. Choose File, Save from the Configuration Editor menus to save the configuration.

5. Select File, Exit from the menus to close the Configuration Editor.

6. In Visual Studio 2005, in the trading service solution, choose Debug, Start Debugging from the menus.

7. Wait until there is activity in the console window of the trade recording service host.

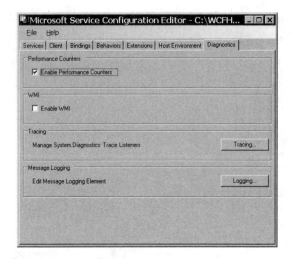

FIGURE 12.72   Enabling performance counters.

8. Choose Run from the Windows Start menu; then enter

   `perfmon`

   and click OK.

9. In the Performance console, right-click on the graph on the right side, and choose Add Counters from the context menu, as shown in Figure 12.73.

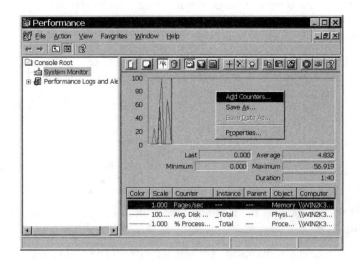

FIGURE 12.73   Adding performance counters to the Performance console.

10. Select `ServiceModelService` from the Performance object list, as shown in Figure 12.74.

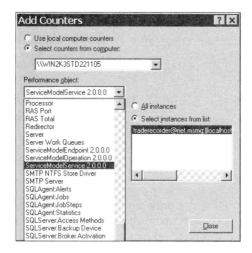

FIGURE 12.74   Selecting a Windows Communication Foundation performance counter category.

ServiceModelService is the name of the category of Windows Communication Foundation performance counters at the service level. Note that there are also categories for performance counters at the level of both endpoints and operations. When the ServiceModelService category is selected, the trade recording service shows up in the list of instances on the right, as shown in Figure 12.74, because that is a service for which performance counters have been enabled.

11. Scroll through the extensive list of performance counters in the ServiceModelService category, as shown in Figure 12.75.

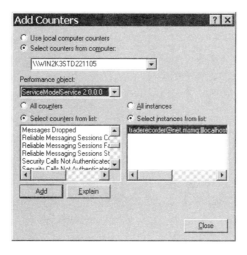

FIGURE 12.75   Examining the Windows Communication Foundation performance counters.

12. Click on the Close button.

13. Choose File, Exit from the Performance Console's menus to close it.

14. In Visual Studio 2005, stop debugging the trading service solution.

WMI Provider

WMI is Microsoft's implementation of the Web-Based Enterprise Management architecture defined by the Desktop Management Task Force. The purpose of the architecture is to define a unified infrastructure for managing both computer hardware and software.

WMI is now built into Windows operating systems, and since its introduction as an add-on for Windows NT version 4.0, not only has it become very familiar to Windows systems administrators, but it also is the foundation for many computer management products. If a piece of software can be examined and manipulated via WMI, system administrators will be able to monitor and adjust it using their preferred computer management tools.

The Windows Communication Foundation takes advantage of that situation, incorporating a WMI provider by which Windows Communication Foundation applications become accessible via WMI. Follow these steps to observe its effects:

1. Start the Configuration Editor; choose File, Open, Executable from the menus, and open the assembly C:\WCFHandsOn\Management\TradingRecordingServiceHost\ bin\Debug\TradingRecordingServiceHost.exe.

2. Select the Diagnostics tab.

3. Check the box labeled Enable WMI, as shown in Figure 12.76, to activate the WMI provider.

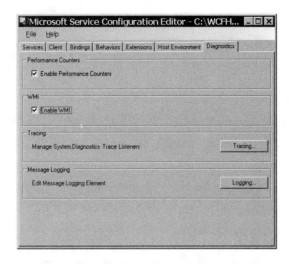

FIGURE 12.76 Activating the WMI provider.

4. Choose File, Save from the Configuration Editor menus to save the configuration.

5. Select File, Exit from the menus to close the Configuration Editor.

6. Download the WMI Administrative Tools from http://www.microsoft.com/
   downloads/details.aspx?displaylang=en&FamilyID=6430F853-1120-48DB-8CC5-
   F2ABDC3ED314.

7. Install the WMI Administrative Tools.

8. In Visual Studio 2005, in the trading service solution, choose Debug, Start
   Debugging from the menus.

9. Wait until there is activity in the console window of the trade recording service
   host.

10. Choose WMI Tools, WMI CIM Studio from the Windows Start menu.

11. Enter `root\ServiceModel` into the Connect to Namespace dialog that appears, as
    illustrated in Figure 12.77. `root\ServiceModel` is the namespace of the classes that
    the Windows Communication Foundation exposes to WMI.

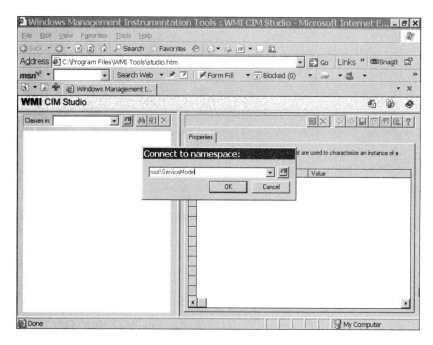

FIGURE 12.77   Connecting to the `root\ServiceModel` namespace.

12. Click OK on the WMI CIM Studio Login dialog, depicted in Figure 12.78, to log in
    as the current user.

FIGURE 12.78   Logging in to the WMI CIM Studio.

13. The classes that the Windows Communication Foundation exposes to WMI are enumerated in the pane on the left. Select ServiceEndpoint, as shown in Figure 12.79.

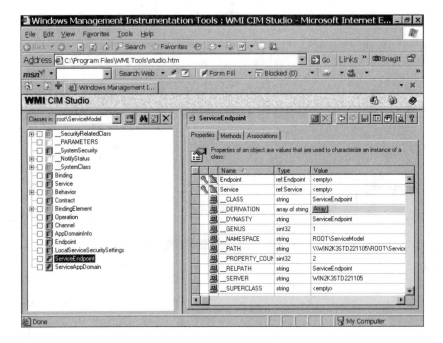

FIGURE 12.79   Selecting a class.

14. Click on the Instances button, which is the fourth button from the left in the row of buttons at the top of the righthand pane. Information is displayed for each endpoint of any running Windows Communication Foundation application for which the WMI provider is enabled, as shown in Figure 12.80 . The WMI CIM Studio is retrieving that information via WMI, which, in turn, retrieves it using the Windows Communication Foundation's WMI provider.

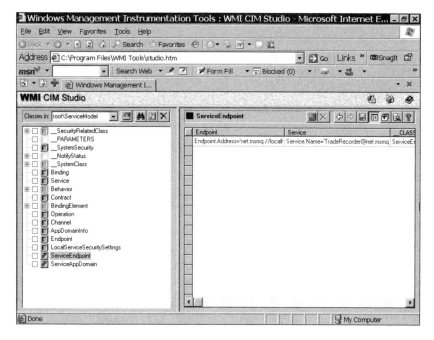

FIGURE 12.80   Viewing data retrieved via WMI.

15. Select the `AppDomainInfo` class in the pane on the right. As illustrated in Figure 12.81, one can modify properties of that class, such as the `LogMessagesAtServiceLevel` property, which configures message logging for a service. This facility allows one to configure properties of services while they are executing. Any modifications made in this way are made to the running instances only and are not persisted in any configuration file. To persist configuration elements in configuration files, use the Configuration Editor.

16. Choose File, Close to close the WMI CIM Studio.

17. In Visual Studio 2005, stop debugging the trading service solution.

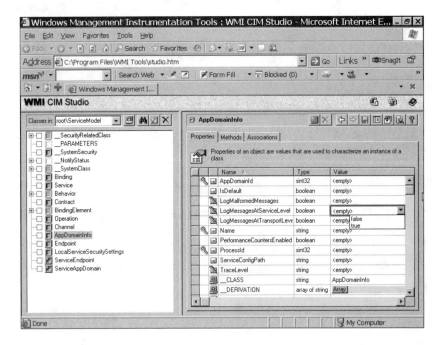

FIGURE 12.81   Configuring running services.

Adding Administration Facilities

Evidently, the Windows Communication Foundation provides a rich set of tools for managing Windows Communication Foundation applications. It also allows software developers to add their own tools for systems, and allows business administrators to monitor characteristics unique to a system.

For example, in the trading service solution, a natural quantity for business administrators to want to monitor is the volume of trades. Among various ways in which that quantity could be exposed for examination, adding a performance counter for trade volume to the trade recording service would allow it to be monitored using the Performance Console that is built into Windows operating systems.

To add this performance counter, or any other management facility, to a Windows Communication Foundation application, a step that is often required is that of accessing a running instance of the application via WMI. To see how to do this to add the trade volume performance counter, follow these instructions:

1. In Visual Studio 2005, open the `Program.cs` file of the TradeRecordingServiceHost project in the trading service solution. After initializing the host of the trade recording service, the code in that file calls a custom `IntializeCounters()` method of the trading service's service type:

```csharp
public static void Main(string[] args)
{
    if (!(MessageQueue.Exists(queueName)))
    {
        MessageQueue.Create(queueName, true);
    }

    TradeRecorder tradeRecorder = new TradeRecorder();
    using (ServiceHost host = new ServiceHost(tradeRecorder))
    {
        host.Open();
        tradeRecorder.InitializeCounters(host.Description.Endpoints);
        Console.WriteLine("The trade recording service is available.");
        Console.ReadKey();
    }
}
```

2. Examine that method, which is in the `TradeRecorder.cs` module of the TradeRecordingService project. It is reproduced in Listing 12.1.

LISTING 12.1   `InitializeCounters()` Method

```csharp
public void InitializeCounters(ServiceEndpointCollection endpoints)
{
    List<string> names = new List<string>();
    foreach (ServiceEndpoint endpoint in endpoints)
    {
        names.Add(
            string.Format("{0}@{1}",
                this.GetType().Name, endpoint.Address.ToString()));
    }

    while (true)
    {
        try
        {
            foreach (string name in names)
            {
                string condition = string.Format(
                    "SELECT * FROM Service WHERE Name=\"{0}\"", name);
                SelectQuery query = new SelectQuery(condition);
                ManagementScope managementScope =
                    new ManagementScope(
                        @"\\.\root\ServiceModel",
                        new ConnectionOptions());
                ManagementObjectSearcher searcher =
```

LISTING 12.1   Continued

```
                    new ManagementObjectSearcher(managementScope, query);
            ManagementObjectCollection instances = searcher.Get();
            foreach (ManagementBaseObject instance in instances)
            {
                PropertyData data =
                    instance.Properties["CounterInstanceName"];

                this.volumeCounter = new PerformanceCounter(
                    TradeRecorder.CounterCategoryName,
                    TradeRecorder.VolumeCounterName,
                    data.Value.ToString());
                this.volumeCounter.ReadOnly = false;
                this.volumeCounter.RawValue = 0;

                break;
            }
        }
        break;
    }
    catch(COMException)
    {

    }

}

if(this.volumeCounter != null)
{
    Console.WriteLine("Volume counter initialized.");
}
Console.WriteLine("Counters initialized.");

}
```

The code for the method assembles a list of the names for the service's endpoints:

```
foreach (ServiceEndpoint endpoint in endpoints)
    {
        names.Add(
            string.Format("{0}@{1}",
                this.GetType().Name, endpoint.Address.ToString()));
    }
```

Then it uses those names to retrieve the WMI objects corresponding to the endpoints of the running instance of the service:

```
string condition = string.Format(
                "SELECT * FROM Service WHERE Name=\"{0}\"", name);
            SelectQuery query = new SelectQuery(condition);
            ManagementScope managementScope =
                new ManagementScope(
                    @"\\.\root\ServiceModel",
                    new ConnectionOptions());
            ManagementObjectSearcher searcher =
                new ManagementObjectSearcher(managementScope, query);
            ManagementObjectCollection instances = searcher.Get();
```

Those objects are then used to add the trade volume counter to that instance of the service:

```
foreach (ManagementBaseObject instance in instances)
{
    PropertyData data =
        instance.Properties["CounterInstanceName"];

    this.volumeCounter = new PerformanceCounter(
        TradeRecorder.CounterCategoryName,
        TradeRecorder.VolumeCounterName,
        data.Value.ToString());
    this.volumeCounter.ReadOnly = false;
    this.volumeCounter.RawValue = 0;

    break;
}
```

3. Look at the `RecordTrades()` method of the trade recording service's service type, which is in the same module:

```
void ITradeRecorder.RecordTrades(Trade[] trades)
{
    Console.WriteLine("Recording trade ...");
    return;
    lock (this)
    {
        while (this.volumeCounter == null)
        {
            Thread.Sleep(100);
        }
```

```
    }


    foreach(Trade trade in trades)
    {
        this.tradeCount+=((trade.Count != null)?trade.Count.Value:0);

        this.volumeCounter.RawValue = this.tradeCount;

        Console.WriteLine(string.Format("Recorded trade for {0}",trade));
    }
}
```

The method updates the trading volume performance counter with the value of each trade the service records. Currently, however, this return statement,

```
Console.WriteLine("Recording trade ...");
return;
```

causes the method to exit prematurely. The reason is that the performance counter would not have been available until the WMI provider was activated for the service according to the instructions given previously. Only after the WMI provider was activated for the service would the InitializeCounters() method have been able to succeed in retrieving the running instance of the service to which to add the performance counter.

4. Because the WMI provider has now been activated for the service, comment out the return statement:

```
Console.WriteLine("Recording trade ...");
//return;
```

5. Choose Debug, Start Debugging from the menus.

6. Wait until there is activity in the console window of the trade recording service host.

7. Choose Run from the Windows Start menu; then enter

```
perfmon
```

and click OK.

8. In the Performance console, right-click on the graph on the right side, and choose Add Counters from the context menu, as shown in Figure 12.73.

9. Select TradeRecording from the Performance Object list, TradeRecording being the name provided by the InitializeCounters() method for a custom performance

counter category for the trade volume counter. As shown in Figure 12.82, the Trade Volume counter is shown as being available for the running instance of the trade recording service.

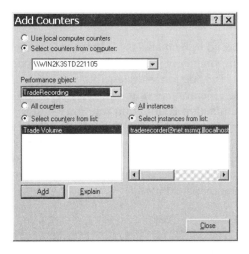

FIGURE 12.82   Adding the Trade Volume performance counter.

10. Click the Add button on the Add Counters dialog, and then the Close button.

11. Enter a keystroke into the console application window of the client application.

12. Observe, in the Performance Console, the movement of the custom trade volume performance counter, as depicted in Figure 12.83.

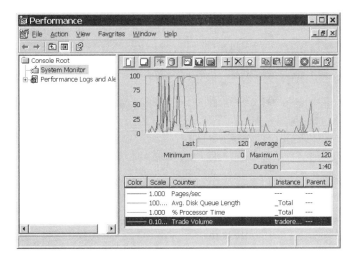

FIGURE 12.83   Monitoring the trade volume performance counter.

13. In Visual Studio 2005, stop debugging the trading service solution.

14. In the Performance Console, choose File, Exit from the menus to close the console.

Summary

Software services are supposed to be manageable, both as software entities by systems administrators, and as components of a business enterprise as budget line items. The Windows Communication Foundation is designed to provide manageable software services. It offers a considerable number of tools for systems administrators to use to manage Windows Communication Foundation solutions, and it allows software developers to add their own. The administration facilities offered by the Windows Communication Foundation all build on familiar management components of the Windows platform, such as WMI and the .NET configuration system, thereby reducing what administrators and developers have to learn about managing Windows Communication Foundation applications.

References

High, Rob, Jr., Stephen Kinder, and Steve Graham. 2005. *IBM's SOA Foundation: An Architectural Introduction and Overview.* http://download.boulder.ibm.com/ ibmdl/pub/software/dw/webservices/ws-soa-whitepaper.pdf. Accessed 21 January 2006.

Newcomer, Eric, and Greg Lomow. 2005. *Understanding SOA with Web Services.* Upper Saddle River, NJ: Addison-Wesley.

Wikipedia. 2006. S.v. "Trace." http://en.wikipedia.org/wiki/Trace. Accessed 26 January 2006.

CHAPTER 13

Representational State Transfer and Plain XML Services

This chapter shows how the Windows Communication Foundation can be used to build and use Representational State Transfer services and also services that communicate with XML files, rather than SOAP messages. In so doing, the chapter also shows how to create a custom encoder binding element for the Windows Communication Foundation, and how to allow custom binding elements to be selected and modified in an application configuration file.

Representational State Transfer

Representational State Transfer, commonly referred to as *REST*, is sometimes misrepresented, as it is by Paul Prescod (2002) as a "new model for [W]eb services construction." Actually, it is a style of building Web applications that was first formally described by Dr. Roy Fielding in his 2000 Ph.D. dissertation at the University of California at Irvine (Fielding 2000). Dr. Fielding is a co-author, along with Sir Timothy Berners-Lee, of many of the core specifications of the World Wide Web, and a co-founder of the Apache Foundation. In his dissertation, he was attempting to describe the architectures of applications commonly in use on the Internet at the time, and REST was one of the architectures he identified. He wrote, "Over the past six years, the REST architectural style has been used to guide the design and development of the architecture for the modern

Web" (Fielding 2000). Dr. Fielding was not proposing a way of building Web services; he was providing a formal description of how the specifications defined by him and Sir Timothy Berners-Lee and others were being used.

A REST server accepts a request from a client via an HTTP POST method. It responds with the URI of a resource, which is retrieved via an HTTP GET method.

XML documents may be used as input to, and output from, REST servers; indeed, they often are. However, those XML documents need not be SOAP XML documents; they typically are not.

There is no standard, machine-readable language for describing REST services, like the Web Services Description Language (WSDL). Security is typically limited to the use of secure HTTP.

Nonetheless, the Windows Communication Foundation, as the universal infrastructure by which Windows software entities can communicate, supports the construction and use of REST services.

Really Simple Syndication

Really Simple Syndication (RSS) aggregation is a common application for REST. The aggregating application retrieves data via an HTTP GET method, which it is able to display and manipulate because the data conforms to a known RSS XML format. Users of RSS aggregators benefit by receiving a feed of information from the World Wide Web, rather than having to expend effort to retrieve information through browsing. RSS aggregation has already dramatically democratized and increased the flow of information and opinion to private individuals, and it is poised for application to the burgeoning problem of knowledge management within organizations.

The 2.0 version of the RSS specification included support for multimedia enclosures, which has led to the phenomenon of podcasting. In podcasting, information retrieved via an aggregator is transferred to a portable media device, such as an Apple iPod, for offline consumption while one is on the go.

A growing concern for parents is awareness of, and control over, the content that their children are able to access via podcasts, which may well be adult-oriented (Ojeda-Zapata 2005). Wanting to facilitate that awareness and control by no means implies an endorsement of censorship. Only once parents are reassured of their control over their children's access to a medium can that medium be safely used by adults for whatever purposes they wish.

Objective

This chapter shows the Windows Communication Foundation being used to build a REST service that exposes an RSS information feed. It also shows the Windows Communication Foundation being used to build an RSS aggregator that allows parents to control the type of content that children can access from an RSS feed.

Designing the Solution

In the Windows Communication Foundation, everything about how software entities communicate is controlled through the specification of addresses, bindings, and contracts. Addresses identify where software entities are located on the network. Bindings specify protocols by which messages may be transmitted between a service and its clients. Contracts describe the messages that the service can understand, and how the service will respond to the messages it receives.

In building a REST service using the Windows Communication Foundation, a unique address will be provided for the service, as well as a binding that specifies the use of the HTTP protocol to communicate with the service, because all REST services use HTTP to exchange messages. Also, because the service will be used to publish an RSS feed, the binding will have to be configured for the exchange of XML messages that are not in the SOAP format. Henceforth, messages that are not in the SOAP format will be referred to as *plain old XML*, or *POX*, messages. The contract for the service should be one by which an empty request from an RSS aggregator receives the POX message of the RSS feed in response.

Note that Wikipedia defines the term *POX* in such a way that one might conceivably not count an RSS feed as being an instance of POX (Wikipedia 2005a). However, there is some evidence that the original use of the term was to refer to XML messages in any format other than the SOAP format (Box 2005).

To allow the RSS aggregator to control what a child can see of the contents of the RSS feed, the RSS 2.0 specification's support for adding new tags, or *extensions*, to the basic RSS format will be leveraged (Winer 2005). One extension tag that will be added is one for specifying a rating for the content of the field: whether it is for all ages, or only for adults. Of course, parents cannot rely on the authors of RSS feeds to accurately rate their content independently. So the content ratings will be digitally signed, along with links to content, with the private key of the certificate of some organization that parents might trust to rate the content of RSS feeds. The RSS aggregator will use the public key of that organization's certificate to verify the certificate of the digitally signed content rating of the feed, and thereby know that it can trust the rating and the links to content, and behave accordingly to show or not show the content to a child. With these simple extensions to RSS, one could establish a system not entirely unlike the Comics Code Authority that reassured parents of the content of mainstream American comic books for almost half a century from the mid-1950s to 2001 (Wikipedia 2005b).

Constructing the REST RSS Server

Complete the steps in the following sections to construct a REST RSS server.

Create the RSS Feeds

The first step is to create the RSS feeds that the server will publish:

1. Copy the code associated with this chapter that you downloaded from www. samspublishing.com to the folder C:\WCFHandsOn. The code is all in a folder called

RepresentationalStateTransfer, and it contains a single Visual Studio solution with the same name. After the code has been unzipped, there should be a folder that looks like the one shown in Figure 13.1.

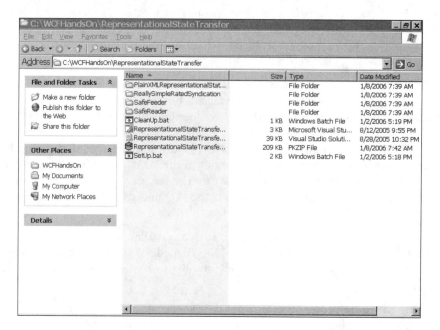

FIGURE 13.1   Representational State Transfer solution folder.

2. Open the solution C:\WCFHandsOn\RepresentationalStateTransfer\ RepresentationalStateTransfer.sln. The solution includes the projects SafeFeeder, which is for building the REST RSS service that delivers RSS feeds with digitally signed content ratings, and SafeReader, which is for building the child's RSS aggregator that can process those ratings and behave in accordance with them.

3. Examine the file Feed.xml in the SafeFeeder project:

```xml
<?xml version="1.0"?>
<rss version="2.0" xmlns:rating="http://blog.code.com/ContentRating">
    <channel>
        <title>"Harry Potter" author's homepage.</title>
        <link>http://www.jkrowling.com/textonly/en/</link>
        <description>See the homepage of the author
            of the Harry Potter! books.</description>
        <language>en-us</language>
        <rating:contentRating>AllAges</rating:contentRating>
    </channel>
</rss>
```

The only formal stipulation on the addition of extensions to RSS made by the RSS 2.0 specification is that the extension tags are included in their own namespace (Winer 2005). Thus, the declaration of a namespace for the content rating extensions, `http://blog.code.com/ContentRating`, appears in the RSS file, along with the content rating element itself. The feed defined by this RSS file is rated `AllAges`, signifying that the RSS feed is fine for children to see.

4. Now look at the file `NaughtyFeed.xml`, in the SafeFeeder project:

```xml
<?xml version="1.0"?>
<rss version="2.0" xmlns:rating="http://blog.code.com/ContentRating">
    <channel>
        <title>"Jessica Rabbit" from "Who Framed Roger Rabbit?"</title>
        <link>http://www.retrocrush.com/babes/babes2004/jessicarabbit/01.jpg
        </link>
        <description>A picture of Jessica Rabbit.</description>
        <language>en-us</language>
        <rating:contentRating>AdultsOnly</rating:contentRating>
    </channel>
</rss>
```

This RSS file contains a link to a picture of Jessica Rabbit, a corrupting influence if there ever was one. So it is rated `AdultsOnly`, to indicate that it is not suitable for viewing by children.

Define the Contract for the REST RSS Service

The REST RSS service will have a contract, like any other Windows Communication Foundation service:

1. Add a class module called `IReallySimpleSyndication.cs` to the SafeFeeder project.

2. Modify the contents of the file so that it looks like this:

```csharp
using System;
using System.ServiceModel;

namespace RepresentationalStateTransfer
{
    [ServiceContract]
    public interface IReallySimpleSyndication
    {
        [OperationContract(Action="*")]
        Message Get(Message input);
    }
}
```

IReallySimpleSyndication is a common .NET interface. The addition of the Windows Communication Foundation's ServiceContract attribute identifies it as a Windows Communication Foundation contract.

In Chapter 10, "Publish/Subscribe Systems," it was explained that specifying Action="*" as the parameter to the OperationContract attribute signifies that the operation with that attribute is the unmatched message handler, which means that operation will be used to process all messages that are not matched with another operation. A REST service like the RSS service being constructed here must provide an unmatched message handler. The SOAP specifications include HTTP bindings that provide standard ways of expressing, within the header of an HTTP POST method, which operation on the server is the intended destination of the message, although different versions of the SOAP specification provide different ways of incorporating that information. REST does not provide any such standard mechanism for mapping incoming messages to service operations, so all the messages directed at the REST service need to be processed by the same handler, which will be the unmatched message handler.

The Windows Communication Foundation's Message class represents messages as messages, rather than as messages of a particular type. WSDL provides a standard way, which leverages the XML Schema language, of specifying the types of messages processed by a given operation. REST has no such mechanism, so in constructing REST services, one must resort to using the Message class to represent the messages. Thus, the definition of the Get() operation that will process the messages of the REST service represents the inputs and outputs of the method simply as instances of the Message class.

Implement the Contract for the REST RSS Service

Having defined the contract, the next step is to implement it:

1. Add a class module called ReallySimpleSyndicationServer.cs to the SafeFeeder project. Modify the file so that it looks like Listing 13.1. The code in Listing 13.1 is provided in the file C:\WCFHandsOn\RepresentationalStateTransfer\SafeFeeder\ ReallySimpleSyndication.txt.

LISTING 13.1   The REST RSS Service Type

```
using System.IO;
using System.ServiceModel;
using System.Text;
using System.Xml;

namespace RepresentationalStateTransfer
{
    public class ReallySimpleSyndicationServer : IReallySimpleSyndication
    {
        private string feedFilePath = null;
```

LISTING 13.1   Continued

```
public ReallySimpleSyndicationServer(string feedFilePath)
{
    this.feedFilePath = feedFilePath;
}

private ReallySimpleSyndicationServer()
{
}

Message IReallySimpleSyndication.Get(Message input)
{
    Message message = null;
    if (File.Exists(this.feedFilePath))
    {
        XmlDocument document = new XmlDocument();
        document.Load(this.feedFilePath);

        ReallySimpleRatedSyndication.AddContentRating(document);

        message = Message.CreateMessage(
            "*",
            new XmlNodeReader(document.DocumentElement));

    }
    else
    {
        message = Message.CreateMessage(Constants.DefaultAction);
    }

    return message;
}
}
}
```

In the argot of the Windows Communication Foundation, a class that implements an interface with the Windows Communication Foundation's ServiceContract attribute is a *service type*. The interface IReallySimpleSyndication, which was added in the preceding step, has that attribute. So the class that we have added now, ReallySimpleSyndicationServer, to implement that interface is a service type, the service type for the REST RSS service.

In its implementation of the IReallySimpleSyndication interface's lone Get() method, ReallySimpleSyndicationServer loads one of the two RSS files that we looked at earlier, and calls on the static AddSignedContentRating() method of the

ReallySimpleSyndication class to sign the content rating and the link in the RSS file. Then it creates a message with the RSS file incorporating the signed content rating and link as the body, and returns that message to the caller.

2. Examine the AddSignedContentRating() method of the ReallySimpleRatedSyndication class, which is in the ReallySimpleRatedSyndication.cs module of the ReallySimpleRatedSyndication project, and reproduced in Listing 13.2.

LISTING 13.2   Method for Adding a Content Rating

```csharp
using System;
using System.Collections.Generic;
using System.IO;
using System.Security.Cryptography;
using System.Security.Cryptography.Xml;
using System.Security.Cryptography.X509Certificates;
using System.Text;
using System.Xml;

namespace RepresentationalStateTransfer
{
    public enum ContentRating
    {
        Unknown = -1,
        AllAges = 0,
        AdultsOnly = 1
    }

    public class ReallySimpleRatedSyndication
    {
        private const string personalCertificateStoreLocation
            = @"My";
        private const string trustedPeopleCertificateStoreLocation
            = @"TrustedPeople";
        private const string contentRatingCertificateSubjectName
            = @"Woodgrove";
        private const string contentRatingExtensionTagName
            = @"contentRating";
        private const string linkTagName
            = @"link";
        private const string signedContentRatingExtensionTagName
            = @"signedContentRating";
        private const string contentRatingExtensionNamespace
            = @"http://blog.code.com/ContentRating";
```

LISTING 13.2   Continued

```
private const string signatureValueTagName
    = "SignatureValue";
private const string contentRatingIdentifier
    = "ContentRatingIdentifier";
private const string linkIdentifier
    = "LinkIdentifier";
private const string universalResourceIdentifierPrefix
    = @"#";
private const string signatureTagName
    = @"Signature";
private const string xmlDigitalSignatureNamespace
    = @"http://www.w3.org/2000/09/xmldsig#";

private static XmlElement CreateWrappedSignature(
    AsymmetricAlgorithm signingKey,
    XmlElement contentToSign,
    string identifier)
{
    SignedXml signedXML = new SignedXml(contentToSign);
    signedXML.SigningKey = signingKey;
    DataObject dataObject = new DataObject(
        identifier,
        null,
        null,
        contentToSign);
    signedXML.AddObject(dataObject);
    Reference reference = new Reference();
    reference.Uri = string.Concat(
        ReallySimpleRatedSyndication.universalResourceIdentifierPrefix,
        identifier);
    signedXML.AddReference(reference);
    signedXML.ComputeSignature();
    return signedXML.GetXml();
}

private static bool VerifySignature(
    X509Certificate2 certificate,
    XmlElement signatureElement)
{
    SignedXml signedXML = new SignedXml(signatureElement);
    signedXML.LoadXml(signatureElement);

    bool checks = signedXML.CheckSignature(certificate, true);
```

LISTING 13.2   Continued

```
        return checks;
    }


    public static void AddSignedContentRating(XmlDocument document)
    {
        X509Store store = new X509Store(
            ReallySimpleRatedSyndication.personalCertificateStoreLocation,
            StoreLocation.LocalMachine);
        store.Open(OpenFlags.ReadOnly);
        X509CertificateCollection certificateCollection =
            store.Certificates.Find(
                X509FindType.FindBySubjectName,
ReallySimpleRatedSyndication.contentRatingCertificateSubjectName,
                false);
        X509Certificate2 certificate =
            (X509Certificate2)certificateCollection[0];

        XmlElement ratingElement =
            (XmlElement)document.GetElementsByTagName(
                ReallySimpleRatedSyndication.contentRatingExtensionTagName,
ReallySimpleRatedSyndication.contentRatingExtensionNamespace).Item(0);
        XmlElement signedElement =
            ReallySimpleRatedSyndication.CreateWrappedSignature(
                certificate.PrivateKey,
                ratingElement,
                ReallySimpleRatedSyndication.contentRatingIdentifier);
        ratingElement.InnerXml = signedElement.OuterXml;

        XmlElement linkElement =
            (XmlElement)document.GetElementsByTagName(
                ReallySimpleRatedSyndication.linkTagName).Item(0);
        signedElement = ReallySimpleRatedSyndication.CreateWrappedSignature(
            certificate.PrivateKey,
            linkElement,
            ReallySimpleRatedSyndication.linkIdentifier);
        linkElement.InnerXml = signedElement.OuterXml;

    }


    public static bool ValidateSignedContentRating(
        XmlDocument document,
        out ContentRating rating,
        out string link)
```

LISTING 13.2   Continued

```
        {
            rating = ContentRating.Unknown;
            link = string.Empty;

            X509Store store = new X509Store(
ReallySimpleRatedSyndication.trustedPeopleCertificateStoreLocation,
                StoreLocation.CurrentUser);
            store.Open(OpenFlags.ReadOnly);
            X509CertificateCollection certificateCollection =
                store.Certificates.Find(
                    X509FindType.FindBySubjectName,
ReallySimpleRatedSyndication.contentRatingCertificateSubjectName,
                    true);
            X509Certificate2 certificate =
                (X509Certificate2)certificateCollection[0];

            XmlNodeList nodes =
                document.GetElementsByTagName(
                    ReallySimpleRatedSyndication.signatureTagName,
                    ReallySimpleRatedSyndication.xmlDigitalSignatureNamespace);
            foreach(XmlNode signedNode in nodes)
            {
                if(!(ReallySimpleRatedSyndication.VerifySignature(
                    certificate,(XmlElement)signedNode)))
                {
                    return false;
                }
            }

            nodes = document.GetElementsByTagName("Object");
            foreach (XmlNode node in nodes)
            {
                foreach (XmlAttribute attribute in node.Attributes)
                {
                    switch (attribute.Value)
                    {
                        case "ContentRatingIdentifier":
                            rating =
                                (ContentRating)Enum.Parse(
                                    typeof(ContentRating),
                                    ((XmlElement)node).InnerText);
                            break;
                        case "LinkIdentifier":
                            link = ((XmlElement)node).InnerText;
```

LISTING 13.2 Continued

```
                            break;
                    }


                }
            }

        return true;

    }

}
}
```

The method retrieves an X.509 certificate from the My store location within the local machine store, and uses the private key of that certificate to sign the content rating. The signed content rating is added to the RSS feed document as the contents of the contentRating element.

3. Install the Woodgrove certificate used by the ReallySimpleRatedSyndication class to sign the content ratings of the RSS feeds by executing the batch file C:\WCFHandsOn\ RepresentationalStateTransfer\SetUp.bat. It is assumed that the certificate belongs to an organization that parents will trust to certify the content ratings of RSS feeds. The Setup.bat batch file assumes that the tools included with the version of the Microsoft Windows SDK for use with WinFX are installed in the folder C:\Program Files\Microsoft SDKs\Windows\v1.0\Bin. If they are not installed there, modify the batch file accordingly. If their location is unknown, search the hard disks for the tool CertKeyFileTool.exe; the other tools should be in the same location. A second batch file, C:\WCFHandsOn\RepresentationalStateTransfer\ CleanUp.bat, is provided for removing the certificate after the exercise has been completed.

Host the REST RSS Service in an Application

A host is provided for the REST RSS service type in these next few steps:

1. Open the file PlainXMLRepresentationalStateTransferServiceHost.cs, in the SafeFeeder project, and modify the Main() method of the PlainXMLRepresentationalStateTransferServiceHost class so that it reads as shown here:

```
static void Main(string[] arguments)
{
    ReallySimpleSyndicationServer serviceType
        = new ReallySimpleSyndicationServer(arguments[0]);
    ServiceHost service = new ServiceHost(
        serviceType, new Uri[] {new Uri(@"http://localhost:8888/") });
```

```
service.Description.Behaviors.Remove(
    typeof(ServiceMetadataBehavior));

service.Open();

Console.WriteLine(
    @"The service is available.  Press any key to terminate it.");
Console.ReadLine();
}
```

The additional code uses the Windows Communication Foundation's `ServiceHost` class to host the `ReallySimpleSyndicationServer` service type within the SafeFeeder console application.

The base address of the service is given as http://localhost:8888/. Shortly, a specific address will be added, relative to that base address, for messages destined to be processed by the operations of the `IReallySimpleSyndication` contract of the REST RSS service.

2. Notice the statement

```
service.Description.Behaviors.Remove(
    typeof(ServiceMetadataBehavior));
```

By default, the Windows Communication Foundation responds to an HTTP GET method directed at the address of a service with the WSDL for the service. That behavior is facilitated by the Windows Communication Foundation's `ServiceMetadataBehavior` class. Now, not only is there no way to describe a REST service like the REST RSS service with WSDL, but HTTP GET methods directed at the address of our service should also not be intercepted by the `ServiceMetadataBehavior` class. Those commands should pass through to the service. So the role of the statement

```
service.Description.Behaviors.Remove(
    typeof(ServiceMetadataBehavior));
```

is to disable the `ServiceMetadataBehavior` class for the REST RSS service.

Is it unfortunate that one should have to explicitly disable the `ServiceMetadataBehavior` class in order to build a REST service with the Windows Communication Foundation? Well, having to do so aptly illustrates the nature of the choice one makes in adopting REST to build services. Rich tools for building SOAP services have been freely available for several years. Those tools not only support SOAP and its extensions, but also automate the process of providing perfectly accurate machine-readable descriptions of services in WSDL, and automate the process of retrieving those descriptions and generating clients from them. Given all of that, the choice of eschewing SOAP services in favor of REST is a deliberate one to forego a wealth of features. So having to deliberately turn off the feature by which the Windows Communication Foundation automatically provides WSDL as metadata to describe services, in order to build a REST service, seems most appropriate. Think of it as a final warning.

Configure the Address and the Binding of the Service

The next steps are to specify an address and a binding for the REST RSS service:

1. Add an application configuration file called App.Config to the SafeFeeder project, and modify its contents as shown in Listing 13.3.

LISTING 13.3   REST RSS Service Configuration

```xml
<?xml version="1.0" encoding="utf-8" ?>
<configuration>
    <system.serviceModel>
        <services>
            <service type=
"RepresentationalStateTransfer.ReallySimpleSyndicationServer,SafeFeeder">
                <endpoint
                    address="Service"
                    binding="customBinding"
                    bindingConfiguration=
                        "PlainXMLRepresentationalStateTransferBinding"
                    contract=
"RepresentationalStateTransfer.IReallySimpleSyndication, SafeFeeder"/>
            </service>
        </services>
        <bindings>
            <customBinding>
                <binding name="PlainXMLRepresentationalStateTransferBinding">
                    <plainXMLEncoder/>
                    <httpTransport mapAddressingHeadersToHttpHeaders="true"/>
                </binding>
            </customBinding>
        </bindings>
        <extensions>
            <bindingElementExtensions>
                <add name="plainXMLEncoder"
            type=
"System.ServiceModel.PlainXMLEncoderBindingElementExtensionSection,
                PlainXMLRepresentationalStateTransfer"/>
            </bindingElementExtensions>
        </extensions>
    </system.serviceModel>
</configuration>
```

Here the specific address, Service, is provided for messages meant to be processed by the operations of the IReallySimpleSyndication contract. That address is relative to the base address of http://localhost:8888/ that was specified for the service earlier, in providing the host. So the absolute address for messages to be processed by the operation of the IReallySimpleSyndication contract is http://localhost:8888/Service.

As it was just explained, because all REST services use HTTP to exchange messages, in configuring the binding for the REST RSS service, it will be necessary to specify the use of the HTTP protocol to communicate. Also, because the service will be used to publish an RSS feed, it will be necessary to configure the binding for the exchange of plain XML messages. The Windows Communication Foundation does not provide a built-in binding with those characteristics, but it is very easy to create one's own bindings, which are called custom bindings.

The name that is assigned, in the configuration of the REST service, to the custom binding is PlainXMLRepresentationalStateTransferBinding. Recall that bindings are simply a composition of one or more binding elements. Two binding elements are used to compose the PlainXMLRepresentationalStateTransferBinding: one that provides for the exchange of plain XML messages, and another that specifies the use of the HTTP protocol.

Use of the HTTP protocol is specified by including HttpTransportBindingElement within the custom binding. The value of its MapAddressingHeadersToHttpHeaders property must be set to true for REST services. Recall that whereas the SOAP specifications include HTTP bindings that provide standard ways of expressing which operation on the server is the intended destination of the message, REST does not provide any such standard mechanism. Setting MapAddressingHeadersToHttpHeaders to true causes the value of the To property of the Message instance representing an HTTP request to the REST service from a client to be set to the URI of the request. That will, in turn, result in that Message instance being passed to the unmatched message handler of the contract associated with the URI of the request. In the particular case of the REST RSS service, the IReallySimpleSyndication contract has been associated with the address http://localhost:8888/Service, and its unmatched message handler is its Get() method; so, by default, all Message instances with http://localhost:8888/Service as the value of their To property will be sent to the implementation of that method. Because the value of the MapAddressingHeadersToHttpHeaders property of the HttpTransportBindingElement is set to true, when HTTP requests are directed to http://localhost:8888/Service, the Windows Communication Foundation will create instances of the Message class to represent those requests, and set their To properties to http://localhost:8888/Service. Hence, those messages will then be dispatched to the Get() method of ReallySimpleSyndicationServer that implements the IReallySimpleSyndication contract.

The binding element that provides for the exchange of plain XML messages by the REST RSS service is the PlainXMLEncoderBindingElement. As its name implies, it is a binding element that specifies that messages exchanged with the service are to be encoded as plain XML.

The PlainXMLEncoderBindingElement is not among the message encoder binding elements that are built into the Windows Communication Foundation. So a custom one has been constructed using the tools that the Windows Communication Foundation provides for that purpose. Because it is not a built-in binding element, one needs to tell the Windows Communication Foundation where to find it, and that is the purpose of this configuration information that is included in the configuration file in Listing 13.3:

```
<extensions>
    <bindingElementExtensions>
        <add name="plainXMLEncoder"
    type=
"System.ServiceModel.PlainXMLEncoderBindingElementExtensionSection,
            PlainXMLRepresentationalStateTransfer"/>
    </bindingElementExtensions>
</extensions>
```

It tells the Windows Communication Foundation to use the PlainXMLEncoderBindingElementExtensionSection in the PlainXMLRepresentationalStateTransfer assembly to configure and provide the binding element referred to by the plainXMLEncoder element of the binding provided for the service:

```
<plainXMLEncoder/>
```

2. Examine the PlainXMLEncoderBindingElementExtensionSection class that is in the PlainXMLEncoderBindingElementExtensionSection.cs class module in the PlainXMLRepresentationalStateTransfer project, and also reproduced in Listing 13.4.

LISTING 13.4   Plain XML Encoder Binding Element Section

```
using System;
using System.Collections.Generic;
using System.ServiceModel.Configuration;
using System.Text;

namespace System.ServiceModel
{
    public class PlainXMLEncoderBindingElementExtensionSection:
        BindingElementExtensionSection
    {
        private const string sectionName = @"plainXMLEncoding";

        public override Type BindingElementType
```

LISTING 13.4   Continued

```
        {
            get
            {
                return typeof(PlainXMLEncoderBindingElement);
            }
        }

        protected override BindingElement CreateBindingElement()
        {
            return new PlainXMLEncoderBindingElement();
        }

        public override string ConfiguredSectionName
        {
            get
            {
                return PlainXMLEncoderBindingElementExtensionSection.sectionName;
            }
        }
    }
}
```

The `PlainXMLEncoderBindingElementExtensionClass` derives from the abstract
`BindingElementExtensionSection` class:

```
using System;
using System.ServiceModel;

namespace System.ServiceModel.Configuration
{
    public abstract class BindingElementExtensionSection :
        ServiceModelExtensionSection
    {
        protected BindingElementExtensionSection();

        public abstract Type BindingElementType { get; }

        public virtual void ApplyConfiguration(BindingElement bindingElement);
        protected internal abstract BindingElement CreateBindingElement();
        protected internal virtual void InitializeFrom(
            BindingElement bindingElement);
    }
}
```

That class defines the abstract method `CreateBindingElement()`. Therefore, the Windows Communication Foundation knows that the `PlainXMLEncoderBindingElementExtensionClass` has a `CreateBindingElement()` method that the Windows Communication Foundation can invoke to retrieve the custom binding element referred to by

```
<plainXMLEncoder/>
```

in the configuration of the binding for the service.

3. Study the `PlainXMLEncoderBindingElement` class that is in the `PlainXMLEncoderBindingElement.cs` class module in the PlainXMLRepresentationalStateTransfer project, and also shown in Listing 13.5.

LISTING 13.5   Plain XML Encoder Binding Element

```
public class PlainXMLEncoderBindingElement :
    BindingElement,
    IMessageEncodingBindingElement
{
    public override IChannelFactory BuildChannelFactory(
        ChannelBuildContext context)
    {
        if (context == null)
            throw new ArgumentNullException("context");

        context.UnhandledBindingElements.Add(this);
        return context.BuildInnerChannelFactory();     }

    public override IChannelListener<TChannel> BuildChannelListener<TChannel>(
        ChannelBuildContext context)
    {
        if (context == null)
            throw new ArgumentNullException("context");

        context.UnhandledBindingElements.Add(this);
        return context.BuildInnerChannelListener<TChannel>();
    }

    public override bool CanBuildChannelListener<TChannel>(
        ChannelBuildContext context)
    {
        if (context == null)
            throw new ArgumentNullException("context");

        context.UnhandledBindingElements.Add(this);
        return context.CanBuildInnerChannelListener<TChannel>();
    }
```

LISTING 13.5 Continued

```
public override BindingElement Clone()
{
    return new PlainXMLEncoderBindingElement();
}

public override ChannelProtectionRequirements GetProtectionRequirements()
{
    throw new Exception("The method or operation is not implemented.");
}

#region IMessageEncodingBindingElement Members

AddressingVersion IMessageEncodingBindingElement.AddressingVersion
{
    get
    {
        throw new Exception("The method or operation is not implemented.");
    }
}

MessageEncoderFactory
    IMessageEncodingBindingElement.CreateMessageEncoderFactory()
{
    return new PlainXMLMessageEncoderFactory();
}

#endregion
}
```

This class is the custom binding element for supporting plain XML messages. As any binding element does, it derives from the abstract base class for binding elements, which is BindingElement:

```
public abstract class BindingElement
{
    protected BindingElement();
    protected BindingElement(BindingElement other);

    public virtual IChannelFactory BuildChannelFactory(
        ChannelBuildContext context);
    public virtual IChannelFactory<TChannel> BuildChannelFactory<TChannel>(
        ChannelBuildContext context);
    public virtual bool CanBuildChannelFactory<TChannel>(
        ChannelBuildContext context);
```

```
    public abstract BindingElement Clone();
    public virtual T GetCapabilities<T>(
        IList<BindingElement> lowerBindingElements) where T : class;
    public abstract ChannelProtectionRequirements GetProtectionRequirements();
    public virtual ChannelProtectionRequirements GetProtectionRequirements(
        CustomBinding context);
}
```

As a non-abstract derivative of BindingElement, PlainXMLEncoderBindingElement must implement the abstract methods of BindingElement. The implementations that it provides do no more than what is necessary to include the capability of processing plain XML documents within the sequence of binding elements that are applied in processing incoming or outgoing messages.

As any binding element that is for message encoding does, PlainXMLEncoderBindingElement implements the interface IMessageEncodingBindingElement:

```
public interface IMessageEncodingBindingElement
{
    AddressingVersion AddressingVersion { get; }

    MessageEncoderFactory CreateMessageEncoderFactory();
}
```

The implementation of the CreateMessageEncoderFactory() method of that interface returns an instance of a MessageEncoderFactory derivative called PlainXMLMessageEncoderFactory, which the Windows Communication Foundation uses to construct plain XML message encoders to process incoming and outgoing messages.

4. Look at the PlainXMLMessageEncoderFactory class in the PlainXMLBindingElement.cs class module of the PlainXMLRepresentationalStateTransfer project:

```
public class PlainXMLMessageEncoderFactory : MessageEncoderFactory
{

    public override MessageEncoder Encoder
    {
        get
        {
            return new PlainXMLEncoder();
        }
    }
```

```
    public override MessageVersion MessageVersion
    {
        get
        {
            return MessageVersion.Soap11Addressing1;
        }
    }
}
```

The `PlainXMLMessageEncoderFactory` class overrides the base
`MessageEncoderFactory` class' `MessageEncoder` property to allow the Windows
Communication Foundation to retrieve instances of PlainXMLEncoder, a custom
encoder for encoding messages in plain XML.

An encoder in the Windows Communication Foundation has two duties. One is to
accept a stream or an array of bytes that have been received, and to yield from those
an instance of the `Message` class, which will be the form in which the data that
has been received will be processed internally by the Windows Communication
Foundation. The other duty of an encoder is to accept instances of the `Message` class
representing output, and to transform those into an array or a stream of bytes.

5. Examine the `ReadMessage()` of the `PlainXMLEncoder` class in the
   `PlainXMLBindingElement.cs` file of the PlainXMLRepresentationalStateTransfer
   project. It is shown in Listing 13.6. It implements the abstract `ReadMessage()`
   method of the PlainXMLEncoder's abstract base `MessageEncoder` class.

LISTING 13.6 The Plain XML Encoder's ReadMessage() Method

```
public override Message ReadMessage(
    ArraySegment<byte> buffer,
    BufferManager bufferManager)
{
    Message message = null;

    if (buffer.Count > 0)
    {
        MemoryStream stream = new MemoryStream(buffer.Array);
        XmlTextReader reader = new XmlTextReader(stream);
        message = new PlainXMLMessage(
            MessageVersion.Soap11Addressing1,
            "*",
            reader);
        return message;
    }
```

LISTING 13.6   Continued

```
message = new PlainXMLMessage(
    MessageVersion.Soap11Addressing1,
    "*");

return message;
}
```

The ReadMessage() method is invoked to transform received data into an instance
of the Message class. The method takes the array of bytes that it receives, which
it is expecting to be plain XML, and creates from those an instance of the
PlainXMLMessage class, which is a derivative of the Message class, reproduced in
Listing 13.7.

LISTING 13.7   Plain XML Message Type

```
public class PlainXMLMessage : Message
{
    private const string MissingRootError = "Root element is missing.";

    private MessageHeaders headers;
    private MessageProperties properties;
    private XmlReader reader;

    public PlainXMLMessage(MessageVersion version, string action, XmlReader body)
        : base()
    {
        headers = new MessageHeaders(version);
        properties = new MessageProperties();
        properties.Add(
            Constants.HttpRequestMessageProperty,
            new HttpRequestMessageProperty());
        reader = body;
    }

    public PlainXMLMessage(MessageVersion version, string action)
        : base()
    {
        headers = new MessageHeaders(version);
        properties = new MessageProperties();
    }

    public override MessageHeaders Headers
    {
        get
```

LISTING 13.7   Continued

```
        {
            return headers;
        }
    }


    protected override void OnWriteBodyContents(XmlDictionaryWriter writer)
    {
        if (reader != null)
        {
            while (!reader.EOF)
            {
                try
                {
                    writer.WriteNode(reader, true);
                }
                catch (XmlException exception)
                {
                    if (exception.Message.Contains(
                        PlainXMLMessage.MissingRootError))
                    {
                        return;
                    }
                    else { throw exception; }
                }
            }

        }
    }


    public override MessageProperties Properties
    {
        get
        {
            return properties;
        }
    }


    public override MessageVersion Version
    {
        get
        {
            return Headers.MessageVersion;
        }
    }
}
```

From the constructor of that class,

```
public PlainXMLMessage(MessageVersion version, string action, XmlReader body)
        : base()
{
    headers = new MessageHeaders(version);
    properties = new MessageProperties();
    properties.Add(
        Constants.HttpRequestMessageProperty,
        new HttpRequestMessageProperty());
    reader = body;
}
```

it is apparent that all the data read from the array of incoming bytes is assigned to the field that represents the body of the message. That is appropriate, because, as a plain XML message rather than a SOAP message, none of the data in the message should constitute a SOAP header.

6. Examine the `WriteMessage()` methods of the `PlainXMLEncoder` class in the `PlainXMLBindingElement.cs` file of the PlainXMLRepresentationalStateTransfer project. It is reproduced in Listing 13.8. It implements the abstract `WriteMessage()` method of the PlainXMLEncoder's abstract base `MessageEncoder` class.

LISTING 13.8   The Plain XML Encoder's WriteMessage() Method

```
public override ArraySegment<byte> WriteMessage(
    Message message,
    int maxMessageSize,
    BufferManager bufferManager,
    int messageOffset)
{
    byte[] buffer = bufferManager.TakeBuffer(maxMessageSize);
    MemoryStream stream = new MemoryStream(buffer);
    XmlTextWriter innerWriter = new XmlTextWriter(stream, Encoding.UTF8);
    XmlDictionaryWriter outerWriter = XmlDictionaryWriter.CreateDictionaryWriter(
        innerWriter,
        false);
    message.WriteBodyContents(outerWriter);
    outerWriter.Flush();
    int position = (int)stream.Position;
    outerWriter.Close();
    return new ArraySegment<byte>(buffer, 0, position);
}
```

The `WriteMessage()` method of the `PlainXMLEncoder` is invoked to turn outgoing instances of the `Message` class into an array of bytes. To produce an array of bytes containing nothing besides plain XML, the method only serializes the body of the message into the array of bytes. Any headers incorporated in the Message instance are ignored, because, as a plain XML message rather than a SOAP message, the message should not contain any headers.

See a Windows Communication Foundation Plain XML REST Service in Action

To use the REST RSS service, follow these simple steps:

1. Compile the SafeFeeder project.

2. Right-click on the project and choose Debug and then Start New Instance from the context menu. Doing so should serve to start the console application that has been configured to host the REST RSS service.

3. When there is some activity in the console of the SafeFeeder application, open a browser and browse to http://localhost:8888/Service. One of the RSS feeds should appear in the browser, as shown in Figure 13.2, the browser having sent an HTTP GET method request to the service, which responded with the plain XML of one of the RSS feeds.

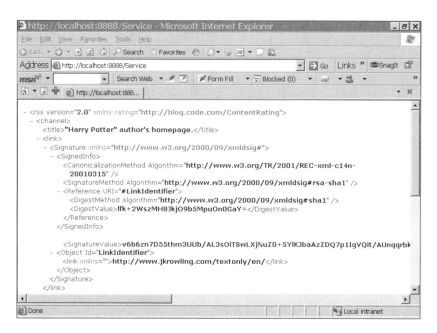

FIGURE 13.2   An RSS feed provided by the SafeFeeder application.

Constructing the RSS Aggregator

Now follow these steps to begin constructing the RSS aggregator client for the REST RSS service:

1. Open the `MainForm.cs` module of the SafeReader project of the `RepresentationalStateTransfer` solution in the Windows Forms Designer. It should appear as shown in Figure 13.3. It has a WebBrowser control, named `browser`, that will be used to display the content referred to by the link field in RSS feeds retrieved from the REST RSS service that we have constructed, provided, of course, that the content rating indicates that the content is suitable to be shown to children.

FIGURE 13.3   The design of the Safe Reader RSS aggregator's main window.

2. Add a copy of the module `IReallySimpleSyndication.cs` in the SafeFeeder project to the SafeReader project.

3. Add an application configuration file called `app.config` to the SafeReader project, and modify it as shown in Listing 13.9.

LISTING 13.9   RSS Aggregator Configuration

```
<?xml version="1.0" encoding="utf-8" ?>
<configuration>
    <system.serviceModel>
        <client>
            <endpoint name="ReallySimpleSyndicationService"
                    address="http://localhost:8888/Service"
                    binding="customBinding"
                    bindingConfiguration
                      ="PlainXMLRepresentationalStateTransferBinding"
                    contract
="RepresentationalStateTransfer.IReallySimpleSyndication,SafeReader"/>
        </client>
```

LISTING 13.9   Continued

```
        <bindings>
            <customBinding>
                <binding name="PlainXMLRepresentationalStateTransferBinding">
                    <plainXMLEncoding/>
                    <httpTransport mapAddressingHeadersToHttpHeaders="true"/>
                </binding>
            </customBinding>
        </bindings>
        <extensions>
            <bindingElementExtensions>
                <add name="plainXMLEncoding"
type="System.ServiceModel.PlainXMLEncoderBindingElementExtensionSection,
                    PlainXMLRepresentationalStateTransfer"/>
            </bindingElementExtensions>
        </extensions>
    </system.serviceModel>
</configuration>
```

This Windows Communication Foundation configuration provides the information that the Windows Communication Foundation requires to enable the SafeReader RSS aggregator to communicate with the SafeFeeder REST RSS service. Specifically, the configuration provides the address where the REST RSS service is located, identifies the contract implemented by the service at that address as the IReallySimpleSyndication contract, and, finally, defines a custom binding specifying how to communicate with the plain XML REST RSS service that is identical to the binding defined for the service itself.

4. Modify the handler of the form's Load event, which is the method MainForm_Load(), in the module MainForm.cs, as shown in Listing 13.10.

LISTING 13.10   Form Load Event Handler

```
private void MainForm_Load(object sender, EventArgs e)
{
    IReallySimpleSyndication client =
        new ChannelFactory<IReallySimpleSyndication>(
            "ReallySimpleSyndicationService").CreateChannel();
    System.ServiceModel.Message message =
        System.ServiceModel.Message.CreateMessage(
            Constants.DefaultAction);
    System.ServiceModel.Message output = client.Get(message);

    XmlDocument document = new XmlDocument();
    XmlDictionaryReader reader = output.GetReaderAtBodyContents();
    document.LoadXml(reader.ReadOuterXml());
```

13

LISTING 13.10 Continued

```
ContentRating rating;
string link = null;
bool validRating =
    ReallySimpleRatedSyndication.ValidateSignedContentRating(
        document,
        out rating,
        out link);

if ((validRating) && (rating == ContentRating.AllAges))
{
    try
    {
        this.browser.Url = new Uri(link);
    }
    catch (Exception)
    {
        this.browser.DocumentText = string.Empty;
    }
}
else
{
    this.browser.DocumentText = Resources.Prohibited;
}
}
```

This code for the handler of the form's Load event uses the Windows Communication Foundation's ChannelFactory<T> generic to create a proxy for communicating with REST RSS service. It uses that proxy to send an empty instance of the Message class to the service to retrieve the RSS feed from the service. Then it passes the RSS feed to the ReallySimpleRatedSyndication class's ValidateSignedContentRating() method to confirm that the content rating incorporated in the feed was digitally signed with the private key of a trusted content ratings organization. If the signature of the content rating is confirmed and the rating indicates that the content is suitable for children, the content referred to in the RSS feed is shown to the user. Otherwise, the user is told that the content is not suitable for viewing.

5. Examine the ReallySimpleRatedSyndication class' static ValidateSignedContentRating() and VerifySignature() methods in the ReallySimpleRatedSyndication.cs module of the ReallySimpleRatedSyndication project. Listing 13.2, earlier in this chapter, shows the methods.

The ValidateSignedContentRating() method accepts the RSS feed retrieved from the REST RSS service, gets the public key of the trusted content rating organization from the trusted people store of the current user's certificate store, and passes that certificate, along with the signed data containing the content rating and the links to content, to the `VerifySignature()` method. That method confirms that the data was signed with the private key corresponding to the public key of the trusted content rating organization. Then the `VerifiySignedContentRating()` method extracts the signed content rating and links to content from the RSS feed.

6. Build the solution.

7. Modify the SafeFeeder project's Debug properties, as shown in Figure 13.4, so as to provide `Feed.xml` as the command-line argument.

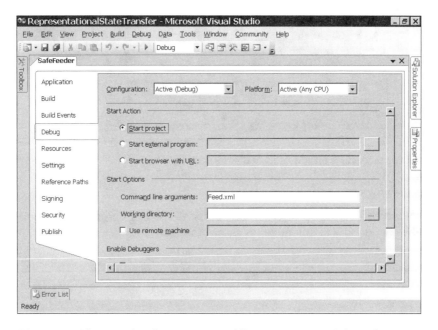

FIGURE 13.4   Providing Feed.xml as a command-line argument to SafeFeeder.

8. Right-click on the SafeFeeder project, and choose Debug, Start New Instance from the context menu. The SafeFeeder console application that hosts the REST RSS service should start.

9. After you see activity in the console of the SafeFeeder application, right-click on the SafeReader project, and choose Debug, Start New Instance from the context menu.

   The content of the feed should appear in the SafeReader, as shown in Figure 13.5, because the content rating specified in the `Feed.xml` RSS document indicates that the content is suitable for all ages. Now the service will be modified to provide an RSS feed that is suitable only for adults.

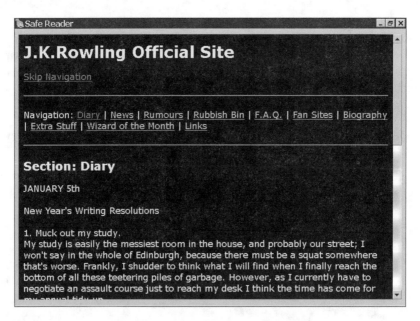

FIGURE 13.5　Accessing an RSS feed that is safe for children.

10. Stop debugging.

11. Modify the SafeFeeder project's Debug properties so as to provide `NaughtyFeed.xml` as the command-line argument, as shown in Figure 13.6.

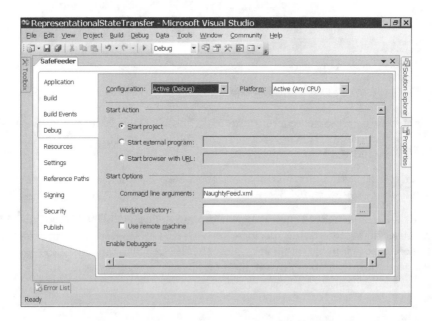

FIGURE 13.6　Providing NaughtyFeed.xml as a command-line argument to SafeFeeder.

12. Right-click on the SafeFeeder project, and choose Debug, Start New Instance from the context menu. The SafeFeeder console application that hosts the REST RSS service should start.

13. After you see activity in the console of the SafeFeeder application, right-click on the SafeReader project, and choose Debug, Start New Instance from the context menu.

This time the RSS aggregator should display a message like the one shown in Figure 13.7, saying that the content of the RSS feed is too naughty to be shown. The reason is that the content rating of the NaughtyFeed.xml RSS document indicates that it is suitable for viewing only by adults.

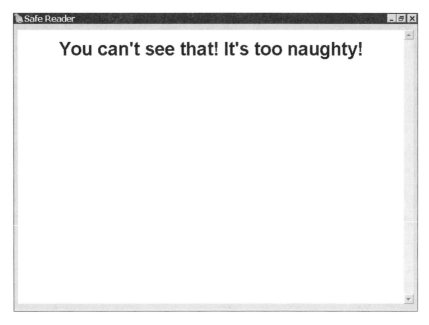

FIGURE 13.7   Prohibited from accessing an RSS feed that is only for adults.

Summary

The Windows Communication Foundation supports plain XML REST services in addition to services that communicate using SOAP messages. All that is required to communicate with such services is a simple custom encoder to handle plain XML messages. In explaining how that custom encoder was built and made configurable, this chapter has also shown how to extend the Windows Communication Foundation with the addition of custom binding elements, and how to allow those custom binding elements to be configured using an application configuration file.

References

Box, Don. 2005. *POX Enters the Lexicon.* http://pluralsight.com/blogs/dbox/archive/2005/02/10/5764.aspx. Accessed 7 January 2006.

Fielding, Roy Thomas. 2000. Architectural Styles and the Design of Network-based Software Architectures. Ph.D. diss., University of California, Irvine. http://www.ics.uci.edu/~fielding/pubs/dissertation/top.htm. Accessed 7 January 2006.

Ojeda-Zapata, Julio. 2005. *Parents have a new problem: 'iPorn' on demand.* http://jewishworldreview.com/1105/ipod_brings_new_worries_to_parents.php3. Accessed 7 January 2006.

Prescod, Paul. 2002. *REST and the Real World.* http://webservices.xml.com/pub/a/ws/2002/02/20/rest.html. Accessed 7 January 2006.

Wikipedia. 2005a. S.v. "POX." http://en.wikipedia.org/wiki/POX. Accessed 7 January 2006.

Wikipedia. 2005b. S.v. "Marvel Rating System." http://en.wikipedia.org/wiki/Marvel_Ratings_System. Accessed 7 January 2006.

Winer, Dave. 2005. *RSS 2.0 Specification.* http://blogs.law.harvard.edu/tech/rss. Accessed 7 January 2006.

CHAPTER **14**

InfoCard

Background

In the promised land of Connected Systems, we will be able to build a service using our favorite tools and technologies without introducing constraints as to who might be able to consume that service. It follows that in this WS-* world, where my service can be accessed by anyone or anything with an Internet connection, who that caller *is* and what he can access becomes rather important.

Unfortunately, as I write, at the dawn of 2006, Information Technology is suffering from an identity crisis that threatens the evolution of Connected Systems and "Web 2.0." What is at stake here? Well, to quote Ray Ozzie:

> "The environment has changed yet again—this time around services. Computing and communications technologies have dramatically and progressively improved to enable the viability of a services-based model. The ubiquity of broadband and wireless networking has changed the nature of how people interact, and they're increasingly drawn toward the simplicity of services and service-enabled software that "just works." Businesses are increasingly considering what services-based economics of scale might do to help them reduce infrastructure costs or deploy solutions as-needed and on [a] subscription basis."

The environment has changed but we are missing one major piece: There is no identity layer for the Internet. The Internet was built without a way to know who you are dealing with. The consequences of this omission are evident: Users are beset by the perils of identity theft, "phishing," and "pharming." Day to day, we face either struggling with a growing list of usernames and passwords or compromising our security by reusing them. To add insult to injury, every time we register with a new site we are made to type in the same information we've supplied to every other site while—coincidentally or not—we endure nauseating quantities of spam in our in-boxes and blogs!

Businesses, on the other hand, are blessed with a veritable busload of identity technologies—a number exceeded only by the profusion of identity integration products that promise to help bring order out of the chaos of identity balkanization. Single Sign-On (SSO) is an elusive goal and Identity Management is a complex process. When you add the challenges of regulatory compliance to the mix, you can almost hear the cries of pain and frustration. It's no wonder the idea of outsourcing has become so attractive!

The banks are facing losses from online fraud. A directive from the Federal Financial Institutions Examination Council (FFIEC)—comprising the United States' five federal banking regulators—recommends that financial institutions deploy security measures such as multifactor authentication to authenticate their online banking customers *by the end of 2006.*

Many governments, notably in Belgium, the U.K. and Ireland, plan to introduce smart-card-based identity cards, augmenting existing eGovernment systems such as online tax returns. In the realm of healthcare, the obvious potential of electronic patient records is undermined by the challenges around patient privacy and access control.

How on earth can we hope to make progress in this complex minefield?

Well, there is hope. Some people, both talented and experienced, have been thinking hard about these issues. Crucially, there has been a continual open discussion and feedback from experts across the industry.

What are the requirements of an open and inclusive "user-centric" identity system? What are its properties? What might it look like? Given the diverse backgrounds, interests, and goals of the participating parties, there has been a remarkable degree of consensus.

There is even a technology (the chapter title gives it away somewhat) that helps us build an identity infrastructure for the Web. But before we get to that, let's take a step back and look at what identity is in the context of IT systems.

What Is Identity?

Someone's identity includes his or her physical appearance, beliefs, interests, likes and dislikes, reputation, and history. It can cover everything vaguely interesting about the person.

At the risk of boring you stupid, I'll take myself as an example. I am thus the *subject* and my identity can be (partially) expressed using the following statements:

- I am English.
- I am married.
- I am over 21.

- I live in Seattle.

- I am employed by Microsoft.

- I have an excellent reputation as a buyer on eBay.

- I am a member of Netflix.

- I read the *Guardian* newspaper.

- I have a blog at http://blogs.msdn.com/nigelwa.

- I have Frequence Plus Carte Rouge.

If we express this information digitally I become the *digital subject*:

> *A digital subject is a person or thing represented in the digital realm which is being described.*

Humans are not the only possible digital subjects. We might equally deal with groups, devices, policies, resources, or relationships (such as between a user and a device).

With a sprinkling of XML, each of the claims above can help form my *digital identity*:

> *A digital identity is a set of claims made by one digital subject about itself or another digital subject.*

Claims can take many forms: a simple identifier such as `REDMOND\nigelwa`, personal information (my name and address), membership of a group (Netflix), a capability (my credit limit is $5,000) or knowledge of a key.

Do you believe all of them? Why? Why not? Would showing you my passport or my driver's license increase your level of belief in my proposed age? What if the Human Resources department at Microsoft were asserting that I was an employee?

By using the word *claim* in the definition of digital identity, we make a subtle but deliberate choice. In a closed directory-based domain (for example, a Windows Server 2003 domain), we typically deal in security *assertions*, meaning "confident and forceful statements of fact or belief." This confidence is well-merited: It is a closed, administered system. However, if we want to have an open and broad-reaching identity system (we do), it helps to reflect the element of doubt inherent in dealing with parties on the Internet. How confident you are in the veracity of these claims depends on who the *identity provider* is, their reputation, and your relationship with them. Oh, and whether the claims have reached you intact and without being tampered with! In this case, I am the identity provider (and my security token is a Sams book). Perhaps you might have greater confidence in my age if shown my passport or my *certificat de mariage*—or digital versions of those documents signed by a government authority. You might have less faith if you saw them in an English tabloid newspaper.

This claim model is extremely flexible—we can express a subject's identity in pretty much any way we choose to. It has another very valuable property: It enables us to tackle the concerns of the general public around privacy and anonymity. On the Internet—even more than elsewhere—our natural desire is to remain anonymous until the moment *we* choose to reveal our identity, and even then we want to disclose the *minimum* amount of information possible (for example, revealing that I am over 21 without revealing my age). But how can an identity system preserve anonymity? Surely "anonymous identity" is an oxymoron?!

Well, anonymity is as much a part of identity as recognition. Anonymity is the null set of identity—and is very much a part of what we're trying to achieve. Many existing identity systems rely on unique identifiers. This is a critically useful constraint (to say the least) but not necessarily one we always want to apply. This is a flaw in URL-based systems—by their very definition, they resolve to a location.

The key idea is that identifying a subject needn't have anything to do with knowing who that subject is "in the real world." We can use a pseudo-identity to represent a user, not a real identity, and associate that with zero or more claims. The fact that a certain user has a consistent pseudo-identity over time allows us to gauge the quality of that user without having any idea of who he really is.

Summarizing, we are going to represent a subject's digital identity using a set of claims supplied in a secure and verifiable way by an identity provider. The claims are packaged in a security token that can travel over process and machine boundaries to wherever they are required.

Existing Identity Solutions ("Getting to Where We Want to Be from Where We Are Today")

If you are a corporate developer, then likely you will be intimately familiar with the world of pain that is Single Sign-On. The amount of time spent getting applications to accept a corporate standard authentication mechanism is astounding. Although there seems to be a trend for enterprises to consolidate around Active Directory—the twin lures of Exchange Server and Group Policy proving too strong to resist—it will be many years, if ever, before one directory service becomes a de facto standard.

Regardless of which directory an organization standardizes on, the entries in that directory are best limited to the employees and resources of that organization. We really don't want to have to maintain a directory entry for every single employee of every business partner we deal with. The right way to do it is via identity *federation*.

Microsoft's Active Directory Federation Services (ADFS) uses WS-Trust and WS-Federation to build a bridge between two companies' Active Directories. In effect, Company A is set up to trust certain security tokens from company B and/or vice versa.

To give a concrete example, Microsoft has a company store where you can buy gorgeous Microsoft-branded merchandise such as mugs and umbrellas. Employees can order these collectors' items via a hosted website run by an outside company—with its own directory. In the past, Microsoft employees have had to be issued—and worse, had to remember—a separate username and password for this site. By setting up a trust relationship between an account ADFS server on the Microsoft side and a resource ADFS server on the hosting company side, Microsoft employees can now authenticate using their habitual AD credentials, seamlessly gain access to the company store website, and buy 10 mugs and a cordless mouse to celebrate.

The separation of responsibilities here is entirely logical. Microsoft maintains its directory of employees and their spending limits. The hosting company concentrates on processing orders without the hassle of maintaining a shadow account for every Microsoft employee who buys a T-shirt. The employees, meanwhile, have the pleasure of a seamless experience and the untold joy of one fewer username and password to remember.

Federation is a powerful solution for cooperating businesses—but what about identity outside of corporate domains? What about identity for Internet users?

As I mentioned before, there is no identity infrastructure built into the Internet and thus no way to know who you're dealing with. Attempts at a solution have been ad hoc kludges, difficult to understand, hard to automate, and vulnerable from a security point of view. Furthermore, every new solution creates another identity silo we have to connect to.

Our digital identities end up locked into these silos. There is no way for me to move my Amazon book-purchasing history or my Netflix movie-viewing history to, say, Barnes & Noble or Blackwells. My excellent reputation with eBay is hard earned; I would like to be able to use it with other sites.

Obviously, what we really need is for everyone to agree on just one solution. Fat chance, I hear you say, but the industry has a history of moving away from proprietary siloed technologies such as X.400 and Token-Ring toward standardized, simple, open protocols like TCP/IP, HTML, and SMTP. The WS-* protocols have broad industry support; why can't we just devise an identity system for the Internet and have done with it?

Although this would be a great relief for everybody, it is important to realize that each of the technologies available today has its compelling use cases, its merits, and its faults. In short, it is an extremely difficult task to select a single identity technology that can satisfy all existing scenarios and, furthermore, anticipate every single future one.

There are two classic approaches to complex computing problems like this. One is to have a very simple system with an extensibility mechanism so that it can be adapted to each problem domain (for example, SOAP); the other is to add a level of indirection that provides a consistent experience and hides multiple underlying technology implementations (for example, TCP/IP over Ethernet and Token-Ring).

But before we decide on which fundamental approach to take—and each has its advocates—it would be wise to examine previous efforts at solving the identity problem. We can learn from their successes and their failures—both technological and sociological—in a range of contexts. From that analysis we hope to identify the characteristics that our identity system must possess in order to be successful.

Although there have been a number of efforts in this area, the two that spring to mind are Microsoft's (much-maligned) Passport and Public Key Infrastructure (PKI).

What prevented the Passport identity system from being successful? Well, that question's a bit harsh: There are currently more than 250 million Passport users and more than a billion Passport logons per day. So it *is* a success as an identity provider for MSN. However, as an identity provider for the Internet, it simply didn't cut the mustard.

The problem is that Microsoft is the identity provider for every transaction. Regardless of whether you trust the company—or believe it to be the very incarnation of evil—this arrangement is not always appropriate or desirable. When I disclose my digital identity, only those parties whose presence is truly justified should be involved. We can formalize this requirement as follows:

> *Digital identity systems must be designed so [that] the disclosure of identifying information is limited to parties having a necessary and justifiable place in a given identity relationship.*

This is the *law of justifiable parties* and it is one of seven "laws of identity" published and refined online at www.identityblog.com. The ability of identity experts to directly influence the formation of these laws via the "blogosphere" has produced an industry-wide consensus that the laws are sound, accurate, and complete. These laws are the best tools available to us for evaluating new and existing identity systems.

I will uncover the rest of the laws in a moment, but first let's take a look at PKI.

PKI, as many of those immersed in it will tell you, is a wonderful technology that is set to take the world by storm. Unfortunately, PKI's advocates have been saying this for a long time! There is no doubt that it *is* an extremely powerful and useful technology, but it can be costly, it can be complex to manage, and it is overkill in simple contexts.

Despite its flaws, PKI is the nearest we have to a universal identity system today. It is PKI that provides us with the security backbone of the Internet. It is SSL certificates that allow us to conduct secure transactions over the Web. If we are to build an Internet identity layer and are not averse to a bit of reuse, it might be prudent to take advantage of this existing infrastructure—provided it doesn't cause us to fall afoul of the laws.

It is revealing that even a strong technology like PKI, with a choice of vendors and identity providers (namely, the certificate authorities), has not been universally deployed. Without being overly pessimistic, there probably isn't a "one size fits all" identity solution.

It is this point, combined with the reality of a large existing installed base of identity silos, that helps us decide whether the "simple and extensible" or the "level of indirection" approach is most likely to gain traction and succeed.

In short, the indirection method has the greater potential. What's more, it has the advantage of not precluding the simple/extensible approach. Nascent identity technologies can evolve naturally under the all-encompassing wing of indirection. Perhaps, over time, a simple/extensible solution will become dominant—but it will still be able to interoperate with legacy technologies.

Therefore, what we require is an identity metasystem, or system of systems, that provides that level of indirection, encompasses existing identity technologies, and obeys the laws of identity.

And now to the rest of the laws....

The Laws of Identity

Here are the laws of identity as stated at www.identityblog.com:

1. **User Control and Consent**

   Technical identity systems must only reveal information identifying a user with the user's consent.

2. **Minimal Disclosure for a Constrained Use**

   The solution which discloses the least amount of identifying information and best limits its use is the most stable long-term solution.

3. **Justifiable Parties**

   Digital identity systems must be designed so the disclosure of identifying information is limited to parties having a necessary and justifiable place in a given identity relationship.

4. **Directional Identity**

   A universal identity system must support both "omni-directional" identifiers for use by public entities and "unidirectional" identifiers for use by private entities, thus facilitating discovery while preventing unnecessary release of correlation handles.

5. **Pluralism of Operators and Technologies**

   A universal identity system must channel and enable the inter-working of multiple identity technologies run by multiple identity providers.

6. **Human Integration**

   The universal identity metasystem must define the human user to be a component of the distributed system integrated through unambiguous human-machine communication mechanisms offering protection against identity attacks.

7. **Consistent Experience across Contexts**

   The unifying identity metasystem must guarantee its users a simple, consistent experience while enabling separation of contexts through multiple operators and technologies.

The laws, I hope, are pretty self-explanatory, but I'll attempt to clarify or emphasize where appropriate. For a more detailed explanation, take a look at the *Laws of Identity* whitepaper.

The first law states that the user must be in control, be informed, and give their consent before the system releases personal information. This law is at the heart of the oft-used term *user-centric* identity management (as opposed to domain-centric).

The second and third laws are common sense: Identity information is sensitive so reveal the minimal amount to the fewest people necessary.

The fourth law says that an identity system should support both public and private identities. A website like Amazon has a public identity. The more people who know that identity the better, as far as Amazon is concerned: The Amazon people are happy for it to be broadcast everywhere. A private individual, on the other hand, wants to share her identity only in a point-to-point fashion, not broadcast it to the whole world.

The fifth law we've already covered. The sixth law emphasizes that the user is a fundamental part of the system, not an afterthought.

The seventh law derives from the preceding two. If we accept that the human factor is crucial and there will be a mixture of operators and technologies, then there must be a unified experience across contexts for the system to be usable.

The Identity Metasystem

So we need an identity metasystem. What does it look like? Well, it has to obey the laws of identity, expose the strengths of its constituent identity systems, provide interoperability between them, and enable the creation of a consistent and straightforward user interface over all of them.

Just to emphasize the point, it should be completely open and nonproprietary: It is "the identity metasystem" not "the Microsoft or IBM or whoever identity metasystem."

There are three roles in the metasystem:

- *Subjects*, the entities about whom claims are made
- *Identity Providers (IPs)*, which issue digital identities
- *Relying Parties (RPs)*, which require digital identities

To give but one example to illustrate the roles, when I buy a book online I am the subject, my bank is the identity provider giving my credit-card details, and the online bookstore is the relying party consuming those details to enable me to buy a copy of *The Idiot's Guide to PKI*.

If you remember, our identity is packaged in a security token containing claims made by an identity provider. In the preceding example the online bookstore might specify that it requires a token that contains my name, address, and credit-card claims. I can then ask my bank to provide the required security token with proof that it was issued by them and a way to prove I am the rightful possessor of the token. When I give this token to the online bookstore, they verify that it came from my bank, and that I am the rightful purchaser, and they extract the claims and complete the transaction.

Notice here that the user is at the center. Potentially the token could have gone directly from bank to bookstore—from identity provider to relying party—but instead it goes via the user so that she has control and consent over the release of identity information.

Expanding a little on the example, you can see a number of requirements for the system to work.

First, the relying party needs a way to specify the claims it requires in a way that everyone understands: "I need first name, surname, and address claims." Likewise, the identity provider needs a way to specify the claims it is able to supply.

Second, the relying party and the identity provider may use completely different identity systems with different token formats—this is a metasystem, remember! So both parties need a technology-agnostic way to express the kinds of security tokens that they understand: "I need a SAML 1.1 or SAML 2.0 security token."

Furthermore, it would be useful if the identity provider and relying party could negotiate the types of claims they can use: "I can provide tokens of these types: X, Y"; " I can receive tokens of these types: Y, Z"—"Okay, let's use token type Y because we both understand that."

This is a bit like people communicating via languages and raises an interesting idea. If I speak English and French but you speak only Japanese, Swedish, and German, we can still communicate provided we can find someone who can understand, say, French and Japanese. Provided we trust that person not to make things up or fall victim to Chinese Whispers (as in the game of Telephone), we can interoperate perfectly well.

Within the context of our identity system, we may need to translate not only the type of token but also the claims themselves. For example, my identity provider may provide a "date of birth" claim, but the relying party may require an "older than 21" claim. Or my company may provide an "is at job level 1000" claim, but the relying party needs an "is a manager" or "is an executive" claim.

What we need is a token translation service: a trusted service that can receive tokens of one type and convert them to tokens of another type. Such beasts exist and they are commonly known as *security token services* (or STSs).

Furthermore, the user cannot "just" ask an identity provider for a security token—that's not very secure! The user has to authenticate to the identity provider in some way and prove who she is. Put another way, the user must supply some kind of security token (asserting her identity) in order to get a security token back (also asserting her identity) that she can give to the relying party.

Thus it becomes clear that

- Identity providers are security token services.
- All interactions with security token services involve giving one kind of security token and getting another one back.

Meanwhile, at the center of everything lies the user. Regardless of the complex flow of claims, tokens, and token types between the different systems within the metasystem, we want the user to have a simple, consistent experience and be able to control the release of information.

These requirements can be summarized as stated here:

- **Negotiation**—Way to enable relying party, subject, and identity provider to negotiate technical policy requirements

- **Encapsulation**—Technology-agnostic way to exchange policies and claims between identity provider and relying party.

- **Claims transformation**—Trusted way to change one set of claims regardless of token format into another.

- **User experience**—Consistent user interface across multiple systems and technologies.

The architecture that enables the identity metasystem to be implemented—allowing us to meet the preceding requirements and link together identity providers, subjects, and relying parties—is the WS-* Web Services architecture (http://msdn.microsoft.com/webservices/). This set of open specifications is available for anyone to use on a reasonable and nondiscriminatory basis and has been adopted across the industry. For our purposes, the key specifications for the metasystem are WS-SecurityPolicy, WS-MetadataExchange (WS-MEX), and WS-Trust.

WS-SecurityPolicy allows us to describe the security token and claim requirements of a service in policy, and WS-MetadataExchange allows us to query and retrieve these service policies. WS-Trust defines the mechanism for requesting and receiving security tokens. In other words, it defines how a security token service communicates to the world. As you have seen, this is very simple: There is a Request for a Security Token (RST) and a subsequent Request for a Security Token Response (RSTR). Figure 14.1 helps show how everything fits together.

There are multiple relying parties, each with different token and claim requirements expressed using WS-SecurityPolicy. If we want to access one of these relying parties, we can find out their policy using WS-MEX. After we know their requirements, we can select a matching identity provider (or chain of providers).

For example, a relying party may require SAML 1.1 tokens containing my name and SSN from "any" identity provider. I can then select one of the identity providers that is able to provide the right token for the job.

The *identity selector* in the diagram is the "consistent user experience" part of the metasystem. After being invoked by an application, the identity selector performs the negotiation between the relying party and identity provider(s), displays the matching identity providers and relying parties to the subject, allows the user to select appropriately, obtains a security token containing the requested claims, and releases it to the requestor—all under the supervision of the subject (that is, the user).

Furthermore, the identity selector should be agnostic to specific security token types and identity mechanisms. You could use the most esoteric security token imaginable and the identity selector will just pass it on. It is a conduit for identity flow under user control between identity providers and relying parties.

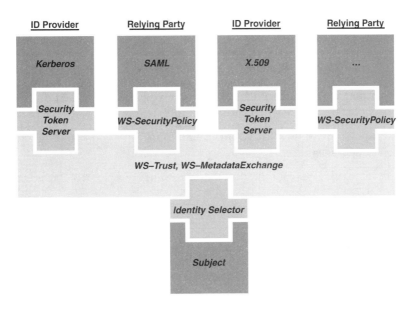

FIGURE 14.1   Identity metasystem architecture.

The InfoCard System

InfoCard is an identity selector that runs on Windows Vista, Windows XP SP2, and Windows Server 2003 SP1. It ships as part of WinFx along with WCF. However, it is both hoped and expected that there will be identity selectors on other operating systems such as the Apple Mac and Linux. The identity metasystem is inclusive of all technologies and platforms and, to the amazement and disbelief of some, it is entirely possible to build an end-to-end solution without having any Microsoft software whatsoever.

There will, of course, be an Active Directory Security Token Service (AD/STS), but there will also be STSes from other vendors and on other platforms. Indeed there is already an STS implementation on Linux by Ping Identity. To test the true interoperable nature of the technology, Kim Cameron runs his blog on the LAMP stack and uses InfoCard to log in!

Now that we're a few pages into a chapter on InfoCard, it's high time I provided a one-paragraph definition of InfoCard that tries to encapsulate its qualities:

The InfoCard system is a new feature of Windows that allows users to control the use of their digital identity via the simple and familiar metaphor of a set of cards. When a user wants to access an online service, rather than providing his username and password or filling in a form, he selects an appropriate card from a special, security-hardened UI. This "InfoCard" represents the digital identity of the user and enables the service to receive the data it needs to authenticate and authorize the user. This information is provided in a secure and consistent way by identity providers such as the user's employer, his bank, his government, or indeed the user himself. It is an interactive system and the user can determine exactly what information is disclosed and to whom, while the identity provider asserts the validity of the information. By utilizing standard interoperable protocols such as WS-Security and WS-Trust, the system is able to provide users with a simple, consistent, and secure sign-on experience to trusted websites and Web services.

In other words, in the same way I might present my driver's license in an American bar to prove I'm older than 21, or use my gym card to prove I'm a member of my gym, or provide my passport to prove I'm British, I can use a *virtual* card to assert one or more claims (for example, "I *am* older than 21") when interacting with a website or service.

Perhaps the easiest thing to do at this point is to create a card and then you'll get a better idea of what I'm talking about.

When you install WinFX, you should find a new icon in your Control Panel (classic view please):

If you double-click this, you should get the dialog shown in Figure 14.2.

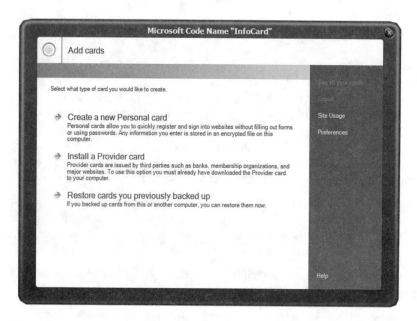

FIGURE 14.2 The InfoCard Add Cards dialog.

As you can see, there are two types of cards, personal cards and provider cards. The names are reasonably descriptive: *provider* cards (also known as managed cards) are given to you by an identity provider such as your bank, your company, or your government; *personal* cards (also known as self-issued cards) are created by you personally. Their most common use is to log in to websites that you use usernames and passwords with today. If you have a user account at a website today, you can use an InfoCard tomorrow—the site just needs to add InfoCard support to the existing username and password support it already has, and this process has been designed to be as simple and as nondisruptive as possible.

You can create several personal cards to represent your identity in different contexts. For example, your Xbox Live identity is likely to be different from your Amazon identity. You can also use the same card in different contexts—for example, a card providing minimal information for use at sites where you don't want to reveal things like your address or email address. The same principles apply to provider cards: You can have more than one card from a single identity provider and use the same card in many different places (an InfoCard representing your credit-card details would be pretty useless otherwise!).

Go ahead and create some personal cards and experiment with exporting and importing them. Open the exported .crds file in Notepad to see what it looks like.

There are only 12 claims associated with personal cards:

14

    GivenName

    Surname

    EmailAddress

    StreetAddress

    Locality

    StateOrProvince

    PostalCode

    Country

    PrimaryPhone

    DateOfBirth

    Gender

    PrivatePersonalIdentifier

It is up to you what values you put in the 11 claims that appear in the UI. The one that doesn't appear in the UI is the PrivatePersonalIdentifier (PPID). It is generated by the InfoCard system and is what, when you're using a personal card, uniquely identifies you to a site. Without a PPID it would be impossible to provide a consistent, personalized experience if the only claims you provided were GivenName = "Maria", Surname= "Gonzalez", and StateOrProvince="CA"—there are 10,000 Maria Gonzalezes in LA county alone (this is known in identity circles as the "Maria Gonzales problem"!).

InfoCard's main purpose in life is to help users to authenticate and be authorized at websites and services in a simple, secure, and flexible way. It enables identity providers to supply claims for those sites to consume. It's important to understand that InfoCards enable the user to retrieve personal identity information from identity providers but InfoCards do not contain claims.

InfoCards contain metadata concerning *which* claims can be provided and *where and how* to get them. They do *not* contain identity data, but only metadata (that is, data about the data). Nor do cards actually go anywhere off the user's machine (across the wire). They stay on the client machine unless the user decides to export them or they are roamed within a domain.

Let's go through an example to make this clearer. Suppose my bank gives me an InfoCard to represent my credit-card information. The bank emails me a signed .crd file and I import it (naturally, since InfoCards are metadata, their ultimate expression is as an XML document). When I use that card to make a payment at a website, the InfoCard system sends an RST to the bank's security token service (the IP/STS) and I get back an RSTR with a signed, encrypted security token with the credit-card data in it, ready to pass on to the website (the RP) provided that I, the user, give my consent to release that information. It is security tokens containing claims that pass over the wire, not cards. In the end, choosing an InfoCard is just an elegant way to get hold of a security token.

The semantics of using a personal card are exactly the same as for a provider card. The card contains details about which claims can be retrieved, where they are, and how to get them—only in this case the security token service is local and the data is sitting on my hard disk.

Extending this model further, in the near future we will have portable security token services (pSTSes) that contain personally identifiable information. These will come in all shapes and sizes: thumb drives, mobile phones, and Pocket PCs. There might even be a use for those fancy digital wristwatches that Bill Gates promotes every couple of years or so. These solutions will provide both mobility and security but the concept is exactly the same: The InfoCard points to an STS that provides security tokens containing claims.

Personal cards provide some of the most commonly used claims, but it is hardly an exhaustive list (er, 12). This is by design. By including these basic claims, InfoCard helps the user avoid some tediously repetitive typing, but these are not exactly interesting claims. And that is the whole point: There's not much incentive for a bad guy to go looking for this information. It would be easier to look in the phone book! We are purposely avoiding having a honeypot of personal information on the user's machine. The cards that represent the really interesting data are the provider cards, and all that they have in them is metadata. It's my bank's server that has my account details and it's the government-run server that has my Social Security information—which is, of course, exactly how it should be.

InfoCards in Action

We've covered how to create InfoCards and what's in them (metadata!) but how are they actually used in practice? Figure 14.3 shows the interaction between the user, the identity provider, and the relying party.

Now let's dig into the next layer of detail. Figure 14.4 shows the message flow sequence from the *Guide to Integrating with InfoCard*.

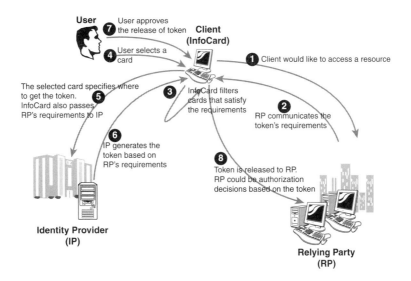

FIGURE 14.3   Basic flow between parties.

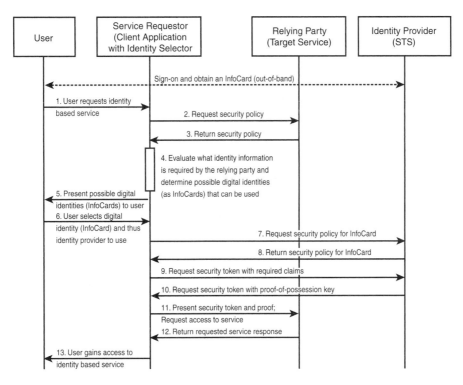

FIGURE 14.4   Message flow.

This basic message flow is the same for all InfoCard interactions, with variations based on the number of security token services. For example, the relying party can have an STS controlling access to a resource. This is typically the case with websites where access control is commonly regulated using cookies. Also, as with our language example earlier, there can be any number of identity provider STSes where one security token is exchanged for another until the security token required by the relying party is obtained and presented (this is easily configured in WCF config files).

Let's use a real-world example to make this STS chaining a little clearer. Suppose I want to buy an HP computer from an online retailer and I know that my employer, Microsoft, has an employee purchase arrangement with HP. The retailer also has a relationship with HP; he orders stock from them and accepts HP partner discounts. The retailer needs to see a security token from HP in order for me to get my discount. In turn, to get that, I need to provide HP with proof that I work for Microsoft. So this is what happens:

1. I select my Microsoft provider InfoCard and authenticate to the Microsoft STS using my domain credentials or my smartcard. I receive a security token that has a claim that I am a Microsoft employee.

2. This token is presented to the HP STS. Because the HP STS has a trust relationship with the Microsoft STS, it can see that the token is valid (it's signed using a private key known only to Microsoft), and it checks a proof-of-possession key that helps prove that I am the rightful user of the token.

3. The HP STS issues another security token (signed using an HP cert and with a proof-of-possession key from HP).

4. This security token is presented to the retailer service. The retailer checks the token for validity, sees that it comes from HP and that I am the rightful owner, and gives me my $1 discount.

It is worth clarifying how one authenticates to an STS (you have to prove who you are in order to be issued a security token!). InfoCard supports four ways to authenticate users to the initial identity provider STS: Kerberos, X.509 (software and hardware based), a personal InfoCard, and a username and password. When you select a provider card, you can be prompted for the associated credentials such as a password, a personal InfoCard, a smartcard and pin—or the InfoCard system may use a client certificate or your Kerberos credentials, in which case the authentication is seamless.

The identity provider specifies which authentication method to use in the security policy that InfoCard retrieves using WS-MEX. It also obtains security binding information, endpoint information, and the like.

For fine details on interactions between the identity provider, the user, and the relying party, the best place to look is in the *Guide to Integrating with InfoCard* (aimed at vendors interoperating with InfoCard) and the *Technical Reference for InfoCard v1.0 in Windows*.

The Kerberos authentication method dovetails nicely with Microsoft's Active Directory Security Token Service when it becomes available. System administrators will use an admin console to set up trust relationships with organizations and define which Active

Directory attributes are exposed as claims. Then a user just selects his company's provider InfoCard to gain access to a trusted partner's application or website. All the necessary authentication and access control is done seamlessly and painlessly in the background.

InfoCard Architecture and Security

The InfoCard system installed with WinFx consists logically of three things:

- An InfoCard service responsible for creating self-issued security tokens and retrieving security tokens from security token services

- An InfoCard data store

- A user interface component that is used to manage and select InfoCards

Figure 14.5 shows the logical architecture of the InfoCard system.

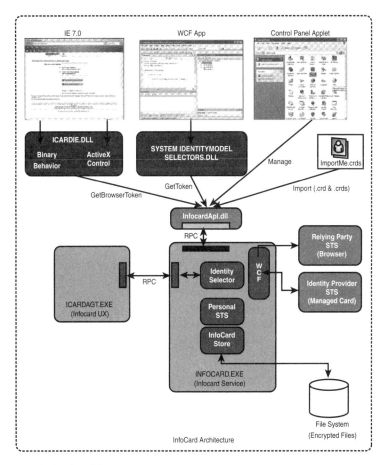

FIGURE 14.5   InfoCard architecture.

The central part of the system is the `infocard.exe` service, which handles all token and management requests and runs as Local System. It creates the UI Agent process, `icardagt.exe`, to interact with the user, and this runs as the user on a private desktop, communicating with `infocard.exe` via RPC.

Running the UI in a separate desktop helps ensure that personal identity information is displayed in a secure way, protecting against phishing and shatter attacks and disclosure of personal information.

There is one component, `infocardapi.dll`, that handles all entry points into the InfoCard system and is loaded into the client process (the browser, a WCF app, or the Control Panel applet). It has no public types but is dynamically loaded by `System.IdentityModel.Selectors.dll` in WCF clients and by `icardie.dll` in IE7.

The only other process is created when the user needs to use the Open File dialog, such as when importing or exporting a card or choosing an image. This process runs in the context of the user on the normal user desktop.

The `icardie.dll` component is the bridge between IE7 and the InfoCard system and it ships with IE7 (from the IE7 Beta 2 Preview onward). The InfoCard system is exposed to web developers in two ways, a binary behavior and a COM object, but they have a shared implementation for accessing `infocardapi.dll` using the `GetBrowserToken()` API.

Both binary behaviors and ActiveX objects are compatible with other browsers (a mandatory requirement for any browser solution), have minimal impact on existing sites, and provide a seamless user experience should InfoCard not be present on the user's system, that is, if WinFx has not been installed.

ActiveX controls have the advantage of being well-known to web developers but can be disabled in high-security environments. Binary behaviors, though less familiar, are available even when the browser is configured to use high security settings and ActiveX controls are disabled.

WCF applications access InfoCard via `System.IdentityModel.Selectors.dll`. This `.dll` is installed in the global assembly cache (GAC), and the API used is `GetToken()`. However, as far as WCF developers are concerned, they simply need to add a reference to `System.ServiceModel` and select the IssuedToken client credential type to launch the InfoCard process.

Both the `GetToken()` and the `GetBrowserToken()` methods return signed and encrypted (using the identity of the recipient) security tokens ready to be dispatched to the server/service.

The identity selector module in `infocard.exe` is the component that does all the hard work. It retrieves IP and RP policies using WS-MetadataExchange, evaluating what identity information is required and determining which possible digital identities (that is, InfoCards) can be used. It then calls the UI process, `icardagt.exe`, to display those cards to the user (cards not meeting the RP's policy are greyed out).

If the user selects a card, the identity selector knows which identity provider (and STS) to contact from the card's metadata. It may have to ask the IP/STS for its security policy via WS-MEX, but in any case the identity selector does the WS-Trust dance with the IP/STS. It sends an RST asking for a security token containing the claims required by the relying party's policy. The IP/STS then returns an RSTR containing a signed security token for the RP, a proof-of-possession key, and, optionally, a display token to show the user what's in the security token proper. As the name implies, the proof key enables the user to prove to the relying party that he/she/it is the rightful bearer of the security token.

The identity provider STS can be an external service (for example, my bank or my company), in which case it is represented by a provider card supplied to me by the identity provider. Or it can be my personal STS that provides the security token, in which case it is represented by a personal card. In either case, the logical semantics are the same—and furthermore, extend to portable, device-based STSes—but in the case of personal cards it is the InfoCard system, `infocard.exe`, that creates a SAML 1.1 security token using data stored locally in the InfoCard store.

After the InfoCard system has received a security token from the IP, the user is prompted (via the UI agent) whether to send the token to the relying party to gain access to the site or service.

Relying parties are required to have an X.509 certificate (preferably a high-assurance certificate) to identify themselves but also so that security tokens sent to them can be encrypted using the certificate's public key. What this means is that a security token destined for a relying party is totally opaque to the InfoCard system. This is by design: Identity selectors need to be security token agnostic, and it follows that there shouldn't be a requirement for InfoCard to understand every token that passes by. However, the user needs to have a way to see the contents of the token in order to know what personally identifiable information is being sent to the RP.

The solution is to have an optional display token sent by the identity provider to the user along with the normal security token (which is destined for the relying party). It is the display token that is displayed to the user so that the user makes an informed decision on whether to proceed.

At the relying party, the recipient of the security token can be either a service endpoint or a relying party STS (aka a resource STS) which controls access to the relying party's site or service. The relying party cracks open the token and authenticates and authorizes the user based on the claims in the token (and the provider of those claims). In the browser case, the RSTR from the resource STS is a browser cookie. This means that access to a website after authenticating via InfoCard is exactly the same as an existing solution using username and password authentication.

WCF services can also use a resource STS. That way, once the user has authenticated using a security token from an IP, access to a service is controlled by the relying party and there is no longer a requirement for an IP security token. Although the client app can cache the IP's security token as a performance optimization—at least until the token is no longer fresh—this gives the relying party control.

After you receive a provider InfoCard from an identity provider—in a way that enables you to trust that the card is authentic—you can use the cryptographic information it contains to authenticate to the identity provider and communicate securely.

Personal InfoCards and their (limited) information are created by the user and stored locally, but they also contain an RSA key pair to enable security tokens to be signed by the personal IP. I will cover how this is generated in a moment.

The InfoCard system is an interactive system (not programmatic) that does not authorize release of personal information without explicit user approval. It is therefore the user who is responsible for protecting his personal information. The system aids the user in making intelligent decisions by providing an intuitive user interface and detailed information about the entity requesting a security token. Information is gathered from the recipient's X.509 certificate including logos (when present) and displayed to the user. This UI, combined with the use of high-assurance certificates, enables the user to make an informed decision to trust the recipient. Furthermore, all UI and display of this info is done using a private desktop accessible only by the LSA that hides the user's desktop. This helps to prevent phishing and screen-scraping attacks.

There is an encrypted and signed InfoCard store per user and it is ACL'd for Local System access only. Data in the store is encrypted using AES256, and the symmetric key used is doubly encrypted using DPAPI (256-bit AES keys), first using the user's DPAPI key and then again using the System DPAPI key. InfoCard allows only one level of role access—normal user access. This way only the user can access the data and only via a System process (that is, `Infocard.exe`) that impersonates the user. Even when this data is loaded into memory, it remains encrypted until it is needed.

Individual InfoCards can also be protected by a password, which is useful for cases in which a Windows login is shared. However, this feature notwithstanding, if someone learns your Windows password, they will have access to your InfoCards. The mitigation here is to have a device like a portable STS or a smartcard to provide multifactor authentication. I should also point out that if you log in with admin privileges and run some malware, it doesn't matter how well designed a piece of software is—but there's nothing new here. The mitigation is to try to not log in as an administrator (the default in Vista) and to avoid running software of dubious origin.

InfoCards are XML documents issued by identity providers (including self-issued) and stored by the user on the storage device of their choice. An InfoCard does not contain any security sensitive data per se. It simply represents the security token issuance relationship of the user with an identity provider. The actual request and issuance of the corresponding security tokens will be authenticated and secure. You should note that the metadata exchanges to retrieve policy are in plain text.

Each card includes in its metadata an element called CardID that is a globally unique URI for that card. It is generated by, and only meaningful to, identity providers. For personal cards, the CardID is assigned by the system automatically at the time of card creation. For provider cards, the identity provider assigns a unique CardID for each card it issues, and this is included in requests for security tokens by the user.

As mentioned earlier, with personal cards the user is represented by a PrivatePersonalIdentifier (PPID) claim. This is created by hashing together the CardID and the relying party's organizational ID (the OLSCID derived from the X509 certificate of the site or service). This means a user can use the same card at multiple sites and there will be a different PPID for each one: Sites are unable to collude and track the user. It is this claim that is used when a user authenticates to an identity provider STS using a personal card.

Identity providers may or may not need to provide a user identifier to the relying party. The identity provider may just need to supply a security token with, say, an "over 21" age claim. However, if the identity provider *does* need to provide a user identifier, the PPID claim is a good choice. An identity provider can choose to use any mechanism of its choice to generate the PPID for the user as long as it can consistently reproduce it for that user.

Ultimately it is at the discretion of the relying party and identity provider in any given business context as to what is suitable as a persistent user identifier. For a government-run identity provider, a Social Security number may be a good identifier and an ISP could provide an email address. Both could also support PPID as a generic identifier (and a method to generate it) if they chose to.

Security tokens generated by an identity provider have to be signed with a trusted/well-known key that the recipient of the token can validate. For provider cards this is done by the identity provider using an X.509 certificate.

However, with personal cards we have two technical problems to overcome. We need an asymmetric key pair to sign security tokens but, more than that, we would like a key pair *per site* to again avoid correlation issues between sites. Also, once we have these keys, we need a way to roam them with the cards for a consistent user experience.

The solution is to use a master key per card. This is a 256-bit random number that is hashed with the relying party's organizational ID to create a seed for the Crypto API to generate per-site, per-card (and ANSI X9.31–compliant) RSA key pairs. To be able to roam the store itself, InfoCard uses the Crypto API and PKCS#5 to generate a 256-bit AES key from the user's password.

Relying parties must have a public key pair for identity and encryption. The public key is used to encrypt security tokens destined for the relying party. Similarly, any tokens from an identity provider that are destined for the user (such as display tokens) must be encrypted to ensure that the claims are visible to the IP, the RP, and the user only. When username and password authentication is used with an IP/STS, the channel must be secured using SSL. For Kerberos a symmetric key is used, and for hardware- and software-based X.509 an asymmetric key pair is used. Authentication to an STS using a personal card can use either a symmetric or an asymmetric key pair for the security binding. Authentication to an STS using a provider card is not permitted.

One final security feature to note: InfoCard is able to obtain a security token from an identity provider without revealing the identity of the relying party to the identity provider. This is the default mode and we refer to the security token as an *unscoped* token. This is Law 2 at work!

Now let's write some code to see how InfoCard is accessed.

Basic WCF App

I like to provide very simple examples ("as simple as possible but no simpler" to quote someone who should know) to illustrate a feature, so my apologies to those who prefer something more complex or interesting. It is best practice to use svcutil for creating client proxies, but I have coded by hand for brevity and clarity.

It is important to stress that the code presented here was written and tested using a beta 2 build of WinFx. Unfortunately, features such as browser integration are not available before the February CTP (Community Technical Preview), so I have used an early version of that (the latest that was available to me at the time of writing). The upside for you is that this sample code—or something very similar—should work with all builds from the February CTP onward. The downside is that there is a chance that by some quirk of fate my code will not work on the final beta 2 build. If this is the case, please accept my abject apologies. I hope the difference is not so great as to impair your enjoyment of getting the code to work and seeing InfoCard in action.

So let's take a very basic WCF app and add InfoCard support. We're not going to use an STS—in either this example or the browser example that follows—it's just about showing how InfoCard works at a basic level.

The application consists of a service—which will be our *relying party*—and a client app that communicates with the service via WCF. Both are very simple console apps. You'll need to create a solution (InfocardHelloWorld, say) and two console application projects (InfocardHelloClient and InfocardHelloService, say).

Here are the code listings of the applications we're going to add InfoCard to. For each project you will need to add a reference to `System.ServiceModel`.

First the contract, `contract.cs`, a copy of which is in both the client and the service projects:

```
using System.ServiceModel;

namespace HelloService
{
    [ServiceContract]
    interface IHello
    {
        [OperationContract]
        string Say();
    }
}
```

Now the service code, `program.cs`:

```csharp
using System;
using System.ServiceModel;

namespace HelloService
{
    class Hello : IHello
    {
        public string Say()
        {
            return "Hello World";
        }
    }

    class Program
    {
        static void Main(string[] args)
        {
            ServiceHost sh = new ServiceHost(typeof(Hello),
              new Uri("http://localhost:4123/helloService"));
            sh.Open();
            Console.WriteLine("Listening....");
            Console.ReadKey();

            sh.Close();          // close the service
        }
    }
}
```

And the service configuration file, `app.config`:

```xml
<?xml version="1.0" encoding="utf-8" ?>
<configuration>
  <system.serviceModel>

    <services>
      <service name="HelloService.Hello">
        <endpoint address="helloEndpoint"
          contract="HelloService.IHello"
          binding="wsHttpBinding"
          bindingConfiguration="helloBinding">
        </endpoint>
      </service>
    </services>
```

```
    <bindings>
      <wsHttpBinding>
        <binding name="helloBinding">
        </binding>
      </wsHttpBinding>
    </bindings>

  </system.serviceModel>
</configuration>
```

Now the client pieces. First, the client code, program.cs (note that this is the same file-name as the server-side code—as with contract.cs and app.config—but it resides in a different project and directory):

```
using System;
using System.ServiceModel;

namespace HelloClient
{
    class Program
    {
        static void Main(string[] args)
        {
            ChannelFactory<HelloService.IHello> cnFactory =
              new ChannelFactory<HelloService.IHello>("helloClient");
            HelloService.IHello chn = cnFactory.CreateChannel();
            Console.WriteLine(chn.Say());

            // Clean up
            cnFactory.Close(); // close the client's channel
            Console.ReadKey();
        }
    }
}
```

And finally the client configuration file, app.config:

```
<?xml version="1.0" encoding="utf-8" ?>
<configuration>
  <system.serviceModel>

    <client>
      <endpoint
          name="helloClient"
          address="http://localhost:4123/helloService/helloEndpoint"
```

```
        contract="HelloService.IHello"
        binding="wsHttpBinding"
        bindingConfiguration="helloBinding">
    </endpoint>
  </client>

  <bindings>
    <wsHttpBinding>
      <binding name="helloBinding">
      </binding>
    </wsHttpBinding>
  </bindings>

 </system.serviceModel>
</configuration>
```

14

There, we're done. This should compile and successfully run a basic WCF "Hello World" application.

Adding InfoCard

What do we need to do to add InfoCard to our application? Well, the key point is that we don't have to write any *code* to enable InfoCard. We can enable InfoCard via the client and server app.config files.

This is consistent with the WCF vision of enabling administrators to make configuration changes without having to recompile. Everything you can do in config you can still do in code, but by using config files you add deployment flexibility to your application. If you want to limit that flexibility, you can use binding requirements and custom channels to prevent inappropriate changes.

Here we are selecting InfoCard as a credential type in the WCF classes, a way to transfer credentials from the client to the server. Let's start with the server app.config:

We need to update the service binding to use message-level security and the InfoCard credential type, which is IssuedToken:

```
<bindings>
  <wsHttpBinding>
    <binding name="helloBinding">
      <security mode="Message">
        <message clientCredentialType="IssuedToken" />
      </security>
    </binding>
  </wsHttpBinding>
</bindings>
```

Now we'll adjust the client's `app.config` to match the server. This is *identical* to the server binding:

```
<bindings>
  <wsHttpBinding>
    <binding name="helloBinding">
      <security mode="Message">
        <message clientCredentialType="IssuedToken" />
      </security>
    </binding>
  </wsHttpBinding>
</bindings>
```

We've specified that the client should use InfoCard to pass credentials to the service, but how does the service identify itself to the client app? How does the client—or, more specifically, the user of the client app—*trust* the server?

One of the bedrock requirements of the InfoCard system is that any potential recipients of my digital identity must identify themselves to me using cryptographically verifiable but human-friendly means. Only then can I make a rational decision on whether to trust that party and provide them with information.

The way servers identify themselves on the Internet today is by using PKI certificates—typically purchased from Certificate Authorities such as VeriSign or Thawte.

InfoCard takes advantage of this. A service must identify itself using an SSL certificate. Furthermore, the relying party behind the service should identify itself by the use of high-assurance certificates (this is preferred but not mandatory). After all, the user does not trust a service endpoint per se but rather the company or organization providing the service endpoint.

Consequently, the X.509 certificate should identify the organization behind the server and, to help the human in the system, the certificate should utilize *logotypes* [RFC 3709] for the issuer organization (the Certificate Authority) and the subject organization (the relying party). Logotypes provide a mechanism by which signed JPEG or GIF images are bound to the certificate to help us recognize the relevant parties and make an informed decision to trust or not to trust. It is these logos that are displayed in the trust (or RIP) dialog.

Let's install a certificate for our service to use. You're welcome to try your own, but one place you can find a certificate that uses logotypes is in the *Microsoft Federated Identity and Access Resource Kit for Sept 2005 Community Technology Preview*. This can be found at http://www.microsoft.com/downloads. However, the code in the Resource Kit will work only with the earlier September WinFx CTP. It will not work with beta 2. We are using it only as a source for some certificates.

When you extract the Resource Kit MSI file, a `Certificates-and-Logos` folder is created in `C:\Program Files\Microsoft Federated Identity and Access Resource Kit - Sept 2005 CTP\InfoCardWalkthrough\StepByStepSamples`.

`Fabrikam-Contoso.pfx` contains the public/private key pair so it needs to be installed on the server (password xyz). `Fabrikam-Contoso-Public.cer` has just the public key and will need to be installed on the client.

To import, launch the Microsoft Management Console (MMC) from a command prompt and choose Add/Remove Snap-in from the File menu. Next click the Add button and double-click the Certificates snap-in. Choose My user account and Finish, then double-click the Certificates snap-in again and choose Computer account, then Local computer and Finish. Close the dialog and click OK.

We import the `.pfx` file by expanding the Certificates (Local Computer) node, right-clicking the Personal node, and choosing All Tasks and Import. In the wizard make sure you select `Fabrikam-Contoso.pfx` (the default file type is `.cer`). As you go through the wizard, keep the defaults, but select Automatically Select the Certificate Store Based on the Type of Certificate. You should get a warning dialog saying that Windows cannot confirm the origin of the certificate and asking whether you still want to install the certificate (you say yes!). This will place the Fabrikam certificate in Local Computer Personal Certificates and an INFOCARD certificate in Trusted Root Certification Authorities Certificates. You will need to do a refresh for the certificates to show up in the MMC UI.

For the client we need access to a certificate containing (just) the public key. So we import the `.cer` file by expanding the Certificates—Current User node, right-clicking the Trusted People node, and doing an import of the `Fabrikam-Contoso-Public.cer` file, making sure that the certificate gets placed in the Trusted People store.

Now we can modify the client and service `app.config` files so that WCF and InfoCard can locate and use these certificates. Let's start with the service and its `app.config`.

The correct mechanism for hooking up WCF to a resource on the local machine is to use a *behavior*. This should sit beneath the entire `<bindings>` section (that is, between `</bindings>` and `</system.serviceModel>`):

```
<behaviors>
  <behavior name="helloServiceBehavior"
    returnUnknownExceptionsAsFaults="true" >
    <serviceCredentials>
      <serviceCertificate
        findValue="Fabrikam"
        storeLocation="LocalMachine"
        storeName="My"
        x509FindType="FindBySubjectName" />
    </serviceCredentials>
  </behavior>
</behaviors>
```

Here you can see we are using a certificate called Fabrikam in the LocalMachine Personal ("My") store. If you've used your own certificates (for example, from a certificate authority, Certificate Services, or the makecert utility), you will need to make the appropriate changes.

We refer to the behavior by adding a `behaviorConfiguration` attribute to our service description:

```
<service
  name="HelloService.Hello"
  behaviorConfiguration="helloServiceBehavior">
```

We have now enabled WCF to access the certificate and the private key so that it can now use it for signing and decryption. However, we are not quite finished because we need to allow access to the certificate via an endpoint reference to enable identity and token encryption. Our entire `<services>` section now looks like this:

```
<services>
  <service
    name="HelloService.Hello"
    behaviorConfiguration="helloServiceBehavior">
    <endpoint
      address="helloEndpoint"
      contract="HelloService.IHello"
      binding="wsHttpBinding"
      bindingConfiguration="helloBinding">
      <identity>
        <certificateReference
          findValue="Fabrikam"
          storeLocation="LocalMachine"
          storeName="My"
          x509FindType="FindBySubjectName" />
      </identity>
    </endpoint>
  </service>
</services>
```

After this is in place, we have finished our service configuration. Next is the client's `app.config`. On the server side we need a behavior to access the private key. On the client we can either add a behavior or use the `MetadataResolver` class to retrieve the certificate information via WS-MetadataExchange. Let's take the behavior approach:

```
<behaviors>
  <behavior name="helloClientBehavior">
    <clientCredentials>
      <serviceCertificate>
        <authentication
          certificateValidationMode="PeerOrChainTrust"/>
        <defaultCertificate
          findValue="Fabrikam"
          storeLocation="CurrentUser"
```

```
        storeName="TrustedPeople"
        x509FindType="FindBySubjectName" />
      </serviceCertificate>
    </clientCredentials>
  </behavior>
</behaviors>
```

And add a reference to that behavior:

```
<client>
  <endpoint
    name="helloClient"
    address="http://localhost:4123/helloService/helloEndpoint"
    contract="HelloService.IHello"
    binding="wsHttpBinding"
    bindingConfiguration="helloBinding"
    behaviorConfiguration="helloClientBehavior">
  </endpoint>
</client>
```

And again we need to allow the InfoCard system access to encrypt the identity so our
<client> section looks like this:

```
<client>
  <endpoint
    name="helloClient"
    address="http://localhost:4123/helloService/helloEndpoint"
    contract="HelloService.IHello"
    binding="wsHttpBinding"
    bindingConfiguration="helloBinding"
    behaviorConfiguration="helloClientBehavior">
    <identity>
      <certificateReference
        findValue="Fabrikam"
        storeLocation="CurrentUser"
        storeName="TrustedPeople"
        x509FindType="FindBySubjectName" />
    </identity>
  </endpoint>
</client>
```

Now comes the moment of truth: Run the application and see what happens. If all goes
well, you should get the Trust dialog, looking something like what's shown in Figure 14.6.
You'll see how to display the logos in a moment.

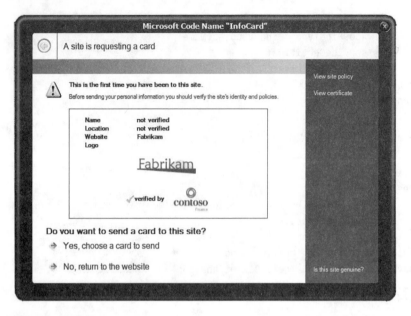

FIGURE 14.6   Trust dialog.

You click Yes, Choose a Card to Send; then, if you already have some cards, you will get what is shown in Figure 14.7.

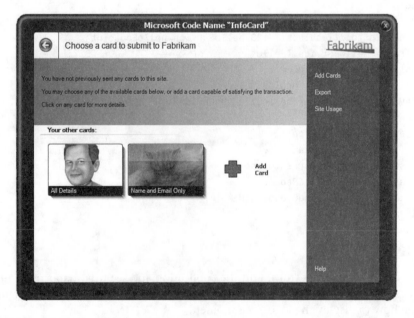

FIGURE 14.7   Choosing an InfoCard.

If you have yet to create any cards, you will see a dialog similar to the Add Cards dialog shown earlier where you have the choice of creating a new Personal ("self-issued") card, installing a card provided to you by an identity provider (a .crd file), restoring an exported card (a .crds file), or simply returning to the website without doing anything—the user is in control!

After you choose a personal card, a security token is created by the personal STS and, with your approval, sent to the service. The service doesn't actually do anything with the security token at this point and simply displays "Hello World."

Step through the code so that you understand at exactly which point the InfoCard dialog is launched.

If you don't choose a card, you will get an ugly Unhandled Exception error, so let's add some code to the client to catch the exception and handle it gracefully. In the HelloClient project, add a reference to System.IdentityModel.Selectors and open Program.cs. Next add the following statement at the top of the file:

```
using System.IdentityModel.Selectors;
```

Then in the body of Program.cs modify Main() so that it looks like the following:

```
static void Main(string[] args)
    {
        try
        {
            ChannelFactory<HelloService.IHello> cnFactory =
                new ChannelFactory<HelloService.IHello>("helloClient");
            HelloService.IHello chn = cnFactory.CreateChannel();
            Console.WriteLine(chn.Say());
            cnFactory.Close();
        }
        catch (UserCancellationException)
        {
            Console.WriteLine("User has cancelled");
        }
        catch (UntrustedRecipientException)
        {
            Console.WriteLine("User does not trust the recipient");
        }
        catch (ServiceNotStartedException)
        {
            Console.WriteLine("InfoCard service not started");
        }
        catch (InfoCardException ice)
        {
            Console.WriteLine("Generic InfoCard exception :" + ice.Message);
        }
```

```
catch (Exception e)
{
    Console.WriteLine("Other exceptions :" + e.Message);
}
finally
{
    Console.ReadKey();
}


}
```

Experiment a bit and see whether the exceptions are caught properly.

As stated previously, the service's certificate includes links to the subject and issuer logos. To verify this, you can open up MMC and the Certificates snap-in and look at the properties of the Fabrikam certificate. Under the 1.3.6.1.5.5.7.1.12 field there are links to the subject and issuer logos.

http://localhost/ServiceModelSamples/fabrikam.gif is the link for the subject logo; http://localhost/ServiceModelSamples/contoso.gif is the link for the issuer logo. These logos cannot be modified because a hash of each logo is also a part of the certificate. However, for these logos to be accessed, we need to place them in an http://localhost/ServiceModelSamples virtual directory.

Use the Internet Manager (inetmgr.exe) MMC snap-in to create a virtual directory called ServiceModelSamples under the Default Web Site (choose context menu, New, Virtual Directory) and point it at the directory containing the certificates. Accept the default settings elsewhere in the wizard.

Launch Internet Explorer and make sure that the logos display correctly using the URLs given earlier:

http://localhost/ServiceModelSamples/fabrikam.gif

http://localhost/ServiceModelSamples/contoso.gif

Now run the application again and you should see the logos appear in the Trust dialog.

Where would these logos be hosted in real life? Normally, a relying party would host its logo (the subject), and the issuer's logo would be hosted by the Certificate Authority. Alternatively, a third party could provide the hosting service.

Federation with InfoCard

The next step is to write some service code to crack open the security token selected by the user and passed to the service.

In the HelloService project, add a reference to System.IdentityModel.Claims.

Next we'll modify the service implementation in `program.cs`.

Add two using statements:

```
using System.IdentityModel.Claims;
using System.IdentityModel.Policy;
```

Next modify the `Hello` class to display the claims in the service console window:

```
class Hello : IHello
    {
        public string Say()
        {
            GetIdentity();
            return "Hello World";
        }

        private void GetIdentity()
        {
            AuthorizationContext ctx =
              OperationContext.Current.ServiceSecurityContext.
              AuthorizationContext;
            foreach (ClaimSet claimSet in ctx.ClaimSets)
            {
                foreach (Claim claim in claimSet)
                {
                    Console.WriteLine();
                    Console.WriteLine(claim.ClaimType);
                    Console.WriteLine(claim.Resource);
                    Console.WriteLine(claim.Right);
                }
            }
            return;
        }
    }
```

Now run the application and see what you get in the service console window.

You probably expected to see more claims. The reason you didn't is that we are using `wsHttpBinding`. This binding only allows a restricted claim set. To take advantage of all the claims in a security token, we need to use a federated binding.

Open the service `app.config` and add the following binding inside the `<bindings>` section after the existing `<wsHttpBinding>` section:

```
<wsFederationHttpBinding>
  <binding name="helloFederatedBinding">
    <security mode="Message">
```

```
      <message issuedTokenType="urn:oasis:names:tc:SAML:1.0:assertion">
        <claims>
          <add claimType=
➡"http://schemas.microsoft.com/ws/2005/05/identity/claims/emailaddress"/>
          <add claimType=
➡"http://schemas.microsoft.com/ws/2005/05/identity/claims/givenname"/>
          <add claimType=
➡"http://schemas.microsoft.com/ws/2005/05/identity/claims/surname"/>
          <add claimType=
➡"http://schemas.microsoft.com/ws/2005/05/identity/claims/
➡ privatepersonalidentifier"/>
          <!-- add more claims here-->
        </claims>
        <issuer address=
➡"http://schemas.microsoft.com/ws/2005/05/identity/issuer/self"/>
      </message>
    </security>
  </binding>
</wsFederationHttpBinding>
```

Here we are specifying a policy that will only accept security tokens containing the EmailAddress, GivenName, Surname, and PrivatePersonalIdentifier claims and we are accepting self-issued security tokens.

We also need to modify our service endpoint to use this binding:

```
binding="wsFederationHttpBinding"
bindingConfiguration="helloFederatedBinding"
```

That's our service app.config. Now let's turn our attention to the client app.config.

Cut and paste the <wsFederationHttpBinding> section you just entered into the <bindings> section or the client app.config, again after the existing <wsHttpBinding> section. Then change the binding and binding configuration under the client <endpoint>:

```
binding="wsFederationHttpBinding"
bindingConfiguration="helloFederatedBinding"
```

Now run the application again and see what you get. This time you should get the EmailAddress, GivenName, Surname, and PrivatePersonalIdentifier claims displayed in the service console window.

InfoCard from the Browser

Implementing InfoCard in websites is, if anything, easier than adding it to a WCF application. InfoCard is supported by Internet Explorer 7.0 and will work with builds after the IE7 Beta 2 Preview (the magic ingredient is icardie.dll, but you must also have the rest of the InfoCard system installed via WinFx). I hope also that by the time this book gets into your hands you will be able to try this code (successfully) on other browsers.

Go into IIS Manager and create a virtual directory, called, say, infocard. Into that directory we will put four files, but first we will use the Fabrikam certificate from the preceding WCF sample to provide an SSL certificate for the site to provide a secure channel. Right-click Default Web Site and select the Directory Security tab. Then click the Server Certificate button and choose Assign an Existing Certificate. Provided you have imported the .pfx file into your certificate store, the Fabrikam certificate should be visible in the Available Certificates dialog. Select it and finish the wizard.

If you want to see the spectacular way IE7 warns you when an SSL certificate name does not match the URL of a website, you can omit the next step, which is to modify the hosts file in C:\WINDOWS\system32\drivers\etc to have the following entry:

```
127.0.0.1 localhost fabrikam
```

This makes it a slightly smoother experience because you can refer to the site as http://fabrikam. If you omit this step, be sure to modify the code and config that follow to use the correct URLs.

Now, provided you have ASP.NET installed (if you installed .NET 2.0 before IIS, you won't), you can now create the four files that illustrate the InfoCard experience on a web page. Again, the following examples are as simple as possible but no simpler.

The first file is the default web page, default.htm:

```html
<html>
  <head>
    <title>InfoCard</title>
  </head>
  <body>
    <form name="ctl00" method="post" action="https://fabrikam/infocard/Main.aspx"
id="ctl00">
      <input type="submit" name="InfoCardSignin" value="Log in using InfoCard"
id="InfoCardSignin" />
      <OBJECT type="application/infocard" name="xmlToken">
        <PARAM Name="tokenType" Value="urn:oasis:names:tc:SAML:1.0:assertion">
        <PARAM Name="issuer"
Value="http://schemas.microsoft.com/ws/2005/05/identity/issuer/self">
        <PARAM Name="requiredClaims"
Value="http://schemas.microsoft.com/ws/2005/05/identity/claims/givenname,
http://schemas.microsoft.com/ws/2005/05/identity/claims/surname">
      </OBJECT>
    </form>
  </body>
</html>
```

This is an HTML page with a button that posts to the next page, `main.aspx`. The magic is in the `<OBJECT>` tag (we are using the ActiveX control in `icardie.dll`), which has a special type, `application/infocard`, and three `PARAM` tags specifying the token type (SAML 1.0), the token issuer (self-issued), and the required claims (first name and surname).

Next is `main.aspx`:

```
<%@ ValidateRequest="false" Language="C#" AutoEventWireup="true"
➡ CodeFile="Main.aspx.cs" Inherits="_Default" %>

<!DOCTYPE html PUBLIC "-//W3C//DTD XHTML 1.0 Transitional//EN"
➡"http://www.w3.org/TR/xhtml1/DTD/xhtml1-transitional.dtd">

<html xmlns="http://www.w3.org/1999/xhtml" >
  <head runat="server">
    <title>Main</title>
  </head>
  <body>
    <form id="form1" runat="server">
      <asp:Label ID="Label1" runat="server" Text="Label" Font-Size="X-Large"
➡ ForeColor="Navy"></asp:Label> 
    </form>
  </body>
</html>
```

And `main.aspx.cs`:

```
using System;

public partial class _Default : System.Web.UI.Page
{
  protected void Page_Load(object sender, EventArgs e)
  {
    string tokenString = Request["xmlToken"];

    if (null == tokenString)
    {
      Response.Redirect("default.htm?error=logonFailed");
    }
    else
    {
      this.Label1.Text = "Hello, world!";
    }
  }
}
```

Finally there is the `web.config` file (actually, our example is so simple that this can be omitted):

```
<?xml version="1.0"?>
<configuration>
  <appSettings/>
  <connectionStrings/>
  <system.web>
    <compilation debug="true">
      <assemblies>
        <add assembly="System.Xml, Version=2.0.0.0, Culture=neutral,
➥ PublicKeyToken=b77a5c561934e089"/>
        <add assembly="System, Version=2.0.0.0, Culture=neutral,
➥ PublicKeyToken=b77a5c561934e089"/>
        <add assembly="System.Security, Version=2.0.0.0, Culture=neutral,
➥ PublicKeyToken=B03F5F7F11D50A3A"/>
      </assemblies>
    </compilation>
    <authentication mode="Windows"/>
    <customErrors mode="Off"/>
  </system.web>
</configuration>
```

Try browsing directly to http://fabrikam/infocard/main.aspx. You will be redirected to http://fabrikam/infocard/default.htm because you do not have the security token. However, if you click on the button and select a card, you will able to get to `main.aspx`. We are not doing anything with the claims in the security token, but we could crack open the token, examine the claims, and make authentication and authorization decisions based on them. There will be functionality for doing this easily in a future WinFx CTP. A full website solution would have a relying party STS return a cookie for the browser to use to access pages on the site.

The IE7 Beta 2 Preview doesn't yet support the binary behavior implementation of InfoCard, but I'll include the code here for your information and for later builds. This is the binary behavior equivalent of `default.htm`. Again, it's pretty simple:

```
<html XMLNS:ic>
  <body>
    <form  method="post" action="https://fabrikam/infocard/Main.aspx" >
      <ic:informationCard  name='xmlToken'
➥ style='behavior:url(#default#informationCard)'
➥ issuer='http://schemas.microsoft.com/ws/2005/05/identity/issuer/self'
➥ tokenType='urn:oasis:names:tc:SAML:1.0:assertion'>
        <ic:add
➥ claimType='http://schemas.microsoft.com/ws/2005/05/identity/claims/givenname'
➥ optional='false'/>
```

```
      <ic:add
➥claimType='http://schemas.microsoft.com/ws/2005/05/identity/claims/surname '
➥optional='false'/>
        <ic:/informationCard>
      <input type="submit" name="InfoCardSignin" value="Log in using InfoCard"
➥id="InfoCardSignin" />
      </form>
  </body>
</html>
```

Summary and Next Steps

The primary goals of the InfoCard system are to do the following:

- Enable the use of digital identity in the form of claims in security tokens as authentication and/or authorization data using Web service mechanisms.

- Allow users flexibility in their choice of digital identities they want to employ, and put users squarely in control of the use of their identities in digital interactions.

- Support cryptographically verifiable but human-friendly identification of the recipients of a user's digital identities.

- Enable interoperability with identity providers and relying parties using open protocols to allow an identity ecosystem to thrive.

- Remain agnostic of specific security token types and identity mechanisms so as to effectively be a conduit for identity flow under user control between identity providers and relying parties.

- Safeguard user privacy by providing privacy-friendly identity mechanisms to help thwart tracking of users' online behavior and unsolicited collusion.

- Provide a simple identity provider to allow users to construct and employ self-issued identities in Web service interactions when acceptable.

I hope you can see that InfoCard does a good job of meeting these goals. We're not even at beta 2 and there is still some work to be done. The next release of the Microsoft Federated Identity and Access Resource Kit will have more samples of using IE, managed cards, and security token services, showing end-to-end InfoCard solutions. Stay tuned!

References

The Identity Blog:

http://www.identityblog.com/

The Laws of Identity:

http://msdn.microsoft.com/windowsvista/building/infocard/default.aspx?pull=/library/
en-us/dnwebsrv/html/lawsofidentity.asp

Microsoft's Vision for an Identity Metasystem:

http://msdn.microsoft.com/windowsvista/building/infocard/default.aspx?pull=/library/
en-us/dnwebsrv/html/identitymetasystem.asp

A Guide to Integrating with InfoCard v1.0:

http://download.microsoft.com/download/6/c/3/6c3c2ba2-e5f0-4fe3-be7f-c5dcb86af6de/
infocard-guide-beta2-published.pdf

A Technical Reference for InfoCard v1.0 in Windows:

http://download.microsoft.com/download/5/4/0/54091e0b-464c-4961-a934-
d47f91b66228/infocard-techref-beta2-published.pdf

A Guide to Supporting InfoCard v1.0 Within Web Applications and Browsers:

http://msdn.microsoft.com/winfx/reference/infocard/default.aspx?pull=/library/
en-us/dnwebsrv/html/infocardwebguide.asp

Index

A

O

P

Q

Queued Messaging, 161-163

creating clients for the service, 183-184

creating WCF applications, 180-183

implementing, 177

testing, 185

queues, 177

QuizChild class, 370

BuildBinding() method, 366-379

constructor of, 369-370, 379-381

IResponse service contract, 371

QuizItem struct (Peer Channel example), 346

QuizManagement path, 370

QuizResponse struct (Peer Channel example), 346

QuizTeacher class, 355-356

BuildBinding () method, adding, 357

BuildBinding() method, 362-363, 375

constructor of, 362, 375-378

endpoints, defining, 367-368

R

RandomDataPoint class, 312

RandomDataPoint project, 312

Read() method

custom streams, 334-338

CustomStream class, 332, 334

ReadMessage() method, 278

PlainXMLEncoder class, 465-466

Really Simple Syndication (RSS), 446

ReallySimpleRatedSyndication class

AddSignedContentRating() method, 452-456

ValidateSignedContentRating() method, 472-473

VerifySignature() method, 472-473

Woodgrove certificate, 456

RecordTrades(), 441

referencing clients, COM+ as WCF Web services, 214-216

Register method (Peer Channel example), 358

reliability, 159

Queued Messaging, 161-163

Reliable Sessions, 161-162

Reliable Sessions, 161-163

WS-RM, 160

Reliable Sessions, 161-162

implementing, 163

adding WCF SOAP Reliable Messaging, 163

Relying Parties (RPs), 484, 498

Replicator activity (XSI example), 146

purpose of, 147

ReplyAction parameter (OperationContract attributes), 123

report queues, 178

Representational State Transfer. *See* REST

representing data. *See* data representation

RequestIdentifier property (XSI example), 150

requests, creating WCF Web Services that integrate with MSMQ, 217

Resolve class (Peer Channel example), 358

Resolver class (Peer Channel example), 359-362

Resolver property, 363

ResolverClient class (Peer Channel example), 358, 363-366

Resource Access client application, 126. *See also* XSI, Resource Access client application

performance, improving, 114-119, 121

role-based authorization, 106, 108, 110-114

U

V

X-Y-Z